P9-CKI-961

$825

ELECTRICITY AND ELECTRONICS

BASIC

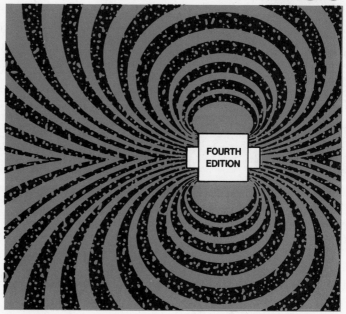

FOURTH
EDITION

William B. Steinberg
Director of Vocational Education
San Diego Community Colleges

Walter B. Ford
Professor Emeritus, Electronics
Industrial Arts Department
San Diego State College

AMERICAN TECHNICAL SOCIETY
Chicago, Illinois 60637

COPYRIGHT, © 1957, 1961, 1964, 1972 BY

American Technical Society

COPYRIGHTED IN GREAT BRITAIN
ALL RIGHTS RESERVED

LIBRARY OF CONGRESS CATALOG CARD NUMBER: 77-174341
ISBN: 0-8269-1402-0

FIRST EDITION
1st Printing May, 1957
2nd Printing November, 1957
3rd Printing July, 1958
4th Printing September, 1960

SECOND EDITION
5th Printing 1961
6th Printing 1962

THIRD EDITION
7th Printing August, 1964
8th Printing November, 1966
9th Printing November, 1970

FOURTH EDITION
10th Printing, 1972
11th Printing, 1973
12th Printing, 1974

No portion of this publication may be
reproduced by *any* process such as photo-
copying, recording, storage in a retrieval
system or transmitted by any means
without permission of the publisher.

PRINTED IN THE UNITED STATES OF AMERICA

PREFACE

Electricity and Electronics—Basic, now in its fourth major edition, has been enthusiastically accepted by schools throughout the country. This new edition incorporates not only the new advances in the field but also the many valuable suggestions of hundreds of teachers who have used this book in the past. New material has been added and the text updated to include the latest developments in the field of electricity and electronics.

The awe-inspiring achievements of nuclear science and the spectacular advancements in aviation, as well as the innumerable discoveries that have added comfort and convenience to daily life, lead to increasing dependence upon electricity and electronics. It may never be necessary for the student to operate an atom-smasher or guide a space ship, but electric lights, the automobile, the telephone, radio, and television demand at least some knowledge of basic principles involved.

Anyone who wishes to feel at home in the world of modern technology must be familiar with the fundamentals of electricity and electronics. To make it possible to acquire this familiarity quickly and easily is the purpose of this book. The necessary information is presented in a direct and simple manner. Each step is clearly illustrated by photographs and drawings.

Color is used in the illustrations to provide clarity and as an asset in the learning process. Experience has shown that color, properly used, is a valuable tool in illustration. Its overuse, for effect, is distracting and destroys its value. The use of color simply for decoration has been studiously avoided.

Throughout, the text provides the convenient symbols used by engineers and technicians in all fields to represent electrical and electronic equipment on diagrams. At the end of each unit of study, there is a group of "Review Questions." These are provided to assist the reader to test his knowledge and to check his progress.

"Interesting Things to Do" is what the authors have called the many fascinating projects that demonstrate and apply what has been learned in the text.

These projects are not only interesting but produce useful articles and develop practical skills. Few tools are necessary and generally only materials commonly found in a home or school shop are required. The fourth edition includes eleven new projects.

The knowledge of electricity and electronics gained from this book will open new and inviting paths. A great number of vocational opportunities exist and they are multiplying rapidly in the area that is leading progress in most occupational fields. A variety of exciting hobbies offer themselves. And you will have the keen satisfaction of grasping the essentials of an important part of your everyday life.

CONTENTS

THIS ELECTRICAL AND ELECTRONIC AGE

MAKING USE OF MAGNETISM

HOW ELECTRICITY IS PRODUCED

BASIC ELECTRICAL CIRCUITS

ELECTRICITY FOR EVERYDAY LIVING

USING ELECTRONICS FOR COMMUNICATION

INTERESTING THINGS TO DO

MAKING USE OF MAGNETISM

HOW ELECTRICITY IS PRODUCED

BASIC ELECTRICAL CIRCUITS

ELECTRICITY FOR EVERYDAY LIVING

USING ELECTRICITY FOR COMMUNICATION

Man's first landing on the moon, July 20, 1969. This historical event was made possible through the magic of electronics.

This Electrical and Electronic Age

UNIT 1
THINGS ELECTRICITY CAN DO

Electricity and Electronics

When we think of the terms *electricity* and *electronics*, we may wonder which one to use when we speak of the operation of an electrical device. The field of electricity is usually thought of when electricity is used to operate electromagnets, generators, motors, lights, and heaters.

The field of electronics is usually thought of when electricity is used to operate radio, television, and other devices where electron tubes and transistors are used.

In the Home

We are so accustomed to operating a switch in our homes and having a room instantly flooded with light that we seldom think of what is happening behind the scenes to make this possible. Yet back of every home lighting system there are a number of interesting devices. The names of these devices are strange to most of us. As we proceed with the study of electricity, we shall become very familiar with the names and electrical equipment they represent and learn what an important part they play in bringing electricity into our homes.

Probably the most important use of electricity in the home is for producing light with either the common light bulb or fluorescent lamps. Ultraviolet type lamps can bring the effects of sunshine into the home and also kill harmful germs in the air. Infrared type lamps can provide us with radiant heat.

Fig. 1-1. Electronics help to make kitchen chores a pleasure. With the microwave oven shown above, a frozen dinner can be made ready to serve in 3½ minutes, instead of the usual 20 to 50 minutes. To bake a potato requires only 5 minutes. (International Crystal Mfg. Co.)

zor, clock, furnace blower, and workshop equipment. Electric mowers and hedge trimmers lighten the work outside the home.

The uses for electricity in the home do not end with furnishing light and motor power. Electrical heating provides comfort for the family by operating the range, toaster, waffle iron, water heater, coffee maker, heating pad, iron, ironer, and electric blanket. See Figs. 1-1 and 1-2.

On the Farm

Electricity is just as important to the farm as it is to the modern city dwelling.

Fig. 1-2. Transistorized intercom units provide communication between all rooms of a modern home. Requiring little current to operate, they may be left on over long periods of time to monitor a sleeping child or serve to call the family to dinner. (Allied Radio Corp.)

How many electric motors are working in your home to lighten household tasks and provide for your comfort? If you gave an offhand answer without counting them, you would probably fall far short of the correct number. In the average modern home, electric motors operate the clothes washer, drier, refrigerator, garbage disposal, fan, electric ra-

About two-thirds of all farms use electricity to lighten the chores, as well as to serve in the home. Many of the jobs that were formerly done by hand and required many "man-hours," may now be done with electricity in a fraction of the time. These include pumping water, grinding feed, and milking to name but a few.

In Industry and Business

When we think of the many ways in which electricity helps to run a modern home, we are apt to overlook the part it plays in keeping the wheels of industry moving. Actually, only about one third of all of the electricity produced in our power plants is used by farms and homes. The remaining two-thirds supplies the needs of commercial and industrial plants. The average modern manufactur-

ing establishment uses over 10,000 kilowatt-hours of electrical power a year in the machines it operates. Let us consider some of the ways in which this tremendous amount of power is used in industry.

In the great steel industries, electricity is used in practically every process from the time the crude iron ore is taken from the earth to when the finished product in the form of flat steel sheet is ready for delivery to manufacturing plants across

Fig. 1-3. Up to 40 remote operations—lights, motors, heating and air conditioning systems, as well as clocks, time recorders and signals—can be automatically controlled by a central control system. Before the plant opens . . . during the working day . . . after close down, the electronic control system will maintain automatic and efficient 24-hour supervision. (IBM)

the nation. Electric shovels are used to remove the ore, and electric cranes load it into freight cars or ships and unload it at the steel plant. Electric conveyors carry the iron ore to furnaces where it is converted into steel. The rolls which form the steel into sheets, are driven by electric motors. When the finished sheets of steel reach the manufacturing plants, electric motors operate the machines which shape them into some of the appliances that contribute so much to our way of living. These electric motors help produce radio and television chassis and many household aids.

Automation has become a common word in industry. See Fig. 1-3. Jobs which were formerly done by handpower, are now being performed with electricity. Many manufacturing plants are now being made ready for the day's operation before the first worker arrives on the job. Lights, motors, heating and air conditioning systems, as well as clocks, time recorders, and signals are automatically controlled from a central control system. Before the plant opens, during the working day, and after close-down, the electronic control system maintains automatic and efficient 24-hour supervision.

The manufacture of many products is now being done with the aid of com-

Fig. 1-4. Businessmen find the pocket-size electronic calculator a time-saving aid in their daily operations. This versatile unit will add, subtract, multiply, divide or calculate percentage accurately with answers up to eight figures. (Radio Shack)

puters. For example, circuit boards for electronic equipment can be assembled with little manual assistance. The components are placed in a machine where they are automatically tested, selected for proper sequence, and secured and soldered in place. The assembled unit is then given a final test and passed from the machine.

Banks and commercial institutions have found computers to be indispensable tools for conducting their business operations. With their use, mathematical calculations and keeping of records which formerly required hours, may now be handled in a matter of seconds by the use of computers.

Industry and business are using more and more calculators, stationary and portable, battery operated. The relative inexpense and versatility of some models makes them popular in the home and in the school. See Fig. 1-4.

Manufacturing plants can now guard their property against undesired intruders. Electrically operated detectors that can see in the dark, can detect a man at 1,000 feet, and a truck at 3,500 feet, and sound an alarm instantly.

For Communication

Primitive man depended upon fire, smoke, or drum signals to communicate with his neighbor. Modern man has only to lift the receiver of his telephone and dial a series of numbers to send his voice to the most distant point of our nation. And as we learned from man's first landing on the moon, the distance he can communicate through outer space is limited only by the distance he can travel from the earth. See Fig. 1-5.

Through the means of man-made satellites such as Telstar, orbiting in space, it is now possible to span the oceans with ultra-high frequency TV signals to view programs from distant lands. At the point where a program originates, the signals

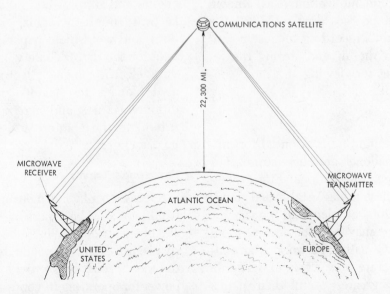

Fig. 1-5. At a height of 22,300 miles above the earth, the orbital speed of a communications satellite will coincide with the speed of the earth's rotation. This places it in a fixed position relative to positions on earth, and provides a reliable relay service between continents for voice and television transmissions.

are transmitted to a satellite many miles above the earth, where they are received and amplified, then transmitted to the distant point where they are received. Power for operating the communicating equipment in the satellite is obtained from solar cells.

Within the past few years, a new communication system known as the "Citizen's Band" has grown to over 1,000,000 stations and is still increasing at the rate of about 10,000 units a month. The power of each transmitter is limited to 5 watts. The system was authorized by the Federal Communications Commission to provide business and other necessary communications between citizens. Owing to the large number of Citizen Band units in use, a stranded motorist so equipped, can usually summon aid within minutes. A license is necessary to operate a unit, but an examination is not required to obtain it.

A new application of tape recording is now available for home entertainment and other communication uses. Known as "video tape recording", (VTR) the device permits recording television programs from the air and storing the recorded tapes for viewing at a more convenient time.

For Lighting

Adequate lighting is essential for preventing accidents and eye strain. For those reasons, the National Fire Protection Association has established minimum amounts of electrical power for lighting that may be used in any room where people gather or work. Many industries operate on a 24 hour schedule to make the greatest use of their plants. Only adequate lighting makes this possible. While the largest electric lamp in the home rarely consumes over a few hundred watts of power, the power required for an industrial lamp may be in the thousands.

Major sporting events such as baseball and football games are frequently held at night to permit day workers to attend. Electricity provides the light to make the playing fields as bright as daylight.

Cities depend on electricity to light streets and highways and to operate signals to control traffic.

For Transportation

Hardly any form of transportation exists today which does not require electricity to keep it going. Diesel-electric locomotives, ocean liners, subway and elevated trains, and propeller and jet type aircraft, all require electrical power for their operation.

Although gasoline supplies the driving power for today's modern automobiles, they could not function without electricity. Electric power is required to start its engine and supply the ignition spark to keep it running. Lights, turn signals, horn, and windshield wipers which provide for the driver's safety, are operated with electric power. Electrically operated blowers for heaters and air conditioners, radios, and stereo players contribute to the comfort and pleasure of its passengers.

For Space Travel

Success in placing men on the moon would not have been possible without the aid of electricity. When the unmanned spacecraft, Surveyor, made its journey to the moon, solar cells provided electrical power for operating its controls and sending valuable information back to earth. This information made possible the eventful landing of the manned spaceship, Apollo 11, which followed later. Millions of viewers on earth were able to watch this historical occasion by means of ultra-high frequency television signals which bridged the 240,000 mile span of outer space.

In Medicine

Electricity is rapidly gaining a place in the field of medicine. By means of a computer, a hospital patient can be monitored to keep track of more than 20 physical variables which include blood pressure, breathing rate, and body temperature. From such measurements, the computer can determine the amount of blood pumped with each heart beat, and the extent of lung movement during each breath of the patient. This information is recorded in the floor monitoring office

Fig. 1-6. The recently developed Jet Flying Belt enables man to soar like a bird, crossing canyons, rivers, and ground traffic at will. Using the world's smallest ramjet engine weighing only 65 pounds, the vehicle can attain speeds up to 60 miles an hour. Safety features include a parachute that will permit landing from an elevation as low as 65 feet, two-way radio, and a telemetry system for transmitting flight data to a ground station. (Bell Aerosystems Co.)

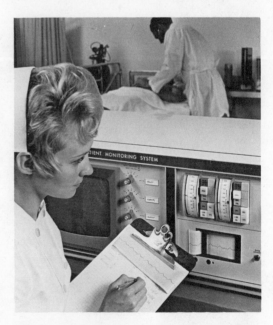

Fig. 1-7. Electronically operated patient monitoring system simultaneously displays data as it is monitored at bedside to assist hospital staff in quickly determining and responding to critical changes in the patient's condition. (Honeywell Instrument Division)

and makes it unnecessary for the patient to have a nurse in constant attendance. See Fig. 1-7. Electrically operated lasers can now permit delicate eye operations which formerly required complex surgery and long periods of recuperation.

A disease-detecting camera that makes use of radioisotopes, now makes it possible for doctors to diagnose malfunctioning of vital parts of the body in a fraction of the time required by the older X-ray method. Radioisotopes are formed when a neutron is added or taken away from the nucleus of a radioactive element. Harmless radioisotopes which permit taking pictures from radiation from within the body are injected into the patient's bloodstream. Known as *scintograms*, the pictures show far greater detail than X-rays and permit complete diagnostic procedures within less than 30 minutes.

REVIEW QUESTIONS

1. List the ways in which you have used electricity since getting out of bed this morning.

2. Make a list of the number of electric motors that you have in your home.

3. What is the size of the largest lamp used for lighting in your home?

4. Name several uses for the electric lamp.

5. What part of all of the electric power produced is used by farms and homes?

6. What is meant by the word *automation?*

7. How do satellites assist long distance communications?

8. Name several ways in which electronics aids in the practice of medicine.

UNIT 2
FUTURE DEVELOPMENTS IN ELECTRONICS

In the Home

When we think of the many ways electronics has added comfort and ease of living to our homes, we may wonder what further improvements the future will bring. Research personnel are working constantly to produce more efficient electric lamps and controls to operate them.

One day we may turn our lamps on or off merely by passing into or out of a room. Postcard size wireless transmitters will add safety and convenience to our homes by permitting us to flood them with light from a bedside table or any other location within the home.

The Picturephone, (Fig. 2-1), a device by which we may see the person to whom

Fig. 2-1. A television telephone that will make it possible to see the person at the other end of the line. (Kay Laboratory)

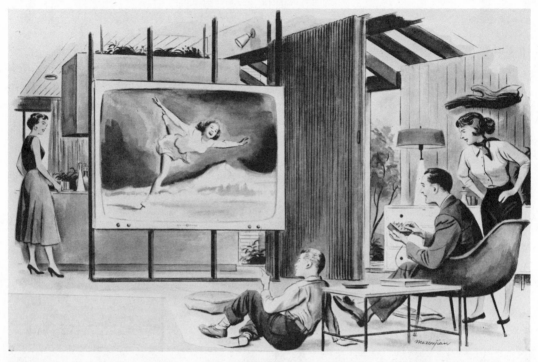

Fig. 2-2. A practical method of direct light amplification may be the key to large-screen television sets, which are thin enough to hang on a wall or to be used as room dividers. (General Electric Co.)

we are talking over a telephone, is expected to be placed in nation-wide service in the near future. This device has been under development for several years, but with the aid of integrated circuits it has recently been tested successfully between cities several hundred miles apart. Another telephone convenience scheduled for the future, is a device with which we may transfer incoming calls to another location. For example, if you are about to leave your home to visit a friend and are expecting some important calls, you merely press the required buttons on your telephone and the calls will be transferred automatically to your friend's home.

In the field of entertainment, we will have television receivers with regular size screens, and several smaller ones operat-ing on different channels. We may see what programs are being shown on other stations, then transfer the more desirable one to the larger screen. Other television receivers of the future will store and index on electronic memory circuits, news that is transmitted continually during the day. When you press one button, an index of the day's happenings will appear on the screen. Decide what you wish to see, press another button and the news event flashes on the television screen before you. See Fig. 2-2.

In Industry

With travel into outer space now a reality, scientists are looking forward to establishing giant orbiting space stations which will serve as factories for products that may be built under the zero gravity and high vacuum conditions of outer space. Two such products among the many possibilities might be bars made of steel foam many times stronger than ordinary steel bars with equal cross-section and steel ball bearings that are perfect spheres.

Back on earth, industry is progressing toward developing a storage battery with which gasoline driven automobiles may be converted to electric motor drive. Air pollution in our cities from car exhaust makes this project one of great importance.

In Automobile Traffic Control

With the number of automobiles traveling on our streets and highways growing larger daily, authorities are seeking ways to reduce the number of accidents arising from the increasing flow of traffic. A future contribution to highway safety will be electronically controlled signs above street intersections which display a "count down" on the seconds of time remaining before the traffic signal changes from green to red. This will allow an approaching driver to adjust his speed accordingly.

The traffic officer of the future, may be a computer controlled device installed in an automobile which will automatically photograph driver and car approaching at excessive speed from the roadside. It will record the miles-per-hour, maximum permissive speed for the area, location, date, and time of day of violation. All of this information, recorded on a computer card, will become the driver's citation.

A New Source of Power

From recent tests, scientists claim to have detected and measured gravity waves from outer space, traveling with the speed of light, 186,000 miles a second. Gravitational energy is very weak,

Fig. 2-3. Another possible source of future power, electricity produced directly from heat, lights small lamps in the laboratory of General Electric scientist Dr. Volney Wilson, inventor of the thermionic converter. (General Electric Co.)

but there is about 100 times as much of it in the universe as there is nuclear energy and at some future day, scientists predict, man will be able to tap this new source of power and adapt it to his use. See Fig. 2-3.

In Communications

On May 9, 1962, a laser beam of brilliant red light was flashed on the moon and reflected back to earth in slightly more than two and a half seconds. See Fig. 2-4. An amazing feature of the dem-

onstration was the fact that after its 240,000 mile journey through outer space, the beam had spread only to a diameter of about one mile when it hit the moon's surface. A beam from a powerful searchlight, if it could be built, would have spread to a diameter of over 10,000 miles when it reached the moon.

Since the day of the successful laser-moon experiment, scientists have worked toward using laser beams for communication. Progress has been rapid, but there are still some problems to be solved be-

Fig. 2-4. A laser beam strikes the moon with an increase of about only one mile in diameter through its 240,000 mile journey. The low ratio of beam spreading to distance traveled has encouraged scientists into further research toward the day when a laser beam can serve as a carrier for most long distance communications. (Bell Telephone System)

fore their goal is reached. Most of our long distance communications such as voices, computer data, and television, are carried presently by coaxial cables and microwave systems. However, the loads on those systems are increasing so fast that scientists estimate that within ten years they will reach their maximum capacities. By that time they predict that the laser beam, with its fantastic ability to handle millions of voices at one time, will be ready to take over most of the nation's long distance communication needs.

REVIEW QUESTIONS

1. What new electrical device might be developed for the home?

2. What new source of power is a future possibility?

3. For what purposes, other than lighting, can electric lamps be used?

4. What new development may replace our present day television tube?

5. What electronic device may someday be used to make highway travel safer?

6. What recent electronic development may aid future long distance communication?

UNIT 3
OPPORTUNITIES IN ELECTRICITY AND ELECTRONICS

Electricity and Electronics as a Vocation

Probably no other industry provides better job opportunities than the field of electricity and electronics. New electronic developments are made almost every day, and each of these developments provides new jobs. Everywhere we look, electricity and electronics are being used more and more. The tremendous growth of electrical devices means that more people are needed to design, install, and repair these items.

Basic jobs in electricity and electronics may be divided into seven classifications: (1) Assembler, (2) Construction, (3) Maintenance and repair, (4) Communication, (5) Technician, (6) Engineer, and (7) Scientist. See Fig. 3-1.

Fig. 3-1. This portable videotape recording system, consisting of a backpack recorder and hand-held camera, was designed mainly for on-the-spot recordings for television where conventional equipment cannot be used. Since the operator may be required to service his equipment in the field, it is essential that he have a good electronics background. (Ampex Corp.)

Assembler

Assemblers can be found in any plant that manufactures electrical or electronic equipment or components. Assembling jobs include such positions as chassis assembler in a radio manufacturing plant, coil winder in an electric motor plant, or a cable installer in an aircraft factory. Each position requires special training for each specific job. Some very intricate work is required of the assemblers who place small parts on a printed circuit board used in a television set.

Most of these jobs require good finger dexterity, ability to follow directions closely, using hand tools, and an understanding of the types of schematic drawings required for a particular job. Many assemblers must also learn how to use certain test equipment to determine whether or not the finished product will function properly. See Fig. 3-2.

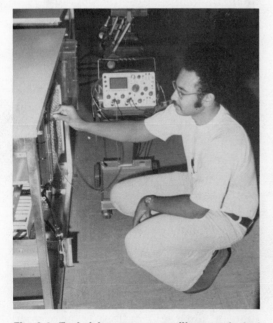

Fig. 3-2. Technician uses an oscilloscope to test section of a computer unit. (Honeywell)

Construction

Construction electricians perform the various tasks relating to electrical work on all types of building projects. They install electrical fixtures, heating devices, lighting circuits, and other types of equipment using electricity. The ability to read blueprints is important in electrical installation work as well as skill in the use of tools. The construction electrician is important to all building trades.

Other jobs that might be classified with construction are: the ship electrician who installs the wiring and electrical equipment in ships, the telephone installer who runs the telephone lines into homes and factories, and the stage electrician who provides lighting and wiring in motion picture studios and on theater stages.

All construction jobs must follow specific electrical code requirements, and the ability to read wiring diagrams, and calculate electrical formulas are all essential for the construction electrician's job.

One of the best ways to learn the electrician's trade is through an apprenticeship program. Apprenticeship is an approved program of supervised on-the-job training supplemented by related trade instruction. Most apprenticeship programs require a high school diploma with course work in mathematics, electricity, and science.

Maintenance and Repair

More people are employed in the maintenance and repair of electrical and electronic equipment than in any other phase of the industry. Maintenance electricians are responsible for keeping in good working order the tremendous amount of electrical equipment and machinery used in the home and in the nation's industrial, commercial, and government buildings. This field of work includes the skilled craftsman who inspects, repairs, and maintains electrical wiring, motors, generators, transformers, and other types of electrical equipment. A very important individual in the maintenance field is the electrical appliance repair man who works on home equipment such as electric toasters, waffle irons, washing machine motors, and electric clothes dryers. Each of these maintenance jobs requires special training, tool skills, and a knowledge of electrical principles.

In electronics, one of the best known repair fields is the servicing of radio and television sets. All types of electronic equipment require specially trained service men. Hearing aids, computers, transmitters, test instruments, and stereo amplifiers need the attention of a skilled maintenance man when they fail to operate properly. These men have a high degree of skill, a good understanding of electronic theory, and they must know how to use the many types of special test equipment.

Training for maintenance and repairmen of electrical and electronic equipment may be obtained from special technical schools, military service schools, and from some industrial training programs. Most of these training schools require a high school diploma and desire students who have enrolled in mathematics, science, electricity, and electronics courses.

Communication

Probably the best known use of electronics is found in the field of communi-cations which includes radio, television, radar, radio relay systems, telemetering, ship radio, telephone, and facsimile transmission. The ability to communicate using electronic equipment plays an important part in the safety services provided by aviation, coast-guard, police, fire, forestry conservation, highway maintenance, and special emergency service. Many types of positions involving the use of electronics can be found in each of the areas of communication. For example, a television station employs operators to maintain and repair the transmitter, to control the sound and adjust the picture, to operate the camera, to run the motion picture projector and adjust the lighting. Each of these highly skilled individuals must work together when the station is transmitting a program.

It is often difficult to separate the communication operator and the technician, as they have a great deal in common. In many cases the operator of a particular piece of communication equipment is also the technician who designs and repairs the equipment. The general speed-up in the communications field has resulted in an increased need for individuals to operate and to maintain a variety of equipment for communication.

Many of the positions in communications require a special operator's license which can be obtained by examination from the Federal Communications Commission. High school courses in mathematics, science, and electronics provide a valuable background in planning such a career. Obtaining an amateur radio station license and building and operating an amateur station is also good training.

Technician

The term "Electronic Technician" is used to designate a worker performing electronic activities requiring technical and related training, which provides direct support to the engineer or scientist in specialized areas of work. It includes those jobs involving research, design, and the development of electrical and electronic circuits. Testing and modifying experimental electronic devices is also part of the technician's job.

The electronic technician field is one of the most rapidly growing occupations. In general, they do work similar to that of the engineer and scientist but with greater emphasis on the practical. They must be able to solve problems and present written reports about their work. Testing and calibrating electronic instruments, installing components, and using tools and machinery are all part of a technician's job. See Fig. 3-3.

In addition to working on all types of communication equipment, technicians become specialists in such fields as industrial measuring, recording, indicating and controlling devices, navigational equipment, missile and space-craft guidance, electronic computors, and many other types of equipment using vacuum tubes and semiconductor circuits.

There are many types of technician positions, and a number of different titles are used, such as, electronic computor technician; electronic circuit technician; electronic instrument technician;

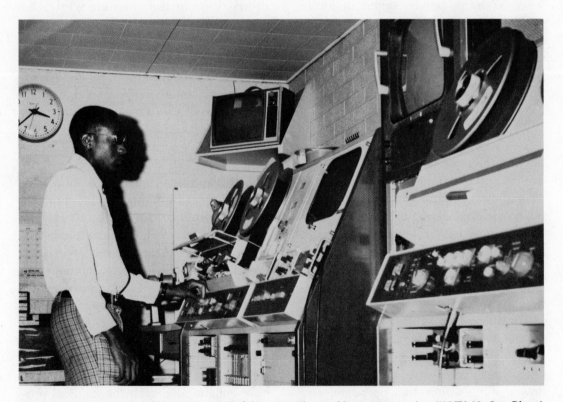

Fig. 3-3. A television broadcast station technician operating a video tape recorder. (KGTV 10, San Diego)

electronic research technician; and systems testing technician. Technicians are employed by industry and the government to conduct tests direct installation experiment and operate equipment using electrical and electronic principles. For example, a technician working on a proposed printed circuit must first experiment with the arrangement of wires and components, so that they may be properly assembled. He plans methods of testing the unit by using test instruments and changes the arrangement of parts, so that the device operates correctly. To do all of this, he must understand electronic theory and use the mathematical computations necessary to plan, operate, and test the circuit.

Technicians usually qualify by obtaining training above the high school level. Training can be found in junior colleges, technical institutes, vocational schools, in-plant training, and the armed forces. Typical courses include electrical and electronic theory, mathematics, physics, and drafting.

Engineering

The engineer is responsible for conducting research, designing, experimenting, and creating new ideas with electrical and electronic devices. Electrical and electronic engineering is one of the most rapidly growing professions, and with the advances made in our technology and the increased use of electronics, the demand for electronic engineers continues to grow.

The major areas of work in this branch of engineering include electrical or electronic machinery and equipment manufacturing, telephone and telegraph, power, illumination, transportation, and communication. Areas of work such as nuclear energy, missile guidance systems, servomechanisms, computors, and automation require large numbers of electronic engineers.

The electronic engineer's work is exacting, and he must learn to work alone or as a member of a team. Much of his time is used working on ideas, sketches, mathematical calculations, and in writing reports and specifications. Engineering requires considerable above average ability, exceptional aptitude, and achievement in mathematics and science.

There are many areas of specialization within the field that may appeal to persons with particular interests. For example, the illumination engineer who has a keen artistic sense may find his ideal occupation in the motion picture industry or in the theater, while the electronics engineer with an appreciation of music may find his greatest opportunity in one of the many positions concerned with the recording and reproduction of high fidelity music. Similar interests might be stated in other areas of specialization.

Scientist

The electronic scientist is primarily concerned with experimental projects that will produce new products. He has a thorough knowledge of electronic theory and uses this information to create or design new devices. He has been responsible for developing many exotic products through the application of electronic technology. The techniques and equipment for manned flights to outer space were developed mostly by electronic scientists. Electronic scientists have collaborated with the medical profession to develop some revolutionary aids for diagnosing ailments and assisting the functions of the human body. The most successful electronic scientist is one who is interested in the challenge of research. His educational background generally includes a master's or doctor's degree.

A good high school background in the fields of mathematics and science are essential to enter the field of engineering. Most electrical or electronic engineers obtain a college degree in engineering. To those who have the ability, the opportunities in the field of engineering seem to be unlimited.

REVIEW QUESTIONS

1. What field of electronics would you choose as a vocation?

2. Why should jobs in electricity and electronics be plentiful in the future?

3. List the jobs that a good service electrician should be able to do.

4. What type of electronics work requires a government license?

5. Name as many electrical or electronics engineering jobs as you can.

Making Use
of
Magnetism

Everyday Uses of Permanent Magnets

To understand electricity we must first know something about magnetism. *Magnetism* is not the same as electricity, but it plays a very important part in the construction and operation of many electrical devices.

Almost everyone has picked up pieces of iron with a magnet or has seen a small magnet hold itself to a metal surface. This simple principle, of holding on to certain metals, is used for many practical purposes around the home. The tack hammer shown in Fig. 4-1 is a magnet used to hold tacks firmly to the hammer head so that the user will not have to hold the tacks with his fingers. In the kitchen, magnets are attached to potholders so that they will "stick" to the

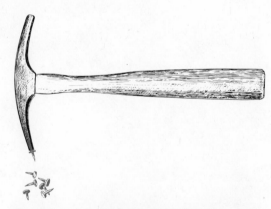

Fig. 4-1. The magnetic tack hammer is a very useful tool for upholstering or where tacks must be driven in hard-to-get-at places. The magnetic head is usually in a horseshoe form and the opposite end of the head is nonmagnetic.

stove, refrigerator, or other metal surfaces. Magnetic strips are used to hold sharp knives, small magnets hold notes

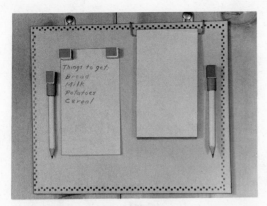

Fig. 4-2. This note pad holder consists of a steel back plate and several small permanent magnets. These magnets hold paper and pencils when placed on the metal back.

to a metal plate on cabinet doors (Fig. 4-2),and cabinet doors are held closed with magnets. Some games use magnets to keep miniature players on a metal playing board.

All around us magnets are used; however, most people do not know how materials are magnetized. Figs. 4-1 thru 4-3 are examples of how some permanent magnets are used. They are really artificial magnets because they were not magnets in their natural form. Something had to be done to the material to change it into a magnet.

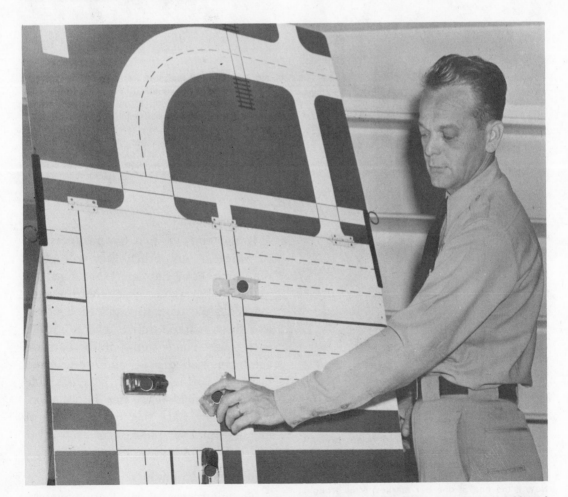

Fig. 4-3. In traffic courts, magnets in miniature plastic automobiles will hold the vehicles to a metal board so that positions of various automobiles that have been involved in an accident may be illustrated.

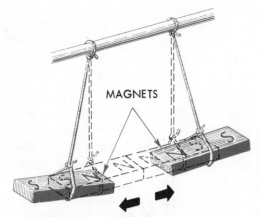

REPULSION BETWEEN LIKE POLES

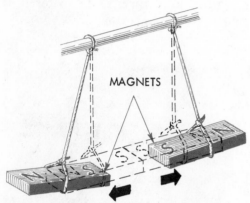

REPULSION BETWEEN LIKE POLES

Fig. 4-5. The top magnets were placed so that the like poles were near each other. When iron filings were sprinkled on them, a pattern formed, which shows that the two like magnetic fields push each other away. In the lower magnets, with unlike poles placed close together, the magnets have a strong attraction for each other. The iron filings form the path of the magnetic field.

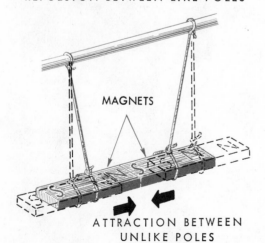

ATTRACTION BETWEEN
UNLIKE POLES

Fig. 4-4. When the ends marked *N* are brought together, there is a tendency for the two bars to move apart or push each other away. The same is true if the ends marked *S* are brought together. Now if the end of one bar marked *N* is brought near the end of the other bar marked *S*, the two bars will pull themselves together.

Magnetic Action

If the ends of two bar magnets are placed near each other, they will either pull together or stay apart. See Figs. 4-4 and 4-5. We can easily see that the ends marked alike tend to repel each other, and those marked unlike tend to attract each other. The *N* and *S* on the bars are commonly called *poles* and are referred to as the *north pole* and the *south pole* of the magnet. With this information, we can now state the first principle of magnetism: *Like poles repel each other and unlike poles attract each other.*

Structure of Magnets

Not all pieces of steel are magnets. Two pieces may look exactly alike but

Fig. 4-6. The ball bearings shown in the photograph represent the molecules in a piece of steel. A magnetized piece of steel has all of the molecules aligned so that the like poles are all in the same direction.

one may attract other steel objects and one may not. The one that attracts another steel object is called a *magnet*. What makes the difference between the magnetized and unmagnetized pieces of steel?

Steel, like all things, is composed of very small particles called *molecules*. It is believed that each molecule has a north and a south pole the same as a whole magnet. In a piece of steel that is magnetized, these very small magnets have arranged themselves in an orderly fashion. Fig. 4-6 illustrates how the molecules have been arranged so that all north poles point in the same direction and, of course, all south poles will be pointing in the opposite direction. In the unmagnetized steel the molecules are arranged in a very irregular manner, as shown in Fig. 4-7. In this random arrangement of the tiny magnets, they

tend to neutralize each other and thus the steel is unmagnetized.

Magnetic Induction

The unmagnetized steel may be magnetized if we stroke it with a magnet, as demonstrated in Fig. 4-8. The magnet will make the tiny molecules arrange themselves so that all of the poles bear in the same direction. This is called *magnetic induction*.

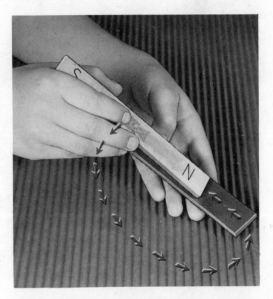

Fig. 4-8. This piece of steel is being magnetized by stroking it with a permanent magnet. One pole of the permanent magnet is placed at one end of the piece of steel and pulled the full length of the steel. At the end of the stroke the magnet is lifted away from the steel and before starting the second stroke the magnet is again placed at the original starting position. After repeating this several times the steel will become magnetized. This is called *magnetic induction*.

Fig. 4-7. Each ball or molecule is marked to show that it has a north and south pole. In this unmagnetized piece of steel the molecules are not arranged in an orderly pattern.

Magnetic Compass

If a piece of magnetized steel is suspended and left free to rotate, it will turn so that one end points north and the other end points south. This is because the earth is a huge magnet with

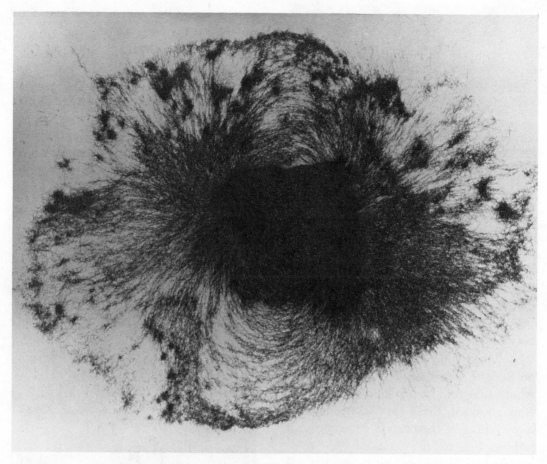

Fig. 4-9. Bits of steel wool show magnetic field of a piece of *lodestone*.

north and south poles that attract the poles of the suspended magnet. This is the principle of the *magnetic compass*. The compass uses a very light, thin magnet that rotates freely on its pivot. The end of the compass that points north is commonly referred to as the *north-seeking pole*. The magnetic compass is an important aid to all types of navigation. Through its use, ships at sea are guided safely to port, explorers are protected from becoming lost, and airplanes are kept on their course.

The first compasses made by man centuries ago used a piece of *lodestone*, which means "leading stone." It is an iron ore that is naturally magnetic. See Fig. 4-9.

The north magnetic pole is not always in the same position; it shifts slightly from year to year. It is in the vicinity of Hudson Bay in northern Canada, as indicated in Fig. 4-10. The changes in location of the poles are quite small and for most purposes the pole is considered to be approximately 12° west of the geographical north when a compass is read in New York City, and approximately 18° east of the geographical north when read in San Francisco. In a narrow strip

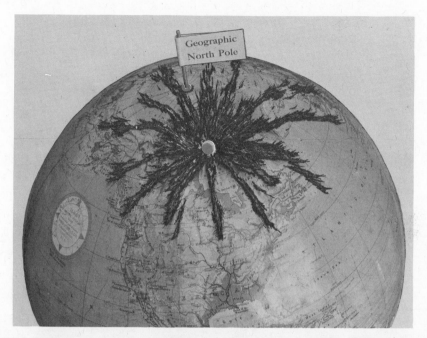

Fig. 4-10. The iron filings on the top of the globe illustrate the magnetic field of the earth. Not everyone realizes that the earth's geographic north pole and its magnetic pole are not the same. They are approximately 1400 miles apart and the compass points to the magnetic pole. The fact that these two poles are not the same makes it necessary for air or sea navigators to recognize this difference when plotting courses.

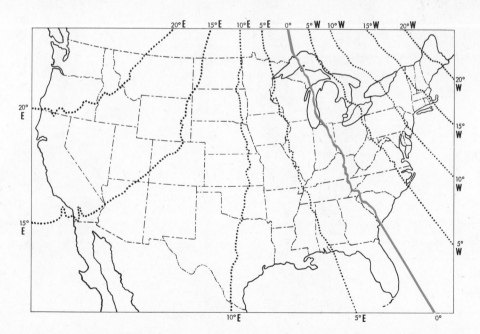

Fig. 4-11. With this chart you will be able to determine the variation from true north that is indicated by a compass in your locality. The heavy line passing diagonally through right side of the chart is known as an *agonic* line. This is an imaginary line which passes through points where a compass needle shows no variation.

through the United States, from Michigan to Georgia, the compass will point true north and south all of the time, because the magnetic pole is directly in line with the north pole. See Fig. 4-11. The difference between true north and the compass reading at any place on the earth is called *variation*.

A permanent magnet may lose its magnetism by being hammered, dropped, or heated. All of these means cause the molecules to change their positions and thus the steel will lose its magnetism.

On the other hand, an ordinary piece of steel will acquire magnetism if it is pointed north and hammered. The attraction of the earth's magnetism aligns the molecules.

Metals That Make Magnets

The Bell Telephone Laboratories have developed powerful magnets which contain the rare metal samarium. This new magnetic material has the highest resistance to demagnetization of any other material of comparable magnetic proper-

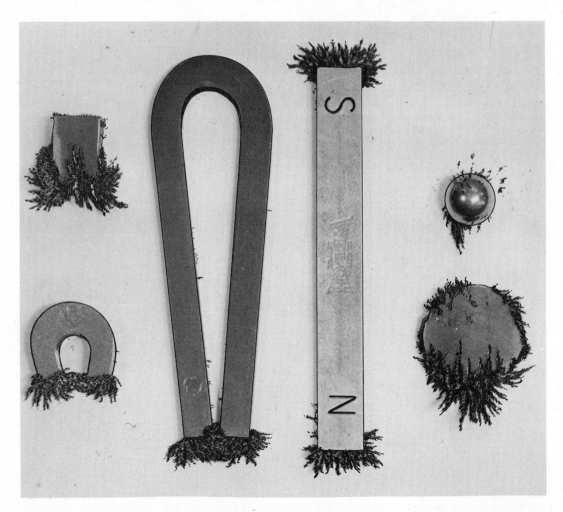

Fig. 4-12. Typical examples of commercial magnets. Each magnet has definite north and south poles regardless of its shape.

ties. Other ingredients of the magnetic material include solid cobalt, copper, and iron.

Permanent magnets are made in many shapes and sizes, as seen in Fig. 4-12. The common types are *horseshoe* and *bar* magnets. They are made of hardened steel, because it retains its magnetism for a long period of time. Soft steel can easily be magnetized but will not hold its magnetism. It is believed that soft steel loses its magnetism easily because the molecules of steel are free to move and thus change position readily. In hard steel the molecules are not so free to move.

A steel alloy, which is steel mixed with other metals such as tungsten, chromium, cobalt, or nickel, will make a very strong permanent magnet. Recent developments in the use of alloy steels have produced magnets which have a much greater magnetic field than the hard steel magnets. One of the best alloys for making magnets contains aluminum, nickel, and cobalt. This type of alloy is commonly called *alnico*. Uses for permanent magnets other than those shown in the illustrations are in radio speakers, electrical measuring instruments, telephone receivers, generators, and motors. We shall learn more about these uses later.

Magnetic Materials

Metals which are attracted by a magnet are called *magnetic materials*. These are iron, from which steel is made, cobalt, and nickel. Other metals, including pure aluminum and copper, zinc, and lead will not be attracted by a magnet and are called nonmagnetic. Materials other than metals, such as wood, textiles, etc., are never magnetic.

Magnetic Field

Magnetism will pass through all materials which are nonmagnetic. This can be illustrated by placing a piece of paper or glass on top of a magnet and sprinkling iron filings on it. The iron filings will become magnetized and drawn toward the magnet even though the paper or glass is between the filings and the magnet. Fig. 4-13 shows how the filings will form a definite pattern which is similar to the invisible magnetic field produced by the magnet. This magnetic field is always present around any magnet.

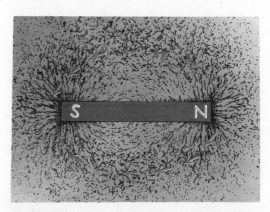

Fig. 4-13. The iron filings show the lines of force that are always present between the poles of any magnet.

We can get a stronger magnetic field if two unlike poles are brought closer together. The closer the two poles are together without touching each other, the shorter the path will be for the magnetic field to travel. Each pole will have a greater attraction for the other and also they will have a stronger pull for other magnetic materials. If we should bend a bar magnet into the shape of a horseshoe, we would then find the magnetic field to be stronger.

INTERESTING THINGS TO DO

1. Showing the Magnetic Field Surrounding a Single Magnet.

a. Place a bar magnet on a flat wooden surface and cover it with a sheet of paper. Sprinkle iron filings on the top of the paper and tap it lightly until a pattern forms. You now have the picture of a magnetic field. Observe that the lines tend to go from one pole to the other. Also note that the strongest field is close to the ends of the poles.

b. Sprinkle iron filings on a horseshoe magnet covered with a sheet of paper. You will notice that the magnetic field is now concentrated between the two poles. Why is there a greater magnetic field shown by the horseshoe magnet than by the bar magnet?

2. Showing the Magnetic Field Formed by Two Magnets.

a. Place two bar magnets on a flat surface, end to end, so that the north poles are approximately 1″ apart. Cover the bars with a sheet of paper and sprinkle iron filings on the paper the same as in *1a*. Observe the pattern of the magnetic field. What is happening to the magnetic field?

b. Place two bar magnets on a flat surface, end to end, so that the north pole of one and the south pole of the other are approximately 1″ apart. Cover the bars with a sheet of paper and sprinkle iron filings on the paper. Observe the pattern of the magnets. How does it differ from the pattern of *2a*?

3. Making a Permanent Magnet by Induction.

a. Place an old hacksaw blade in a vise and with a pliers break off a piece about 2″ long. (To avoid having the blade break into several pieces do not let it extend over 2½″ beyond the vise jaw.) Obtain a permanent magnet and stroke the blade with the magnet. Test the blade to see if it is magnetic by trying to pick up some small nails. Why has the blade become a permanent magnet?

b. Obtain two ¼″ straight-shank twist drills, and magnetize them by induction, using a very strong magnet. Be sure to stroke each drill with the same pole of the magnet and keep each drill pointed in the same direction. Then place the two drills parallel on a flat surface about ⅛″ apart. Keep the sharpened ends pointed in the same direction. Observe what happens to the drills. Why do the drills push each other apart? Reverse the direction of one of the drills. What happens and why?

4. Making a Compass.

Obtain a piece of spring steel approximately ³⁄₁₆″ wide and 1″ long (an old

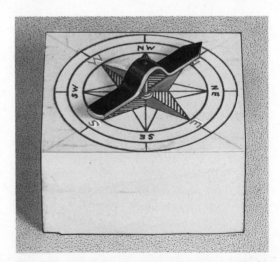

Fig. 4-14. Compass constructed from a clock spring.

clock spring is excellent for this purpose). Shape the spring to a point on one end. Center-punch the spring in the middle so that it will balance on a pivot. It is easier to balance the compass if the center of the spring is raised as in Fig. 4-14. The pivot can be made by sharpening a brad on each end and forcing one end into a block of wood. The wood block should be about ¾" thick and 1½" square. A small hole can be made in the block with another brad, making it possible to push the pointed pivot in with your fingers. A drawing of the points of the compass can be made on a piece of paper and glued to the block. Magnetize the spring steel by induction. Place the magnetized spring on the pivot. If it does not balance, grind the heavy end until the steel compass needle balances perfectly. Compare the direction in which the spring points with that of a standard compass. Why does it point towards the north magnetic pole? What happens if the north pole of a bar magnet is brought near the north-seeking pole of the compass?

5. Making a Magnetic Field Pattern Developer.

Materials needed:
1 Tin can (size of 3 lb. shortening can or a 2 lb. coffee can)
1 Lamp socket
6 ft Lamp cord
1 ft Wood dowel, ¼"
1 Wood base
2 Pieces wood for can support
2 Pieces wood for pattern platform
1 Piece heavy cardboard
1 Attachment plug
1 Rubber grommet, ⅜"

Make a platform approximately 3" high with two pieces of wood and a piece of heavy cardboard and secure it to the wood base. In securing the parts of the platform together and to the wood base, use glue instead of nails or screws. Mount the lamp socket on a wood block and drill a ¼" hole lengthwise through the center of the block for the wood dowel. Drill two ¼" holes through the sides of the can near the bottom, so that the piece of wood dowel can be inserted in the holes, and through the hole in the wood block which holds the lamp socket. Glue the piece of wood dowel to the wood block and secure the lamp socket to the bottom of the can. See Figs 4-15 and 4-16.

Drill a ¼" hole in each of the can supports so that when the can is mounted and rotated the edge of the can will clear the top of the pattern platform by ¼". Drill a ⅜" hole in the bottom of the can near the lamp socket for the rubber grommet. Attach one end of the lamp cord to the lamp socket, extend

Fig. 4-15. Sprinkling steel wool on the wax paper held under the lamp of the magnetic field pattern developer.

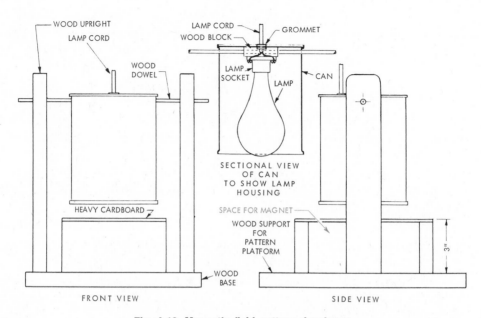

Fig. 4-16. Magnetic field pattern developer.

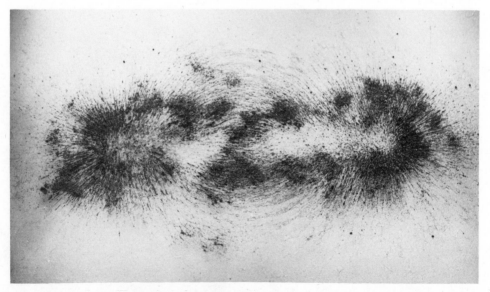

Fig. 4-17. The magnetic pattern is permanently impressed on the wax paper.

the cord through the grommet and attach a plug cap on the opposite end. Insert a lamp in the socket and the field pattern developer is ready to operate. The size of the lamp may vary from 75 to 150 watts, depending upon the type of wax paper used in making the patterns.

To make a permanent magnetic field pattern, place a magnet, either permanent or electromagnetic, under the platform and close to the cardboard top. Place a piece of waxed paper on top of the platform and sprinkle fine iron filings on the paper. Pieces of steel wool rubbed together will produce very satisfactory results. Tap the cardboard top of the platform gently until the desired pattern is formed, then swing the can with the lamp lighted over the pattern. Within one minute the heat from the lamp will cause the filings or pieces of steel wool to sink into the wax on the paper. When the heated lamp is removed a permanent pattern of the magnetic field will remain on the waxed paper. See Fig. 4-17.

REVIEW QUESTIONS

1. List the uses that have been made of permanent magnets in your home.

2. Why are man-made permanent magnets called artificial magnets?

3. What are the poles of a magnet called?

4. State the basic law of magnetism.

5. When a piece of steel becomes magnetized what change takes place?

6. What is meant by *magnetic induction?*

7. What do we call the end of the compass that points towards the north?

8. What is the difference between the geographic north pole and the magnetic north pole?

9. Explain why a compass is important to all types of navigation.

10. Find out the approximate compass variation for your locality.

11. Why does the compass point true north and south in certain locations?

12. Why does hard steel retain magnetism?

13. What materials are used in making very strong permanent magnets?

14. List some nonmagnetic materials.

15. What is meant by a *magnetic field?*

16. What material did ancient navigators use for a compass?

17. What is meant by the term *agonic line?*

UNIT 5
ELECTROMAGNETS

How Permanent Magnets Are Made

We have discussed how a permanent magnet may be made by stroking a section of hard steel with another magnet. Another method of making a permanent magnet is by *electromagnetism*. If insulated wire is wrapped around a hard piece of steel and the two ends of the coil are then connected to a source of electricity, such as a battery, we have what is called an *electromagnet*. If the battery is left connected for a short time, the steel will become magnetized and, when withdrawn from the coil, will be found to be a magnet.

Coil Polarity

What caused the coil of wire to magnetize the steel? We can find out if, after removing the steel core from the coil, we reconnect the coil to a battery source of electricity. Now iron filings may be sprinkled around the coil and a pattern will develop like that shown by the bar magnet. A compass may be placed near the coil and it will point in the direction of the magnetic field. See Fig. 5-1. This field can also be called the *lines of force*. The lines of force around the coil have a north and south pole just like the permanent magnet. The south pole of the coil will attract the north pole of the compass.

Fig. 5-1. Compasses have been placed in the magnetic field of a coil that has been connected to a dry cell. Each compass points in the direction of the magnetic field. We can see that one end of the coil attracts the south pole of the compass. This shows us that the coil has definite north and south poles the same as a bar magnet.

Importance of Electromagnets

Of all the functions of electricity, one of the most important is in the *electromagnet*. Many devices use the principle of electromagnetism in their construction. Without its use our entire industrial world would stop functioning. All electric motors are dependent upon it. Automobiles use it to start and to keep running. The sound coming from a radio is dependent upon it. The television picture is focused by it. The power that provides heat and light for our homes is generated by it. Many more uses could be listed, as electromagnets are working for us continually. See Figs. 5-2 and 5-3.

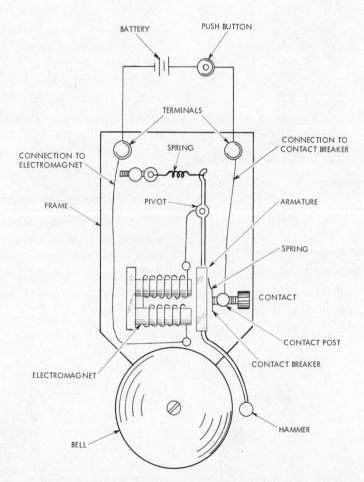

Fig. 5-2. The bell is an application of an electromagnet. Its vibrating motion is made through the use of a contact point. When the bell is connected to a source of electricity, the electromagnet attracts the armature. As soon as the armature is pulled toward the electromagnet, the contact points open and the coil loses its magnetism. The armature then returns to its original position where the contact points again make contact. At this time the electromagnet once more pulls the armature of the coil. The bell rings each time the hammer, which is attached to the armature, strikes the bell. The vibrating motion is the result of the electricity being continually turned off and on.

Fig. 5-3. Huge electromagnets used in industry simplify the job of loading and unloading scrap steel. (Cutler-Hammer)

How an Electromagnet Is Made

When we made a permanent magnet with electromagnestism, we used hard steel for the magnet. This was done because we wanted to retain the magne-tism in the steel. Electromagnets are used in many electrical devices which require a very strong magnetic field and also require the magnetism to be started and stopped rapidly.

If we connect a coil of wire to a source of electricity, we will find that it will have a very weak attraction for iron. Now if we insert a piece of soft steel into the center of the coil, we will find that the electromagnet will lift a number of steel objects. This increase in magnetic strength is due to the soft steel core, which provides a better path for the magnetic field. Disconnecting the battery from the coil will cause the steel objects to drop from the core. This shows us that a soft steel core loses its magnetism easily. It also illustrates that when the coil is disconnected from the source of electricity, the electromagnet is no longer operating.

Basic Principles of Electromagnets

We have now stated the two principal requirements of an electromagnet: (1) It must have a strong magnetic field which can be concentrated through the use of a steel core. (2) It must have a soft steel

OR

INDUCTANCE
(AIR CORE)

Both coil symbols are now in common use.

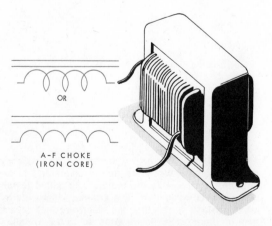

OR

A-F CHOKE
(IRON CORE)

Two lines always indicate a magnetic core.

core so that the magnetism can readily be controlled.

The electromagnet can be made stronger or weaker, depending upon how strong the source of electricity is and upon the number of turns of wire around the core. We can increase the strength of the magnetic field if we can increase the power of the electricity. Likewise, if the number of turns of wire around the core is increased, this too will increase the strength of the electromagnet. These two factors will be more fully explained in another section of this book.

Coil and Moving Plunger

Devices that require opening, closing, pushing, and pulling by remote control usually use an electromagnet consisting of a coil and steel plunger, commonly called a *solenoid*. See Fig. 5-4. If we wind a coil of wire on a nonmagnetic hollow form, such as cardboard tubing, and connect it to a battery, it will set up a magnetic field around the coil. This field consists of lines of force that pass through the center of the coil. A small piece of soft steel placed near the hollow

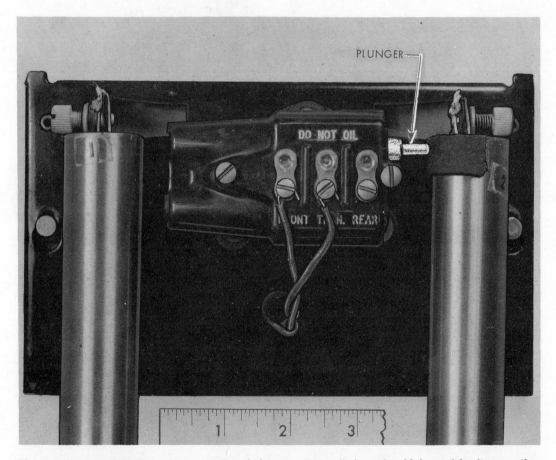

Fig. 5-4. In a modern door chime a coil-and-plunger, often called a *solenoid,* is used for its operation. When the door button is pushed, the plunger is pulled into the coil against one of the chime tubes. As the button is released a spring pulls the plunger back out of the coil against the other chime tube. From this starting and stopping of the electricity we are able to get the two different tones from the chimes.

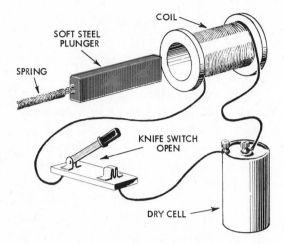

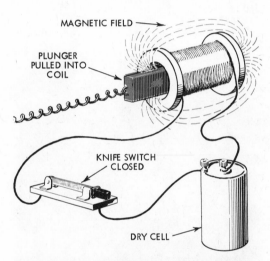

Fig. 5-5. When the battery is connected to the coil, the plunger is magnetized and pulled into the center of the coil. When the battery is disconnected, the coil and plunger lose their magnetism and the spring pulls the plunger back.

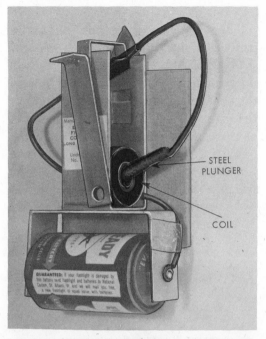

Fig. 5-6. A rear view of the coil-and-plunger used to provide motion in a commercial advertising sign. In operation the flashlight cell is connected to the coil of wire so that it pulls the steel core toward the center of the coil. As the plunger goes through the coil the battery is disconnected by the movement of the plunger. This permits the plunger to pass through the coil and after reaching the top of its swing it returns to the starting position. At this time the coil is reconnected to the dry cell and the plunger action starts over again. The device must be started by hand.

opening of the coil will be drawn into the coil, as shown in Fig. 5-5. This attraction, which causes the piece of steel to be pulled into the center of the coil, is due to the magnetism of the coil magnetizing the steel core. The molecules of the steel align themselves because they are attracted by the magnetic poles of the coil. We then have a coil acting like a magnet and magnetizing a steel core— the coil and the steel core attract each other. When the battery is disconnected, the coil loses its magnetism and, since it is made of soft steel, the plunger also loses its magnetism. This moving plunger can be used to push or pull various devices whenever the electricity is connected to the coil. If a spring is hooked onto the plunger, it will return the plunger to its original position as soon as the electricity is turned off. See Fig. 5-6.

Superconducting Electromagnets

A characteristic of an electrical conductor such as copper is that its resistance to the flow of electrons through it varies with its temperature. High temperatures tend to restrict their flow, while low temperatures provide an easier path for them to follow. From the relationship between carrying capacity of the conductor and temperature, scientists reasoned that if temperatures could be lowered sufficiently, a conductor would lose its resistance to electron flow. From the results of that study, known as "cryogenics," the world's largest superconducting electromagnet was developed and is now being operated in the Atomic Energy Commission's Argonne National Laboratory. The magnet is termed "superconducting" because no power is lost as heat in its coils. Only a small amount of electric power is required for the initial charging of the magnet which takes two and one half hours. After the initial charge, the only power used will be that required by the liquid helium refrigerator to keep the temperature of the coils down to −451.3° F, (about 400 watts). A conventional magnet used in place of the superconducting magnet would require enough power to supply a town of 10,000 inhabitants. See Fig. 5-7.

Fig. 5-7. Assembling a *superconductive* electromagnet. The magnet contains 30 energizing coils, half of which may be seen. Each coil is made up of 4400 feet of conductor strip, two inches wide and 1/10 inch thick. Six strands of niobium-titanium alloy are imbedded in the strips to serve as a superconductor. (Argonne National Laboratory.)

INTERESTING THINGS TO DO

1. Making a Permanent Magnet by Means of Electricity.

Make a hollow tube by wrapping a piece of thin cardboard (tagboard) 2" x 2" around a ¼" wood dowel. Using a fast drying glue, secure the overlapping cardboard. Be sure to avoid gluing the tubing to the dowel so that it can be removed easily. Out of heavy cardboard or ⅛" masonite, shape two round washers about 1" in diameter. Drill a hole in the center of each washer so that they can be fitted snugly over the ends of the cardboard tubing. Drill a ¹⁄₁₆" hole in one washer close to the center hole. A second ¹⁄₁₆" hole should be drilled near the outside edge of the same washer. Glue one washer to each end of the tubing. Insert one end of a spool of No. 22 magnet wire through the inner ¹⁄₁₆" hole in the washer. Wind four, close-spaced, even layers of wire on the tubing and bring the end out through the outer hole in the washer. The two coil leads should be left about 6" long. See Fig. 5-8.

Obtain a piece of hard steel approximately ¼" x 3". This can be a section of hacksaw blade, clock spring, or tool steel. Insert the steel into the center of the hollow coil. Connect the two ends of the coil to a dry cell for about ten seconds. Disconnect the cell and remove the hard steel core. Test the steel to see

if it will attract small nails. What has happened to the steel? Hold one end of the steel near the north-seeking pole of a compass. Mark the polarity of your magnet.

2. Using a Plunger Type Solenoid.

Obtain a piece of soft steel ¼" in diameter and about 2½" long. Insert the soft steel about halfway into the center of the coil made in Number 1. Connect one end of the coil to a dry cell, and momentarily make contact with the remaining coil lead to the other terminal of the cell. What happened to the soft steel core? Why did this occur? How can this principle be used on other electrical devices?

The coil that you have wound can be used on a number of different electrical projects such as a buzzer, door chime, motor, electrical lock, relay, or switch.

3. Making a Powerful Electromagnet.

This electromagnet will hold a weight of nearly 200 pounds when connected to a small flashlight cell.

Materials needed:

1 Piece iron pipe, 4" pipe size, 2⅛" long
1 Piece sheet steel, mild, ¼" x 5" x 5"
1 Piece sheet steel, mild, ⅜" x 5" x 5"
1 Piece steel rod, mild, round, 1½" diameter, 2½" long
2 Eye bolts, steel, ⅜"
2 Hexagon nuts, steel, ⅜"
8 Machine screws, R. H. steel, 8-32, ¾" long
360 Feet magnet wire, 18 ga., enamel or cotton covered
1 Piece sheet metal, 20 ga., 6" x 8", for wire spool (see text)
1 Piece plastic tubing, size 18, 2" long.

The secret of this electromagnet's tremendous holding force on very small battery power, shown in Fig. 5-3, is the

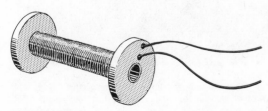

Fig. 5-8. Electromagnetic coil.

nearly perfect magnetic contact between the top plate and pipe and a similar contact between the bottom plate, core, and pipe. This requires that the parts which go together be turned and faced on a lathe to a mirror-like surface. For those who have the ability to perform the necessary lathe operations, and also the welding experience to weld the center core to the top plate, the magnet will open up the fascinating field of electromagnetism with many exciting experiments.

Four inch pipe usually has an outside diameter of about $4\frac{1}{2}''$, but since that measurement may vary somewhat the steel pieces for the top and bottom plates are specified larger so that they may be placed in a lathe chuck with ample clearance.

Turn and face the parts in a lathe to get the smoothest possible surfaces on the parts which fit together. The bottom plate should be about $\frac{1}{4}''$ wider than the diameter of the pipe. Drill the center of the top plate for a press fit with the center core, press the core into place and weld the two pieces together, as shown in Fig. 5-9. Secure the top plate and core to the pipe with steel machine screws, as shown in the drawing. Place the magnet shell in a lathe and face the

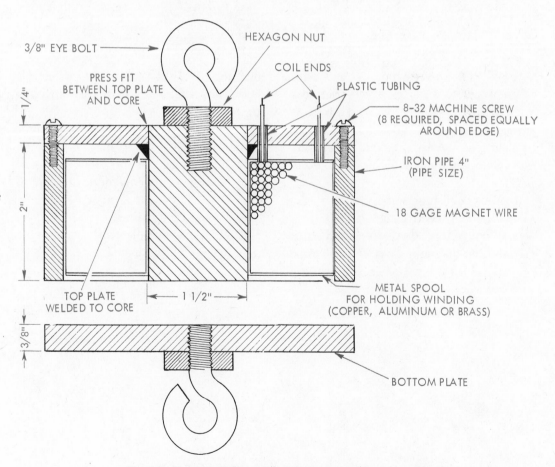

Fig. 5-9. Cross-section drawings of a powerful electromagnet.

ends of the core and pipe so that the two pieces will be perfectly in line. Drill and tap the magnet core and bottom plate and secure the eye bolts in place with hexagon nuts. Drill two ⅛" holes in the top plate for coil leads.

Make a form out of copper, aluminum, or brass, on which to wind the magnet wire. *Do not use iron or steel.*

This form should fit snugly over the center core and should be slightly shorter than the iron pipe. Wind 360 feet of magnet wire on the form and insulate the coil leads with pieces of plastic tubing. To prevent breakage of the coil leads they may be joined to pieces of stranded wire within the form, or they may be brought out to an insulated terminal strip mounted on top of the magnet.

If the magnet is to be used to lift one or more persons, it is advisable to link the top and bottom plates together with a loose piece of chain. This will prevent the bottom plate from striking the person being lifted in case a weak dry cell allows the two parts to separate.

REVIEW QUESTIONS

1. What happens when a coil of wire is connected to a source of electricity?

2. When a piece of hard steel is placed in a coil connected to a source of electricity, what happens to the steel?

3. Give another name for *magnetic field*.

4. Make a list of some electrical devices that use electromagnets.

5. What effect does the steel core have on the magnetic field in an electromagnet?

6. Why isn't hard steel used in electromagnets?

7. What is a coil and moving plunger usually called?

8. Explain why a soft steel core will be pulled into the magnetic field of a coil.

9. Define *cryogenics*.

10. How is an electrical conductor made *superconductive?*

How Electricity

Is

Produced

UNIT 6
THE ELECTRON THEORY

Structure of Matter

Matter is anything that has weight and occupies space. It may be in the form of a solid, such as copper in an electrical conductor; a gas, such as hydrogen; or a liquid, such as water.

Using water as an example, let's analyze the structure of matter. If we took a drop of water and continued to divide it until it could not be divided further and still maintain the chemical properties of water, the smallest particle remaining would be a *molecule* of water.

Next, let's take this molecule of water and pass an electric current through it.

This action will break down the molecule still further into its two component gases, hydrogen and oxygen. But these gases no longer have the properties of water. A substance that can be broken down into two or more basic parts, such as water, is called a *compound*.

The hydrogen and oxygen which combined to make the water and which cannot be broken down further are known as *elements*. The smallest particle of an element which still has the chemical and electrical properties of that element is an *atom*. To make a molecule of water, two atoms of hydrogen and one atom of oxygen are needed. See Fig. 6-1.

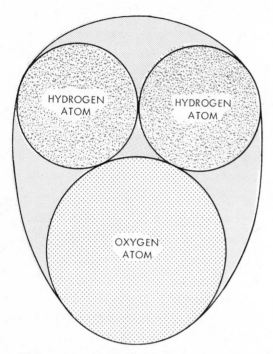

Fig. 6-1. Hydrogen and oxygen atoms unite to form a molecule of water.

The Nature of Electricity

Before the acceptance of the electron theory, the effects of electricity could be seen, felt, and measured but could only be described as a mysterious force that traveled through a conductor at a speed of 186,000 miles per second. The electron theory is widely accepted today as an explanation of the flow of electricity through a conductor.

According to the electron theory, the atoms which make up all matter are composed of 3 types of particles, *protons, electrons,* and *neutrons*. Atoms of different materials vary only in number and arrangement of these particles.

The electron is a particle of negative electrical charge revolving around the center of the atom, similar to the earth revolving around the sun. The center of the atom contains the positively charged

particles called protons and the neutral particles (neutral in that they bear no charge) called neutrons. This center is termed the *nucleus* of the atom.

We have noted that there are two types of charged particles, positive and negative. Since the positive charge of the nucleus of the atom attracts the negative charge of the electron, we can say that *opposite charges attract.* In other words, there is a force of attraction between positive and negative charges.

When considering weight, we must note that the proton and neutron weigh about 1847 times as much as the electron. Thus the total weight of the proton and the neutron will determine the weight of the material.

Strength of Atoms

For the sake of clarity, the structure of an atom is usually represented by a series of progressively larger orbits or shells, with the electrons following their inside circumference. The force which holds the electrons in their paths, preventing their breaking outward, is the attraction between the positively charged protons in the nucleus and the negatively charged electrons. The force which prevents the electrons from moving inward is centrifugal force, which is the force tending to make a rotating body move away from the center of rotation.

Except for the electrons in the outer shell, the particles of an atom are held tightly together and tremendous forces are required to pry them apart. Since the electrons in the outer shell are farthest from the nucleus they are least attracted by its positive charge. In materials such as silver and copper which have only one electron in their outer shell, the electron may be dislodged easily from its orbit by electrical pressure. This characteristic makes silver and copper very good electrical conductors.

We have learned that having only one electron in the outer shells of silver and copper atoms make them very good electrical conductors, but for an understanding of how a single electron reaches the outer shell we must study further the interior construction of an atom.

Distribution of Electrons

Scientists have determined that rather than rotating in a single shell, the electrons of an atom divide into sub-shells, each of which will hold a limited number of electrons. These groups of sub-shells, known as *energy levels*, are assigned the letters K, L, M, N, O, P, and Q. Fig. 6-2 shows the grouping of the sub-shells in an atom of silver. The capacity of the sub-shells is shown below. While these sub-shells will hold any less number of electrons than indicated, any greater number will be rejected and forced into the next outward shell.

If we examine Fig. 6-2 and the table,

CAPACITY OF SUB-SHELLS IN FIRST FOUR ENERGY LEVELS OF AN ATOM

	K	2 Electrons
Inner	L	2 Electrons
Outer	L	6 Electrons
Inner	M	2 Electrons
Second	M	6 Electrons
Outer	M	10 Electrons
Inner	N	2 Electrons
Second	N	6 Electrons
Third	N	10 Electrons
Outer	N	14 Electrons

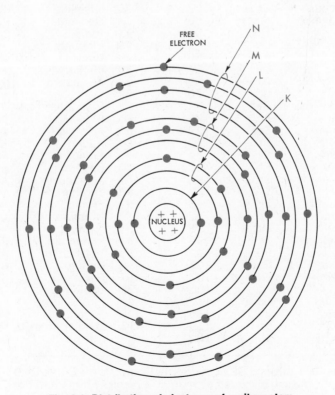

Fig. 6-2. Distribution of electrons of a silver atom.

TABLE OF ELEMENTS

Atomic Number	Name of Element	Symbol of Element	Atomic Weight	Atomic Number	Name of Element	Symbol of Element	Atomic Weight
1	Hydrogen	H	1	52	Tellurium	Te	128
2	Helium	He	4	53	Iodine	I	127
3	Lithium	Li	7	54	Xenon	Xe	131
4	Beryllium	Be	9	55	Cesium	Cs	133
5	Boron	B	11	56	Barium	Ba	137
6	Carbon	C	12	57	Lanthanum	La	139
7	Nitrogen	N	14	58	Cerium	Ce	140
8	Oxygen	O	16	59	Praseodymium	Pr	141
9	Fluorine	F	19	60	Neodymium	Nd	144
10	Neon	Ne	20	61	Promethium	Pm	147
11	Sodium	Na	22	62	Samarium	Sm	150
12	Magnesium	Mg	24	63	Europium	Eu	152
13	Aluminum	Al	27	64	Gadolinium	Gd	157
14	Silicon	Si	28	65	Terbium	Tb	159
15	Phosphorus	P	31	66	Dysprosium	Dy	162
16	Sulfur	S	32	67	Hilmium	Ho	165
17	Chlorine	Cl	35	68	Erbium	Er	167
18	Argon	A	39	69	Thulium	Tm	169
19	Potassium	K	39	70	Ytterbium	Yb	173
20	Calcium	Ca	40	71	Lutecium	Lu	175
21	Scandium	Sc	45	72	Hafnium	Hf	179
22	Titanium	Ti	48	73	Tantalum	Ta	181
23	Vanadium	V	51	74	Tungsten	W	184
24	Chromium	Cr	52	75	Rhenium	Re	186
25	Manganese	Mn	55	76	Osmium	Os	190
26	Iron	Fe	56	77	Iridium	Ir	193
27	Cobalt	Co	59	78	Platinum	Pt	195
28	Nickel	Ni	59	79	Gold	Au	197
29	Copper	Cu	64	80	Mercury	Hg	201
30	Zinc	Zn	65	81	Thallium	Tl	204
31	Gallium	Ga	70	82	Lead	Pb	207
32	Germanium	Ge	73	83	Bismuth	Bi	209
33	Arsenic	As	75	84	Polonium	Po	210
34	Selenium	Se	79	85	Astatine	At	211
35	Bromine	Br	80	86	Radon	Rn	222
36	Krypton	Kr	84	87	Francium	Fr	223
37	Rubidium	Rb	85	88	Radium	Ra	226
38	Strontium	Sr	88	89	Actinium	Ac	227
39	Yttrium	Y	89	90	Thorium	Th	232
40	Zirconium	Zr	91	91	Protactinium	Pa	231
41	Columbium	Cb	93	92	Uranium	U	238
42	Molybdenum	Mo	96	93	Neptunium	Np	239
43	Technetium	Tc	99	94	Plutonium	Pu	239
44	Ruthenium	Ru	102	95	Americium	Am	241
45	Rhodium	Rh	103	96	Curium	Cm	242
46	Palladium	Pd	107	97	Berkelium	Bk	245
47	Silver	Ag	108	98	Californium	Cf	246
48	Cadmium	Cd	112	99	Einsteinium	E	253
49	Indium	In	115	100	Fermium	Fm	256
50	Tin	Sn	119	101	Mendelevium	Mv	256
51	Antimony	Sb	122	102	Nobelium	No	253-254?

Note: Elements 1 through 92 occur normally in nature. Elements 93 and above are those discovered by man as a result of transmutation.

we will see why silver is an excellent electrical conductor. The Table of *Elements* states that a silver atom contains 47 electrons. The capacity chart shows us that shells K, L, M, and the inner, second, and third sub-shells of N will accept only 46 electrons. The 47th electron is forced into the outer N sub-shell where it may be attracted to an adjacent atom with little electrical pressure.

In a similar manner we can learn why copper is a good electrical conductor but ranks below silver in conductivity. See Fig. 6-3. The Table of Elements shows that a copper atom has 29 electrons orbiting around its nucleus. Referring again to the Capacity Table, we learn that shells K, L, and M accept only 28 electrons. The 29th electron is forced into

the inner sub-shell N, where it orbits as a *free* electron. The electrical conductivity of a metal is determined by the ease with which electrons in the outer orbit of its atom can move into an adjacent atom. We learned that the forces which control such movement are the attraction of the nucleus which tends to draw the electron toward it, and centrifugal force which pushed the electron outward. Since the free electron of a copper atom is closer to its nucleus than the free electron of a silver atom, more electrical energy is required to dislodge it and move toward another atom. For that reason copper rates below silver as an electrical conductor.

Aluminum has a lower electrical conductivity than copper, but it is frequently

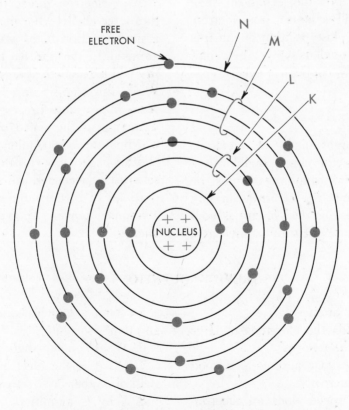

Fig. 6-3. Distribution of electrons of a copper atom.

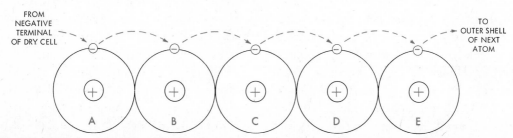

FROM NEGATIVE TERMINAL OF DRY CELL

TO OUTER SHELL OF NEXT ATOM

A   B   C   D   E

Fig. 6-4. When the negatively charged electron moves from the dry cell to atom *A* it forces the electron from the outer shell of atom *A* to atom *B*. The electron from atom *B* moves on to atom *C* where it displaces the outer electron and forces it to atom *D*. This movement continues on to atom *E* and through the remainder of the circuit to the positive terminal of the dry cell.

used when lightness in weight is more important than electrical conductivity. An aluminum atom contains only 13 electrons. If we distribute the electrons according to the capacity table, we learn that shells K, L, and the inner sub-shell M will accept only 12 electrons. The 13th electron must enter the second sub-shell M, where it will orbit as a free electron. The relatively close position of the free electron to the nucleus shows why aluminum ranks below copper in electrical conductivity.

Electron Flow

Since the movement of electrons along a conductor corresponds to the flow of electricity, some means must be provided to start the electrons in motion. When an electrical circuit is connected to a source of supply, such as a dry cell, negatively charged electrons tend to flow from the negative terminal of the dry cell through the conductor. This movement dislodges a negatively charged electron from the outer shell of an atom within the conductor and forces it to the next atom. The newly arrived electron forces the electron in the outer shell to the next atom where a similar action takes place in adjacent atoms until the positive terminal of the dry cell is reached, as shown in Fig. 6-4. While this step-by-step movement may seem like a slow process it is actually occurring at the speed of light, or approximately 186,000 miles per second. In another section, we shall learn how scientists succeeded in separating the particles of certain atoms to create the awesome power known as *nuclear energy*.

REVIEW QUESTIONS

1. Define an atom.
2. What holds the electrons in their paths around the nucleus?
3. Why are silver and copper good electrical conductors?
4. At what speed does an electron move from atom to atom in a conductor?

5. What is known as energy levels in an atom?
6. What is a sub-shell of an atom?
7. What is the electron in the outer shell of copper or silver called?
8. Why is aluminum not as good a conductor as copper?

UNIT 7
MAKING ELECTRICITY WITH CHEMICALS

A Simple Cell

Chemical action is one method of providing a source of electricity. Certain materials, usually metals and carbon, when placed in a liquid solution can produce electricity. A simple cell for producing electricity can be made by placing carbon and zinc in a solution of salammoniac. Salammoniac is used to clean soldering coppers and is available in powder or bar form. Salammoniac is known chemically as *ammonium chloride* and may be obtained in powder form at any drugstore. If the bar salammoniac is used it will be neces-

sary to break off several small pieces and pound them into a powder. The powder can then be mixed with the water in a glass.

A piece of zinc is placed in the glass with the salammoniac solution and a rod of carbon is put in so that it does not touch the zinc. A short length of insulated wire is then connected to the zinc and another wire to the carbon. The other ends of these wires are hooked to a 1½-volt flashlight bulb. The bulb will light, and the cell of zinc, carbon, and salammoniac is developing electricity. See Fig. 7-1.

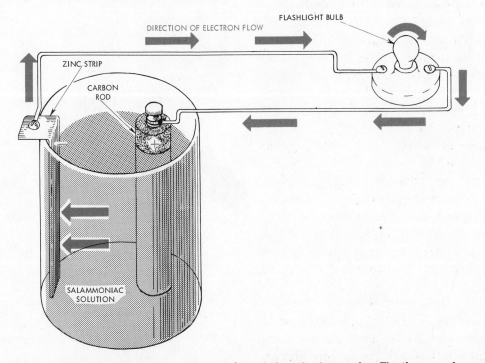

Fig. 7-1. A simple cell made of zinc, carbon, and a solution of salammoniac. The three requirements for a complete electrical circuit are all connected together—a source of electricity, the cell; the two connecting wires; and the object that works from the electricity, the bulb. The flashlight bulb is connected to the zinc and the carbon. The electrons start flowing from the zinc through the wire and the bulb so that they can get to the carbon. This flow of electrons is what is called a flow of electricity. The flow of electricity is then negative particles, called electrons, going from a point where there are many extra electrons to a point where there are very few.

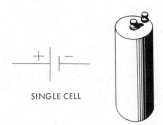

SINGLE CELL

Terminals of a cell are identified by the length of lines.

Electrons

What makes our cell produce electricity? The solution of salammoniac and water, called an *electrolyte,* starts acting on the piece of zinc so that very small particles, not visible to the human eye, gather all around the zinc. These particles are called *electrons.* All electrons are considered to be negative particles of electricity. The electrons will pile up around the zinc until there is not room for any more to get on it. The zinc which has all of the electrons around it is called the *negative electrode.* A minus sign (−) is usually used to indicate the negative electrode. See Fig. 7-1.

Since all the electrons in the solution have gone to the zinc, the carbon is without electrons. We call this point where there is a shortage of electrons the *positive electrode.* A plus sign (+) is usually used to indicate the positive electrode. In electricity when we have a large number of electrons at one place they tend to try to move to a place where there is a shortage of electrons. The electrons in the electrolyte solution flow to the zinc. In order to allow the electrons on the zinc to reach the carbon, an outside path must be provided.

Primary Cells

Cells which cannot be recharged are called *primary cells.* When we made the

cell of zinc, carbon, and salammoniac it was a primary cell because it could not be recharged. The cell went "dead" because the zinc was dissolved in the electrolyte.

Direct Current

The flow of electrons from a cell through a circuit is called *direct current.* Direct current is a flow of electricity that is always in the same direction. A primary cell has one terminal that is negative (−) and the other that is positive (+). When the terminals were connected to a flashlight bulb, the electrons flowed from the negative terminal through the wire and bulb to the positive terminal. This is a direct current source of electricity because the electrons always travel in the same direction. The abbreviation for direct current is DC.

The Dry Cell

A primary cell that can be carried easily and handled without spilling the

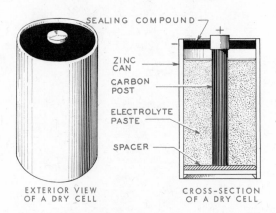

SEALING COMPOUND

ZINC CAN

CARBON POST

ELECTROLYTE PASTE

SPACER

EXTERIOR VIEW OF A DRY CELL

CROSS-SECTION OF A DRY CELL

Fig. 7-2. The outside of a flashlight cell is covered with cardboard but the container is a zinc can. The center post is a carbon rod held in place at the top by an insulating material. Under the insulating top and in the zinc container can be found the electrolyte, which is salammoniac in paste form with black manganese dioxide added.

electrolyte is called a *dry cell*. See Fig. 7-2. These dry cells are used in flashlights, pen lights, radios, telephone circuits, and in many other places where direct current is needed. They differ mainly from the wet cell, in that the electrolyte is made of a paste instead of a liquid.

The dry primary cell will have about 1½ volts. See Fig. 7-3. As in the wet cell, the carbon is the positive (+) terminal and the zinc is the negative (−) terminal. The action is the same as in the wet cell. When the zinc is dissolved the cell goes dead.

in flashlights, they are made small so that they are light in weight.

The Alkaline-Manganese Cell

An undesirable characteristic of ordinary dry cells is the forming of gas bubbles on the surface of the electrodes. This reduces the active area in contact with the electrolyte and limits the current output from the cell. This action is called *polarization* and a depolarizer in the form of manganese-dioxide is usually combined with the electrolyte to reduce its effect. The polarizing effect frequently gets ahead of the action of the

Fig. 7-3. This experiment demonstrates that regardless of the size a single dry cell will produce only 1½ volts.

Single dry cells are found in many shapes and sizes. Large cells are used where longer service is needed. Usually the larger the cell the longer it will last. Of course, when cells must be carried, as

depolarizer and then the cell requires a period of rest to return it to a working condition.

Recent developments in dry cells have brought about improvements which re-

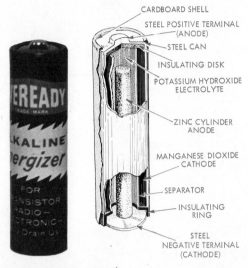

Fig. 7-4. Typical construction of an alkaline-man-ganese cell. The effects of polarization have been reduced by increasing the areas of the anode and cathode elements.

duce materially the effect of polariza-tion, thereby increasing current output capability and useful life several times over that of a similar size zinc-carbon type cell. One such cell, known as an *alkaline-manganese* type is shown in Fig. 7-4. This type of cell has a potassium-hydroxide electrolyte of high conduc-tivity which provides low internal resist-ance, and electrodes with large surface areas which reduce polarization to a minimum. These features provide a dry-cell capable of withstanding reasonably heavy current drain with little change in terminal voltage and one that will operate satisfactorily even under ex-treme low temperature conditions.

The Mercury Cell

Like the Alkaline-Manganese cell, the mercury cell is capable of maintaining a reasonably high current output with no appreciable change in its terminal volt-age. It has a longer useful life than other

type dry cells, extending up to two years, according to the claims of one manufac-turer. It is capable of withstanding extreme hot and cold temperatures, which makes it an excellent source of power for portable electronic equipment where those conditions prevail. One ad-vantage of the mercury cell over other types of dry cells is that it may be ob-tained in small button-like sizes which make them desirable for hearing aids and other electronic devices where space is limited. A sectional view of a mercury cell is shown in Fig. 7-5. Note the similarity in construction with that of an alkaline-manganese cell. Both cathodes are near the outside of the cells and the same type of electrolyte, potassium hy-droxide, is used for each cell. One of the main differences between the two cells is that the mercury cell uses mercuric oxide for a depolarizer while the alka-line-manganese cell uses manganese di-oxide. Since both the mercury cell and the alkaline-manganese cell use highly caustic potassium hydroxide, *never* at-

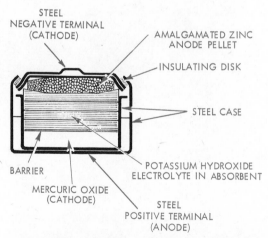

Fig. 7-5. The mercury cell takes its name from the mercuric oxide used as a cathode. This type of cell provides a useful life of several times over that of a similar size dry cell.

tempt to cut one of these cells open, otherwise serious injury to the eyes or skin may result. The chemical action which causes current to flow in a mercury or alkaline-manganese cell is similar to what we learned when we studied the chemical action of a simple cell. The voltage of a mercury cell is 1.35 volts.

Batteries

When more than 1½ volts is needed, dry cells are connected so that the voltage of the cells can be added together. In a flashlight using two dry cells, the voltage produced by the two cells is 3 volts. When dry cells are placed together in one container and are connected to provide more voltage we call this a *battery*. These cells may be round in shape much as the pen light cell or can be made flat so that they will pack more compactly. Radio batteries are made to deliver various voltages, usually 1½, 6, 22½, 45, or 90 volts.

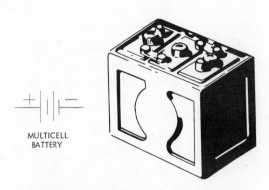

MULTICELL
BATTERY

Cell symbols are combined to represent a battery.

Transistor Radio Batteries

A new type of dry cell, known as "Mini-Max", has been developed for today's portable transistor radio receivers. In contrast with the construction of a conventional dry cell as shown in Fig. 7-6, left, the Mini-Max cell, Fig. 7-6, right, uses a zinc plate covered with carbon on one side to serve as a duplex electrode. The zinc serves as the negative electrode of one cell and the carbon as

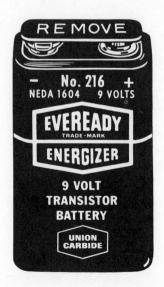

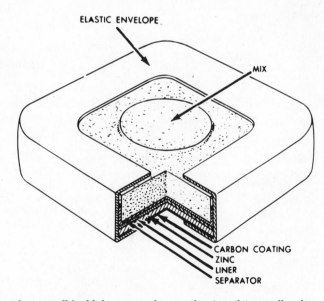

ELASTIC ENVELOPE

MIX

CARBON COATING
ZINC
LINER
SEPARATOR

Fig. 7-6. Left: compact cell construction makes possible high energy in popular transistor radio size. Right: cross section of "Mini-Max" flat cell. (Union Carbide Corp.)

the positive electrode of the adjacent cell. This increases the amount of polarizing mix available for each cell with a comparable increase in its energy content. In addition, the flat cell, because of its rectangular shape, reduces wasted space in assembled batteries.

The Storage Cell

One of the disadvantages of the dry cell is that when it has been used for a period of time the cell becomes discharged and must be thrown away. A cell that can be used over and over again by recharging is called a *secondary cell*. This is the type of cell found in the storage battery that is used in automobiles. A storage cell that is being used as a source of electricity will run down, but after recharging it is ready for use again.

In the simple primary cell we used two unlike materials such as zinc and carbon in an electrolyte solution. The most common type of secondary cell is called a *lead-acid cell* since it contains plates of lead for both the positive and the negative terminals, and sulfuric acid and distilled water for the electrolyte. We can construct a simple storage cell by putting a dilute solution of sulfuric acid in a glass container. Extreme care must be used in handling sulfuric acid as it is very dangerous. If the acid comes in contact with any part of the body it will burn the skin, and it will also burn holes in clothing. The acid should be diluted by first pouring the water into the glass and then adding the acid very slowly. Two strips of lead are next placed in the acid solution so that they do not touch each other. These metal strips are both alike and the cell will not produce electricity until we do something to change one of the pieces of lead.

The cell needs to be *charged;* this can be done by using a source of direct current electricity such as that found in two dry cells. The dry cells should be connected so that they will produce 3 volts, the positive terminal being connected to one strip of lead and the negative terminal to the other strip. We can see that some action is taking place in the electrolyte as bubbles start to appear in the solution. As the charging process continues, the lead plate connected to the positive terminal of our dry cell will start to turn brown. The negative plate will show little change in color. After about ten minutes we can disconnect our dry cells and test the storage cell to see if it produces electricity.

Charging and Discharging a Storage Cell

When the cell has run down we can recharge it and use it again. During the charging process, two changes occurred in the cell. The plates became different in color, with the positive plate turning brown. The brown coating on the positive plate is chemically called *lead peroxide*. See Fig. 7-7. This charging has made the two lead plates different, one of the requirements of a primary cell. The electrolyte solution changes from a weak solution of sulfuric acid to a stronger solution of the acid. The change in the metals and the formation of stronger acid always occur during charging. The voltage of the fully charged cell is about 2 volts.

Commercial Storage Batteries

Besides the advantage of recharging, the storage cell is much better than the dry cell where continuous heavy use is

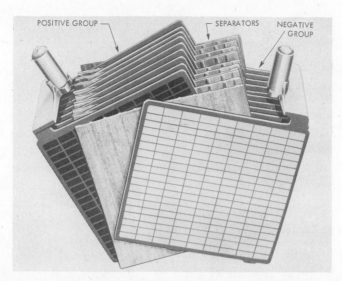

Fig. 7-7. Each cell of a commercial battery is made up of several negative plates and several positive plates held apart from the others, by insulated separators. These separators may be made of such insulating materials as wood, fiber glass, or rubber, and they keep the negative plates from touching the positive plates. In the cell all of the negative plates are connected together and all of the positive plates are connected together so that the cell will be able to handle heavy demands for electricity. The plates are made of a lead grid framework. The negative grids are filled with spongy lead and the positive plates are filled with lead peroxide.

1. TERMINAL POST

2. VENT CAP

3. SEALING COMPOUND

4. CELL COVER

5. FILLING TUBE

6. ELECTROLYTE LEVEL MARK

7. INTERCELL CONNECTOR WELDED TO LEAD INSERT

8. LEAD INSERT IN COVER AND PLATE STRAP

9. PLATE STRAP

10. SEPARATOR PROTECTOR

11. NEGATIVE PLATE

12. SEPARATOR

13. POSITIVE PLATE

14. NEGATIVE PLATE WITH ACTIVE MATERIAL REMOVED TO SHOW PLATE GRID

15. PLATE GRID

16. CONTAINER

Fig. 7-8. The illustration shows the interior construction of a typical 12-volt automobile battery. (The Electric Storage Battery Co.)

required. In automobiles the storage battery (Fig. 7-8) is used to start the engine, provide power for the ignition circuit, and as a source of electricity for lights and accessories. Since more than 2 volts are usually necessary for these purposes, the battery is made of six lead-acid cells connected to provide 12 volts. In some automobiles a 6-volt storage battery is used.

Testing a Storage Battery

One method of testing a storage battery is to test the acid in each of the cells by means of a *hydrometer*. The hydrometer contains a float inside of a glass tube. The float will rise with liq-uids heavier than water. A term, *specific gravity*, is applied when comparing the weight of different liquids with that of water. Water is given a value of 1.000 in weight, which is called its specific gravity. See Fig. 7-9.

When a battery has been in use for some time the electrolyte becomes lower in the cells. This is due to evaporation. Pure water, called *distilled water,* must be used to refill the cell. After a battery has been in service for a long time it will lose its capacity for being recharged. This is because the paste becomes loose in the grids of the plates, and the plates start to buckle. At this time the battery must either be rebuilt or replaced by a new one.

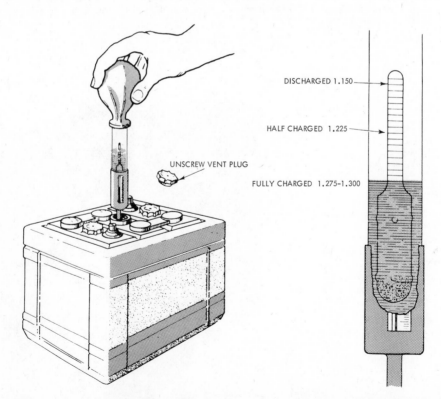

DISCHARGED 1.150

HALF CHARGED 1.225

UNSCREW VENT PLUG

FULLY CHARGED 1.275-1.300

Fig. 7-9. When electrolyte from a fully charged cell is drawn into a hydrometer it will read about 1.300, as the acid is heavier than water. This heavy acid made the float stay up higher in the liquid than it would with water. When a battery is discharged, part of the acid has returned to the plates. The solution in the cell now has less acid than before and the specific gravity will read about 1.150.

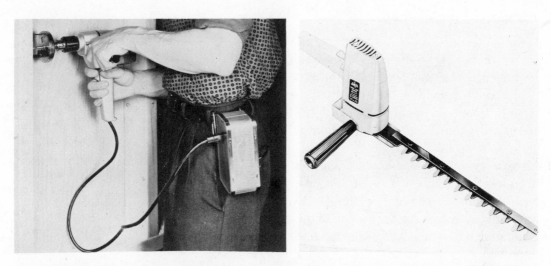

Fig. 7-10. Photographs above show a drill and hedge trimmer which are independent of long power cords. Their source of energy is nickel-cadmium batteries which are very compact, produce energy for many hours, and are easily recharged.

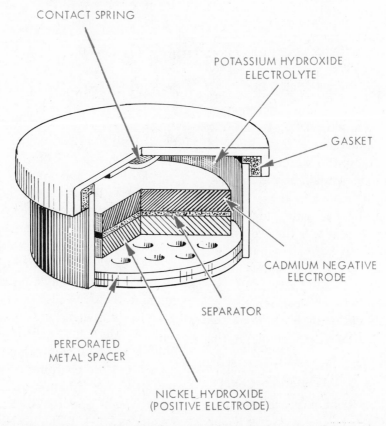

CONTACT SPRING

POTASSIUM HYDROXIDE
ELECTROLYTE

GASKET

CADMIUM NEGATIVE
ELECTRODE

SEPARATOR

PERFORATED
METAL SPACER

NICKEL HYDROXIDE
(POSITIVE ELECTRODE)

Fig. 7-11. Cross-section view of a button-type nickel-cadmium storage cell showing basic elements. Improvements which have done away with replacing water and allowing gas to escape from the cell have made it an excellent source of power for portable equipment.

The Nickel-Cadmium Cell

The introduction of small portable power tools, Fig. 7-10, and electronic equipment that require more current than can be provided by dry-cells has brought about the improvement of the nickel-cadmium storage cell to where it may be used as readily as a dry cell. Like a conventional lead-acid storage cell the nickel cadmium cell in its original form required occasional refilling with water and provision for the escape of gas generated within the cell. The modern improved cell contains a nickel and a cadmium electrode with a potassium-hydroxide electrolyte. In operation the nickel electrode reaches full charge before the cadmium electrode thereby preventing the generating of hydrogen gas from the cadmium. Oxygen generated at the nickel electrode reacts with the cadmium and forms the electrochemical equivalent of cadmium oxide. Since no provision need be made for the escape of gases, the cell may be sealed and used like a conventional dry cell. Nickel-cadmium cells are very popular with transistor radio owners, since they can be recharged by means of a simple transformer, half-wave dry rectifier combination. See Fig. 7-11.

INTERESTING THINGS TO DO

1. Making a Simple Wet Cell.

In a pint glass jar mix a solution of water and salammoniac. Keep adding powdered salammoniac to the water and stir the solution until no more salammoniac will dissolve. Obtain an old dry cell and remove the center carbon rod. Cut a strip of zinc about 1″ wide and 6″ long. Place both the zinc and the carbon in the solution so that they do not touch each other. Connect a wire to the carbon and another wire to the zinc strip. Attach the other ends of the wires to a 1½-volt flashlight bulb. Why does the bulb light? What is happening in the cell?

2. Making a Simple Storage Cell.

Pour a dilute solution of sulfuric acid into a pint glass jar. Use EXTREME CARE IN HANDLING THE ACID. If the acid needs to be diluted, be sure to put the water into the jar first and add the acid slowly. Obtain two lead strips approximately 1″ x 6″. Place these two strips in the electrolyte solution so that they do not touch each other. Connect one wire to one lead strip and another wire to the other strip. Two dry cells should be connected so that they produce 3 volts.

To do this connect the negative terminal of one cell to the positive terminal of the other cell. One wire from the lead strips goes to the remaining negative terminal of the two cells and the other wire goes to the remaining positive terminal. The storage cell is now being charged. Notice what is happening to the lead plates. Let the charging action continue for about ten minutes. In place of the two dry cells, connect the wires from the storage cell to a flashlight bulb or a buzzer. See Fig. 7-12. What is happening? Why do we call this a *secondary cell?*

Fig. 7-12. A simple storage cell.

REVIEW QUESTIONS

1. What are the three requirements for a complete circuit?

2. Explain the difference between a wet and a dry cell.

3. What is the difference between a primary and a secondary cell?

4. What is meant by *electron flow?*

5. In a primary cell what happens when the cell goes dead?

6. Explain what we mean when we say that a direct current is flowing.

7. How does the size of a dry cell affect its operation?

8. What happens when a storage cell is being charged?

9. State the purpose of the separators in a commercial storage battery.

10. How can you determine the charge of a storage cell?

11. Why do commercial storage batteries have more than one plate per cell?

12. What is the main difference between a standard dry-cell and an alkaline-manganese cell?

13. State some advantages of a mercury cell over a standard dry cell.

14. Is a nickel-cadmium cell a primary or a secondary cell? Explain.

15. What advantage does a Mini-Max cell have over a conventional dry cell?

UNIT 8
GENERATING ELECTRICITY WITH MAGNETISM

Batteries are very useful for providing a source of electricity but they are limited in the amount of electricity that they can produce. To produce great quantities of electricity, a method of making it by means of a magnetic field is generally used. The generators and dynamos found in electric plants throughout the world use the principle of electromagnetism to make electricity.

Moving Bar Magnet

To produce electricity by a magnetic field we need a coil of wire and a magnet. A coil can be wound of about 25 turns of wire around a 1″ hollow tubing. To indicate that electricity is being produced we need a very sensitive instrument called a *galvanometer*. A galvanometer is used to show that a very small quantity of electrons is flowing in a circuit. Usually the pointer or needle of the meter points to the center of the dial when not in use. When electricity flows through the meter, the needle will move either to the left or right.

Each time we push the magnet toward the center of the coil the galvanometer needle will move in one direction, and each time we pull the magnet out, the needle will move in the other direction. If we leave the magnet inside of the coil the galvanometer needle does not move. To produce electricity, as shown by the galvanometer, we need to have the magnet moving in or out of the coil. See Figs. 8-1 and 8-2.

Turn the bar magnet around so that the other pole is pushed into the coil first. Now we will notice that the needle moves in the opposite direction. This

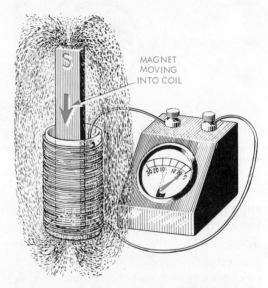

Fig. 8-1. The galvanometer is connected to the two ends of the coil. Holding the bar magnet in one hand, we should then push it through the center of the coil of wire. Immediately we will notice that the pointer of the galvanometer moved in one direction and then comes back to zero in the center of the dial.

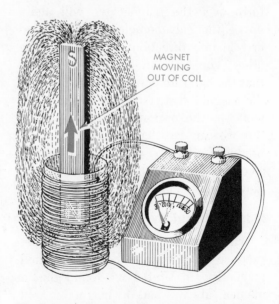

Fig. 8-2. When we pull the magnet back out of the coil the meter pointer moves in the opposite direction and then comes back to zero.

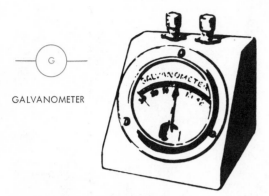

GALVANOMETER

Letter symbols in a circle are used to identify any instrument.

shows us that the direction of the galvanometer needle movement depends upon which direction the magnet is pushed or pulled. The direction that electricity flows depends upon which direction the bar magnet is moving.

Moving Coil

If we hold the bar magnet steady in one hand and place the coil so that the hollow center can be moved back and forth over the magnet we will again notice the galvanometer needle moves first in one direction and then in the other. The coil can be turned over so that the opposite end starts moving over the magnet first. Now the needle will move in the opposite direction. From this we can see that electricity can be produced either by moving a magnet in a coil of wire or by having a coil of wire move over a magnet.

Induced Electricity

Why did the coil and bar magnet produce electricity? When we studied magnetism in Unit 4 we found that a magnet always had a magnetic field around it. When either the magnet is moving or the coil is moving, the wires

in the coil are cutting through the magnetic field of the magnet. Cutting through the magnetic field by the coil produces what is called *induced* electricity. Electricity can be induced in the coil only when either the magnet or the coil is in motion.

Alternating Current

The bar magnet, when pushed in or out of the coil, made the galvanometer needle move first in one direction and then in the other. This was due to the cutting of the magnetic field which induced electricity in the coil. This induced electricity is a flow of electrons through the coil and galvanometer. When the bar magnet was pushed into the center of the coil, the electrons began to flow in one direction. As soon as the magnet was stopped, the electrons stopped flowing in the circuit. Electrons started to flow again in the opposite direction when the magnet was pulled out of the coil. The flow of electrons, first in one direction, then stopping and starting to flow again in the opposite direction, is called *alternating current*. This is different from direct current, which always flows in the same direction.

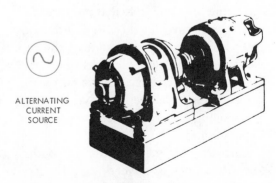

ALTERNATING CURRENT SOURCE

This symbol is used to indicate any source of alternating current.

Alternating current electricity, which is abbreviated AC, always flows first one way through the circuit and then reverses and starts flowing in the other direction. We later shall find that there are many reasons why alternating current is used.

Frequency

The faster that we move the bar magnet in and out of the coil the faster the electrons must change direction of flow through the coil and galvanometer. The electron flow changes direction every time the magnet changes direction. We say that the electrons have completed one *cycle* of flow when the magnet has been pushed into and pulled out of the coil once. One cycle of electricity might be compared to an automobile engine that turns over once. The engine in making one revolution has completed one cycle of its motion before it starts the second revolution. To make a second cycle of alternating current we must plunge the magnet in and out of the coil again. Each time we do this we complete one cycle of alternating current.

The number of cycles completed in one second is called the *frequency*. We can develop a frequency of 10 cycles per second alternating current by pushing the magnet in and out of the coil ten times every second.

The frequency of alternating current coming into most homes is 60 cycle. This means that the alternating current is changing direction 120 times every second.

A Simple Generator

If a coil of wire is moved in a magnetic field we know that the cutting of the lines of magnetic force will produce

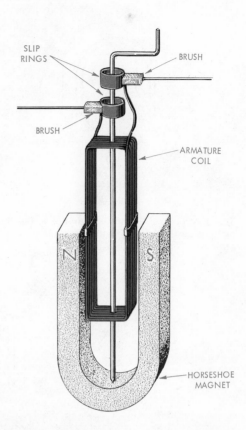

Fig. 8-3. To obtain electricity from the rotating coil we must be able to connect onto the two ends of the coil. This requires the construction of special devices called slip rings or a commutator. The contact to the slip rings or commutator is made by two brushes. The drawing shows how the brushes are always in contact with the two ends of the coil through the use of slip rings.

electricity. This is the principle of the *generator,* which is used to produce most of the electricity that we use. A generator has a moving coil that can be rotated in a magnetic field. The rotating coil is usually called an *armature.* The magnetic field can be made of two magnetic poles such as found in a horseshoe magnet. See Fig. 8-3.

Alternating Current Generator

To make contact with the coil as it rotates, two separate rings are placed around the shaft of the armature. One

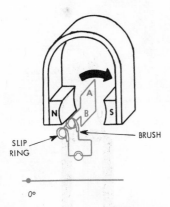

0°

The armature coil is moving parallel to the lines of force so that at this instant no voltage is generated.

90°

The armature is moving across the lines of force. In this position generated voltage is maximum.

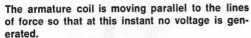

180°

The voltage curve shows zero voltage because in this position the armature is moving parallel to the lines of force.

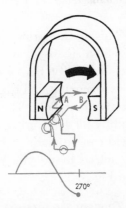

270°

Side "A" and "B" of the armature coil is now moving past opposite poles, and the voltage in the armature coil is reversed.

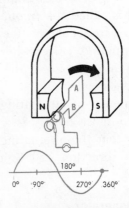

0°   90°   270°   360°
180°

The cycle is complete since the armature is now back in its original position.

Fig. 8-4. AC Generator.

ring is connected to one end of the coil and the other ring to the other end of the coil. The rings must not touch each other and must not touch the armature shaft except through an insulating material. These two rings are called *slip rings* (Fig. 8-4). As they rotate, two *brushes* made either of soft copper or carbon are always in contact with the rings.

When the coil rotates in the magnetic field, made by the two poles of the magnet, the greatest amount of electricity is produced in the coil when it is cutting the largest number of lines of force. The coil is cutting the largest number of lines of force when it is moving directly across the ends of the two poles. See Fig. 8-4.

The coil cuts the fewest lines of force when each part of the coil is moving farthest away from the center of the magnetic field. The amount of electricity produced in the coil is large when the coil is moving between the two magnets. No electricity is produced when the coils are cutting none of the lines of force. See Fig. 8-4.

When a coil was moved in and out of a magnet, we said an alternating current was being produced because it would cut the magnetic field first in one direction and then in the other direction. This same action takes place as the coil rotates between the two poles of the magnet. The induced electricity flows out through the brushes first one way and then the other, as the coil is rotated in the magnetic field. The alternating current is not constant and is changing in amount depending upon where the coil is in the magnetic field. See Fig. 8-5.

Fig. 8-5. This photograph shows how alternating current can be developed with stationary armature coils and a rotating permanent magnet field. As the magnet rotates it induces an alternating current in the stationary coils. Slip rings are not necessary on this generator. Generators used on bicycles are of this type.

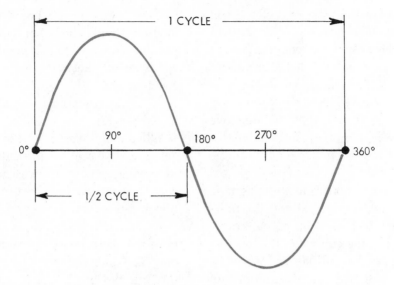

Fig. 8-6. Alternating current wave form.

Alternating Current Wave Form

The action of an alternating current generator can be shown by a graph known as an alternating current wave form, Fig. 8-6. As the armature rotates between the poles of a magnet, the voltage generated rises to a maximum at 90 degrees, then drops to zero at 180 degrees, as shown by the half-cycle wave form. As the armature passes through the 180 degree point to complete the cycle, voltages of the same value as the first half-cycle will be generated, but of opposite polarity because the armature will be cutting magnetic lines of force in the opposite direction. This is represented on the graph by the loop below the line.

Hertz Used For Cycles Per Second

A few years ago it was decided to honor the German physicist Heinrich Rudolph Hertz (1857–1894), who first demonstrated the production and recep-

tion of radio waves, by using his name for cycles per second. The abbreviation Hz (Hertz) is considered a unit of frequency equivalent to 1 cycle per second. Thus a 60 cycle alternating current is called 60 Hertz. In this text many of the future references to frequency will be stated as Hertz instead of cycles per second.

Direct Current Generators

To obtain direct current from a generator we use a *commutator* instead of slip rings. The commutator (Fig. 8-7) consists of a single ring cut in two so that each half is separated from the other on the armature shaft. One side of the commutator is connected to one end of the coil and the other side to the other end of the coil. Brushes make continuous contact with the commutator to pick up the electron flow from the coil. During each half rotation of the armature, the brushes make contact with a different end of the coil. See Fig. 8-7.

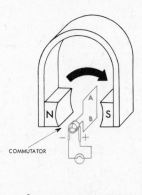

The armature coil is moving parallel to the lines of force so that at this instant no voltage is generated.

The armature is moving across the lines of force. In this position the generated voltage is maximum.

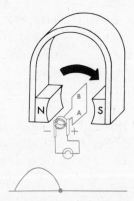

Armature coils "A" and "B" are again moving parallel to the lines of force and the generated voltage falls to zero.

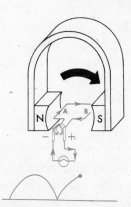

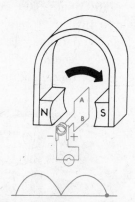

The voltage in the armature is now reversed, but the commutator segments under the brushes are reversed at the same time. The electron flow from the brushes continues in the same direction as in the original first half cycle.

One complete revolution of the armature shows that the current flow is always in the same direction.

Fig. 8-7. DC Generator.

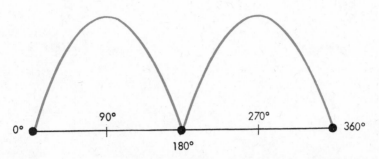

Fig. 8-8. A graph may be used to show a direct current generator wave form. This is similar to the alternating current waveform only both loops are above the line to indicate that the generator output is a pulsating·direct current.

Thus through the use of a commutator we are able to get direct current from the generator. This direct current is varying in strength the same as the alternating current. The difference is in the electron flow, which is always in the same direction for direct current. We call this changing in strength of direct current *pulsating* direct current. See Fig. 8-8.

Commercial Generators

One of the requirements for all generators is that we have some means of power to rotate them. The army uses hand power to turn over some of their portable field generators. Large generators are run by water turbines, or by gasoline, steam, or diesel engines.

GENERATOR

Letter symbols in a circle identify rotating machines.

Most generators built commercially have more than one set of coils in the armature. By having more coils in the armature it is possible to produce a more constant supply of electricity. This is because some of the coils are always directly across from the poles of the magnet. It is at this point that the greatest amount of electricity is induced in the coil.

The automobile generator (Fig. 8-9) uses a commutator to produce direct current electricity. Since the brushes deliver direct current to the field coils each pole always has the same north and south polarity. This type of generator is used for direct current arc welding and many other places where direct current is needed.

Most alternating current generators also use electromagnetic field coils instead of permanent magnets. The magnetic field must always have the same poles and the same polarity. This is not possible with alternating current electricity because the electrons are flowing first in one direction and then the other. We can see that if the field coils were connected to the slip rings of the alternating current generator the poles in the

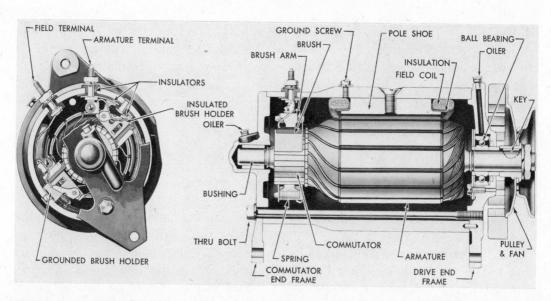

Fig. 8-9. Automobile generators usually have a number of coils on the armature. The end of each coil comes out to a separate section of the commutator. These sections are insulated from each other and are called *segments*. The segments are connected to the coils so that each can deliver its electricity to the brushes. Most automobile generators use an electromagnet for the magnetic field. The electromagnet provides a strong magnetic field for the armature. The coils used to produce the electromagnetism are called *field coils*. These field coils receive their electricity from the armature. (Delco-Remy Div.—General Motors Corp.)

Fig. 8-10. Modern electric power generators are streamlined and compact. This steam-driven generator is capable of supplying electricity to a city of 225,000 people.

field would always be changing. Alternating current generators, like direct current generators, must have constant north and south poles for the electromagnetic field. Some method must be used in alternating current generators to supply direct current to the field coils. This can be done by having a separate generator to produce the direct current, or, by having two generators connected together on one armature as in Fig. 8-10.

INTERESTING THINGS TO DO

Making and Using a Galvanometer.

Use the small compass constructed in Unit 4. The wooden base should be approximately 1½″ square. Cut two pieces of heavy cardboard the same length as the base and wide enough so that the top of the cardboard will be approximately ⅛″ above the top of the compass needle. Glue the two pieces of cardboard on the sides of the base as shown in Fig. 8-11. Wind about 40 turns of No.

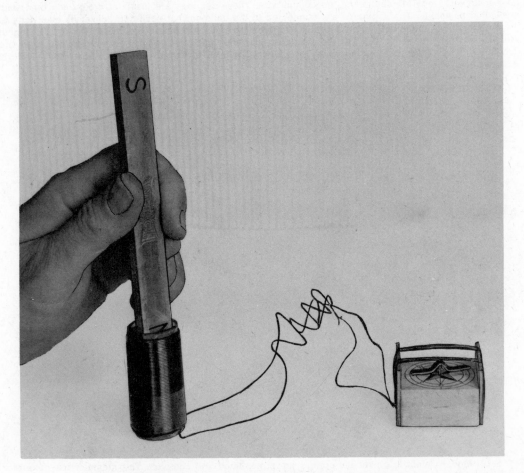

Fig. 8-11. Shop constructed galvanometer indicating electron flow.

28 magnet wire around the compass. In order to be able to see the compass it is best to wind 20 turns on one side of the needle and the other 20 turns on the other side as shown in the picture. This completes the construction of the galvanometer.

Obtain a piece of cardboard tubing about 1″ in diameter and 2½″ long.

Wind approximately 100 turns of No. 22 wire on the form. Connect the two ends of the coil to the two leads on the galvanometer. Keep the coil and galvanometer about 18″ apart. Push a bar magnet into the coil. Now move the magnet back and forth through the coil. What happens to the compass needle? Why?

REVIEW QUESTIONS

1. What is the purpose of a galvanometer?

2. How does reversing the poles of the bar magnet affect the movement of the galvanometer?

3. Why does a coil with a moving bar magnet produce electricity?

4. When alternating current is produced, in what direction do the electrons flow?

5. How does alternating current differ from direct current?

6. What is the number of cycles completed by an alternating current in just one second properly called?

7. In 60 Hz alternating current how many cycles are completed in one minute?

8. What is the difference between commutators and slip rings on generators?

9. When a generator is rotating, at what position is the largest quantity of electricity produced?

10. List the different types of power used to turn generators.

11. In automobile generators how is the magnetic field obtained?

UNIT 9
PRODUCING ELECTRICITY WITH FRICTION, HEAT, LIGHT, PRESSURE, AND GASES

Static Electricity

Probably everyone has had the experience of receiving a shock from touching the door of an automobile just as he started to get out of the car. Possibly you have received a shock when you walked on a heavy rug and then touched another person. These shocks were caused by *static electricity*.

When riding in an automobile your body moves against the seat and back cushions. Rubbing against the cushions gives your body a charge of static electricity. When you touch the door of the automobile, this charge jumps to the door and you feel a shock. The charge was neutralized by the metal of the door. The same is true when you walk across a rug; the friction of your shoes against the rug produces a charge on your body. When you touch someone, the charge is neutralized by the other person.

Static electricity is made by friction which is the result of two different non-metal materials, called *insulators*, rubbing against one another. Most insulating materials are what we call *neutral*. They have an equal number of negative and positive charges. If we rub two different

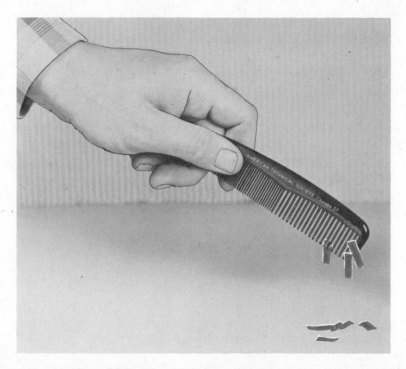

Fig. 9-1. An example of static electricity can be shown by rubbing a comb against a piece of wool clothing. The comb becomes charged as the electrons are rubbed onto it from the wool. When the comb is touched against a small scrap of paper, it will attract the paper and pick it up. The comb, which has a negative charge, repels all of the electrons on the edge of the paper nearest to the comb. The electrons on the paper next to the comb go to the opposite end of the paper. The negative comb now attracts the positively charged edge.

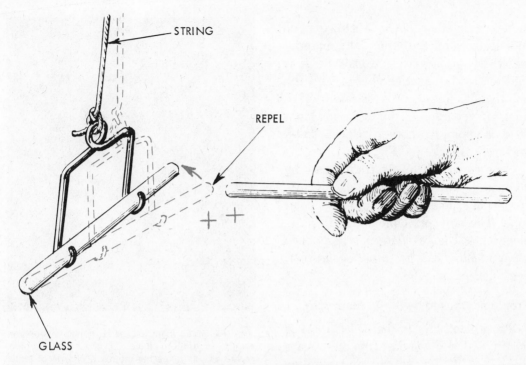

STRING

REPEL

\+ \+

GLASS

Fig. 9-2. Both glass rods have been rubbed with a piece of silk. The silk rubs the electrons off the glass, making them positively charged. Since both glass rods have a positive charge they will repel each other.

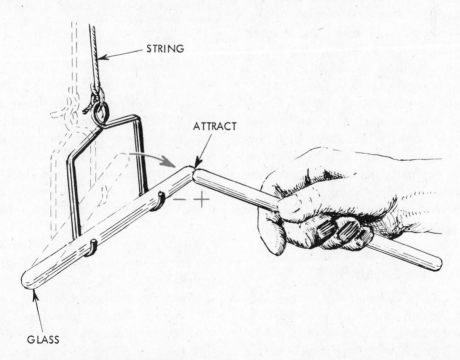

STRING

ATTRACT

− +

GLASS

Fig. 9-3. The glass rod hanging from the string has been rubbed with a piece of fur. The glass takes electrons off the fur, giving it a negative charge. The other glass rod was rubbed with silk, giving it a positive charge. The two unlike charged glass rods will attract each other.

materials together, one will rub some of the electrons off the other. The material which has gathered electrons onto it is said to have a negative charge, and the one that has lost electrons is said to have a positive charge. As the electrons jump from one point to another we see a spark and feel a shock. See Fig. 9-1.

Charges of static electricity can be compared with magnetism. In magnetism unlike poles attract and like poles repel. The same principle is true in static electricity: *Unlike charges attract each other and like charges repel each other.* See Figs. 9-2 and 9-3.

Problems Caused by Static Electricity

Static electricity in many instances is destructive and we need to find ways to control it. Trucks carrying gasoline become charged from the gasoline sloshing around in the tank and from the friction of the tires on the highway. This static charge could result in a spark which might ignite the gasoline. As a result all gasoline trucks have a chain or tape dragging on the ground to prevent the charge from developing. Rotating belts used on machinery can develop a static charge. When these belts are used around explosives it is necessary to ground the parts making contact with the belts. This grounding prevents the charge from developing, and thus prevents a spark that might cause an explosion.

Uses for Static Electricity

Not all of the effects of static electricity are detrimental to man. See Fig. 9-4. Scientists have been able to put its forces to work with very beneficial results. One such application which has become probably more widespread than

Fig. 9-4. Static electricity is responsible for lightning. The friction caused by the small droplets in the clouds gives the clouds a charge of static electricity. When the charge becomes strong enough in the cloud, it discharges to the earth. This discharge of static electricity from the cloud to the earth results in a huge flash and a loud noise. (General Electric Co.)

the others, is the process of copying typed, written, printed, or drawn material by electrostatic means and reproducing perfect copies of the original. A letter, office form, or engineering drawing can be copied in about three minutes. The operation of the process which is known as *Xerography*, is explained in Unit 31.

Another important use for static electricity is the precipitator (Fig. 9-5) which is used in removing dust and smoke from the air. Clothing brushes with plastic bristles pick up the lint from clothing because the plastic bristles become charged with electricity due to the friction caused by rubbing them against clothing.

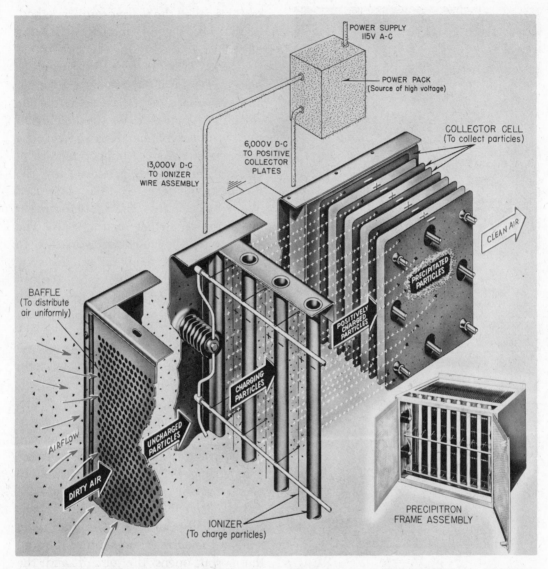

POWER SUPPLY
115V A-C

POWER PACK
(Source of high voltage)

COLLECTOR CELL
(To collect particles)

6,000V D-C
TO POSITIVE
COLLECTOR
PLATES

13,000V D-C
TO IONIZER
WIRE ASSEMBLY

PRECIPITATED
PARTICLES

CLEAN AIR

BAFFLE
(To distribute
air uniformly)

POSITIVELY
CHARGED
PARTICLES

CHARGING
PARTICLES

AIRFLOW

UNCHARGED
PARTICLES

DIRTY AIR

PRECIPITRON
FRAME ASSEMBLY

IONIZER
(To charge particles)

Fig. 9-5. The precipitator is used as an air cleaner. It consists of one set of plates that have a high negative charge and another set of plates that have a high positive charge. The dust or smoke is first given a negative charge as it passes by the negatively charged plates. These particles then flow past a set of plates that have a positive charge. The negatively charged particles are attracted to the positive plates. (Westinghouse Electric Corp.)

Sanding belts are sometimes coated by static electricity. The abrasive is charged by placing the grains in a very strong static electricity field. This charging makes the grains of the abrasive stand on end as iron filings stand in a magnetic field. While the grains are held on end, they are glued onto the belt. The grain ends make a much sharper edge for sanding.

The Thermocouple

Heat can be used to develop very small amounts of electricity. If we twist

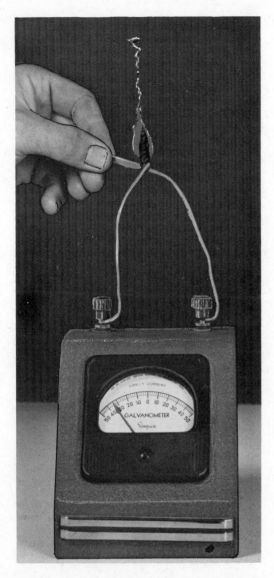

Fig. 9-6. A match will provide enough heat to generate electricity from a thermocouple.

metal is called the *thermocouple* method.

The thermocouple method of making electricity is used to measure high temperatures. Two different metals such as platinum and iridium are joined together and are placed in a heating unit. The electricity developed by the heating of the two different metals is shown by a galvanometer. As the temperature is increased the voltage produced by the thermocouple increases. This increased electricity makes the galvanometer needle move farther on the scale. The scale on the galvanometer is marked to read degrees of temperature. Thus by reading the scale of the meter, we can tell the amount of heat being produced. This type of meter is called a *pyrometer*.

Automatic gas furnaces sometimes use thermocouple electricity to open and close the supply valve. The pilot light of the furnace heats the two different metals to produce the electricity. When the wall thermometer, called a *thermostat*, closes the circuit due to changing of the room temperature, the thermocouple. (Fig. 9-7) develops electricity to operate a coil and steel plunger device called a *solenoid*. This solenoid opens the gas valve. As soon as the room reaches the correct temperature the wall thermostat opens the circuit and the solenoid shuts the gas off.

The Photoelectric Tube

Certain materials such as potassium, sodium, and caesium when held in the light will give off small quantities of electrons. These materials, called *photosensitive*, are used in *photoelectric* tubes. A photoelectric tube (Fig. 9-8) consists of a curved plate coated with the photosensitive material. A rod of metal is placed near the curved plate.

a piece of constantan wire and a piece of iron wire together and heat them where they are joined together, a small quantity of electricity will be developed. See Fig. 9-6. We can indicate that electricity is being produced if we connect a galvanometer to the ends of the two pieces of wire. The producing of electricity by heating two different kinds of

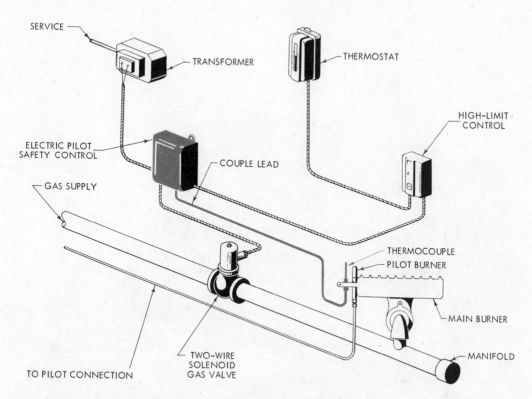

SERVICE

TRANSFORMER

THERMOSTAT

HIGH-LIMIT CONTROL

ELECTRIC PILOT SAFETY CONTROL

COUPLE LEAD

GAS SUPPLY

THERMOCOUPLE

PILOT BURNER

MAIN BURNER

MANIFOLD

TO PILOT CONNECTION

TWO-WIRE SOLENOID GAS VALVE

Fig. 9-7. One use for a thermocouple is to automatically control a gas furnace so as to maintain an even temperature at all times.

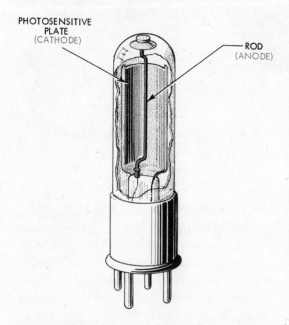

PHOTOSENSITIVE PLATE (CATHODE)

ROD (ANODE)

Fig. 9-8. Photoelectric tubes can be used for many purposes.

Both the rod (*anode*) and plate (*cathode*) are sealed inside of a glass tube. When light shines on the curved plate it gives off electrons. We know that electrons are negative particles of electricity and that they will go to a place that has a positive charge. By connecting the rod to the positive side of a battery it will attract the electrons given off by the plate. The brighter the light that shines on it, the more electrons it will give off. In almost all cases, the phototube must be used with some type of amplifier to make the small flow of electrons strong enough to be useful.

The Photoelectric Cell

More recent research with other photosensitive materials led to the produc-

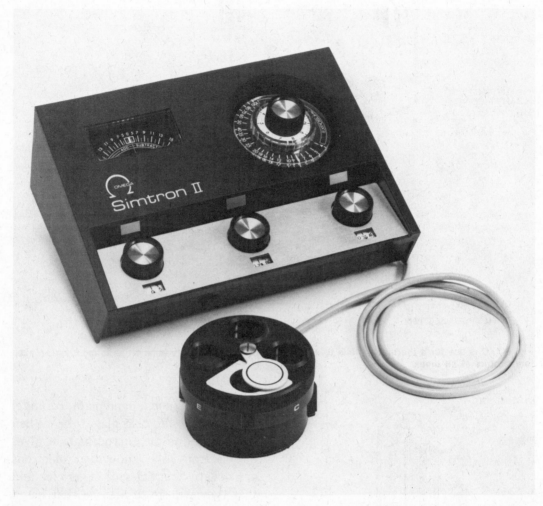

Fig. 9-9. Electronic time-saver for photo laboratories. Photocell attached to cord "reads" negative and determines instantly time required for enlargement.

tion of *photoelectric cells*, which because of their size, have found many applications where the larger photoelectric tube could not be used. Photoelectric cells (Fig. 9-9) may be divided into two basic types: photovoltaic and photoconductive. When light strikes the active element of a *photovoltaic cell*, it produces a flow of electrons within the cell which generates a small voltage. Because of this characteristic, photovoltaic cells are known as *self-generating* cells. These cells may be connected together to increase their voltage and current output. Selenium or silicon is generally used in a photovoltaic cell.

The operation of a *photoconductive cell* (Fig. 9-10) is due to its photosensi-

Fig. 9-10. In a photoconductive type photocell, light-sensitive material such as cadmium-sulfide is formed into a series of loops.

tive material, such as cadmium-sulfide, becoming conductive to a flow of electrons when light strikes its surface. Like photoelectric tubes, photoelectric cells generally require amplifiers to raise their outputs to operating levels.

In addition to the photovoltaic and photoconductive cells, certain arrangements of materials such as silicon and germanium can produce photoelectric effects. Since they are semiconductor and transistor devices, we shall learn about them when we study transistors.

The use of photoelectric tubes and cells affects our daily living in so many ways that it would be difficult to list them all. A few of their applications include automatic control of street lights, fire and burglary protection for the home, accident prevention in industry,

Fig. 9-11. A simple light meter.

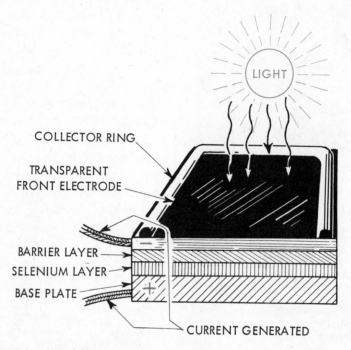

LIGHT

COLLECTOR RING

TRANSPARENT
FRONT ELECTRODE

BARRIER LAYER
SELENIUM LAYER
BASE PLATE

CURRENT GENERATED

Fig. 9-12. Cross-section of a selenium cell. A number of these cells make up sun batteries that provide power for communications satellites.

recording and projecting sound films for television and theaters, camera shutter controls, and photographic enlarging meters. A group of photocells known as a *sun battery* (Figs. 9-11 and 9-12) perform an important function in supplying operating power to our communications satellites.

Pressure Produces Electricity

Very small quantities of electricity can be produced when pressure is applied to some kinds of crystals. These crystals, such as quartz or Rochelle salts, will generate electricity when they are squeezed between two metal plates; and if a very sensitive meter is connected across the plates, voltage will be indicated. The greater the pressure that is placed on the crystals, the greater the resulting voltage. This ability to gen-

erate electricity by compressing a crystal is known as the *piezoelectric effect* of crystals.

PHONO PICKUP

This symbol represents any type of pick-up.

Crystal Phonograph Pick-Up

A good example of the piezoelectric effect is found in crystal phonograph pick-up arms. These pick-up arms use a crystal such as Rochelle salts with a needle attached as shown in Fig. 9-13. As the needle rides in the grooves of the phonograph record, it is vibrated back

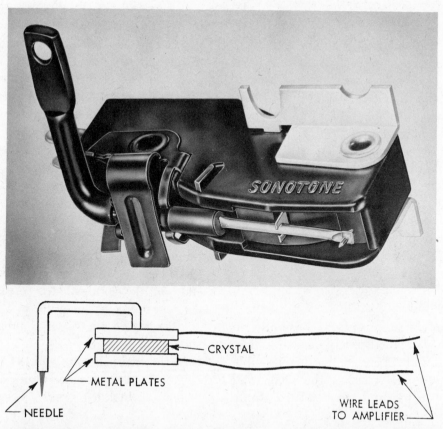

Fig. 9-13. A photograph and sketch of a crystal phonograph pick-up. As the needle vibrates in the record grooves, these vibrations are delivered to the metal plates next to the crystal. These vibrations press on the crystal and a voltage variation is then produced by the crystal between the two metal plates. The varying voltage is then fed into an amplifier.

and forth by small variations that are found in the record grooves. These variations are due to the sound vibrations that were impressed in the record when it was manufactured. Since the needle is connected to the crystal, the vibrations picked up by the needle are applied to the crystal. Thus, a varying pressure is placed on the crystal. This variation in pressure produces a weak voltage change which is then sent to a phonograph amplifier. The phonograph amplifier increases the varying voltage produced by the crystal and the electrical impulses are then converted back into sound waves by the loud speaker.

The Crystal Microphone

Another method of using crystals to generate electricity is found in the crystal microphone, often used in broadcasting stations or public address systems.

When someone speaks into a crystal microphone, the sound waves strike the crystal in the microphone and compress it. The sound waves are converted into a weak electric current by the crystal. This small current is then fed into an amplifier where the signal is made strong enough to operate a loud speaker.

Crystal Vibration

Another piezoelectric effect of a crystal is its ability to vibrate or produce mechanical motion. When a voltage is applied across a pair of plates that have been placed on opposite sides of a crystal, a vibration will be set up by the crystal. The number of vibrations per second that will be produced by the crystal is very constant. These vibrations are called the frequency of the crystal, which is basically determined by the type of crystal and its thickness. Such crystals are usually cut from quartz and are used in broadcasting stations, for example, where fixed frequencies are very important.

The Fuel Cell

Scientists are working constantly to find new methods for generating electrical power. Occasionally, they are able to reach back through the years and pick up a partly developed idea, apply modern research techniques to it and produce a device that has the glamour of a wonderful new discovery. Such has been the case of the recently developed fuel cells, which hold promise of producing electrical power at efficiencies as high as 85 percent. A modern turbine generating station does well to operate at an efficiency of 40 percent.

Sir William Grove, an Englishman, is credited with having built the first primitive model of a fuel cell in 1839. Other workers followed down through the years, but only recently has the fuel cell been brought to its present high state of development by research for efficient source of power for space travel. A drawing of one type of fuel cell is shown in Fig. 9-14.

In the fuel cell shown in the drawing oxygen and hydrogen unite to form water and in the process releases elec-

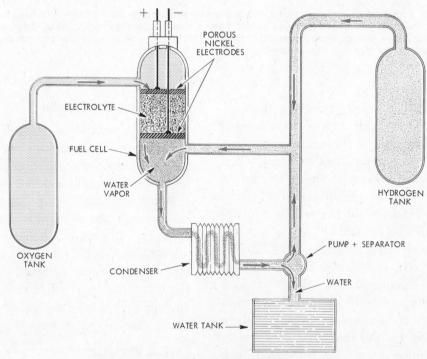

Fig. 9-14. Fuel cell electric power generator.

trons which flow from the negative electrode to the outside terminal when the cell is connected to a load. The water vapor formed by oxygen uniting with hydrogen flows into the radiator-condenser, where heat is removed and the vapor condensed into water. The pump separator forces the water into a tank and sends the exhaust hydrogen back into the hydrogen inlet of the fuel cell.

The fuel cells of this type supplied internal power for the spacecrafts in collecting data that made possible the successful moon landings.

INTERESTING THINGS TO DO

1. Generating Static Electricity.

Cut several small pieces of scrap paper and place them on a flat wooden surface. Charge a comb by rubbing it on woolen clothing. Hold the comb near the scrap pieces of paper. What happens? Why?

2. Making a Thermocouple.

Cut a piece of constantan wire 6″ long and a piece of iron wire the same length. Wire sizes between No. 14 and No. 20 will be satisfactory. Twist the two wires together for a distance of about 1½″. Connect the opposite ends of the wire to a very sensitive galvanometer or a low reading milliammeter, an instrument that measures small currents. Heat the twisted ends of the wires with a match or a gas flame. Why does the needle on the meter move? Reverse the two wire connections to the meter. What happens?

3. Making a Simple Light Meter.

Obtain a selenium photo cell or a sun battery. Connect the two leads from the cell to a milliammeter (0-to-1 or 0-to-5 milliamperes). Be sure to connect the red or positive lead of the cell to the side of the meter marked "positive." Hold the face of the cell toward the window in your room. Observe the reading of the meter. Place the cell directly under a light bulb. How does the meter reading compare with the one taken from the window light? This meter may be constructed and calibrated for use as a light meter for photographic work.

REVIEW QUESTIONS

1. In what ways are static electricity and magnetism similar?

2. List some of the problems caused by static electricity.

3. Name several uses made of static electricity.

4. What are the requirements necessary to produce electricity by the thermocouple method?

5. Name several commercial uses of the thermocouple.

6. How does a photoelectric tube operate?

7. Why is it necessary to have an amplifier when using a photoelectric tube and photoelectric cells?

8. Make a list of purposes for which the photoelectric cell is used.

9. What is the principal material used in the sun battery?

10. Suggest a new type of use that might be made of the sun battery.

11. What is the material used to produce electricity by pressure?

12. Explain how pressure is used to produce electricity in a phonograph pick-up.

13. What chemical action causes electrons to flow in an oxygen-hydrogen fuel cell?

Basic Electrical Circuits

UNIT 10
MEASURING THE VOLTAGE

Voltage and Pressure

We have said that the voltage of a dry cell is 1½ volts and that the voltage of a storage battery may be either 6 or 12 volts. You have probably heard that the

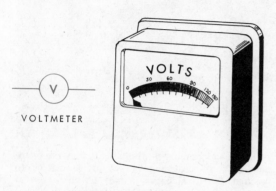

The letter "V" in a circle indicates a voltmeter.

electricity in your home is 115 volts. The various voltages indicate the amount of pressure that each of these sources produces.

Voltage is the pressure or force that pushes electrons through an electrical circuit. A single cell of a storage battery produces a pressure of 2 volts. When six cells are connected together they produce six times as much pressure as one cell. The voltage of the storage battery is 12 volts. The greater the pressure or voltage, the more electrons will be forced to flow through a circuit. See Figs. 10-1 and 10-2.

Voltage might be compared to the water system in a city. Most towns have a large tank that is used to force water through pipes to the houses throughout the community. The water pressure is available whenever the faucet is opened. If the water in the tank gets low, the pressure in the system is low.

In electricity, the source of electricity produces the voltage the same as the water tank provides the pressure. The greater the voltage, the greater the force of the electricity. This force is called the

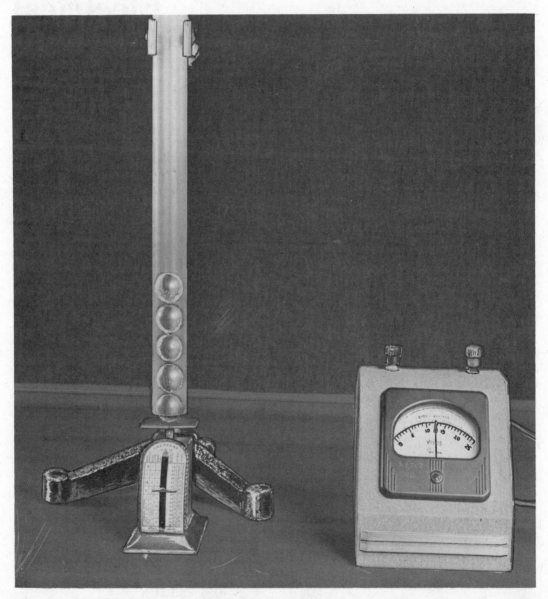

Fig. 10-1. In the photograph the five steel balls have been placed in a clear plastic tube so they are pushing down on the scale used for measuring weights. These balls are providing enough pressure to force the pointer of the weighing scale to the center of the dial. Electrical pressure may be compared to this. The voltmeter is showing electrical pressure forcing the pointer to the center of the scale.

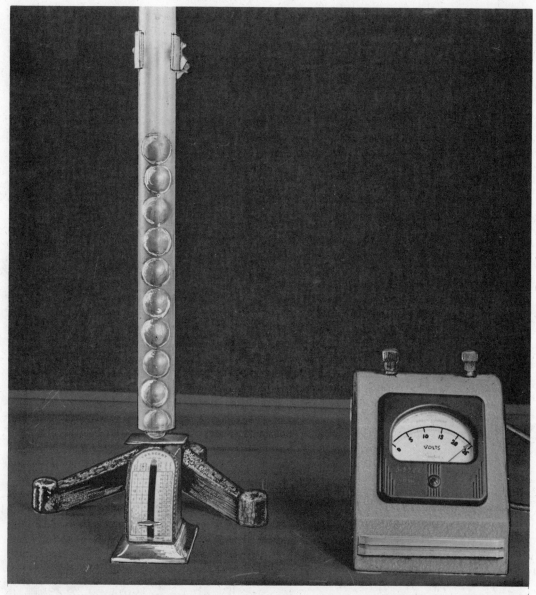

Fig. 10-2. This photograph shows the pointer of the weighing scale almost at the bottom of the dial, indicating that the weight has been increased. The addition of the five steel balls in the plastic tube has increased the pressure and the increase may be measured by the scale. The electrical pressure increase may be compared to this. The voltage was increased and the voltmeter shows this increase.

electromotive force and is measured in *volts*.

Producing an Electromotive Force

The electromotive force, or voltage, may be produced by generators, dry cells, batteries, thermocouples, photoelectric cells, or sun batteries. Of these, generators are the most common source of voltage and are used when higher

COMMON VOLTAGES

Some very common voltages that can be obtained from various devices are listed below:

Thermocouple	Few thousandths of a volt
Dry cell	1½ volts
Storage battery	6 and 12 volts
Door chime transformer	12 to 24 volts
Home outlets	110 to 120 volts
Electric lines into homes	110–220 to 120–240 volts
Transformers on power poles	2,400 to 4,200 volts
Power company substation	12,000 to 69,000 volts
Power company generators	12,500 volts
Long distance transmission lines	287,000 volts

voltages are needed. Batteries are usually used where it is not convenient to use generators and where direct current is needed. The other methods of producing voltage have limited use except in special places where small quantities of voltage are needed.

Using Voltmeters

A voltmeter is used to measure electromotive force. The meter is connected directly across the two terminals where the voltage is to be measured. One connection of the meter goes to one wire of the circuit and the other connection to the other wire as in Fig. 10-3.

When selecting a voltmeter it is necessary to know whether the electricity is alternating current or direct current. Direct current meters will not read alternating current voltages and alternating current meters will give incorrect readings of direct current.

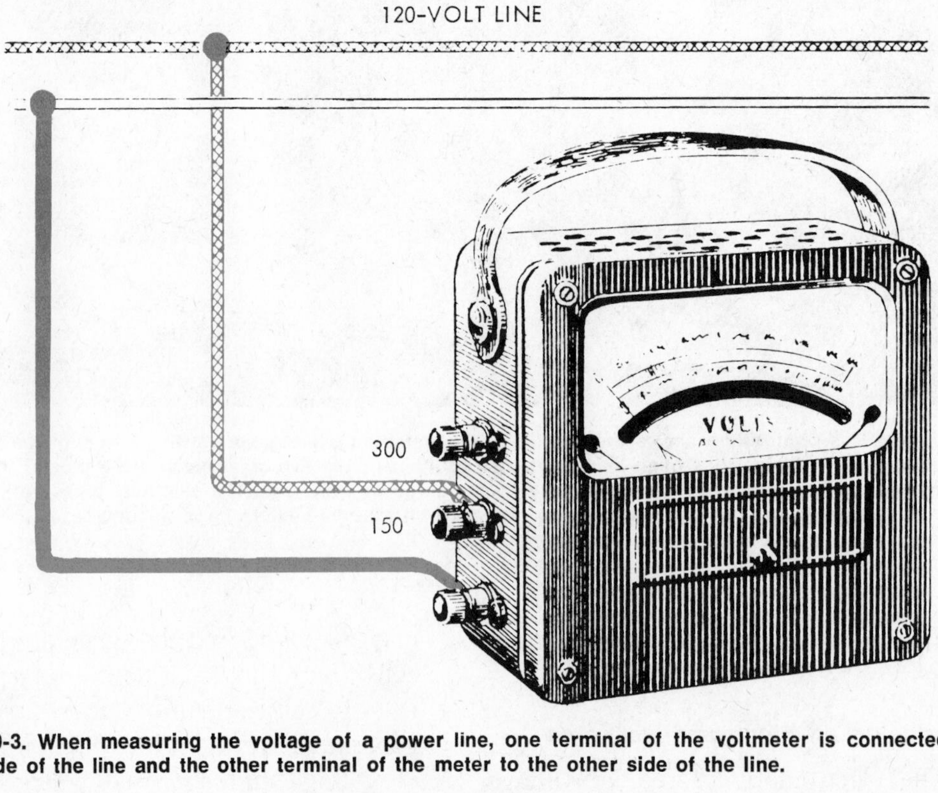

Fig. 10-3. When measuring the voltage of a power line, one terminal of the voltmeter is connected to one side of the line and the other terminal of the meter to the other side of the line.

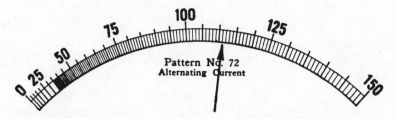

Pattern No. 72
Alternating Current

Fig. 10-4. This is a drawing of one type of meter scale. The divisions found on the scale vary with the type of meter used. The reading on the scale above indicates 111 volts AC.

It is also important that the meter used have the correct scale for the voltage to be measured. If the voltage is too high for the meter it will burn out the meter. See Fig. 10-4.

To measure the voltage of a storage battery that delivers 6 volts, a direct current meter that has a full scale reading of 10 volts is generally used. See Fig. 10-5. If the meter had a 0-to-200–volt scale, the 6 volts of the storage battery would move the meter pointer so

Fig. 10-5. Measuring the voltage of a storage battery with a meter having a 0-to-25—volt scale.

slightly that it would be difficult to obtain an accurate reading. A meter that had a 0-to-1–volt scale could not read the 6 volts and would probably be ruined because it was not designed to read more than 1 volt.

When measuring the voltage of direct current electricity, it is necessary to notice the polarity of the meter. One terminal of the meter is marked with a

+ and is sometimes painted red. This is called the *positive* terminal of the meter and is connected to the positive terminal of the battery. The other terminal of the meter is connected to the *negative* post of the battery. The voltmeter is connected directly across the source of electricity. See Figs. 10-6 and 10-7.

Most homes use alternating current electricity and the voltage of the outlets is from 110 to 120 volts. When measuring the outlet voltage, an alternating current meter must be used. The scale can be a 0-to-150–volt or a 0-to-200–volt. See Fig. 10-8. Alternating current meters do not have a polarity marking as the direction of electron flow is always changing. The meter is connected directly across the outlet with one ter-

Fig. 10-6. A wiring diagram of Figure 10-5. Wiring diagrams, sometimes called schematic diagrams, use electrical symbols to show how the parts are connected.

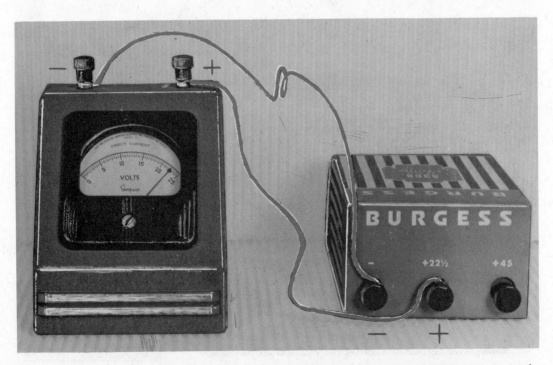

Fig. 10-7. Measuring the voltage of a radio B battery. When connecting the meter it is necessary to observe the polarity of the battery and the meter. Minus goes to minus and plus goes to plus.

Fig. 10-8. Using an alternating current meter to measure the voltage of a wall outlet.

minal of the meter going to one side of the outlet and the other terminal to the other side of the outlet.

Some meters called *multimeters* (Fig.

10-9) can be used for both alternating current and direct current. Separate connections are shown on the cases of the meters where the terminal leads may be

Fig. 10-9. A multimeter that will measure AC and DC voltage, resistance and direct current. (Triplett)

connected for either AC or DC. These meters very often have various scales that can be selected by moving a switch on the front of the meter case.

The Principle of the Moving Coil Meter

Most direct current electricity is measured with a meter using a moving coil. The moving coil meter is often called a D'Arsonval movement meter in honor of the famous French Physicist who introduced the moving coil galvanometer in 1882. The meter operates on the attraction and repulsion effect between magnetic poles.

When direct current flows through a coil of wire it becomes an electromagnet which has a north and south pole. The direction of the magnetic field of a coil may be determined by using what is known as the "left hand rule." This left hand rule is illustrated in Fig. 10-10.

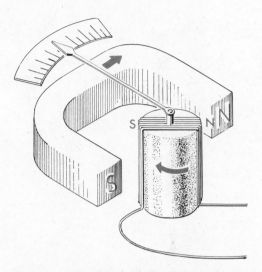

Fig. 10-11. The magnetic forces of attraction and repulsion cause the coil of the meter to turn so that the unlike poles of the coil and the magnet are brought closer together. If the voltage or current is increased, the coil becomes a stronger magnet and it turns further due to the greater magnetic force between the poles of the coil and the magnet. The pointer shows the voltage reading on the scale.

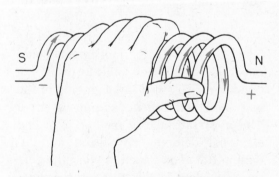

Fig. 10-10. If the fingers of the left hand are wrapped around the coil in the direction of current flow, the thumb will point toward the north pole end of the coil.

If a coil is suspended between the poles of a horseshoe magnet as shown in Fig. 10-11, the coil will turn so that the north pole is near the south pole of the horseshoe magnet and the south pole of the coil will be attracted to the north pole of the magnet. It is this movement of the coil when current is flowing through it that produces the meter readings on most direct current meters.

Construction of the Direct Current Meter

The moving coil of the D'Arsonval meter is made of several turns of insulated wire wound around a rectangular aluminum frame, Fig. 10-12. Aluminum is used so that the weight of the coil will be as light as possible. The coil is placed between the poles of a very powerful permanent magnet, and is mounted so that it is free to turn. Steel pivots at the top and bottom hold the coil between jeweled bearings so that

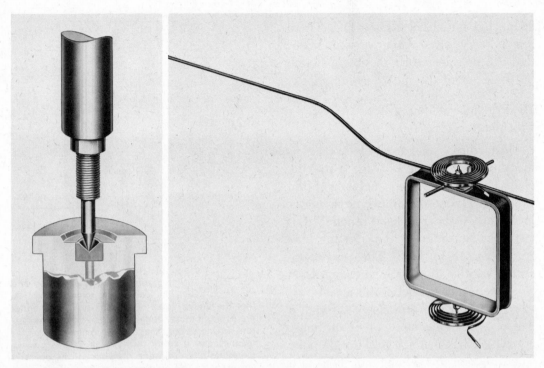

Fig. 10-12. The moving element of the meter must be lightweight. It uses a metal frame for damping. Fig. on left shows bearing. (Weston Instrument Div., Daystrom Inc.)

the coil can turn with very little friction, Fig. 10-12 (left.). Attached to the coil is a lightweight pointer, called the meter pointer, that moves across the scale of the meter. A coiled spring returns the pointer to the zero mark on the scale when the meter is not in use.

Damping the Moving Coil

The moving coil of the meter is mounted between the poles of the horseshoe magnet at a slight angle so that as the current flows through the coil the poles of the coil will be either attracted or repelled by the poles of the permanent magnet. The amount of movement of the coil is determined by the force that the magnetic field exerts against the permanent magnet. The stronger the current flow through the

meter the greater the movement of the coil and needle. See Figs. 10-13 and 10-14.

Since the moving coil is mounted on jeweled bearings its movement could make it swing back and forth like a pendulum. To avoid this swinging of the coil a method called damping is used. The most satisfactory method is called electrical damping. By using an aluminum frame on which to wind the coil, the movement of the frame in the magnetic field causes an electric current to be induced into the frame. The induced magnetic currents are in such a direction that they oppose the motion of the coil and thus the coil comes to rest very quickly. A device called a zero adjustment is used to place the pointer at the zero mark on the meter scale when the meter is not connected in a circuit.

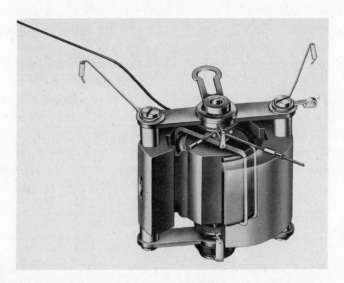

Fig. 10-13. The principal parts of a permanent magnet moving coil meter. The permanent magnet is a circular one called a "core" type magnet. (Weston Instrument Div., Daystrom Inc.)

Fig. 10-14. A representative type of voltmeter which uses the movements shown in Fig. 10-13. (Weston Instrument Div., Daystrom Inc.)

The Direct Current Voltmeter

A voltmeter is always connected directly across the two points to be measured in a circuit as in Fig. 10-15. Since the moving coil has comparatively few turns of wire, it cannot be connected directly across the voltage source as this would burn out the coil. To reduce the current and to obtain the desired scale reading a resistor is always placed in

series with the moving coil when the meter is used as a voltmeter, Fig. 10-16. The resistor is called a multiplier and its size determines the full scale reading of the voltmeter.

In most electrical circuits it is necessary to use a voltmeter that will not place very much of a load on the circuit. If this occurs the meter draws too much current, and will reduce the circuit voltage so that the meter will

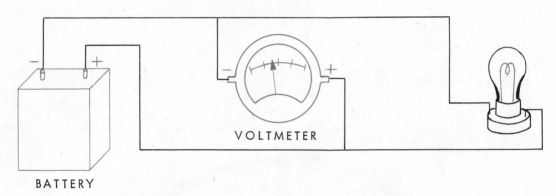

VOLTMETER

BATTERY

Fig. 10-15. A drawing showing how a voltmeter is connected in a circuit.

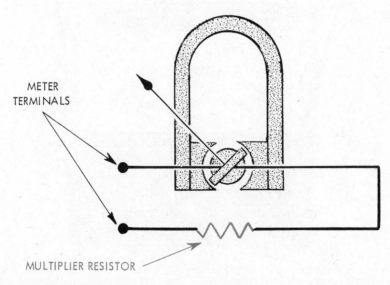

METER TERMINALS

MULTIPLIER RESISTOR

Fig. 10-16. The multiplier resistor is connected in series with the coil of the movement. The resistor is usually located inside the case of the meter.

not give a true reading of the voltage present when the meter is not in the circuit. Voltmeters which use large resistance multipliers are desired since they place a very small load on the circuit.

Voltmeters For More Than One Maximum Voltage

Voltmeters may be used for more than one full scale reading by connect-ing different multiplier resistors into the meter circuit. Fig. 10-17 illustrates a schematic diagram in which a single meter may be used to read full scale direct current voltages of 10 volts, 100 volts, or 1,000 volts. By rotating the selector switch, the maximum full scale reading of the meter may be changed to the desired voltage scale. Fig. 10-18 shows what the meter scale would look like for this meter.

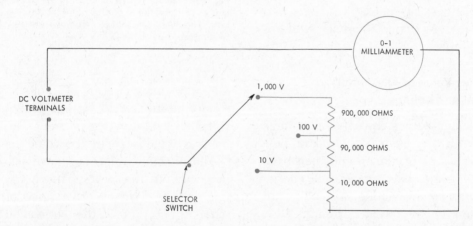

Fig. 10-17. This is a schematic diagram for a direct current voltmeter that will read full scale voltages of 10, 100, or 1000 volts.

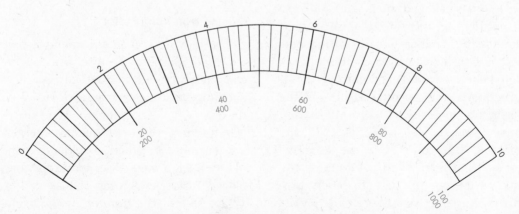

Fig. 10-18. The same meter divisions are used for this three scale direct current meter. The selector switch may be used to select either 10, 100, or 1000 volt maximum scale readings. When the selector switch is changed, the reading of the meter pointer may be determined by selecting the proper maximum scale reading.

Alternating Current Moving Coil Meters

If alternating current is connected directly to a moving coil type meter the needle would just vibrate. Alternating current flows in one direction and then in the opposite direction so rapidly that the meter would be unable to respond to these fluctuations. The moving coil meter can be used to measure low frequency alternating current voltage if a device called a rectifier is used. The rectifier, which will be studied in Unit 29, changes alternating current into direct current so that the meter will operate properly.

Effective Value of Alternating Current and Voltage

Both alternating current and voltage vary with the changing electron flow from zero to a maximum and then back to zero again. The amount of energy produced by alternating current is not the same as for direct current. Direct current usually provides a constant voltage but with alternating current the voltage is continually changing from zero to a peak and then back to zero again. It is necessary to determine what the *effective* voltage of alternating current is. Mathematical calculations show that effective voltage or current of alternating current is equal to 0.707 of the maximum value (Fig. 10-19). Alternating current meters are made to read the effective voltage as it is the effective voltage that helps us in determining the amount of energy that is being produced. An effective voltage of 100 volts alternating current produces the same amount of energy as 100 volts of direct current. In most homes, for example,

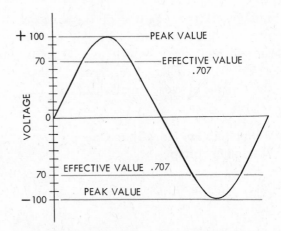

Fig. 10-19. A sine wave illustrating the peak value and effective value in one cycle of alternating current. The peak and effective values are reached twice during each cycle.

the voltmeter will read 117 volts when connected to a wall outlet. The peak voltage of alternating current in the home is actually about 165 volts.

The effective value is known mathematically as the root-mean-square, or *rms* voltage. This effective value of alternating current is the equivalent of a direct current value that will produce the same amount of power. AC meters read the effective value.

Moving Iron Vane Meter

The moving coil meter operates only on direct current. To use the moving coil meter on alternating current it is necessary to use a rectifying device with the meter. A very common type meter used to measure low frequency alternating current is called a *moving vane meter*. Such a meter uses two iron vanes placed inside a circular coil as in Fig. 10-20. One of the iron vanes is stationary, and the other iron vane which is movable is connected to the meter pointer. When the coil is in a circuit so

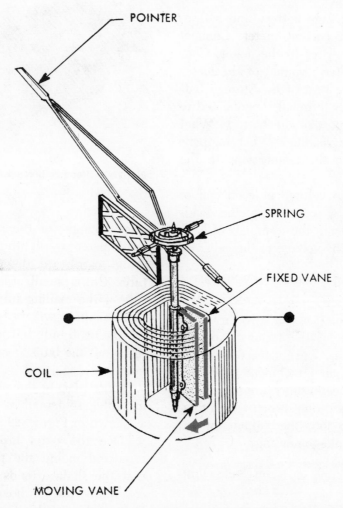

POINTER

SPRING

FIXED VANE

COIL

MOVING VANE

Fig. 10-20. A moving vane meter movement. A repelling force is developed between the two iron vanes when current flows through the coil. One vane is fixed and the other is pivoted so that it will move when the magnetizing current flows.

that the current flows through it the iron vanes are magnetized by induction. The moving vane and the stationary vane become magnetized so that they have like poles at the top and like poles at the bottom. Since like poles repel each other the moving vane is pushed away from the fixed vane. Even when alternating current is connected to the meter coil, the two vanes always have like poles opposite each other so that the pointer will move. A coil spring keeps the two vanes close to each other when current is flowing through the coil.

When it is used as a voltmeter a multiplier resistor is connected in series with the coil the same as for the moving coil meter.

INTERESTING THINGS TO DO

1. Measuring Direct Current Voltage.

Obtain a storage battery and a 0-to-15–volt direct current meter. Connect two insulated wires to the meter. Connect the positive terminal of the meter to the positive post of the storage battery. The other terminal is connected to the negative post of the battery. What is the voltage reading? What happens if you reverse the connections to the meter?

Measure the voltage of each cell of the battery by connecting the leads from the meter to the terminals of each cell. What is the voltage of the cells?

2. Measuring Home Outlet Voltage.

Obtain an AC meter with a 0-to-150–volt scale. Connect two insulated leads to each of the terminals of the meter. The other ends of these leads are connected to an attachment plug cap. Be sure the connectors are tight and that the wires do not touch each other. Plug the cap into the voltage outlet. What is the voltage reading?

3. Constructing a Neon Bulb Voltmeter.

Materials needed to construct the neon bulb voltmeter (Fig. 10-21):

200,000-ohm, ½-watt carbon resistor
500,000-ohm carbon potentiometer
Pointer knob for potentiometer
Neon bulb, type NE-2
One pair of test leads about 3′ long
Hook-up wire
A 2″ length of mailing tube. This tube should be large enough in diameter for the potentiometer to fit in one end.

Cut a piece of cardboard the same diameter as the mailing tube. Make a hole in the center of this round disk

Fig. 10-21. Neon bulb voltmeter.

large enough for the shaft of the potentiometer to fit through. Glue the round cardboard disk to the mailing tube. Cut a small oblong hole in the side of the mailing tube. Check to see that the hole will be large enough to see the neon bulb but not large enough to permit the bulb to come through the hole.

Before placing the parts in the mailing tube, solder all of the connections as shown in Fig. 10-22.

Place the parts inside the mailing tube and mount the potentiometer so that the shaft extends out of the end covered by the cardboard disk. This end of the tube can be covered with white paper as it will be where the dial markings are placed when calibrating the meter. The pointer knob can be tightened on the potentiometer shaft.

Using a clear cement, glue the neon bulb inside the tube so that it is visible through the hole already cut in the tube.

Calibrating the Meter. Radio B batteries or a power supply with different voltages can be used to calibrate the meter. You should be careful when using this meter because the voltages used can

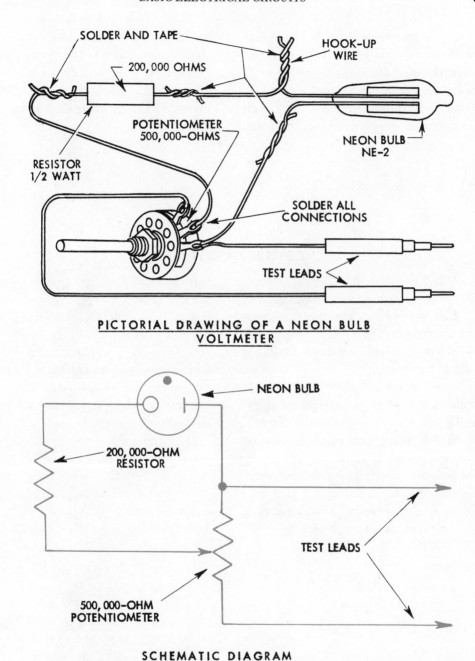

SOLDER AND TAPE

200,000 OHMS

HOOK-UP WIRE

POTENTIOMETER 500,000-OHMS

RESISTOR 1/2 WATT

NEON BULB NE-2

SOLDER ALL CONNECTIONS

TEST LEADS

PICTORIAL DRAWING OF A NEON BULB VOLTMETER

NEON BULB

200,000-OHM RESISTOR

500,000-OHM POTENTIOMETER

TEST LEADS

SCHEMATIC DIAGRAM

Fig. 10-22. Pictorial (top) and schematic (bottom) diagrams of a direct current type neon voltmeter.

cause a bad shock. When measuring voltage, it is important to avoid coming in contact with the terminals. Using a 90-volt B battery connect the two meter leads across the terminals of the battery. Turn the potentiometer to where the neon bulb just starts to glow. If the bulb is already glowing when the leads are connected, turn the potentiometer until the glow is almost out. At this point (where the glow starts to go out) place a mark on the end of the tubing. Label this mark "90 volts." The two test leads can be placed in a wall outlet and this voltage marked on the dial. The wall outlet voltage is usually about 117 volts.

As in the B battery voltage, the dial should be turned to the point when the glow starts to go out. Other known voltages can be marked on the dial. The meter will read up to 650 volts and as low as 70 volts.

REVIEW QUESTIONS

1. What is voltage?

2. Give another name for voltage.

3. List several devices that can produce a voltage.

4. What are the common voltages found in the home?

5. Draw a circuit showing where a voltmeter is placed in a circuit to measure the voltage or electromotive force.

6. When using alternating current voltmeters, why is it not necessary to have polarity markings on the meters?

7. What is the meter called that can measure both alternating and direct current as well as various voltages?

8. List the important parts of a moving coil meter.

9. Why is it necessary to damp a moving coil meter?

10. Why is a resistor used in series with a moving coil voltmeter?

11. What device is used with a moving coil meter when it is used to measure alternating current?

12. If the peak voltage of alternating current is 20 volts what is the effective voltage?

13. List the principle parts of a moving iron vane meter.

UNIT 11
MEASURING CURRENT

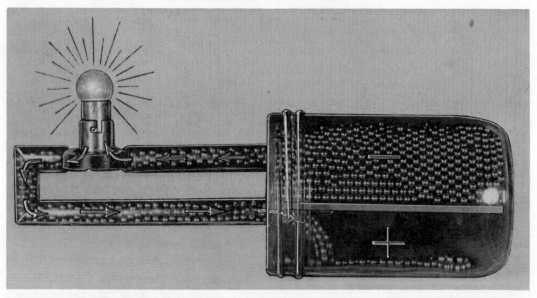

Fig. 11-1. The small steel balls in the photograph represent electrons. The glass jar represents a battery with the negative side of the battery holding a large quantity of electrons (steel balls). The electrons leave the negative terminal of the battery, flow through the plastic tube and light bulb and return through the tube to the positive side of the battery. This flow of electrons from the negative terminal through the light bulb and back to the positive terminal produces light in the bulb. The flow of electrons is called *current.*

Current and Electron Flow

The flow of electricity is the movement of electrons in a circuit. This electron flow in a circuit is called *current* and if the electrons are always going in the same direction it is called *direct current.* *Alternating current* is a flow of electrons that is continuously changing directions.

To have a flow of electrons it is necessary to have a source of electricity, such as a generator, to provide the pressure or voltage to push the electrons through the circuit. These electrons go from the negative pole of the generator through the circuit and return to the positive pole of the generator.

Moving electrons might be compared

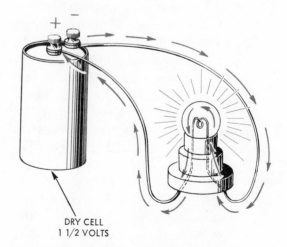

DRY CELL
1 1/2 VOLTS

Fig. 11-2. This drawing indicates with arrows the flow of electrons from the negative terminal of the dry cell through the wire and light bulb back to the positive terminal. The circuit drawn here also shows the same type of circuit that is illustrated with the steel balls in Figure 11-1.

to a bucket brigade used in putting out a fire. The source of water is a well and after the bucket is filled, the people in the brigade pass it from one person to the next. The last person in line receives the bucket and pours the water on the fire. He then passes the bucket to another line of people who return it to the well to be filled again. Buckets are continuously being passed from one person to the next from the well to the fire and from the fire back to the well. This continuous movement of the buckets is like the flow of electrons which leave the source of electricity and flow through the circuit. See Figs. 11-1 and 11-2.

Electron Flow Measured in Amperes

In a city water system it is very common to measure the amount of water that is flowing through a pipe by determining the number of gallons that is flowing through the pipe in an hour. In electricity the electron flow is measured in amperes, which indicate the number of electrons that pass through the circuit in one second. Electrons are so very small that it takes about six million, million, million of them to pass through a circuit in one second to equal one ampere. Since this is such a large figure the quantity of current flow is stated in amperes. *Ampere* is the unit of measurement for current, the abbreviation being *amp* or *amps*.

Using Ammeters

An ammeter is used to measure the electron flow in amperes. All ammeters are labeled as to whether they will read AC or DC. Just as in using a voltmeter, it is important that the ammeter have the correct scale for the current to be measured. See Figs. 11-3 and 11-4.

To measure the current flow in a circuit the ammeter is connected in one wire of the line so that the electrons must flow through the meter as well as all of the rest of the circuit. Extreme care must be used to be sure that the voltage is not on when the meter is being connected.

Most direct current meters have a + marked on the positive connection. The other terminal is negative and should be connected to the negative side of the circuit. Alternating current ammeters do not have a polarity marking as they are made so that the electrons can flow through the meter in either direction.

When measuring current it is usually advisable to start with a meter that has a high ampere range. If the current is not enough to move the pointer so an accurate reading can be made, a smaller range meter can be used. Starting with a large range meter and then replacing with small range meter will avoid burning out the meter.

A common use of an ammeter is on the dashboard of some automobiles. The ammeter is used to show the driver whether the generator is charging or not. The meter is a center scale meter and indicates that no current is flowing through it when the pointer is in the center of the dial. As the generator charges the battery of the automobile the pointer moves to the right, showing that current is being supplied by the generator. When the generator is not charging the pointer moves to the left. This shows the driver that the battery is providing the electricity and usually indicates that the automobile generator is not working. In some automobiles a red light is used in place of an ammeter. The red light comes on when the generator is not

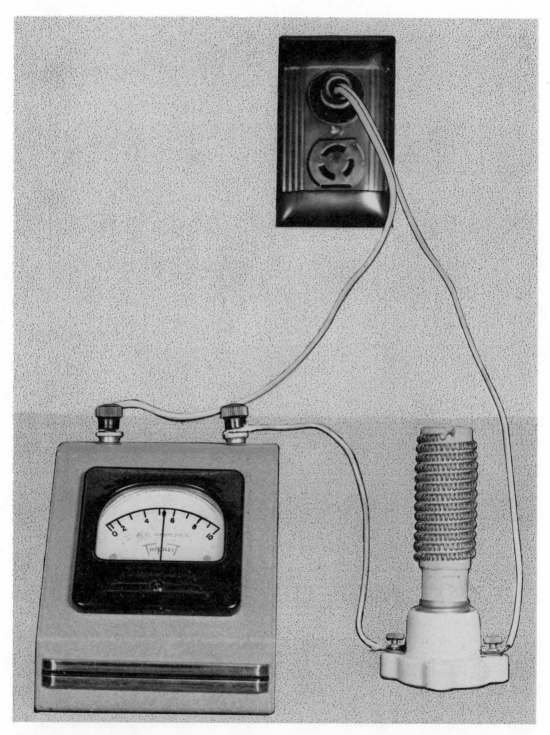

Fig. 11-3. A heater element is plugged into a 115-volt alternating current wall outlet. Notice that one side of the wire going to the heater has been cut so that the ammeter can be connected in the circuit. The ammeter shows that a little more than 5 amperes of current is flowing through the element.

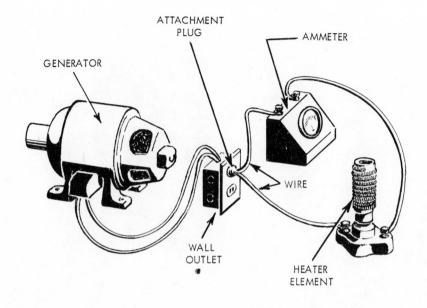

ATTACHMENT
PLUG

AMMETER

GENERATOR

WIRE

WALL
OUTLET

HEATER
ELEMENT

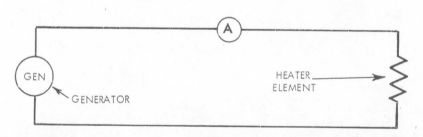

GEN

GENERATOR

HEATER
ELEMENT

Fig. 11-4. The drawing at the top shows the complete electrical circuit of Figure 11-3. The generator is providing the voltage that is delivered by the two wires to the wall outlet. When the heater is connected to the outlet by an attachment plug, current flows in the circuit. The ammeter is connected in one side of the line to measure the current flow. The bottom drawing is a schematic diagram of the entire circuit. Symbols are used to represent the generator, ammeter, and heater element.

charging the battery.

In some circuits, such as a radio circuit, very small amounts of current flow and meters must be used that will read thousandths of an ampere. Meters which read current in thousandths of an ampere are called *milliammeters* (Fig. 11-5). *Milli* means one-thousandth. If a milliammeter has a scale of 0 to 300 this means that the meter will read from zero to three-hundred thousandths of an ampere. Three-hundred thousandths of

an ampere is equal to three-tenths of an ampere.

TYPICAL CURRENT CONSUMPTION

Approximate currents used by some common home appliances are listed below:

Sewing machine	0.80 ampere
Lamp bulbs (100-watt)	0.83 ampere
Radio (small)	0.85 ampere
Refrigerator	2.00 amperes
Television	2.00 amperes
Washing machine	2.50 amperes
Iron	6.60 amperes
¾ hp home air conditioning unit	12.00 amperes

Fig. 11-5. The milliammeter indicates that 185 milliamperes is the amount of current flowing through the 1½-volt light bulb when it is connected to a flashlight cell. The 185 milliamperes are equal to 0.185 ampere.

Construction of the Ammeter

The basic construction of the ammeter is the same as that of the voltmeter described in the previous section. A moving coil movement is generally used and the amount of current flowing through it determines the amount of

AMMETER

The letter "A" in a symbol means ammeter.

pointer deflection. Moving vane movements may also be used in some instruments. Figs. 11-6 and 11-7 show details of typical meters.

An ammeter measures electron flow and must be connected in series with the circuit so that the total current to be measured will flow through it. In order that an accurate reading be obtained, it is important that the *meter* present as little resistance to the current flow as possible. If the meter presents opposition to the electron flow, the amount of current flowing would not be the same as when the meter is out of the circuit and an inaccurate reading would result.

The coil in most meters has very little

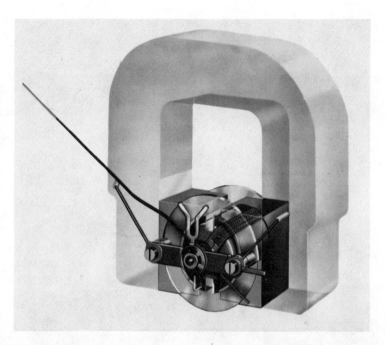

Fig. 11-6. A view of a typical moving coil meter movement. The permanent magnet used is made in a U shape and is referred to as an "outside" magnet. The moving coil is the same as the one shown in Figure 10-2. (Weston Instrument Div., Daystrom Inc.)

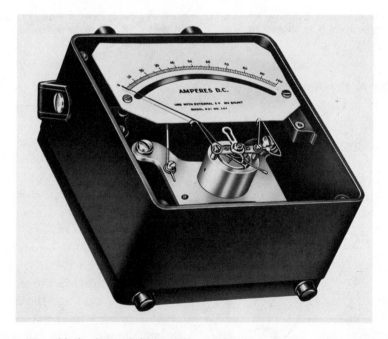

Fig. 11-7. An ammeter with the front of the case removed to show details of the movement. The movement for this meter uses a magnet which fits closely around the coil and is known as a core magnet. (Weston Instrument Div., Daystrom Inc.)

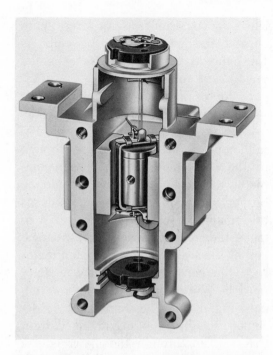

Fig. 11-8. A cutaway view of a coil movement used in a galvanometer. This is a meter used to measure very small amounts of current. (G. M. Laboratories Inc.)

resistance and can be used only for measuring small amounts of current as heavier currents would burn out the coil. See Fig. 11-8. A resistor cannot be connected in series with the movement to reduce the current since this would result in an inaccurate reading of the meter.

Changing Meter Current Ranges

To avoid burning up the coil and to increase the range of the meter, a resistor called a *shunt* is connected across the meter coil. The shunt allows a small amount of the current to flow through the meter coil and a large amount of current flows through the shunt (Fig. 11-9). Thus, the ammeter with the shunt provides very little opposition to current flow in the circuit and makes it possible to have a true reading of the current.

The shunt which is placed across the meter coil is said to be in parallel with

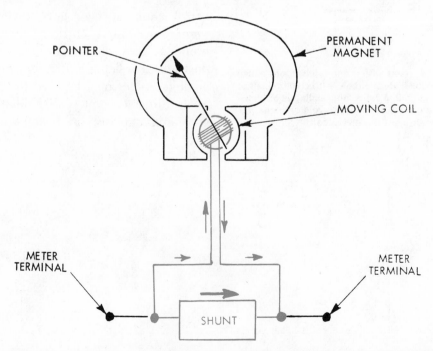

Fig. 11-9. In an ammeter, a shunt is connected in parallel with the moving coil. A small amount of current flows through the meter coil and a large amount of current flows through the shunt.

the coil. Different ranges or maximum scale readings of ammeters may be obtained by changing the size of the shunt. To read large amounts of current a very low resistance shunt is placed across or in parallel with the coil. This very low resistance shunt allows most of the current to flow through the shunt and only a small amount through the coil. Since only a small amount of current flows through the coil it takes a large current flow to effect the movement of the pointer and thus the range of the meter is extended.

To read small amounts of current a larger resistance is used for the shunt.

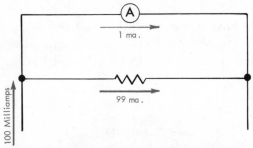

Fig. 11-10. A meter with a one milliampere movement is placed in a circuit with 100 milliamps flowing through it. A full scale reading is obtained if the shunt carries 99 milliamps and only one milliamp goes through the meter coil.

The larger resistance shunt forces more current to flow through the coil. As this happens, the meter reacts to smaller amounts of current.

If, for example, a meter with a one milliampere (0.001 amps) full scale deflection is placed in a circuit with 100 milliamperes (0.1 amp) flowing through it, the pointer would be driven completely off scale and the coil could be burned out. (Full scale deflection means the amount of current that it takes to make the pointer move to the extreme end of the scale). To make such a meter read the correct current flow a shunt must be placed across the meter terminals, Fig. 11-10. The shunt must be designed so that the maximum current that can go through the meter coil is the amount needed for full scale reading. The rest goes through the shunt.

Ammeters With Several Current Ranges

An ammeter may have several different maximum current ranges, the same as for voltmeters. Fig. 11-11 illustrates a schematic diagram in which a single meter may be used to read full scale direct current of 10 milliamperes, 100 milliamperes, or 1 ampere (1000

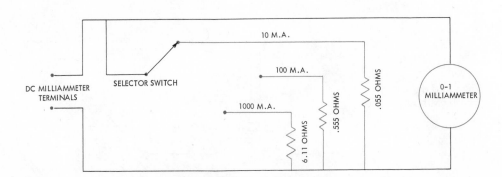

Fig. 11-11. A schematic diagram for a direct current milliammeter that will read full scale current of 10 milliamperes, 100 milliamperes, and 1 ampere (1,000 milliamperes).

milliamperes). By rotating the selector switch, the maximum full scale of the meter may be changed to the desired direct current scale.

Electroplating

Electrons will flow through certain chemical solutions the same as through wire conductors. This principle of current flow in solutions is used in *electroplating*. Electroplating is a very valuable commercial process used when metals need to be coated to prevent rust or to improve their appearance. Copper, nickel, silver, chromium, zinc, cadmium, and gold are the materials most often used in electroplating. The shiny chromium finish found on many automobile

accessories is electroplated onto steel.

Electroplating solutions are usually made of a metallic salt solution such as copper sulfate for copper-plating, or nickel sulfate for nickel-plating. A direct current is always used in the plating process.

The object to be plated is placed in the electrolyte solution and is connected to the negative terminal of the direct current electricity. The positive terminal of the electricity is usually connected to a metal such as copper, nickel, or silver that is being used for the plating process. The object to be plated and the metal used for the plating are placed in the solution as shown in Fig. 11-12.

When direct current electricity is con-

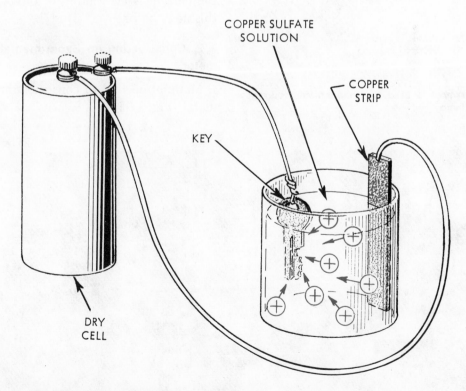

Fig. 11-12. With a brass key and copper strip connected as shown, the positive copper particles dissolve and are then attracted by the negatively charged key. As the key is plated, the copper strip is worn away.

nected to the two metals, a current starts to flow through the metallic salt solution. The plating metal is dissolved into the solution. This makes the solution have an excess of metal particles which are pulled toward the material to be plated. As the metal particles reach the object a thin plating of the metal is placed on the object.

INTERESTING THINGS TO DO

1. Using a Neon Bulb as an Alternating or Direct Current Indicator.

Obtain a 105-125–volt neon lamp and socket for the lamp. Connect two wires from terminals on the socket to a 115-volt alternating current outlet. The lamp will light up immediately and both ele-ments will appear to be lighted. Notice that there is a slight flickering glow from the elements. This flickering is due to the fluctuations of the alternating current.

Now connect the two socket leads of the neon lamp to a direct current source of electricity. This can be obtained from a 90-volt B battery. Notice that only one element of the lamp glows. Reverse the connections to the socket. What happens? How can we determine whether the current is alternating or direct with this neon bulb?

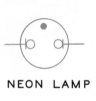

NEON LAMP

This symbol is used for an alternating current neon lamp.

2. Constructing an Experimental Ammeter.

Material needed to construct the ammeter (Fig. 11-13):

Fig. 11-13. Experimental ammeter for measuring the current of a light bulb.

50′ No. 26 magnet wire

Two washers (fiber or masonite), ¾″ diameter

Tubing (cardboard, fiber, hard rubber), with hollow center, about ³⁄₁₆″ to ¼″ diameter x 1½″ long

Pointer of tin, 2¾″ x 3¼″

Base of pine, ¾″ x 3″ x 4½″

Back of plywood (or masonite), ¼″ x 4½″ x 7″

Plunger—round soft iron, ³⁄₁₆″ x 2¼″ (a 20-penny or 40-penny common nail can be used). Plunger must slide freely through the tubing.

Terminals—roundhead (RH) ½″, No. 6 wood screws and soldering lugs or washers.

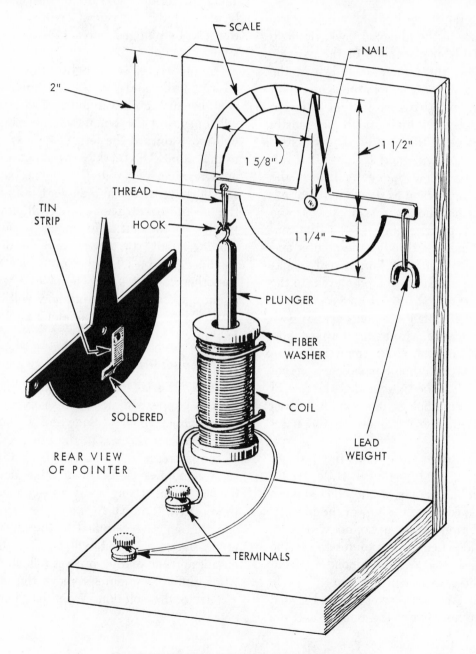

Fig. 11-14. Drawing of the experimental ammeter.

Construction. Drill holes in the two washers so that they will fit snugly over the tubing. Glue the washers to each end of the tubing. Wind the 50′ of No. 26 magnet wire on the tubing. Even layers of wire will make a much nicer looking coil.

Make the meter holder by nailing the pine base to the plywood back. Refer to Fig. 11-14 for placement of the parts.

Cut the tin pointer as shown in the drawing. Punch a hole in the center with a shingle nail. To keep it from tilting, it is necessary to solder a small piece of tin to the back of the pointer. This tin strip is about ¼″ wide and 1″ long. It is soldered just below the center hole of the pointer and is bent as shown in the drawing. A small hole the same size as the pointer is punched in it so that the center nail must go through the pointer and the small tin strip. A shingle nail acts as the pivot and holds the pointer on to the back.

The coil is held to the back by two small pieces of wire at the top and bottom of the coil. Four small holes are drilled through the plywood back so that the wires can be tightened in the rear of the plywood. Solder the two leads from the coil to two terminals on the baseboard.

Check to be sure that the plunger (³⁄₁₆″ x 2¼″ long) will slide freely through the center of the coil. Make a small hookeye on the top of the plunger by soldering a piece of copper wire to it. A thread is tied to the pointer and to the plunger so that when the pointer is centered the plunger will be about ¼″ inside the coil. Another piece of thread is tied to the other side of the pointer and the plunger is balanced by placing small pieces of solder through the thread loop.

Calibrating the Meter. The experimental meter may be calibrated by using a group of light bulbs of a known wattage.

Wire three light bulb sockets in parallel. The terminals on the meter should be connected in one side of a pair of leads that can be plugged into a 115-volt outlet.

Obtain three electric light bulbs—two 25-watt bulbs and one 50-watt bulb.

Screw in the 50-watt bulb. The bulb will burn and the pointer of the meter will move toward the left. Place a mark at that point. This mark shows about 0.41 ampere of current. With the 50-watt bulb still burning, screw in a 25-watt bulb in the second socket. The pointer will move farther to the left. The meter is now reading about 0.62 ampere and the dial should again be labeled. Now screw in the other 25-watt bulb. The pointer will again move and the current flow will be about 0.82 ampere. The ammeter is now calibrated.

3. Copper-Plating an Object.

Fill a glass jar (pint size) with a solution of copper sulfate. Place a strip of sheet copper about 1″ wide and 4″ long in one side of the jar. In the other side of the jar place the object to be plated such as a piece of brass, or other nonferrous metal. Using a dry cell connect the positive terminal to the copper strip and the negative terminal to the object to be plated. Current will flow in the circuit and the plating process will start. After about 15 minutes remove the object from the solution. What has happened?

REVIEW QUESTIONS

1. What is the unit of measurement of electron flow?

2. Explain the difference between alternating current and direct current.

3. Give the name of the meter used to measure current.

4. Draw a circuit of a dry cell connected to a light bulb and show where the ammeter should be connected.

5. Why is it important to have the voltage off when connecting meters?

6. What does the term *milli* mean?

7. If a current has a 0.150 ampere of current flowing in it, how many milliamperes is that?

8. What type of current is used for electroplating?

9. Why is electroplating a very valuable process to many manufacturers of metal objects?

UNIT 12
MEASURING RESISTANCE

Meaning of Resistance

Every complete electrical circuit includes wire and a device that consumes current. The voltage forces the current through the circuit. The wire and the current-consuming device, such as a lamp, provide what is called *resistance*. Resistance is the opposition to electron flow that is found in every circuit.

Electrical resistance can be called friction. Electrical friction might be compared to friction which tends to keep things in motion from moving freely. Automobiles traveling on a highway have friction between the pavement and the tires, boats have friction when moving in water, and friction is developed when an airplane flies through the air. In all of these examples, friction is slowing down the object.

In electricity, the friction or resistance developed by the flow of electrons in a circuit tends to reduce the amount of current flow. The greater the resistance in a circuit, the less the current flow, just as the increased friction developed when an automobile drives off a paved highway onto a dirt road tends to slow it down. The resistance in a circuit can be increased if the length of the wire used in the circuit is made longer, since this will lengthen the path over which the

FIXED
RESISTOR

The resistor symbol begins at the left with an up-stroke.

electrons must flow. If the wire is made smaller this too will increase the resistance since it will provide a smaller path for the electrons to flow through.

How Resistance Produces Heat

Electrical resistance has many uses. One of the most important uses of resistance is its ability to make electricity produce heat. Heat is produced by friction. This can be demonstrated if we rub two wooden blocks together very rapidly. The blocks will become warm owing to the friction caused by the rubbing. In electricity, the electrons that are flowing through the wires hit each other, and this collision of electrons results in heat being developed the same as by the rubbing of the blocks together.

We can increase the heating effect of electricity if we can increase the amount of current flow. Current flow can be increased by adding additional voltage or pressure to the circuit. The greater the electron flow the greater the friction from the electrons coming in contact with each other and thus the greater the heat developed.

We are all familiar with the use of electricity in many types of heating appliances such as electric stoves, hot water heaters, flat irons, waffle irons, toasters, and electric blankets. In these appliances (Fig. 12-1) a special resistance wire called *nichrome* is used to produce heat. Nichrome is an alloy of nickel and chromium and has a high resistance to electron flow. This high resistance plus its ability to be very hot without melting makes it ideal for use as a heater element. In some of the modern type heat-

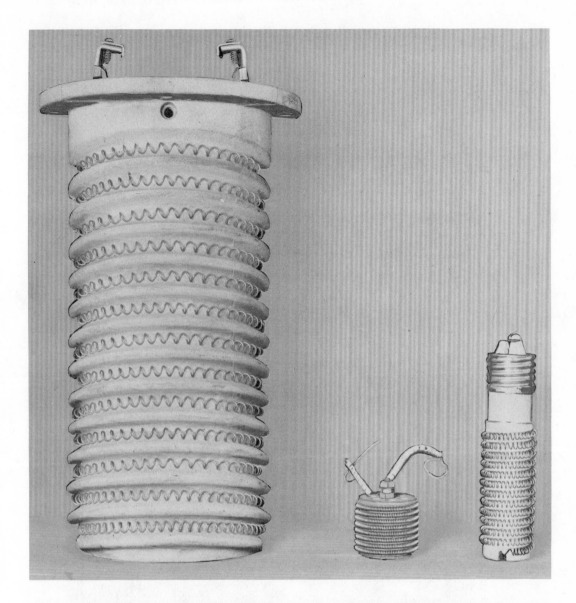

Fig. 12-1. Examples of three types of heating elements. The large element on the left is used in a wall heater; the small element in the center is used to heat a coffee percolator; the element on the right is used in a portable room heater. All of these elements use coiled nichrome mounted on a ceramic base.

ing devices the element of nichrome wire is encased in a tubular sheath. Fins are attached to the tubing for better heat radiation. This method protects the heater element from possible damage. See Fig. 12-2.

The light bulb, called an *incandescent*

lamp (Fig. 12-3), also uses the heating effect of electricity to produce light. The lamp has a wire inside of the glass bulb called a *filament*. This filament is made of a high resistance wire made of tungsten. As the electrons flow through the tungsten the friction of the electrons

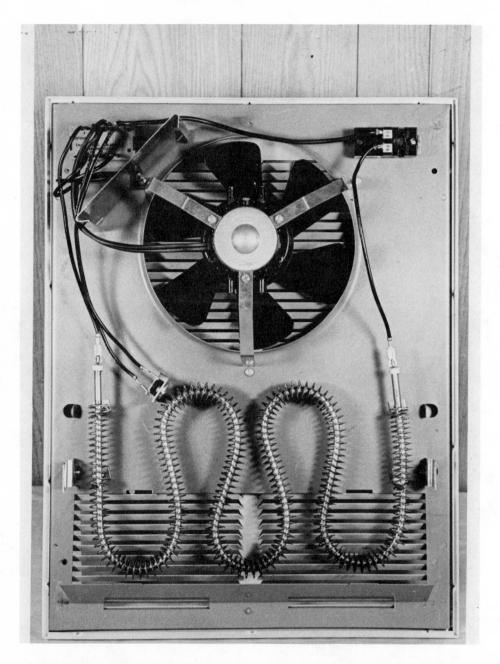

Fig. 12-2. This modern electrical heater has the heater element enclosed in a tubular sheath with bonded fins. An electric fan is used to blow hot air, produced by the heater, into the room.

produces heat. This heat is so great that the filament becomes white hot and gives off light. To keep the tungsten filament from burning up because of the oxygen in the air, it is placed in a glass bulb. All of the air is then removed from the bulb and the filament can get very hot without burning up.

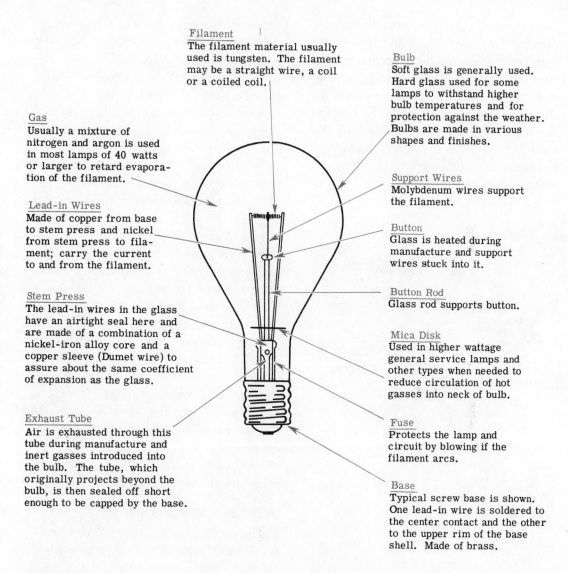

Filament
The filament material usually used is tungsten. The filament may be a straight wire, a coil or a coiled coil.

Bulb
Soft glass is generally used. Hard glass used for some lamps to withstand higher bulb temperatures and for protection against the weather. Bulbs are made in various shapes and finishes.

Gas
Usually a mixture of nitrogen and argon is used in most lamps of 40 watts or larger to retard evaporation of the filament.

Support Wires
Molybdenum wires support the filament.

Lead-in Wires
Made of copper from base to stem press and nickel from stem press to filament; carry the current to and from the filament.

Button
Glass is heated during manufacture and support wires stuck into it.

Button Rod
Glass rod supports button.

Stem Press
The lead-in wires in the glass have an airtight seal here and are made of a combination of a nickel-iron alloy core and a copper sleeve (Dumet wire) to assure about the same coefficient of expansion as the glass.

Mica Disk
Used in higher wattage general service lamps and other types when needed to reduce circulation of hot gasses into neck of bulb.

Exhaust Tube
Air is exhausted through this tube during manufacture and inert gasses introduced into the bulb. The tube, which originally projects beyond the bulb, is then sealed off short enough to be capped by the base.

Fuse
Protects the lamp and circuit by blowing if the filament arcs.

Base
Typical screw base is shown. One lead-in wire is soldered to the center contact and the other to the upper rim of the base shell. Made of brass.

Fig. 12-3. In the incandescent lamp, light results from the heating effect of electrical resistance. (Sylvania Electric Products, Inc.)

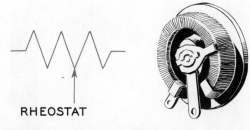

RHEOSTAT

The arrow across the symbol indicates that the resistor is variable.

Resistance Used to Control Current Flow and Reduce Voltage

Very often it is desirable to be able to control the amount of electricity used by a device. A good example of this is stage lighting where it is necessary to dim the lights. If the amount of current flowing through the lights can be reduced then the lights will become dimmer. We can reduce the current flow by putting more resistance in the circuit. The resistance can be a specially constructed resistor of nichrome wire. The resistor is connected in the circuit as shown in Fig. 12-4, so that the current must flow through the resistor and the light bulb. In this way the quantity of electrons flowing through the lamp is reduced by the resistor. The light is

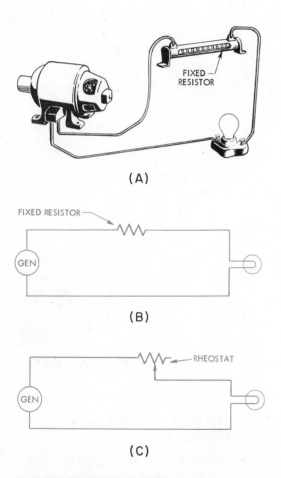

(A)

FIXED RESISTOR

(B)

(C)

Fig. 12-4.(A) The fixed resistor in the circuit reduces the current flow through the lamp bulb. The light from the lamp is dimmer because part of the voltage is used by the fixed resistor. (B) A wiring diagram using electrical symbols to represent the circuit shown in A. (C) This schematic diagram shows how a rheostat is used in a circuit to vary the brightness of a bulb.

dimmed because part of the voltage delivered by the wall outlet is being reduced by the resistor. To vary the brightness of the light a variable resistor called a *rheostat* must be used.

A rheostat has a movable contact arm that makes it possible to change the amount of resistance in the circuit (Figs. 12-5 and 12-6). When the contact arm is moved to the extreme left the entire voltage is available for the lamp and it burns brightly. As the contact arm moves to the right (clockwise) more resistance is placed in the circuit and lamp becomes dimmer. The increased resistance reduces the voltage to the lamp. This drop in voltage reduces the current flow in the circuit.

Rheostats are used to control the speed of motors. The speed of electric sewing machines is controlled through the use of a variable resistor that can be moved with the knee or foot. As the rheostat is pushed down it decreases the amount of resistance and allows more voltage to be used to speed up the sewing machine motor.

Resistance Measurement

The unit of measurement of resistance is the *ohm*. Some circuits have a very few

OHMMETER

This is how to indicate the instrument for measuring resistance in ohms.

Fig. 12-5. The lamp is burning brightly as the contact arm of the rheostat is allowing all of the current to flow directly to the lamp. The voltmeter connected across the lamp reads about 117 volts.

Fig. 12-6. The contact or arm has been moved so that the current must flow through part of the rheostat before going to the lamp. The rheostat has provided enough resistance to reduce the voltage across the lamp to about 60 volts. The light from the lamp is dimmer.

ohms resistance whereas others may have a million ohms resistance. All circuits have resistance in the wire and in the device using the electricity.

Where fairly heavy current is flowing fixed resistors are made of nichrome wire. If small amounts of current are flowing through the circuit, such as in many radio circuits, fixed resistors made of carbon can be used. Variable resistors are also made of nichrome wire or carbon, depending upon the amount of current to be controlled.

Resistance can be measured directly by the use of a meter called an *ohmmeter*. Some multimeters used to measure voltage and current are also used as ohmmeters. A very accurate device used to measure resistance is called a *Wheatstone bridge*.

Care must be used in measuring resistance with an ohmmeter to be sure that the voltage has been disconnected from the circuit. Leaving the voltage on when measuring the resistance will damage the ohmmeter.

In circuits where heat is developed the true resistance cannot be measured with an ohmmeter. As wires heat they increase their opposition to electron flow and the resistance in the circuit is increased. To determine the resistance of circuits where heat is being developed Ohm's law, which will be explained in Unit 14, must be used.

Using the Color Code

The value of the stripes or bands used for color coding composition resistors is shown in Fig. 12-7. To find the size of a particular resistor we must first look at the color bands and by using the Resistor Color Code Chart we can determine its resistance. For example, a resistor has as

Resistor Color Code Chart

Color	Significant Figure	Decimal Multiplier
Black	0	1
Brown	1	10
Red	2	100
Orange	3	1000
Yellow	4	10,000
Green	5	100,000
Blue	6	1,000,000
Violet	7	10,000,000
Gray	8	100,000,000
White	9	1,000,000,000

Tolerance	
No band	= 20%
Silver	= 10%
Gold	= 5%

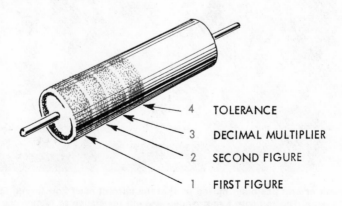

4   TOLERANCE

3   DECIMAL MULTIPLIER

2   SECOND FIGURE

1   FIRST FIGURE

Fig. 12-7. Composition resistor color-coding.

its first band the color red, the second color yellow, the third color orange, and no fourth color band. The first figure (red) is 2, the second figure (yellow) is 4, and

the decimal multiplier (orange) is 1000. The value of the resistance is 24,000 ohms and since there is no fourth color band the tolerance is plus or minus 20%.

INTERESTING THINGS TO DO

Constructing an Experimental Ohmmeter.

Materials needed to construct the ohmmeter (Fig. 12-8):

85' No. 32 magnet wire
Cardboard tubing, 1½" inside diameter
   x 2" long
Wood base, ½" x 3" x 5"
Pointer of sheet brass, 2⅝" x ⅛"
Piece of hacksaw blade, ³⁄₁₆" x 1⅜"
Sheet brass, ½" x 1¾" (2 required)
Sheet brass, ⅝" x 1½" (2 required)

Fig. 12-8. An experimental ohmmeter.

Construction. Shape the two brass pointer bearings as shown in Fig. 12-9. Center-punch the upper ends of the bearings and secure them to the wood base with wood screws ½" apart. Cut the meter pointer to the shape shown in the drawing. Cut a small steel brad and sharpen the ends so that it will turn free-

ly between the pointer bearings. Drill a hole the size of the steel brad through the brass pointer ¾" from the square end. Drill a similar hole through the center of the piece of hacksaw blade. Harden the piece of hacksaw blade by heating it to a cherry red over a flame, then plunging it into cold water. Solder the meter pointer and piece of hacksaw blade to the steel brad so that the two pieces will be at a right angle to each other. Secure a loop of solder to the lower end of the meter pointer, place the pointer between the bearings and test it for balance. The pointer should swing freely between the bearings and come to rest in an exact upright position. If it is necessary to lighten either end of the piece of hacksaw blade it may be done with a grinder or file, but care must be used because the hardened steel may break easily. After the pointer has been checked for balance, the piece of hacksaw blade may be magnetized by stroking it with a magnet as described in another part of this book.

Wind about 200 turns of magnet wire around the center of the cardboard tubing. Drill two small holes through the wood base through which to pass the coil ends and glue the coil to the wood base. Make certain that the coil does not touch the ends of the piece of hacksaw blade.

Shape two pieces of sheet brass to

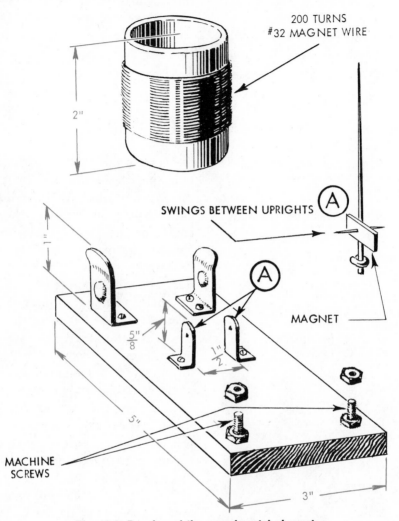

Fig. 12-9. Drawing of the experimental ohmmeter.

hold a flashlight cell and secure them to the wood base as shown in the drawing. Secure two machine screws at the end of the wood base to serve as terminal screws. Connect a piece of magnet wire on the bottom of the wood base between one of the flashlight cell holders and one end of the coil. Connect the other flashlight support to a screw terminal. Connect the other end of the coil to the other screw terminal. Secure a piece of white cardboard to the top of the coil to serve as a meter scale. Secure two pieces of flexible wire to the meter terminals to serve as test leads. The meter is now ready to be calibrated.

Calibrating the Ohmmeter. Place a flashlight cell in the holder and touch the two ends of the flexible leads together. The meter pointer will now swing to an extreme right or left position, depending upon which way the flashlight cell was placed in its holder. This is called the "zero" position and should be marked on the cardboard scale with the figure "0". Secure a 60-watt mazda lamp and touch the ends of the meter test leads to the contacts at the base of the lamp. The meter pointer will swing away from its center position and come to rest at a point toward the "0" position. Since the cold resistance of the 60-watt lamp is 20 ohms, write the figure "20" on the meter scale directly above the meter pointer. Other figures for calibrating the meter may be obtained from other size lamps and household electrical appliances. A 25-watt lamp has a cold resistance of about 50 ohms, while a 100-watt lamp has a cold resistance of only 10 ohms. A spiral heating element such as is used in an electric heater has a cold resistance of about 20 ohms.

REVIEW QUESTIONS

1. What is resistance?

2. What happens to the resistance of a circuit if a large diameter wire is replaced with a smaller diameter wire?

3. How does resistance produce heat?

4. Name the material used for heater elements.

5. Why is it necessary to keep the air away from the filament of an incandescent lamp?

6. What is a variable resistor called?

7. What is the unit of measurement of resistance called?

8. Explain what happens to the resistance of a heater element when the current is turned on.

UNIT 13
USING CONDUCTORS AND INSULATORS

Common Conductors

We have stated that wires are used to provide a path through which electrons flow. These wires are called *conductors* (see Fig. 13-1) because they conduct the electricity through the circuit. Conductors are usually made of metal since most metals permit electrons to flow through them easily. Some liquids are conductors of electricity but are used only for special purposes such as the electrolyte in storage batteries and electroplating.

All metals are conductors of electricity but some have more resistance than others. Copper is one of the metals which has a low resistance. Silver has a slightly lower resistance than copper but because it is more expensive than copper it is used only in special types of circuits. Almost all circuits use copper wire for conductors, as it is an excellent conductor that is fairly plentiful and not too expensive.

Aluminum has a higher resistance than copper but it is often used when extremely light weight is needed. Long power transmission lines are sometimes made of aluminum to reduce the weight of the wire.

Since all metals are conductors, different metals are sometimes used where they can supply special needs. These metals and some of their uses are listed below. They are listed according to their resistance with the first, silver, having the lowest resistance and the last, carbon, having the highest resistance.

Measuring Wire Sizes

All conductors have resistance. Large conductors have less resistance than small conductors because the electrons have more freedom to move in the large conductors. Long conductors have more resistance than short conductors (of the

CONDUCTOR	TYPICAL APPLICATIONS
Silver	Circuit breaker contacts, electronic circuits
Copper	All types of electrical conductors
Gold	Electroscope leaves
Aluminum	Lightweight conductors
Tungsten	Radio and lamp filaments
Zinc	Fuses and dry cells
Brass	Wall plugs and other types of exposed electrical connections
Nickel	Radio tubes
Tin	Solder
Steel	Telephone and telegraph lines
Lead	Solder and storage battery plates
Mercury	Switches
Nichrome	Heater elements
Carbon	Arc lamps and motor brushes

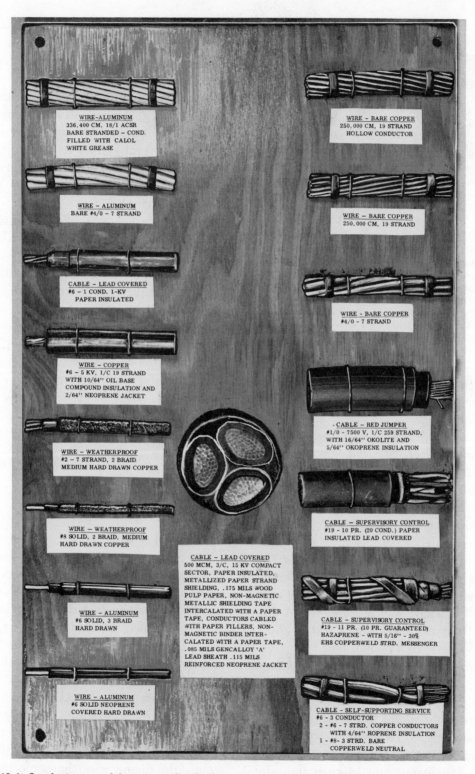

Fig. 13-1. Conductors used for power distribution are made to meet the requirements of different conditions.

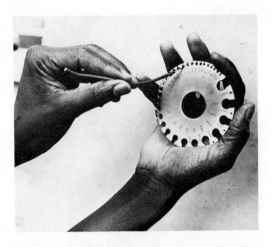

Fig. 13-2. Using a wire gage to determine the size of a wire. The size of wire is found by placing the wire between the slots on the outside edge of the gage. The slot in which the wire fits snugly indicates the gage of the wire. The round hole at the bottom of the slot makes it easier to remove the wire after checking for size.

same size) because the electrons have a longer path to flow through in the long conductor.

Since resistance can reduce the amount of electricity that flows in a circuit, it is often necessary to have conductors which will provide very little opposition to electron flow. To help in selecting the correct conductor all wires are designated according to number size. The smaller the number the larger the wire. A No. 8 wire is about ⅛″ in diameter and is much larger than a No. 14 wire which is about 1/16″ in diameter. A No. 36 wire is extremely small and is about the diameter of a human hair.

Wire sizes may be measured by a gage called a *wire gage* (Fig. 13-2). Gages used in the United States are called *American Standard Wire Gages.*

Use of the correct wire size for different circuits is necessary to prevent loss due to resistance and to keep the wire from heating. If the wire used is too

small for the amount of current flowing in the circuit, heat will be produced. This heat from excess current in wires can produce a fire and has been the cause of many houses burning down. Each electrical device and every circuit in the home uses a size wire that will carry the current safely. It is important to know how much current each circuit will be using in order to select the proper size wire.

The National Board of Fire Underwriters has adopted regulations which are part of what is known as the *National Electrical Code.* These regulations state the maximum amount of current that can be carried by conductors used in home and industrial wiring. The word *ampacity,* derived from *amperes* and *capacity,* is used to indicate those values. *Ampacities* for insulated copper conductors commonly used in home wiring are listed in the table below:

A. W. G.	AMPACITY	
14	15	
12	20	ROOM TEMP. 86°F.
10	30	
8	40	
6	55	

Circular Mil Area

Since the amount of current that a conductor can carry safely depends upon its cross-sectional area, a unit known as a *circular-mil,* abbreviated, *C. M.,* has been selected to give us this information. A mil is equal to 0.001 inch and an area with a dimension of 1 mil on each side, such as Fig. 13-3, would have an area of one square mil. Since most conductors, except those used in special applications, are round we need a unit to express circular area. If we square the diameter of the circle shown in Fig. 13-3, we will get the same answer

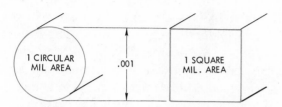

Fig. 13-3. Circular and square mil area.

as we would with the square figure, but it will be in terms of circular mils rather than square mils. Thus, we can see that a circular mil bears the same relation-

ship to a square mil as the area of a circle does to a square, which is 0.7854, and all we have to do to get the circular mil area of a conductor is to square its diameter in mils.

If we compare the current carrying capacity of conductors listed in the table of *National Electrical Code* regulations with those shown in the Copper-Wire Table below, we shall see that there is considerable difference between the two tables. For example, in the *National Electrical Code* table, No. 14 gage wire has a current carrying ca-

COPPER-WIRE TABLE

Gauge No. A.W.G.[1]	Diam. in Mils	Circular Mil Area	Turns per Linear Inch Enamel	Turns per Square Inch Enamel	Feet per Lb. Bare	Ohms per 1000 ft. 25° C.	Ampacity at 1500 C.M. per Amp.
1	289.3	83690	—	—	3.947	.1264	55.7
2	257.6	66370	—	—	4.977	.1593	44.1
3	229.4	52640	—	—	6.276	.2009	35.0
4	204.3	41740	—	—	7.914	.2533	27.7
5	181.9	33100	—	—	9.980	.3195	22.0
6	162.0	26250	—	—	12.58	.4028	17.5
7	144.3	20820	—	—	15.87	.5080	13.8
8	128.5	16510	7.6	—	20.01	.6405	11.0
9	114.4	13090	8.6	—	25.23	.8077	8.7
10	101.9	10380	9.6	84.8	31.82	1.018	6.9
11	90.74	8234	10.7	105	40.12	1.284	5.5
12	80.81	6530	12.0	131	50.59	1.619	4.4
13	71.96	5178	13.5	162	63.80	2.042	3.5
14	64.08	4107	15.0	198	80.44	2.575	2.7
15	57.07	3257	16.8	250	101.4	3.247	2.2
16	50.82	2583	18.9	306	127.9	4.094	1.7
17	45.26	2048	21.2	372	161.3	5.163	1.3
18	40.30	1624	23.6	454	203.4	6.510	1.1
19	35.89	1288	26.4	553	256.5	8.210	.86
20	31.96	1022	29.4	725	323.4	10.35	.68
21	28.46	810.1	33.1	895	407.8	13.05	.54
22	25.35	642.4	37.0	1070	514.2	16.46	.43
23	22.57	509.5	41.3	1300	648.4	20.76	.34
24	20.10	404.0	46.3	1570	817.7	26.17	.27
25	17.90	320.4	51.7	1910	1031	33.00	.21
26	15.94	254.1	58.0	2300	1300	41.62	.17
27	14.20	201.5	64.9	2780	1639	52.48	.13
28	12.64	159.8	72.7	3350	2067	66.17	.11
29	11.26	126.7	81.6	3900	2607	83.44	.084
30	10.03	100.5	90.5	4660	3287	105.2	.067
31	8.928	79.70	101	5280	4145	132.7	.053
32	7.950	63.21	113	6250	5227	167.3	.042
33	7.080	50.13	127	7360	6591	211.0	.033
34	6.305	39.75	143	8310	8310	266.0	.026
35	5.615	31.52	158	8700	10480	335.0	.021
36	5.000	25.00	175	10700	13210	423.0	.017
37	4.453	19.83	198	—	16660	533.4	.013
38	3.965	15.72	224	—	21010	672.6	.010
39	3.531	12.47	248	—	26500	848.1	.008
40	3.145	9.88	282	—	33410	1069	.006

1. American Wire Gauge

pacity (ampacity) of fifteen amperes. The Copper-Wire table lists the carrying capacity of No. 14 gage wire as only 2.7 amperes. The difference in conductor carrying capacity between the two tables is due to the fact that in manufacturing transformers, coils, and other small electrical devices which are enclosed in metal cases, larger conductor to current ratios must be used to reduce heat losses developed in the windings.

The column under "Circular-Mil Area" in the wire table shows the relationship between conductors of different number sizes. If we divide the circular-mil area of one conductor by the area of the next smaller conductor, for example, 10,380 cir-mils (No. 10), by 8234 cir-mils (No. 11) the answer will be 1.26. This ratio holds true throughout the whole scale for any two adjacent wire sizes.

Wire may be obtained either solid or stranded. Solid wire is usually used for wiring homes and in places where the wires do not need to be moved. Stranded wire is made up of several small wires twisted together. By using several small wires together it is possible to have a very flexible wire that can be moved easily. All large cables used for transmission lines are stranded. Cords used on home appliances and extension cords are stranded so that the cords can be moved and coiled readily.

The following table shows several wire sizes and gives some common uses for these sizes.

Size of Wire	Common Use
6 to 10	Service leads for light and power to homes
12 to 14	Interior house wiring
16 to 18	Lighting fixtures
18 to 20	Bell wire, radio circuits
20 to 24	Motors, door chimes
24 to 30	Radio coils, small motors

Purpose of Insulators

Materials which do not permit electrons to flow through them are called *nonconductors* or *insulators*. These insulators are nonmetallic. In electrical circuits insulators are just as important as conductors. Conductors provide a definite path through which electrons will flow; insulators prevent electrons from flowing where they are not wanted.

Insulation is necessary in most electrical wiring to avoid short circuits. Short circuits occur when wires or bare electrical contacts touch each other so that an unwanted path is made through which current can flow. These unwanted paths allow the current to flow through them instead of through the regular circuit. The wires used in electrical circuits in the home are covered with insulation so that they can be placed next to each other without causing a "short circuit." Should the bare copper wires touch each other the electrons would stop flowing through the necessary parts of the circuit. Most wires are covered with enamel, cotton, rubber, or plastic materials. The type of material selected for wire insulation depends upon where the wire is going to be used. Heavy insulation is needed on wires that may contact other objects or where high voltages are used.

Insulation is needed to protect people from coming into contact with electrical circuits. All switches must be insulated so that people may turn them off and on without receiving a shock from the electricity. Wall outlets are insulated so that they will not shock anyone that touches them.

Types of Insulators

There are many types of insulators. See Fig. 13-4. Each is used for a specific

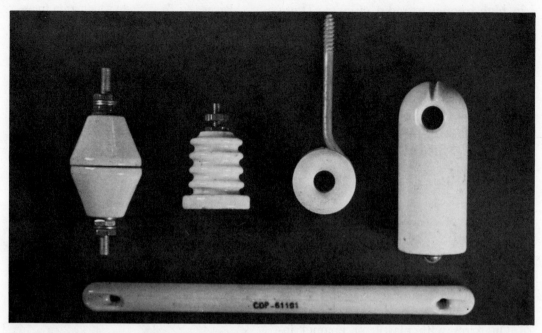

Fig. 13-4. Insulators are designed for special purposes; without them, electricity could not be used.

purpose. Air is a good insulator and is used where space is not a problem and where people cannot touch the circuit. Air is actually the insulation between the wires that are strung on high power transmission lines.

Circuits carrying very high voltages require extremely good insulators. The pressure from high voltages can make the electrons jump from one part of the circuit to another the same as lightning jumps between the clouds and the ground. High-voltage transmission lines use large glass or ceramic insulators on the power poles. These insulators prevent the electricity from flowing through the poles to the ground. Power poles made of wood become very good conductors of electricity when wet.

In circuits where heat is involved asbestos, ceramic, and mica are used for insulation. Wire cords connected to heater elements, such as in flat irons, are

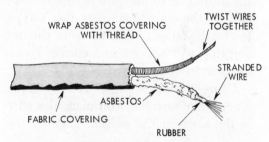

Fig. 13-5. A drawing showing asbestos insulation in a heater cord. Each wire is wrapped in asbestos which will not burn. The drawing illustrates the method used to repair this type of cord.

usually covered with asbestos and cotton. The asbestos will not burn and is a very good insulator for electricity. See Fig. 13-5. Mica and ceramic materials are used as a base to hold the heater elements made of nichrome wire in toasters, flat irons, and all types of electrical heaters. Both materials are good insulators and can withstand tremendous heat without burning or melting.

Special types of insulators are needed

in high-frequency radio circuits. These high-frequency waves have the ability to make electrons flow through some types of insulation. Materials such as steatite and polystyrene are often used in high-frequency circuits since they are good insulators for this purpose.

The following are some common insulators and their uses:

Insulator	Common Use
Air	Between transmission lines
Paper	To separate windings in transformers and motors
Enamel	Covering on magnet wire
Fiber	Motors, solenoids
Mica	Toasters, separation for radio capacitors
Rubber	Wire covering
Bakelite	Electrical outlets and switches
Ceramics	Heater element bases, transmission lines
Plastic	Wire covering
Steatite	Television, radio
Oil	Transformers and capacitors

INTERESTING THINGS TO DO

1. Using a Wire Gage.

Obtain six unknown wires of different sizes. Remove the insulation about one inch from the end of each of the wires. See Fig. 13-6.

On wires with plastic or enamel insulation, be very careful when scraping the insulation so that you do not remove part of the copper wire. If you scrape too hard, you can make the wire thinner and thus will not obtain a correct measurement of the wire.

Using the wire gage, measure each wire. Make sure that you place the wire in the slots on the outside edge of the

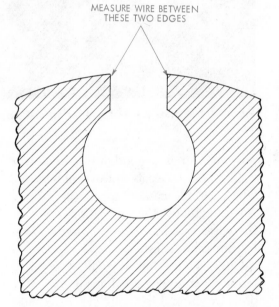

Fig. 13-7. Enlarged drawing of one slot in a wire gage.

gage as shown in Fig. 13-7. The correct wire size can be determined when the wire fits snugly between the slots. Record your results.

2. Making a Western Union Splice.

Remove the insulation from the ends of the wires for a distance of about 3″, A, Fig. 13-8. Cross the two wires, as shown at B. Twist the wires around each other, so as to make two complete turns, C.

Fig. 13-6. When removing insulation with a knife, use a fairly sharp knife and cut the insulation at an angle of about 30 degrees. Do not circle the wire with the blade at right angles to it. Usually, this produces a groove or nick in the wire which will cause it to break easily when bent at this point. Also a nick in the wire may reduce its capacity to carry current. Use a wire stripper to remove insulation whenever possible.

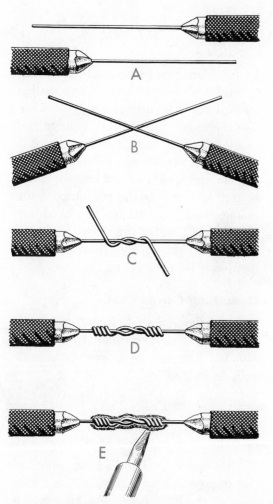

Fig. 13-8. These are steps to follow in making a Western Union splice.

Wrap the projecting ends around the straight sections of the wires so as to make three close turns, *D*. Wind the wire tightly with pliers and cut off the remaining ends. Solder the splice, as shown at *E*. A completed Western Union splice is shown in Fig. 13-9. After the wire has cooled, wipe it with a damp cloth and insulate the splice with Scotch Electrical Tape.

REVIEW QUESTIONS

1. Why is copper used most often as a conductor?

2. Where is aluminum used as a conductor?

3. What metal has the lowest resistance?

4. In wire sizes, which is larger in diameter, a No. 10 wire or a No. 12?

5. Why is it important to use the correct size wire when wiring a home?

6. What is the resistance of 50′ of No. 30 wire?

7. Give the purpose of insulators in a circuit.

8. List several commercial-type insulating materials.

9. What is the difference between conductors and insulators?

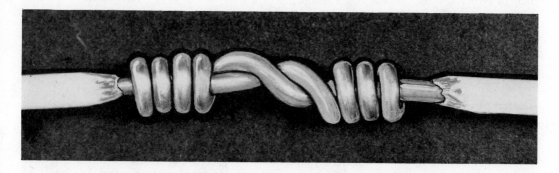

Fig. 13-9. A Western Union splice is used where wire needs to be lengthened.

UNIT 14
SHOWING THE RELATIONSHIP OF VOLTAGE, CURRENT, AND RESISTANCE

Importance of Ohm's Law

In every electrical circuit we have three basic measurements:

1. *Voltage* —The pressure that forces electrons through the circuit.
2. *Current* —The amount of electrons flowing.
3. *Resistance*—The opposition to electron flow.

Before connecting a circuit it is often important to know what each of these measurements will be. By knowing what the current flow is we can select the proper size wire. By knowing what the voltage is we can select the correct size device that will work from the known voltage. It would be very time-consuming if every electrical circuit had to be tried out experimentally before it was possible to determine the amount of voltage, current, or resistance in the circuit. If we are to work efficiently with electricity we must be able to calculate the electrical measurements of the circuit before we hook it up.

There is a definite relationship between the voltage, current, and resistance in every circuit. When the voltage is increased the current will also be increased since more voltage will provide more pressure to push electrons through the circuit. If more resistance is added to a circuit this will reduce the amount of current, as there will be more opposition to electron flow. Whenever any change is made in either the voltage or resistance this changes the current flow.

This relationship that exists between the three electrical measurements can

be calculated mathematically by a law called *Ohm's law*. Ohm's law is a mathematical formula that is used to calculate the current flow if the voltage and resistance of the circuit are known; it is used to determine the voltage if the current and resistance are known; and it is used to calculate the resistance if the voltage and current are known. From this we can see that if any two measurements are known the third measurement can be determined.

Calculating Current Flow

Ohm's law states that the *current is equal to the voltage divided by the resistance*. This can be shown mathematically as follows:

$$\text{Current (in amperes)} = \frac{\text{Voltage (in volts)}}{\text{Resistance (in ohms)}}$$

In the circuit in Fig. 14-1 the voltage of the storage battery is 6 volts. The resistance of the bulb is 3 ohms. How much current will flow in the circuit? Using the formula

$$\text{Current} = \frac{\text{Voltage}}{\text{Resistance}}$$

Voltage is 6 volts
Resistance is 3 ohms

Placing the numbers in the formula:

$$\text{Current} = \frac{6}{3}$$

$$\text{Current} = 2 \text{ amperes}$$

In Ohm's law as in most mathematical formulas symbols are used for each of the measurements.

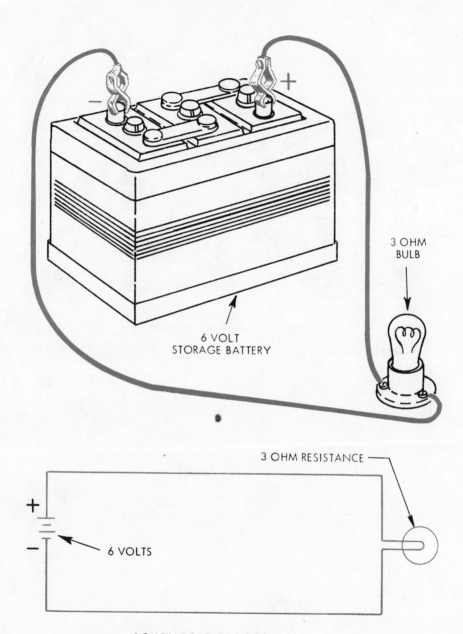

SCHEMATIC DIAGRAM

Fig. 14-1. Six-volt storage battery connected to a light bulb with 3 ohms resistance.

The letter I is used for current in amperes.

The letter E is used for voltage in volts.

The letter R is used for resistance in ohms.

Ohm's law formula:

$$\text{Current} = \frac{\text{Voltage}}{\text{Resistance}}$$

Ohm's law formula with symbols:

$$I = \frac{E}{R}$$

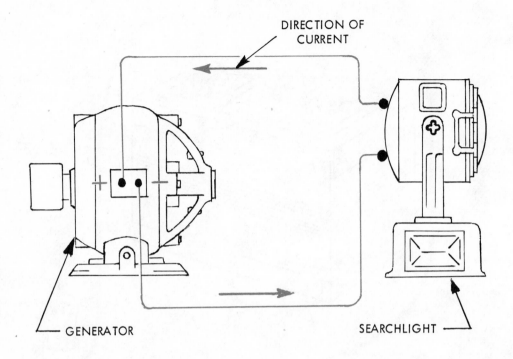

DIRECTION OF
CURRENT

GENERATOR   SEARCHLIGHT

PICTORIAL

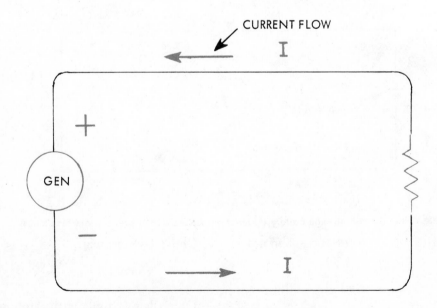

CURRENT FLOW

I

GEN

I

SCHEMATIC

Fig. 14-2. The generator supplies current to the searchlight, which acts as a resistor.

Devices connected to a source of voltage are often shown in a diagram as being a resistor. The pictorial drawing in Fig. 14-2 shows a generator connected to a searchlight. The line drawing using symbols is called a *schematic diagram* and shows the searchlight as a resistor.

If the generator is producing 50 volts and the resistance of the searchlight is 5 ohms how much current would be flowing in the circuit?

Ohm's law formula $I = \dfrac{E}{R}$

Placing numbers
in the formula

$$I = \frac{50}{5}$$

$$I = 10 \text{ amperes}$$

The current flowing in the circuit would be 10 amperes.

Calculating Voltage

Ohm's law can be used to determine the voltage being applied to a circuit provided the current and resistance are known. The formula for determining the voltage is:

Voltage = Current × Resistance
Using symbols $E = I \times R$

In the circuit in Fig. 14-3 the current is 5 amperes. The resistance is 6 ohms. What is the voltage of the generator?

$$E = I \times R$$
$$E = 5 \times 6$$
$$E = 30 \text{ volts}$$

The voltage of the generator is 30 volts.

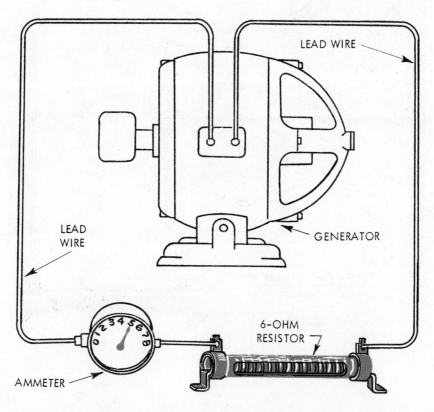

LEAD WIRE

LEAD WIRE

GENERATOR

6-OHM RESISTOR

AMMETER

Fig. 14-3. A current of 5 amperes is flowing through a resistance of 6 ohms.

Calculating Resistance

Ohm's law can be used to calculate the resistance in a circuit if the voltage and the current are known. The formula for calculating resistance is:

Resistance is equal to voltage divided by the current.

$$\text{Resistance (ohms)} = \frac{\text{Voltage (volts)}}{\text{Current (amperes)}}$$

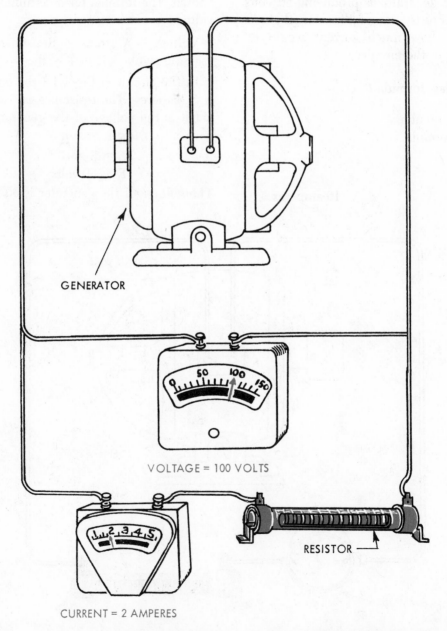

GENERATOR

VOLTAGE = 100 VOLTS

RESISTOR

CURRENT = 2 AMPERES

Fig. 14-4. The generator is producing 100 volts and 2 amperes of current is flowing through the resistor.

Using symbols $R = \dfrac{E}{I}$

In the circuit in Fig. 14-4 the voltage is 100 volts. The current is 2 amperes. What is the resistance of the circuit?

$$R = \dfrac{E}{I}$$

$$R = \dfrac{100}{2}$$

$$R = 50 \text{ ohms}$$

The resistance of the circuit is 50 ohms.

The Three Forms of Ohm's Law

Ohm's law can be used for three different purposes:

To find the current $I = \dfrac{E}{R}$

To find the voltage $E = I \times R$

To find the resistance $R = \dfrac{E}{I}$

If any two of the electrical measurements are known the third measurement can be determined.

Measuring Electrical Power

The amount of electrical energy required to produce heat, light, or motion is often stated in watts.

The *watt* is the electrical unit of power. Power means the ability to do work. We are all familiar with the unit of work called *horsepower* used with automobiles. In automobiles it is customary to state the amount of horsepower that the engine will produce. A 175-horsepower engine is more powerful and will do more work than a 100-horsepower engine. In electricity the wattage indicates the power being used by the electrical device.

Electric light bulbs are marked ac-

cording to the number of watts of electricity they use. The greater the wattage of the bulb the greater the amount of light produced. A 25-watt electric light bulb will not burn as brightly nor will it use as much electricity as a 100-watt bulb. A 75-watt electric soldering iron will not get as hot as a 100-watt soldering iron. A 600-watt electric wall heater will not heat a room as fast as a 1,000-watt heater. In each of these items the lower wattage produces less power in the form of heat or light, and uses less electricity. From this we can see that it is important to look at the wattage rating on all electrical equipment that we plan to buy or use.

Calculating Wattage

The power or wattage used by electrical circuits can be calculated mathematically. The basic formula for determining wattage states that *the number of watts used equals the voltage across the circuit multiplied by the current flowing in the circuit.*

Basic watt formula
  Watts = Voltage × Current

Using symbols
  $W = E \times I$

In the circuit in Fig. 14-5 the toaster has 9 amperes of current flowing through

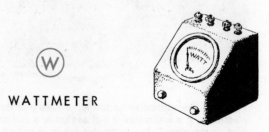

WATTMETER

This symbol indicates an instrument for measuring power.

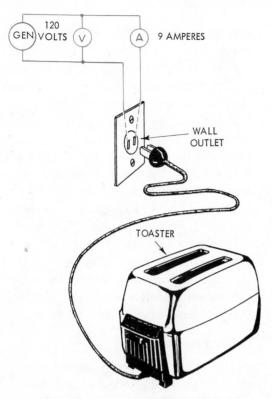

Fig. 14-5. The amount of electricity is measured in watts.

it and the voltage at the electrical outlet is 120 volts. What is the wattage of the toaster?

Basic formula

Watts = Voltage × Current

$$W = E \times I$$

(Placing numbers in the formula)

Volts = 120

Amperes = 9

$$W = 120 \times 9$$

$$W = 1080 \text{ Watts}$$

The toaster is using 1,080 watts of electricity.

The instruments used to calculate the wattage are a voltmeter and an ammeter. A single meter called a wattmeter which is a combination voltmeter and ammeter can be used to measure the wattage of a circuit. With this meter it

Fig. 14-6. The wattmeter on the left shows that the heater element is using a little more than 600 watts of electricity. If a wattmeter is not available a voltmeter and an ammeter may be used to determine the wattage of the circuit. The voltmeter reads about 120 volts. The ammeter reads about 5 amperes. Using the watt formula the power can be calculated by multiplying the voltage times the current. Thus, 120 volts times 5 amperes equals 600 watts.

is not necessary to use the watt formula. When connected in the circuit a watt-meter scale reading shows the amount of wattage being used by the circuit. See Fig. 14-6.

Meaning of Kilowatt

The term *kilowatt* is sometimes used to express power used by electrical equipment. *Kilo* means 1,000. One kilowatt equals 1,000 watts. Ten kilowatts equals 10,000 watts. If an electrical heater has a name plate that states that the heater uses 3 kilowatts of electricity this means that it uses 3,000 watts of electricity.

Using Watt-Hour Meters

The power company that delivers electricity to homes and businesses throughout a community uses a meter called a *kilowatt-hour* meter at each location. See Figs. 14-7 and 14-8. The meter is con-

nected so that all the electricity goes through it before going into the building. Each meter is so constructed that it measures the wattage and also operates

Fig. 14-8. This watt-hour meter will record the amount of electricity used.

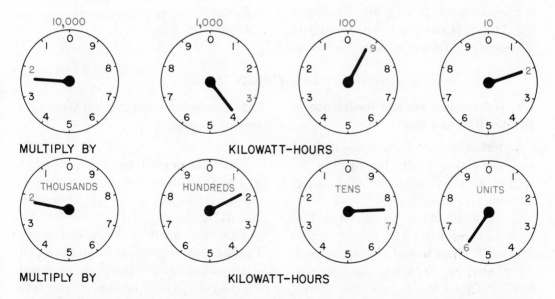

Fig. 14-7. This is how to read a watt-hour meter. Record the figure which the pointer on the right hand dial has last passed and proceed to the left, recording in like manner the respective figure indicated on each successive dial. Thus, the top meter would read, 23,920 (setting numbers down right to left — 20, — 920, — 3,920, — 23,920) and the bottom one 2,176.

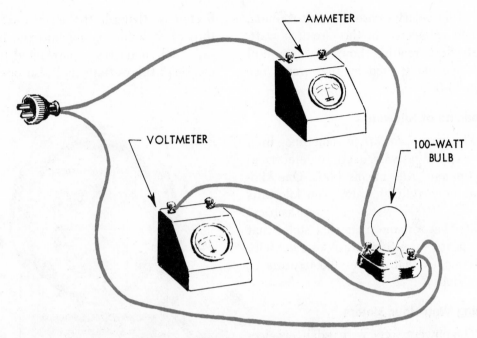

Fig. 14-9. Hot resistance of light bulb.

like a stop watch that runs only when the current is being used. Thus the meter is keeping a record of the amount of time that it is being used. The dials on the face of the meter record the number of kilowatt-hours flowing into the building. The exact number of kilowatt-hours of electricity consumed can be determined at any time by reading the meter. Power companies have a rate that they charge for each kilowatt-hour of electricity. Electric bills are figured by determining the number of kilowatt-hours consumed and multiplying this by the rate charged.

INTERESTING THINGS TO DO

1. Determining the Hot Resistance of an Electric Light Bulb.

Materials needed are a 100-watt light bulb, lamp socket, attachment plug, insulated wire, AC voltmeter and an AC ammeter.

Connect the circuit as shown in Fig. 14-9. The voltmeter and ammeter constructed in Units 10 and 11 may be used. After measuring the voltage and the current use Ohm's law to calculate the resistance of the light bulb. How will this resistance differ from the cold resistance of the light bulb?

2. Determining the Current Used by a Heater Element.

Materials needed are a lamp socket, a screw-base type 600-watt heater element, attachment plug, AC voltmeter, and AC ammeter.

Wire the circuit as shown in Fig. 14-10. The resistance of the heater element is approximately 20 ohms. After measuring the voltage calculate the current flow using Ohm's law. Prove your answer by using an AC ammeter to measure the current.

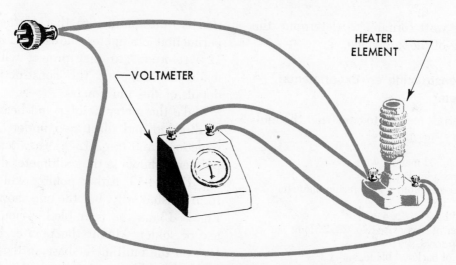

Fig. 14-10. Current used by heater element.

3. Determining the Wattage of a Household Appliance.

Materials needed are an AC voltmeter, AC ammeter, attachment plug, insulated wire, outlet box, and some type of household appliance such as waffle iron, toaster, heater, radio, or flat iron.

Wire a circuit as shown in Fig. 14-11. Plug the household appliance attachment plug into the outlet box. After measuring the voltage and the current

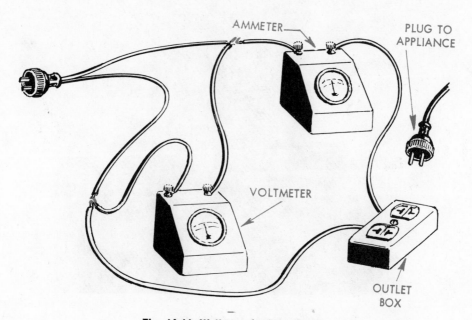

Fig. 14-11. Wattage of an appliance.

use the watt formula to determine the wattage of the appliance.

4. Constructing an Experimental Multimeter.

Materials needed to construct the multimeter (Fig. 14-12):

175′ No. 32 magnet wire
10′ Radio hookup wire
Cardboard tubing, 1½″ inside diameter
   x 2″ long
Wood base, ½″ x 4½″ x 6″
Pointer of brass wire, No. 22, 3″ long
   (optional, see text)
Piece of hacksaw blade, ³⁄₁₆″ x 1⅜″
Sheet brass, ⅝″ x 1¼″ (2 required)
4 Terminal screws
Piece of white cardboard for meter scale

This multimeter will measure resistances from 100 to 4,000 ohms, direct current voltages up to 12 volts, and current up to five amperes. Since its construc-

tion is quite similar to that of the experimental ohmmeter shown in Figure 12-9 reference to that project will be made for some of the constructional details of this multimeter.

Make the meter pointer and bearings as directed and illustrated under "construction" and Fig. 12-9. An alternate pointer is shown in the multimeter drawing, Fig. 14-13. Either pointer will perform satisfactorily, but the one shown in Fig. 14-13 may be assembled without the use of solder. Mount the pointer bearings on the multimeter base so that the pointer will be centered on the base. After the pointer has been balanced, remove it from its bearings. Wind No. 32 and No. 22 wires on the cardboard form as shown in 14-13. Both coils should be wound in the same direction. Pass the ends of the coils through the wood base

Fig. 14-12. Multimeter.

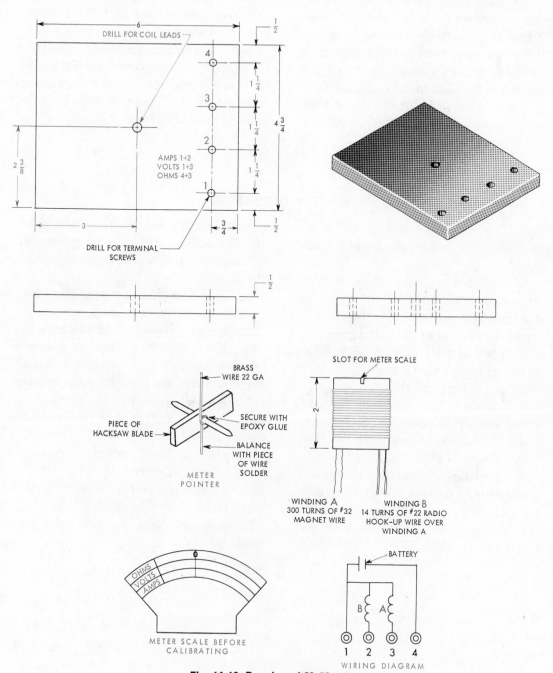

Fig. 14-13. Drawing of Multimeter.

and glue the coil form to the base. Place terminal screws in the wood base, number the terminals as shown, and connect them as indicated in the wiring diagram. Extend the battery leads through a hole in the base back of the coil. Replace the meter pointer. Make a chart showing the connections for the different meter measurements and attach it to the base near the terminals. Make a cardboard scale for the meter as shown in Fig. 14-13, and insert it in the slots in the coil form. Connect 3 to 9 volts (flashlight cells or transistor battery) to the battery leads and calibrate the meter scale by checking the pointer movement against other meters, or by measuring known values such as resistors and voltage sources. The meter pointer will indicate from each side of its center position. If more chart space is required O, V, and A may be substituted for ohms, volts, and amps.

REVIEW QUESTIONS

1. How can a knowledge of Ohm's law help us in making electrical calculations?

2. Explain what is meant by "hot" resistance in an electrical circuit.

3. How can we overcome the effect of high resistance in an electrical circuit?

4. If we increase the voltage in an electrical circuit containing a light bulb what might happen? Why?

5. Explain with a diagram how you would connect a voltmeter and an ammeter in a circuit to determine the "hot" resistance of a light bulb.

6. In what ways could you increase the amount of current flowing in an electrical circuit?

7. What are the three basic measurements usually made in an electrical circuit?

8. An electrical circuit has a voltage of 10 volts and the current flowing through it is 2 amperes. What is the resistance of the circuit?

9. Calculate the current flowing through a circuit that has a voltage of 50 volts and a resistance of 10 ohms.

10. If an electrical circuit has a resistance of 50 ohms and current of 3 amperes flowing through it, what is the voltage being applied to the circuit?

11. Name the unit used to express electrical power.

12. State the basic formula for calculating electrical power.

13. What is the unit for measuring the amount of electricity used?

14. How are home electric bills figured?

UNIT 15
CONNECTING ELECTRICAL CIRCUITS

Series Battery Connections

We know that a single dry cell will deliver 1½ volts and that one cell of a storage battery delivers about 2 volts. We also know that batteries, which are made up of more than one cell, deliver more voltage than a single cell. These batteries have the cells connected so that the voltage of all of the cells can be added together to make the total voltage of the battery.

When cells are connected so that the voltage or pressure is increased the cells are said to be connected in *series*. In a series connection of cells the positive terminal of one cell is connected to the negative terminal of the next cell. In this way each cell adds its voltage to that of the other cells. The total voltage produced by all cells connected in series is equal to the sum of the voltages of all the cells. See Fig. 15-1.

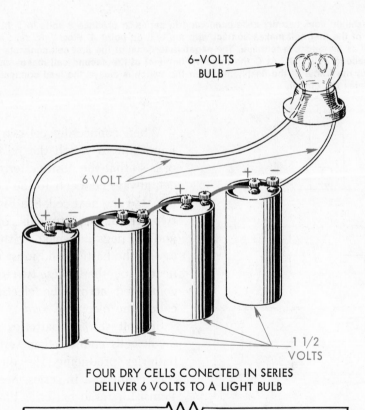

6-VOLTS BULB

6 VOLT

1 1/2 VOLTS

FOUR DRY CELLS CONECTED IN SERIES
DELIVER 6 VOLTS TO A LIGHT BULB

6 VOLT

Fig. 15-1. The voltage of cells connected in series is found by adding the voltages of the individual cells.

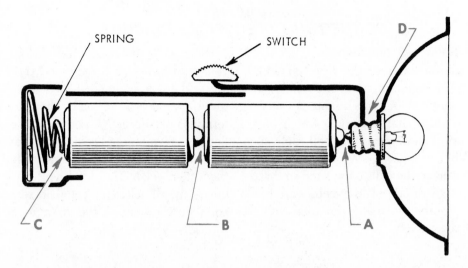

Fig. 15-2. This flashlight uses two dry cells connected in series to produce 3 volts to light the bulb. The positive terminal of the first cell makes contact with the bulb at point *A*. Flashlight cells always use the bottom of the cell as the negative terminal. The negative terminal of the first cell connects to the positive terminal of the second cell at *B*. At *C* the negative terminal of the second cell makes contact with the spring attached to the frame of the flashlight. When the switch is closed the lead connected to the bulb at point *D* completes the circuit.

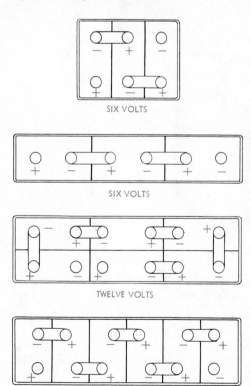

Fig. 15-3. These are typical cell arrangements for automobile storage batteries.

When connecting cells in series it is important to watch the polarity of the cells so that the positive terminal of one cell always connects to the negative terminal of the next cell. See Fig. 15-2. The two remaining terminals, one positive and one negative, make up the total voltage of the battery and must not be connected together. These two terminals are connected across the electrical device called the electrical *load*.

Six-volt storage batteries have three 2-volt cells connected in series. Storage batteries producing 12 volts have six cells connected in series. See Fig. 15-3. Transistor radio batteries that deliver 9 volts have six cells connected in series, and each cell delivers 1½ volts.

Parallel Battery Connections

Dry cells which are very small will not last as long as dry cells which are larger. Even though the voltage of the two cells

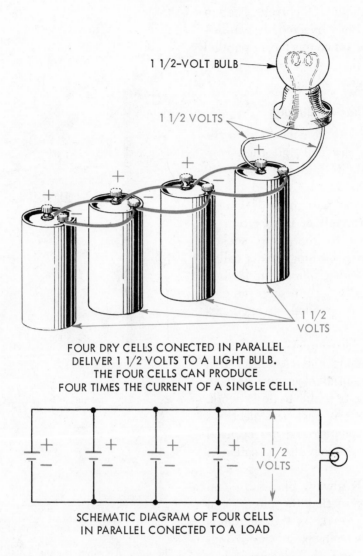

1 1/2-VOLT BULB

1 1/2 VOLTS

1 1/2 VOLTS

FOUR DRY CELLS CONECTED IN PARALLEL
DELIVER 1 1/2 VOLTS TO A LIGHT BULB.
THE FOUR CELLS CAN PRODUCE
FOUR TIMES THE CURRENT OF A SINGLE CELL.

1 1/2
VOLTS

SCHEMATIC DIAGRAM OF FOUR CELLS
IN PARALLEL CONECTED TO A LOAD

Fig. 15-4. Current capacity is increased when cells are connected in parallel.

is the same the large cell will be able to deliver more current.

Sometimes the cells or batteries that are available are not large enough to supply the amount of current needed in a circuit. When this happens the cells or batteries can be connected together so that they each help provide current for the circuit.

Cells are said to be connected in *par-*

allel (Fig. 15-4) when they help each other by providing an increase in the amount of current available. When connecting cells in parallel the negative terminals of all the cells are connected together and all the positive terminals are connected together. Each cell delivers current to the circuit without an increase in the voltage.

If batteries are not large enough to

provide the amount of current needed they too may be connected in parallel. When batteries are connected in parallel it is necessary that each of them deliver the same voltage.

Opening and Closing Circuits

When two wires are connected to the terminals of a dry cell and then connected to a light bulb the light will burn. The light can be turned off by disconnecting one wire from either of the battery terminals or from either of the connections to the lamp socket. When the light is burning this is called a complete or *closed circuit* and when one of the wires is disconnected the current stops and it is called an *open circuit*.

Practically every circuit needs some method of opening and closing. When the circuit is closed electrons start to flow and electricity is able to do its work. When the circuit is open the electrons are no longer flowing. The device used to open and close circuits is called a *switch*.

The switch is always placed in one side of the line so that the circuit can be opened or closed. As the switch is closed the two contacts in the switch come together and the electrons flow through the switch to the rest of the circuit. Opening the switch breaks the contact points on the switch and the electrons are stopped from flowing.

Types of Switches

There are many different types of switches that are used to open and close circuits. One of the most familiar switches is the wall type tumbler switch used in the home to turn lights off and on. When a single circuit is opened and

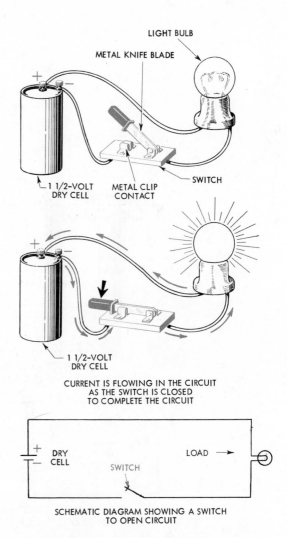

CURRENT IS FLOWING IN THE CIRCUIT
AS THE SWITCH IS CLOSED
TO COMPLETE THE CIRCUIT

SCHEMATIC DIAGRAM SHOWING A SWITCH
TO OPEN CIRCUIT

Fig. 15-5. A switch enables us to start and stop the flow of current.

closed as in Fig. 15-5 the switch is known as a *single pole-single throw* switch. The single pole means that it has one lever and single throw means that it will operate in only one direction. This type switch is often abbreviated as SPST.

Circuits have different requirements for controlling the electron flow and thus a variety of switches is manufactured.

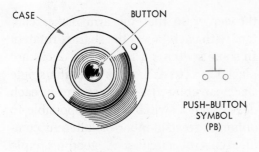

PUSH-BUTTON
SYMBOL
(PB)

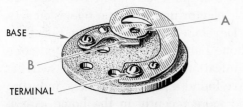

Fig. 15-6. A push button is used as a switch when the circuit needs to be closed for very short intervals. When the button is pushed, contact *A* touches contact *B*, making a complete circuit.

See Figs. 15-6 and 15-7. Symbols of some common switches are illustrated in Fig. 15-8. A double pole, single throw (DPST) switch makes or breaks two circuits simultaneously. The double pole, double throw (DPDT) switch is used where two contacts are simultaneously connected first to one set of circuits and then to another.

The two types of switches most often used in electronic circuits are the toggle and the rotary. The toggle switch is operated by a lever or toggle with an up and down motion, and the rotary switch, operated by a rotating knob or dial, Fig. 15-9. Toggle switches are rated by their current carrying ability and the voltage with which they may safely be used.

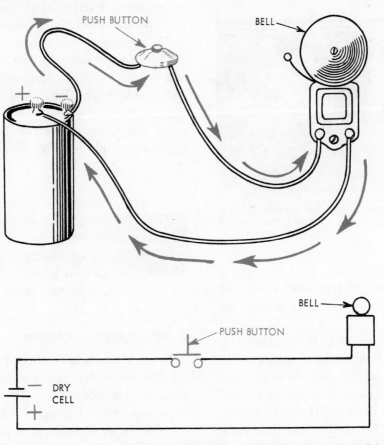

Fig. 15-7. The push button closes the circuit, allowing current to flow from the cell to the bell.

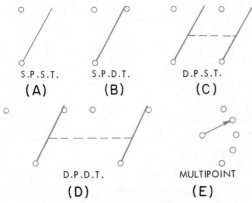

S.P.S.T. (A) S.P.D.T. (B) D.P.S.T. (C)

D.P.D.T. (D) MULTIPOINT (E)

Fig. 15-8. Schematic symbols of several switches.
A — Single Pole Single Throw Switch
B — Single Pole Double Throw Switch
C — Double Pole Single Throw Switch
D — Double Pole Double Throw Switch
E — Multipoint switch. A variety of contacts can be obtained through the use of rotary switches.

Fig. 15-9. Two types of switches used in electronics work. A toggle on the left and a rotary switch on the right.

Radio receivers and television sets use switches with about 3 ampere and 125 volt ratings.

In the rotary switch, the moving arm rotates in a circle, making contact with taps located on the outside edge. The contacts are usually arranged in a circle on a wafer, or deck of bakelite or ceramic material. The moving arm is rotated by means of a shaft running through

the center so that the arm makes contact with each tap as the shaft is rotated. In some switches a number of decks are placed next to each other so that a single shaft can rotate the contact arm in each deck. Such a switch makes it possible to obtain a great number of different combinations of circuits. A good example of a multiple rotary switch is the channel selector used in some television sets.

Developed originally by the Bell Telephone Laboratories for use in their communications equipment, *reed* switches have found a place in business, industry, and more recently in the home experimenter's laboratory. A *reed* switch consists of two overlapping metal strips, sealed in a glass tube filled with inert gas to prevent arcing at its contacts. The ends of the overlapping strips are normally separated, but when a magnetic field is brought near the switch, the ends are drawn together. The action of the switch is so rapid, that in a suitable varying magnetic field, its on-and-off movement can occur as frequently as 1,000 times a second. See Fig. 15-10.

Fig. 15-10. Reed switch.

Parallel Electrical Circuits

If we wish to have three bulbs burn off the same dry cell they should be connected directly across the two terminals as shown in Fig. 15-11. These bulbs are said to be connected in parallel because each bulb provides a separate

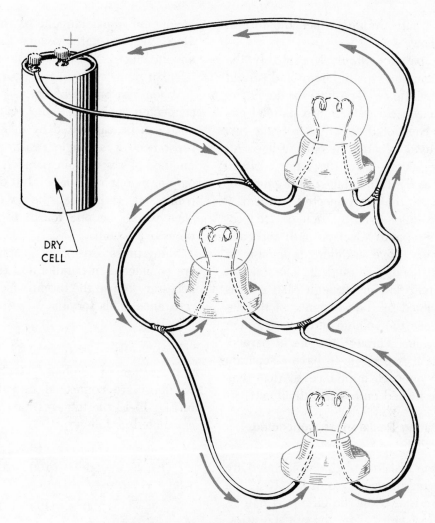

DRY
CELL

THREE BULBS CONNECTED IN PARALLEL.
ARROWS SHOW THREE SEPARATE PATHS
FOR CURRENT FLOW.

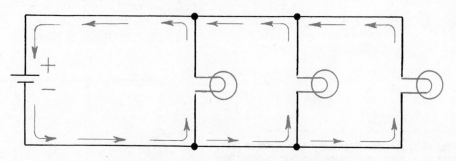

SCHEMATIC DIAGRAM OF THREE BULBS IN PARALLEL

Fig. 15-11. The voltage across each bulb connected in parallel is the same as that of the source of electricity.

parallel path through which the current must flow.

The parallel circuit is probably the most common type of circuit and is used in the wiring of all circuits for the home. Each electrical device in a parallel circuit is connected directly across the two wires used to carry the current flow. All devices must have the same voltage rating as the full voltage of the source of electricity that is connected to them.

In parallel circuits, each device provides a separate electron path and each path may have a different amount of current flowing through it. The amount of current flowing through each path is determined by the resistance of the device since the voltage across every item is the same. Through the use of parallel circuits it is possible to have a separate switch on each appliance so that they can be turned on or off individually.

Calculating Resistances Connected In Parallel

If two resistors of the same value are connected in parallel as in Fig. 15-12 the total resistance in the circuit is half as much resistance as for the single resistor. In such a circuit the current has two paths to flow through with both paths

having an equal amount of resistance. Since the two paths reduce the resistance to electron flow the total resistance is cut in half.

When resistances of equal value are connected in parallel, the total resistance can be calculated by dividing the resistance of a single resistor by the number of resistors in parallel. For example, if four resistors of 100 ohms are connected in parallel the total resistance would be one fourth of the 100 ohms or 25 ohms.

Many times resistors of unequal value are connected in parallel and then it is necessary to use the formula for parallel resistance. This formula is written:

$$\frac{1}{R_{Total}} = \frac{1}{R_1} + \frac{1}{R_2} + \frac{1}{R_3} + \ldots$$

If resistors of 50 ohms, 100 ohms, and 50 ohms are connected in parallel as in Fig. 15-13 the total resistance can be calculated as follows:

$$\frac{1}{R_{Total}} = \frac{1}{50} + \frac{1}{100} + \frac{1}{50}$$

$$\frac{1}{R_T} = \frac{2}{100} + \frac{1}{100} + \frac{2}{100}$$

$$\frac{1}{R_T} = \frac{5}{100}$$

$$5R_T = 100 \quad R_{Total} = \frac{100}{5}$$

$$R_{Total} = 20 \text{ ohms}$$

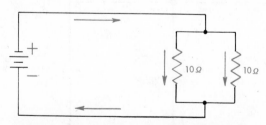

Fig. 15-12. In this circuit the two parallel resistors have equal resistance and the current flow through each resistor will be the same. Since parallel resistance reduces the opposition to electron flow the total resistance in the circuit will be 5 ohms.

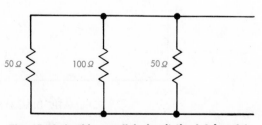

Fig. 15-13. In this parallel circuit the total resistance is 20 ohms.

In the above problem it should be noted that the total resistance of 20 ohms is less than the resistance of any of the resistors connected in the circuit. One important factor to remember about parallel resistance is that the total resistance will always be less than the smallest resistor in the circuit.

Current Flow In Parallel Circuits

In a parallel circuit each resistor may be of different value and thus the current flow in each resistor will be different. The total current flowing in the entire circuit will be equal to the sum of the current flowing through each resistor.

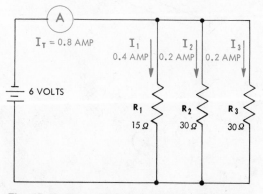

Fig. 15-14. In a parallel circuit the total current flow (I$_T$) is equal to the sum of the current flow through each of the resistors. The total resistance in the circuit is 7.5 ohms.

Three resistors of 15 ohms, 30 ohms, and 30 ohms in Fig. 15-14 are in parallel and connected to a 6 volt battery. By using Ohm's law we can calculate the current flow through each resistor:

$$I = \frac{E}{R}$$

$$I_1 = \frac{6}{15} = 0.4 \text{ ampere}$$

$$I_2 = \frac{6}{30} = 0.2 \text{ ampere}$$

$$I_3 = \frac{6}{30} = 0.2 \text{ ampere}$$

The total current flow in the entire circuit is equal to the sum of the current flowing through each of the resistors.

$$I_{Total} = I_1 + I_2 + I_3$$
$$I_{Total} = 0.4 + 0.2 + 0.2$$
$$I_{Total} = 0.8 \text{ ampere}$$

Another method can be used to find the total current flow in the circuit if the total resistance of the circuit is determined. By using the parallel resistance formula the total resistance is calculated as follows:

$$\frac{1}{R_T} = \frac{1}{R_1} + \frac{1}{R_2} + \frac{1}{R_3}$$

$$\frac{1}{R_T} = \frac{1}{15} + \frac{1}{30} + \frac{1}{30}$$

$$\frac{1}{R_T} = \frac{2}{30} + \frac{1}{30} + \frac{1}{30}$$

$$\frac{1}{R_T} = \frac{4}{30} \qquad R_T = \frac{30}{4}$$

$$R_T = 7.5 \text{ ohms}$$

The total resistance of the circuit is 7.5 ohms. Now the total current can be calculated.

$$I_{Total} = \frac{E}{R_{Total}}$$

$$I_T = \frac{6 \text{ volts}}{7.5 \text{ ohms}}$$

$$I_{Total} = 0.8 \text{ ampere}$$

It should be noted that the current flow of 0.8 ampere calculated by determining the total resistance is the same as when the total current flow was calcu-

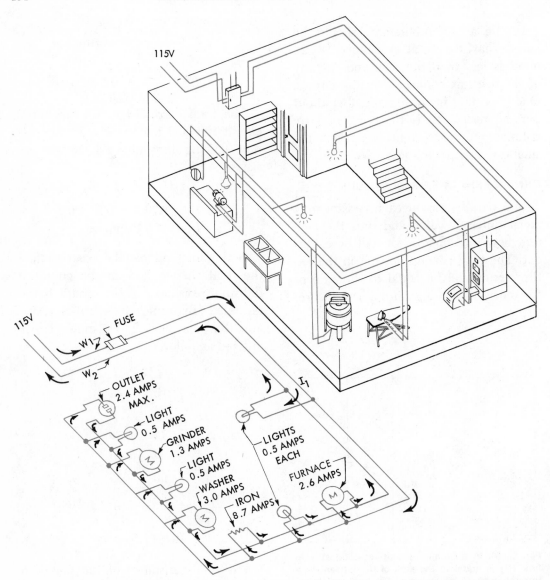

Fig. 15-15. The wiring installed in the basement of this home is a practical example of parallel circuits.

lated by finding the current flow through each resistor. See Fig. 15-15.

Series Electrical Circuits

In a series circuit the electrons must flow through each device before the circuit is completed. If a number of devices are connected in series the voltage is divided among them. See Fig. 15-16.

Should any device be disconnected from a series circuit, the entire electron flow is stopped.

Some small radio receivers often called AC-DC receivers also have the radio tube filaments connected in series. When one of the tubes burns out it is necessary to test all of the tubes to determine which one must be replaced to get the set back into operation.

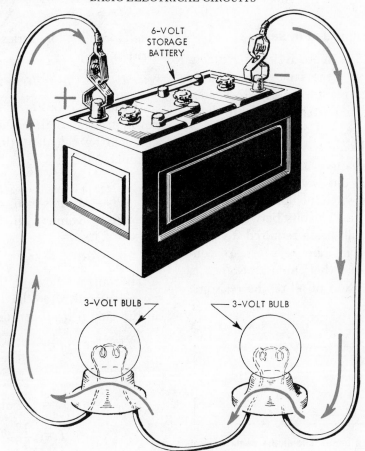

6-VOLT
STORAGE
BATTERY

3-VOLT BULB   3-VOLT BULB

ELECTRONS FLOW FROM THE NEGATIVE POLE
OF THE BATTERY THROUGH ONE BULB
AND THEN THROUGH THE SECOND BULB

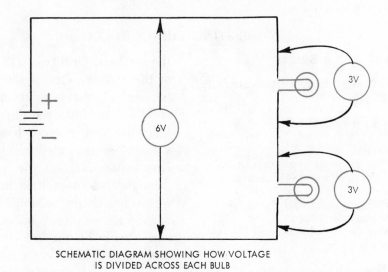

SCHEMATIC DIAGRAM SHOWING HOW VOLTAGE
IS DIVIDED ACROSS EACH BULB

Fig. 15-16. When bulbs are connected in series, the voltage is divided between them.

Resistors Connected in Series

When two or more resistors are connected in series the same current flows through each resistor. In Fig. 15-17 four light bulbs, requiring 3 volts to light them properly, are connected in series and the bulbs are connected to a twelve volt storage battery. If a single bulb was connected to the twelve volts it would burn out, but since the bulbs are in series they divide the 12 volts between them. Thus each bulb has a required 3 volts.

When two or more resistors are connected in series their total resistance is equal to the sum of all of the resistors.

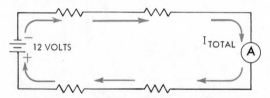

Fig. 15-17. In a series circuit the same current flows through each resistor. The total resistance of this circuit is 12 ohms.

The formula for series resistance is written as:

$$R_{Total} = R_1 + R_2 + R_3 + \ldots .$$

If each bulb in Fig. 15-17 has 3 ohms resistance the total resistance in the circuit can be calculated using the series formula:

$$R_{Total} + R_1 + R_2 + R_3 + R_4$$
$$R_1 = 3 \text{ ohms} \qquad R_3 = 3 \text{ ohms}$$
$$R_2 = 3 \text{ ohms} \qquad R_4 = 3 \text{ ohms}$$
$$R_{Total} = 3 + 3 + 3 + 3$$
$$R_{Total} = 12 \text{ ohms}$$

The current flow in this circuit can be calculated after the total resistance in the circuit has been determined.

$$I = \frac{E}{R}$$
$$E = 12 \text{ volts}$$
$$R_{Total} = 12 \text{ ohms}$$
$$I = \frac{12}{12}$$
$$I = 1 \text{ ampere}$$

INTERESTING THINGS TO DO

1. Constructing a Buzzer.

Material needed to construct the buzzer (Fig. 15-18):

1 Wood base, ½" x 2½" x 2½"
1 Piece of soft steel, round, ¼" x 1¹⁄₁₆"
2 Fiber washers, ⅛" x ¾"
1 Piece of spring brass, 26 gage, ⅞" x 1¼"
1 Piece of soft steel, round, ¼" diameter, ⅛" thick
1 Piece of 20 gage sheet steel, ⅞" x ⅞"
20' of No. 22 magnet wire
1 Piece of tin ¾" wide by 2" long
2 Terminal screws

Bevel edges of block as shown in Fig. 15-19. Drill ¼" holes in the center of the washers. Drill two ¹⁄₁₆" holes in one of the washers. One of the holes should be near the inside edge of the washer and the other hole near the outside edge. Place the washers on each end of the ¼" steel rod so that they will be ¾" apart. Insert one end of the magnet wire through the inside hole in one of the washers allowing about 3" to extend beyond the washer. Wind eight layers of wire evenly on the steel core. The remaining end of the wier should then be pulled through the outside hole in the washer.

Fig. 15-18. Buzzer.

Cut the piece of spring brass to the shape shown in the drawing. This spring is the vibrator of the buzzer. Drill and bend the spring brass as shown in the drawing. Solder the small piece of $\frac{1}{4}''$ round steel to the vibrator.

Cut the piece of sheet steel to shape as illustrated in the drawing. Bend and drill this contact screw support. Solder a 6-32 brass nut to this support. File a blunt point on the end of a roundhead brass 6-32 machine screw. This will serve as the adjusting screw in the contact screw support.

Drill two holes at each end of the

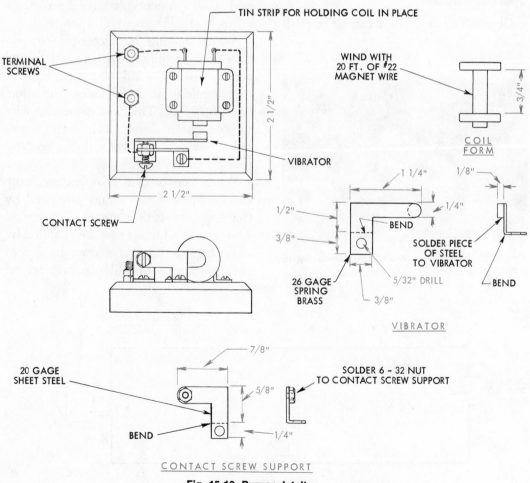

TIN STRIP FOR HOLDING COIL IN PLACE

TERMINAL SCREWS

CONTACT SCREW

2 1/2"

2 1/2"

VIBRATOR

WIND WITH 20 FT. OF #22 MAGNET WIRE

3/4"

COIL FORM

1 1/4"   1/8"

1/2"   1/4"

BEND

3/8"

SOLDER PIECE OF STEEL TO VIBRATOR

BEND

26 GAGE SPRING BRASS

5/32" DRILL

3/8"

VIBRATOR

7/8"

20 GAGE SHEET STEEL

5/8"

SOLDER 6 - 32 NUT TO CONTACT SCREW SUPPORT

BEND

1/4"

CONTACT SCREW SUPPORT

Fig. 15-19. Buzzer details.

tin strap. Shape this strap so that it will hold the coil in place.

Mount all of the parts on the wood base as shown in the drawing. Make connections on the bottom of the wood block as indicated by dotted lines on the drawing. Place a 6-32 brass nut on the adjusting screw and insert the screw into the nut soldered on the contact screw support. The buzzer is now ready to test.

Connect the two terminal screws to 3 to 6 volts either AC or DC. Adjust the contact screw to the desired tone.

2. Connecting Dry Cells in Series to Operate a Buzzer.

Obtain four dry cells, a buzzer, a push

Fig. 15-20. Push button and buzzer connected to a dry cell.

button, and some wire for connections. Connect the dry cells in series as described in the text so that the center or positive terminal of one cell is connected to the outside or negative terminal of the next cell. See Figs. 15-20 and 15-21. When all of the cells have been connected together, a positive terminal of one cell and a negative terminal of another cell will be unconnected. Run a wire from one of those terminals to a terminal on the push button. Connect the other push button terminal to one of the buzzer terminals and connect the other buzzer terminal to the remaining dry cell terminal. Press the push button and if all connections have been made correctly the buzzer will operate.

When making an electrical connection by attaching a wire to a terminal screw, always wind the wire around the terminal in a clockwise direction. See Fig. 15-22. This will cause the wire to wrap more closely around the terminal screw and prevent a loose connection.

When the buzzer is operating, note the loudness of the sound produced by the four dry cells connected in series. The tone of a buzzer may be changed by adjusting the contact screw. If it does not have an adjustable contact screw,

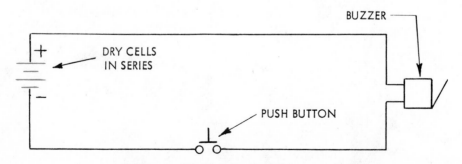

Fig. 15-21. Connecting dry cells in series to operate a buzzer.

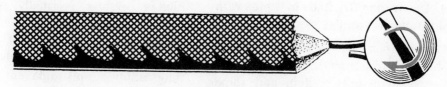

Fig. 15-22. Wind wire clockwise around a terminal.

the fixed contact arm may be bent backward or forward to produce the same result.

3. Connecting Dry Cells in Parallel to Operate a Buzzer.

Connect the four negative terminals of the dry cells together. Connect the four positive terminals of the dry cells together as shown in Fig. 15-23. Connect a wire from the negative terminal of one of the end cells to a push button terminal. Connect a wire from the other push button terminal to one of the buzzer terminals. Connect a wire from the other buzzer terminal to the positive terminal of the end cell. Press the push button and if all connections have been made correctly the buzzer will operate. Is the sound of the buzzer louder or softer than with the series connection? Why?

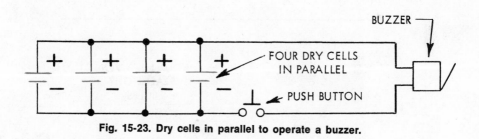

Fig. 15-23. Dry cells in parallel to operate a buzzer.

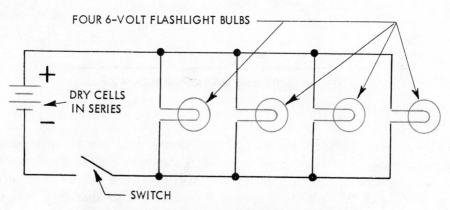

Fig. 15-24. Dry cells in series with light bulbs in parallel.

4. Connecting Dry Cells in Series with Light Bulbs in Parallel.

Obtain four dry cells, four 6-volt flashlight bulbs, four miniature receptacles, a single-pole switch, and some wire for connections. Connect the four dry cells in series. Connect the receptacles together by placing them in line and running a wire to each terminal on the same side as shown in Fig. 15-24. Connect the opposite sides of the receptacles in the same manner. Connect a wire from the unconnected positive terminal of the dry cells to one of the receptacles. Connect the other terminal of the same receptacle to one of the switch terminals. Connect the other switch terminal to the negative termi-

mer or brighter. Normally, when good dry cells are being used there will be no change in the brightness of the bulbs. When the dry cells are nearly worn out they cannot supply sufficient voltage to force the correct amount of current through the light bulbs. When one of the bulbs is removed from the parallel circuit the remaining bulbs are apt to burn brighter, because they will require less current from the dry cells.

5. Connecting Dry Cells and Flashlight Bulbs in Series.

Obtain four dry cells, four 1.5-volt flashlight bulbs, four miniature receptacles, a single-pole switch, and connecting wire. Connect four dry cells in series.

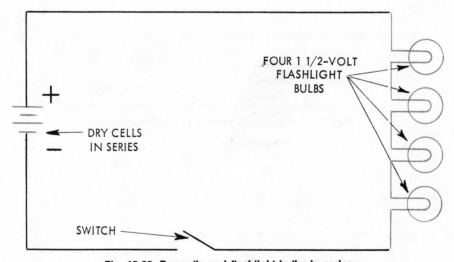

Fig. 15-25. Dry cells and flashlight bulbs in series.

nal of the dry cell. Close the switch and if all connections have been made correctly, the light bulbs should light.

Unscrew one of the bulbs and notice whether the remaining bulbs get dim-

Connect the four receptacles in series, as shown in Fig. 15-25. Run connecting wires between the dry cells, receptacles, and switch so that they will all be in series. Close the switch and if all connections have been made correctly the bulbs will light. Unscrew one of the light bulbs. What happens? Where could this system of connections be used? Replace the 1.5-volt flashlight bulbs with 6-volt bulbs. What happens? Why?

6. Connecting Dry Cells in Series with Push Buttons and Buzzers in Parallel.

Obtain four dry cells, two push buttons, two buzzers, and connecting wire. When you worked with dry cells and buzzers before, you learned that increasing the number of dry cells caused the buzzer to make a louder sound. Although most buzzers will operate on voltage as low as 1.5, when they are used in noisy locations for signaling, a higher voltage is used. The circuit you are about to connect is like the ones used where it is necessary to operate two buzzers from two push buttons which are located at different points.

Connect four dry cells in series. Connect the two push buttons in parallel and the two buzzers in parallel as shown in Fig. 15-26. Connect one of the series dry cell terminals to one of the buzzer

terminals. Connect the other buzzer terminal to one of the push button terminals. Connect the other push button terminal to the remaining series dry cell terminal. Press either push button and if the connections have been made correctly, both buzzers should operate. Place your hand against the armature of one of the buzzers, so that it will not operate and press a push button. Is the operation of the other buzzer affected? Why?

7. Connecting a Three-Wire Return Call Buzzer System.

Obtain four dry cells, two push buttons, two buzzers, and connecting wire. Connect the dry cells in series. Cut two pieces of wire the same length several feet long. Connect one end of each wire to a buzzer. Connect the other end of each wire to a push button. Arrange the wires so that a buzzer and a push button will be at the same ends of the wires. See Fig. 15-27. Connect a short piece of wire between the buzzer and the push button at both ends of the longer wire. Connect one terminal of the dry cells to the short

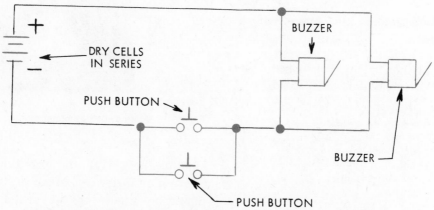

Fig. 15-26. Dry cells in series with push buttons and buzzers in parallel.

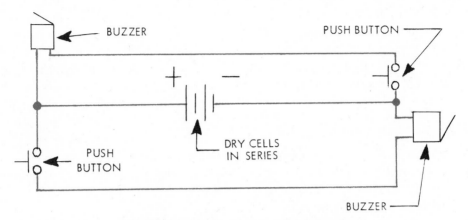

Fig. 15-27. Three-wire return call buzzer system.

piece of wire that connects a push button and a buzzer. Connect another wire from the remaining terminal of the dry cells to the short piece of wire that connects the other push button and buzzer together. The connections should appear as shown in the diagram. If the connections have been made correctly a buzzer at the opposite end will sound when either push button is pressed. Draw a diagram showing how the system could be made to operate using four wires between the stations. What is the advantage of the three-wire system? Where could such a system be used?

8. Demonstrating the Action of a Reed Switch.

Materials needed to demonstrate the action of a reed switch (Fig. 15-28):

1 Small magnet
1 Miniature lamp receptacle
1 Flashlight bulb, 1½ or 3 volts
1 or 2 flashlight cells
1 Reed switch, G. E. Type DR 113
Wood for mounting stand
Connecting wire

This experiment will provide a fas-

Fig. 15-28. Reed switch demonstrator.

cinating insight to the possibilities of this unique device. Make a suitable mounting stand for the switch, light bulb, and flashlight cells. Solder a piece

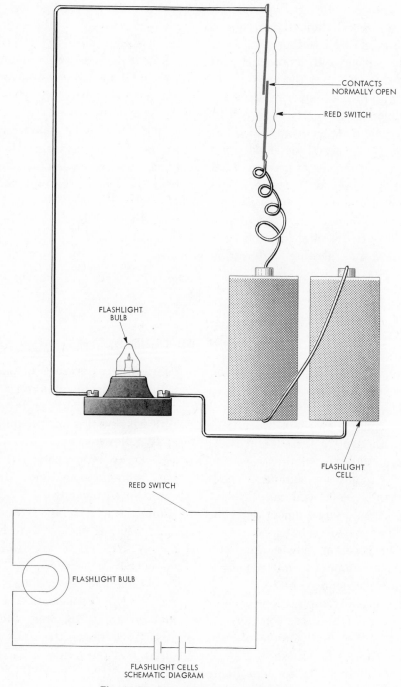

Fig. 15-29. **Connecting a reed switch.**

of wire to each terminal of the switch, but before beginning the soldering operation, grasp the switch terminal close

to the end of the glass tube with a pair of long nose pliers. This will absorb heat from the terminal and lessen the possibility of breaking the glass. Glue the switch to the wood stand if permanent placement is desired. Otherwise, hold the switch in place with loops of thread or fine wire passing over the neck of the glass tube and through holes in the wood backing. Connect the parts as shown in Fig. 15-29. The distance from which the switch can be operated depends upon the strength of the magnet used. A small horseshoe magnet will actuate the switch from a distance of three to four inches.

If you have two similar magnets, you can demonstrate another interesting feature of the reed switch. Hold one magnet in front of the switch to light the flashlight bulb. Bring the other magnet near the back of the mounting board and the light will go out. Move the front magnet away from the switch and the light will go on. What causes this strange action is opposing magnetic forces. When the magnectic forces are equal, due to the distance they are held from the switch, the bulb will not light. However, if one magnet is moved away from the switch, the remaining magnet will actuate it.

REVIEW QUESTIONS

1. Draw a diagram showing how you would connect a group of dry cells to provide 7½ volts.

2. If we connect two No. 6 dry cells in series with two small flashlight cells, what voltage will we obtain?

3. List as many applications of cells connected in series as you can.

4. When would you connect dry cells in parallel?

5. Draw a diagram showing how you would connect four 1½-volt flashlight bulbs to a 6-volt storage battery.

6. Name as many applications of light bulbs connected in series as you can.

7. What is the disadvantage of connecting light bulbs in series?

8. Are the light bulbs in your home connected in series or in parallel?

9. What is the difference between a "short" circuit and an "open" circuit?

10. Make a list of the different types of switches that you know about.

11. Draw a schematic circuit showing how a single pole single throw switch can be used to control a 6 volt light bulb connected to a storage battery.

12. What is the total resistance in a circuit that has four 200 ohm resistors connected in parallel?

13. Calculate the total resistance of four resistors connected in parallel if the first resistor is 16 ohms, the second resistor is 32 ohms, the third resistor is 8 ohms, and the fourth is 32 ohms.

Electricity
for
Everyday Living

Generating Electricity

We learned in Unit 8 that electricity could be generated when a coil of wire is rotated in a magnetic field. We also found that generators can be used to deliver either alternating current or direct current. An alternating current generator uses slip rings to deliver electricity to the brushes and direct current generators use a commutator. See Figs. 16-1 and 16-2.

Most commercial alternating current generators used to provide electricity for the home produce a 60-cycle alternating current. This means that the direction of current flow is changing 120 times every second.

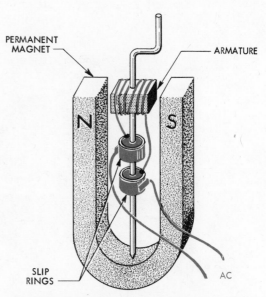

Fig. 16-1. This illustration shows the fundamental parts of an alternating current generator.

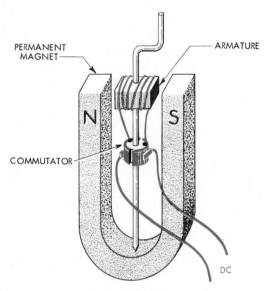

Fig. 16-2. A direct current generator has these basic parts.

Rotating Generators

Every generator needs some method of rotating the armature or rotor. The large generators used to produce electricity for towns and industry are usually rotated by water power or by steam.

These huge generators weighing many tons need a tremendous amount of power to turn them over. The armature or rotor of these generators is usually coupled to a turbine. See Fig. 16-3.

A *turbine* is a device that might be compared to a windmill. A windmill has several blades or vanes that are pushed by the wind. As the blades rotate the center shaft connected to the blades turns so that it can be used to pump water or turn other devices.

When water power is used to turn over a generator it is necessary to have a rapid flow of water. This can be accomplished by a large waterfall such as the Niagara Falls or by having a dam that holds back a huge lake of water. As the water goes over the falls or out through the bottom of the dam it flows through a water turbine. This turbine has vanes called *blades* (or *buckets*) against which the water flows. The force of the water turns the turbine and the turbine rotates the generator.

Steam pressure is used to turn tur-

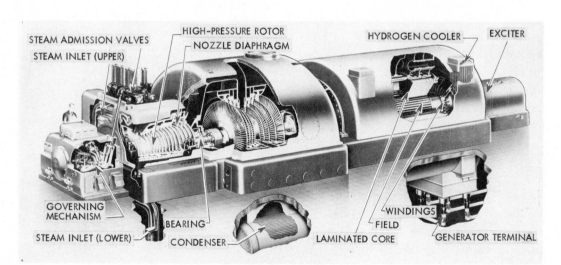

Fig. 16-3. In a modern turbine generator, the steam pushes against many blades to turn the rotor. (General Electric Co.)

bines on many commercial generators. High-pressure steam is directed against the blades on a turbine at the rate of about 1,200 miles per hour. These steam turbines have a series of blade wheels arranged so that steam must pass through from 17 to 20 turbine wheels. The steam passes through the nozzle and strikes a row of blades on the first wheel, it loses some of its pressure, and then passes into another set of nozzles, then through another row of blades, and so on down the line. Sometimes the wheel that holds the last set of blades is 12′ in diameter. See Fig. 16-4.

Since a large volume of water is needed for the water turbine and the steam turbine, most commercial generating plants are located near lakes or other places where water is readily available.

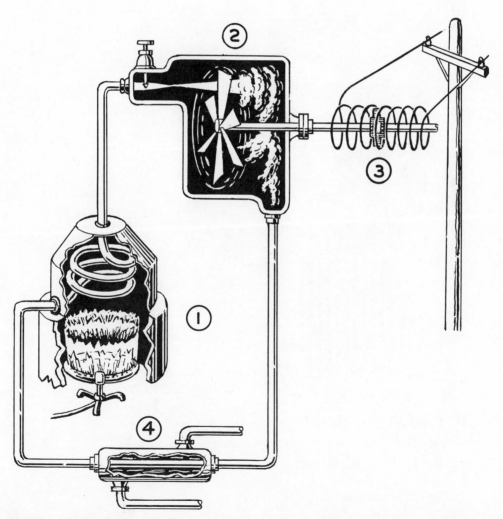

Fig. 16-4. How a steam turbine rotates a generator: 1. Steam is generated in a boiler. 2. Steam passes through a nozzle striking turbine blades. Blade wheel rotates. 3. Turbine turns rotor of generator and electricity is generated. 4. Exhaust steam from turbine is condensed and returned to boiler. (General Electric Co.)

Nuclear Power

We have learned that an atom consists of a number of electrons revolving around a center known as the *nucleus*. The nucleus is made up of positively charged particles called *protons* and neutral particles called *neutrons*. All of the atoms of any one element have the same number of protons in their centers or *nuclei*. Their number of neutrons may vary. For example, in natural or common uranium, 139 atoms out of 140 will each have a total of 238 protons and neutrons in its nucleus. The 140th atom will lack three neutrons. A common uranium atom is known as U238 and the 140th atom, which lacks three neutrons, is known as U235. This difference of three neutrons between U235 and U238 was found to

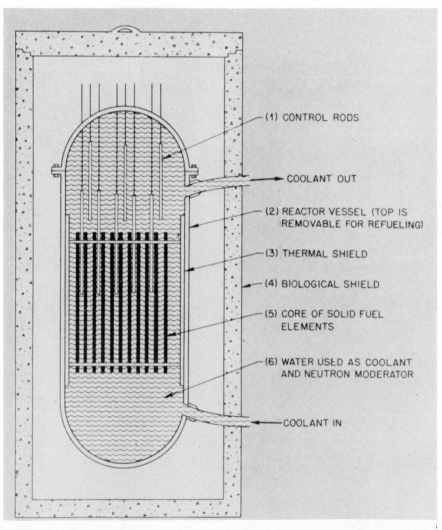

Fig. 16-5. Cross-sectional view of a reactor using water for a coolant. Chemicals or gas serve as coolants in some of the other type nuclear reactors. From *Fundamentals of Electricity*, American Technical Society.

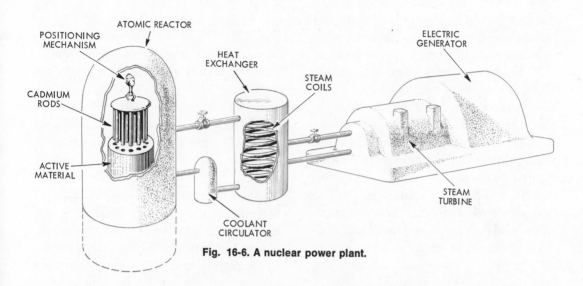

POSITIONING
MECHANISM

ATOMIC REACTOR

HEAT
EXCHANGER

STEAM
COILS

ELECTRIC
GENERATOR

CADMIUM
RODS

ACTIVE
MATERIAL

COOLANT
CIRCULATOR

STEAM
TURBINE

Fig. 16-6. A nuclear power plant.

Fig. 16-7. Automated control room of the San Onofre Nuclear Generating Station. The elaborate system of dials, gages, and colored lights, notifies operators instantaneously of any deviation from normal control until corrective adjustments are made. (San Diego Gas and Electric Co.)

be the key to *nuclear energy*. Scientists learned that U235 could be split, and in the splitting or *fissioning* process as it is known, could be made to release tremendous amounts of energy in the form of heat. Fissioning takes place in a device called an *atomic reactor*. A cross-sectional drawing of one type of reactor is shown in Fig. 16-5.

When the nucleus of active material U235 is struck by a single neutron during the fissioning process in a reactor, two neutrons are ejected from it. The two neutrons bombard two adjacent atoms and release four additional neutrons. This chain reaction increases at such a rapid rate, that the resulting heat would quickly vaporize the reactor if this rise were not controlled. This danger is overcome by the use of cadmium rods which may be raised or lowered in proximity to the active material. Cadmium has the property of absorbing neutrons and may be positioned for the desired rate of fissioning. A typical nuclear power plant, shown in Fig. 16-6, consists of the reactor, heat ex-

changer, steam turbine, and electrical generator. In operation, liquid or gaseous *coolant* is pumped from the reactor chamber to the heat exchanger. Here its heat passes to a coil of water pipe in which steam is generated to drive the turbine.

Millions of us now use electricity derived from nuclear energy and millions more will light their homes and operate their appliances with nuclear power plants (Fig. 16-7) that are already planned or being built. Authorities predict that with the ever increasing demands on conventional electrical power plants, the nation will face a depletion of its supplies of coal, gas, and oil. They are hoping that nuclear power will help to avert such a disaster.

Rotating Small Generators

Generators used to produce electricity where commercial electricity is not available usually are rotated by a diesel engine. Some small generators use a windmill to turn them over. See Figs. 16-8 thru 16-10.

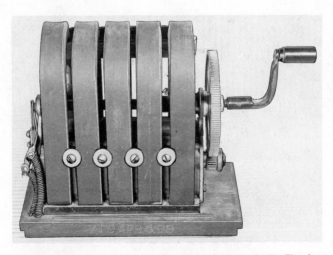

Fig. 16-8. An old-type hand-operated generator used to ring telephone bells. Five horseshoe magnets were used to produce the magnetic field.

Fig. 16-9. A gasoline engine driven generator. The 10,000-watt generator will deliver either 115 volts or 230 volts. (Wincharger Corp.)

Fig. 16-10. A diesel-electric power unit. The 60,000 watt generator will deliver either 115 or 230 volts alternating current. (Katolight Corp.)

Fig. 16-11. A motor-generator set using an electric motor to rotate the generator.

Fig. 16-12. This small dynamotor is a combination motor and generator. It was used to provide power for radio equipment in a Navy airplane.

Fig. 16-13. Large water-driven generators used by the Bureau of Reclamation on the Coulee Dam in the State of Washington. (Westinghouse Electric Corp.)

Large amounts of direct current are often needed for such purposes as electroplating and arc welding. These generators are usually rotated by electric motors. When an electric motor is used with a generator to produce electricity the combination is called a *motor-generator*. Figs. 16-11 thru 16-13 are examples of motor-generators.

Transmission Line Losses

Commercial generating plants must be able to deliver tremendous amounts of electricity to serve the entire needs of a town or city. These generating plants sometimes supply electricity for several communities and often must be located many miles away from where the electricity is used. Power lines called *transmission lines* carry the electricity from the power plant to the towns.

The voltage of these transmission lines is usually very high. Voltages of 66,000 to 110,000 volts are very common. High voltages are used for two reasons: (1) to reduce the voltage loss that would result from the resistance of the wire; (2) to reduce the amount of heat that would result from the large amount of current that would have to flow in the wire.

Loss Due to Resistance

We know that the circuits used in most homes are 115 volts. If the generator located many miles away from the homes delivered 115 volts to the transmission lines there would be a very large loss in voltage by the time it reached the homes. It would take several times the 115 volts to leave the generator so that the correct voltage would be available when it reached the town. The loss would be due to the resistance of the many miles of wire used to carry the electricity. To overcome this loss caused by the wire resistance, it is customary to use high voltages so that plenty of voltage will be available when the electricity reaches its destination.

Heavy Current Flow

If the generator produced only 115 volts of electricity, the amount of current needed to supply all of the homes in a community would be very high. The amount of current would be so great that it would be impossible to build a generator with large enough wire to handle the current flow. It would be very difficult to have transmission wires large enough to take care

of the current needs. By using high voltages it is possible to reduce the amount of current in the circuit.

We learned that electrical power was made up of the voltage multiplied by the current. From this we can see that large quantities of power can be made available if we have: (1) large voltage and a low current; or (2) a low voltage and a high current. Since high current would make the wire heat up it is necessary to reduce the current flow. Transmission lines must have a low current flow and a very high voltage.

Using High-Voltage Transmission Lines

Some commercial generators develop alternating current voltages up to 12,500 volts and higher. Even this is not enough to use on transmission lines that are hundreds of miles long. Voltages are stepped up to 66,000 or even higher after leaving the generator. A special device called a *transformer* is necessary to step up the voltage. We shall learn how transformers function in the next unit.

After the voltage has been stepped up it is carried by the transmission lines to local distributing stations called *substations*. There the voltage is reduced. The amount of voltage reduction varies according to the needs. Voltages of 2,200 volts to 6,000 volts are very common in substations.

From the substation the electricity is carried by power lines to the various sections of the community. Before bringing the electricity into the home it is necessary to again step the voltage down. Transformers located on top of power poles reduce the voltage to 115 or 230 volts. These 115- or 220-volt lines are then brought into the home. See Figs. 16-14 thru 16-17.

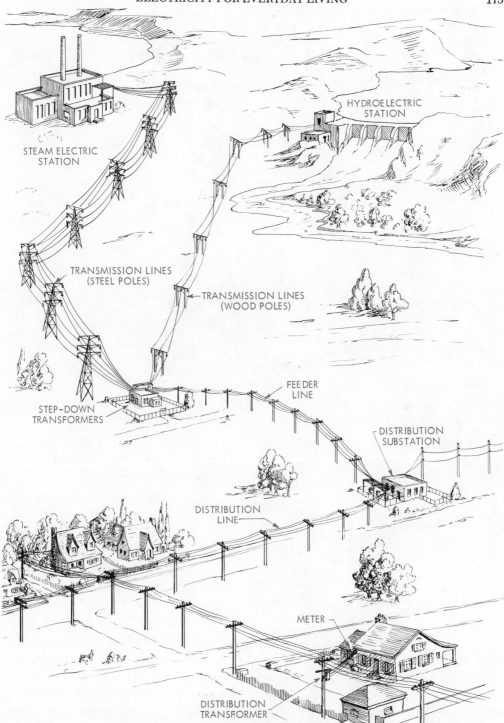

STEAM ELECTRIC
STATION

HYDROELECTRIC
STATION

TRANSMISSION LINES
(STEEL POLES)

TRANSMISSION LINES
(WOOD POLES)

STEP-DOWN
TRANSFORMERS

FEEDER
LINE

DISTRIBUTION
SUBSTATION

DISTRIBUTION
LINE

METER

DISTRIBUTION
TRANSFORMER

Fig. 16-14. This drawing shows how electricity might be produced and delivered to a city. A steam generating plant and a water power generator both produce electricity. After stepping up the voltage at both
plants, the transmission lines deliver this very high voltage to a central station. Here the electrical power
from each plant is brought together. Large step-down transformers reduce the voltage, for safer handling,
as the electricity nears the city. The feeder lines deliver the electricity to a distribution substation where
the voltage is again reduced. From this substation the distribution lines take the electricity to the homes.

Fig. 16-15. Transmission lines deliver 287,000 volts to this substation. These large transformers reduce the voltage before the electricity is sent on to other distribution stations. (Westinghouse Electric Corp.)

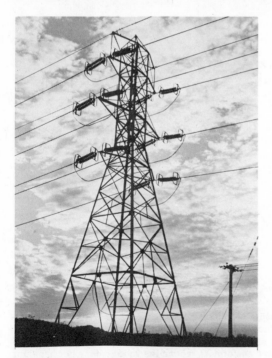

Fig. 16-16. Steel tower supporting electric transmission lines. (General Electric Co.)

High Voltage Direct Current Power Transmission

Typical long distance electrical power transmission requires high voltage and low current which must be produced with alternating current generators and transformers. Since the early days of the electrical power industry, alternating current has been preferred over direct current, for local use. Alternating current motors, generators, and other equipment usually contain fewer parts and are easier to maintain. However, electrical engineers have known that direct current has fundamental advantages for long distance power transmission. For a given area of insulator surface, direct current can operate at a higher voltage. Direct current requires only two line conductors, instead of three as required by alternat-

Fig. 16-17. Electrical power plants have large control panels where technicians monitor and adjust power output. (San Diego Gas & Electric Co.)

ing current. And line losses with similar values of voltage and current are considerably less with direct current. The ideal combination is considered to be direct current for long distance transmission and alternating current local distribution, but generators capable of producing the high voltage direct current required are yet to be developed. Recently, however, Dr. Uno Lamm, a Swedish electrical engineer, developed a system of transmitting extremely high voltage direct current without direct current generators that may revolutionize long distance power transmission the world over.

With the Lamm system, electricity is generated at the source of power such as a dam, then stepped up with transformers to the high voltage required for long distance transmission. The high voltage alternating current is changed to direct current with special mercury-arc valves which Dr. Lamm designed, then transmitted to a distant substation. At the substation, the high voltage direct current is converted back to alternating current with similar mercury-arc valves, then reduced with transformers to voltages required by homes and industry.

The first high-voltage, direct current

transmitting lines and converter stations in the United States using the Lamm system were dedicated in Southern California during September, 1970. Carrying 800,000 volts of direct current, the lines extend from Celilo, Oregon, on the Columbia River, to Sylmar, California, a distance of 856 miles. At Sylmar, the high-voltage direct-current is converted to alternating current, then transformed to lower voltages for distribution to the homes and factories of Southern California. The system is capable of delivering 1.4 million kilowatts of electric power.

Transmission Line Construction

High-voltage transmission lines are made of several strands of heavy wire. Stranded wire makes the cable flexible so that it can swing between the poles without breaking. Also it makes it possible to coil the cable for easy handling.

These cables use several strands of either copper or aluminum wire. Sometimes a kind of hollow tubing is used for transmission lines instead of solid wire. The hollow tubing makes a stronger cable than a solid wire of the same weight. The outside diameter of the entire cable may be as large as 2".

Transmission poles are made of either steel or wood. Often the wire on top of the poles is a ground wire that serves as protection for the transmission wires in the event lightning strikes. If lightning strikes it usually hits the highest point. Since the ground wire is higher than the other wires the lightning is shorted to the ground.

Because of the extreme high voltage on transmission lines, it is necessary to use large insulators on the arms of the poles. These insulators prevent the electricity from shorting between the wires or from shorting to the power pole.

REVIEW QUESTIONS

1. What is the main difference between an alternating current generator and a direct current generator?

2. How are large commercial generators usually rotated?

3. What is the purpose of a turbine?

4. What effect do large transmission lines have on the voltage?

5. Why is it necessary to have a high voltage and a low current on transmission lines?

6. Give two reasons why high voltages are used on transmission lines.

7. What electrical measurements are needed to determine the electrical power in a circuit?

8. Name the device used to step up the voltage after it has been developed by a generator.

9. After delivering the electricity by a transmission line to a city why is it necessary to reduce the voltage?

10. What is the purpose of the ground wire on top of transmission poles?

11. What is a nuclear reactor?

12. State some advantages of direct current over alternating current for transmitting electric power long distances.

UNIT 17
USING TRANSFORMERS TO INCREASE AND DECREASE VOLTAGE

Inducing Current in a Coil

We know that if a bar magnet is pushed into the center of a coil that electricity will be induced in the coil. Electricity can be induced only when the magnet is moving. This induced current was alternating current since each time the magnet was pushed in or out of the coil the direction of current flow changed.

Expanding and Collapsing of the Lines of Force

A magnetic field that is starting or stopping makes the lines of force build up and then collapse around a coil. In Fig. 17-1 when the switch is first closed the lines of force build up or expand all around the coil. In just a fraction of a second all of the lines of force will have been completed and the coil becomes an electromagnet. When the switch is opened as in Fig. 17-2 the magnetic field starts to

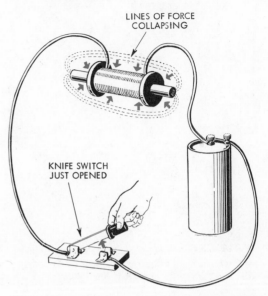

Fig. 17-2. As switch is opened the magnetic field collapses.

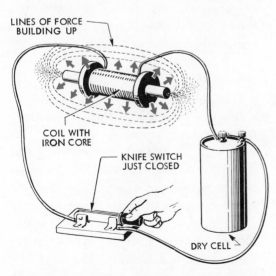

Fig. 17-1. As switch is closed the magnetic field expands.

collapse. When all of the lines of force are gone the coil is no longer an electromagnet. Each time the switch is closed the lines of force build up and each time the switch is opened the lines of force collapse. The closing of the switch completes the circuit and at this time the lines of force start to move out all around the coil forming a path from one pole to the other. Just as soon as the circuit is opened all the lines of force start to move back toward the coil until they disappear.

Inducing Current in a Coil by the Current in Another Coil

A second coil is now placed near the first coil as shown in Fig. 17-3. The leads of this coil are connected to a galvanometer. When the switch is closed the galvanometer pointer moves in one direction and then returns to the zero position. As

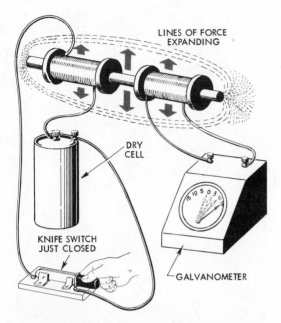

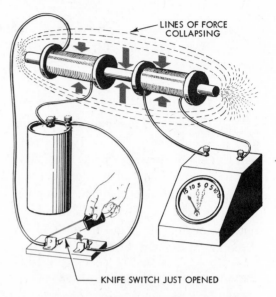

Fig. 17-3. Galvanometer connected to the secondary coil shows that current is induced by the primary coil when the switch is first closed.

Fig. 17-4. When the current in the primary coil is stopped, the collapsing line of force induces a current in the secondary coil. The galvanometer shows that the current in the secondary coil flows in a direction opposite to that in which it flowed when the switch was closed.

long as the switch remains closed the galvanometer pointer remains at zero. As soon as the switch is opened the pointer moves in the opposite direction and then returns to zero as shown in Fig. 17-4.

From this we can see that current is induced in the second coil each time the switch is opened or closed. This is exactly the same as when a bar magnet is moving in or out of a coil. As long as the magnet is moving, current is induced in the coil.

Figs. 17-3 and 17-4 show that current can be induced in a coil by current in another coil. To induce current it is necessary to stop and start the current in the first coil. When the current is started by closing the switch the magnetic lines of force start building up and move so that they cut through the second coil. As soon as all of the lines of force have been completed, the magnetic field is not moving and current is no longer induced in

the second coil. When the switch is opened the lines of force start to collapse and again current is induced in the other coil. As soon as all of the lines of force collapse current stops flowing. Since the current flows first in one direction and then the other direction, the induced current is alternating current.

Transformer Operation

Having one coil induce a current in another coil is the principle of the *transformer*. The first coil is called the *primary* winding. It must have a current that is starting and stopping to induce a current in the second coil. The second coil is called the *secondary* winding.

To improve the operation of a transformer the two windings are placed over a soft iron core as shown in Fig. 17-5. The iron core provides a much better path for the magnetic lines of force to flow

Fig. 17-5. An iron core placed in the center of the primary coil and the secondary coil will improve the efficiency of the transformer.

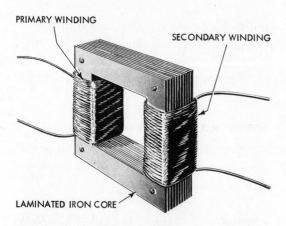

Fig. 17-6. A drawing showing the construction of a transformer. The closed iron core provides a path for the magnetic field to flow through. The laminated core made of thin strips of soft iron improves its efficiency.

Transformer cores are made of many soft iron strips called *laminations* (Fig. 17-6). These laminations help in improving the operation of the transformer.

Using Transformers on Alternating Current

We have just learned that a transformer consists of a primary winding and a secondary winding surrounding an iron core. We also know that to induce a current in the secondary winding it is necessary to have the current in the primary continually starting and stopping.

A type of current that is continually starting and stopping by changing the direction of electron flow is alternating current. When alternating current is connected to the primary of a transformer the magnetic field will be expanding and collapsing each time the current starts and stops. This will induce a current in

through. It also concentrates the lines of force so that they do not spread out but remain close to the coils of wire. By concentrating the lines of force the efficiency of the transformer is greatly improved.

the secondary winding which will also be alternating current.

When direct current is connected to the primary of a transformer it is necessary to have some type of switch that will continually open and close the circuit to induce a current in the secondary winding.

Step-up Transformers

In the study of commercial generators we found that they produce alternating current. We also learned that it was necessary to step up the voltage of these generators so that high voltages would be available for the transmission lines. Transformers are used to step up the voltage. Generating stations use alternating current because the primary of the transformer can be connected directly to the output of the generator.

A transformer is a *step-up transformer* if the secondary winding has more turns than the primary winding. If the secondary has more turns than the primary, the lines of force cut through more turns of wire and the voltage is increased. In a transformer that has 100 turns of wire on the primary and 200 turns of wire on the secondary, the voltage across the secondary will be twice as much as the voltage connected to the primary. The relationship between the number of turns on a primary winding to the number on the secondary is often referred to as the *ratio* between them. In the transformer shown in Fig. 17-7, there is a 1 to 2 ratio.

Step-up transformers are used wherever it is necessary to increase the voltage. It is possible to increase the voltage a little or a great deal, depending upon the need. When it is desired to step up the voltage from 10 volts to 100 volts then the secondary winding must have

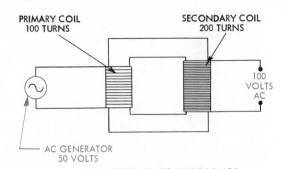

STEP-UP TRANSFORMER

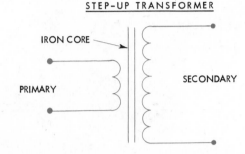

SYMBOL FOR STEP-UP TRANSFORMER

Fig. 17-7. A step-up transformer increases voltage.

ten times as many turns as the primary. Of course, there is some loss in a transformer. To take care of this loss a few extra turns of wire must be added to the secondary winding.

Step-down Transformers

After the high-voltage transmission lines bring the electricity into a town or city, a substation is used to reduce the voltage. These substations use *step-down transformers* to lower the voltage so that it will be safer to handle (Fig. 17-8).

In a step-down transformer the primary has more turns than the secondary. Since the secondary winding has fewer turns than the primary winding the lines of force are cutting through fewer turns and the voltage is reduced.

If we wish to obtain 10 volts from a 100-volt alternating current source of electricity a transformer can be used. The

Fig. 17-8. Large transformers used in a power substation. (General Electric Co.)

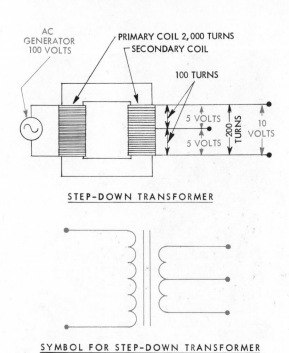

STEP-DOWN TRANSFORMER

SYMBOL FOR STEP-DOWN TRANSFORMER

Fig. 17-9. The voltage from a step-down transformer may be divided as needed.

secondary would have one-tenth as many turns as the primary. See Fig. 17-9.

Mutual Induction

We can see in Figs. 17-3 and 17-4 how a varying magnetic field set up by a current flowing in a coil can induce current in another coil placed close to it. This effect is known as "mutual induction" and all power transformers operate on this principle.

Self-Induction

Another important principle governing the operation of transformers is that of self-induction. When an alternating current flows through the primary winding of a transformer, the varying magnetic field set up by the current will flow through the laminations and through the centers of the primary and secondary coils. This varying magnetic field will induce a voltage in the primary coil which is slightly less than the line voltage, but opposite in direction. Since this induced voltage opposes the line voltage it is referred to as a *counter electromotive force*, and usually abbreviated, *counter-emf*.

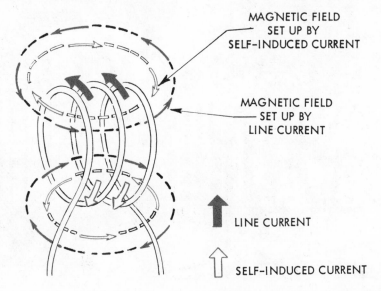

Fig. 17-10. In a transformer primary winding, the self induced current flows in the direction opposite the line current.

Fig. 17-11. Demonstrating the effect of counter electromotive force.

The characteristic of a coil which causes an opposing voltage to be induced in it is known as "self-induction." Self-induction plays an important part in regulating the primary current of a transformer, so that it will vary nearly in direct proportion to the current drawn from the secondary. Fig. 17-10 shows how the self-induced current in a transformer primary opposes the line current. To simplify the drawing the transformer core is not shown.

We learned above how a varying magnetic field causes a counter-emf to be induced in transformer windings. Self-induction also occurs when a switch is opened in a direct current circuit which includes a coil with an iron core. This effect can be demonstrated by connecting a dry-cell, switch, iron-core coil, and 6-8 volt light bulb, as shown in Fig. 17-11. When the switch is closed the bulb will light dimly. When it is opened the bulb will flash brilliantly. During the brief interval when the current through the coil is rising, the increasing magnetic field creates a counter-emf in the coil which diminishes as the current reaches its maximum flow. When the switch is opened the magnetic field collapses so quickly without opposition from the dry cell that it induces a voltage in the coil many times higher than that of the dry cell.

Reactance

If we measure the resistance of the primary of a door chime transformer with an ohmmeter, we will find that it is about 250 ohms. With a line voltage of 117 volts and using Ohm's law, we learn that the apparent current that would flow through the primary would be about 0.47 ampere. On a 24 hour basis this would mean that approximately 1320 watts of electric power would be consumed, which would make the operating cost for a door bell or chime almost prohibitive. If we now connect an AC ammeter in series with the transformer primary and connect the transformer to a 117 volt, AC line there will be little or no visible movement of the meter pointer. Only when we connect a load across the secondary of the transformer will we be able to detect a small movement of the meter pointer. Now, let us see how we can account for the difference between the calculated and measured values of the primary current. When we measured the resistance of the transformer primary with an ohmmeter, the value of 250 ohms was the same as it would be if the wire was stretched out in a straight line. Coiling a wire has no effect on its resistance. When we connected the transformer to a 117 volt, AC line the counter-emf developed opposed any increase or decrease of current with the result that very little current flowed in the winding. The ability of a coil to react against changing current is called "inductive reactance." The value of inductive reactance is expressed in ohms and it is represented by the symbol X_L. The letter, or subscript, L, has no value. It is used only to show that the reactance is due to a coil or inductance. Reactance is also a property of capacitance and we will learn about it when we study capacitors.

Impedance

We have learned how reactance can limit the flow of alternating current in a circuit. If we could make a coil that had no resistance, we could calculate the current that would flow through it by merely substituting X_L for R in ohm's law and saying that $I = E/X_L$. However, since all conductors have resistance, this value must be considered when calculating the current flow in AC circuits containing coils or inductances. The combined opposition of the resistance and the reactance to the flow of alternating current in a circuit is known as "impedance" and is represented by the letter Z. The value of impedance is expressed in ohms. The formula for determining impedance is:

$$Z = \sqrt{R^2 + X_L^2}$$

The Turns Ratio of the Transformer

The ratio between the voltage and the number of turns on the primary and the secondary windings of a transformer is called the turns ratio. By using the turns ratio formula, it is possible to determine either the output voltage or the turns needed on the secondary, providing the input voltage or the number of turns of the primary is known.

The turns ratio formula for a transformer is expressed as:

$$\frac{\text{Prim. Turns}}{\text{Sec. Turns}} = \frac{\text{Prim. Voltage}}{\text{Sec. Voltage}}$$

Using symbols for turns ratio

$$\frac{n_p}{n_s} = \frac{E_p}{E_s}$$

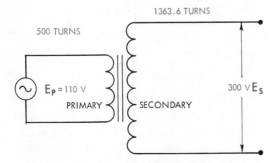

n_p = Number of turns on primary
n_s = Number of turns on secondary
E_p = Primary voltage
E_s = Secondary voltage

To determine how many turns are needed to make a power transformer that will produce 300 volts at the secondary if the primary with 500 turns is connected to 110 volts AC, we can use the turns ratio formula (Fig. 17-12):

$$\frac{500}{n_s} = \frac{110}{300}$$

$$n_s = \frac{150{,}000}{110}$$

n_s = 1363.6 turns on the secondary winding.

Copper Losses in a Transformer

Power transformers are very efficient, but they do have some loss in electrical energy. The wire used to wind the primary and secondary coils has resistance, and this resistance uses up some of the electricity. If excessive current flows through the coils, the wire can become hot, and additional energy may be lost in the form of heat. Because of this loss, called copper loss, transformers are rated according to the voltage and current carrying capacity of each of the windings. When heavy current is needed larger wire is used on the windings.

Eddy Current Losses in a Transformer

Another loss in the transformer occurs in the iron core. Since iron is a conductor of electricity, magnetic lines flowing through the core will cause current to be induced in the core. The current in the core is called *eddy current,* and is a waste of power because heat generated in the core serves no useful purpose in the transformer.

Fig. 17-12. The turns ratio formula was used to calculate the number of turns needed on the secondary winding.

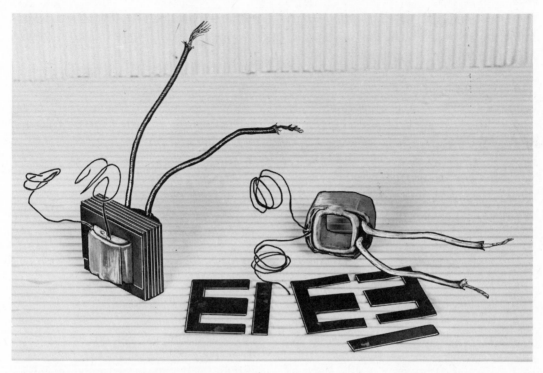

Fig. 17-13. A small step-down transformer is shown on the left. The iron laminations and the primary and secondary coils are shown on the right.

Eddy current losses are reduced by using thin sheets of soft iron, called laminations, for the core, as shown in Fig. 17-13. These strips of iron laminations are painted with shellac or varnish so that they will be insulated from each other. Through the use of these laminations the path to carry the current in the core is reduced; thus the losses due to eddy currents are cut down.

Hysteresis Losses in a Transformer

Each time the alternating current changes direction of flow in a transformer, the magnetic polarity in the iron molecules of the core is changed. This is much the same as when stroking a piece of steel with a bar magnet. The magnet will align the poles of the molecules in one direction when stroked with one of the magnet poles and will reverse the alignment of the molecules if stroked with the opposite magnet pole. Friction produced between the molecules as they change magnetic polarity develops heat in the steel.

As the alternating current acts on the transformer core, a certain amount of energy is needed to continually change the magnetic polarity. This loss in energy is called hysteresis loss. To reduce the hysteresis loss in transformers a very soft iron is used in the core. Silicon steel is one of the materials used as it can change polarity easily and thus reduce the hysteresis loss in the core.

Power Ratio in Transformers

A transformer cannot generate power. By this we mean that if the power used in the secondary is 100 watts, the power in the primary must be at least 100 watts. In other words, we cannot get more power out of a transformer than we put into it. Transformers are not 100% efficient because some loss occurs due to the copper losses, hysteresis, and eddy currents. As a result of these losses, the power used in the secondary will always be less than that in the primary. Well designed commercial power transformers are about 95% efficient.

All power transformers are designed for a definite primary voltage and a maximum primary current. This is known as the power rating of the transformer. By using the power formula, the power input of the transformer can be calculated. For example, a transformer that has a 117 volt primary with a maximum current rating of 2 amperes would have a power input (Fig. 17-14) that would be calculated as follows:

$$\text{Power} = EI$$
$$P = 117 \times 2$$
$$P = 234 \text{ watts}$$

If this transformer was 100% efficient, the secondary power would equal the input power and thus the secondary output would also be 234 watts. Since transformers are not 100% efficient, the power ratio formula is:

$$P_{output} = Pn \text{ input}$$
$$n = \text{Efficiency factor}$$

This formula may also be stated as:

$$E_s I_s = n E_p I_p$$

$$E_s = \text{Secondary voltage}$$
$$I_s = \text{Secondary current}$$
$$n = \text{Efficiency factor}$$
$$E_p = \text{Primary voltage}$$
$$I_p = \text{Primary current}$$

The Autotransformer

A one winding transformer shown in Fig. 17-15 is called an autotransformer. Part of the single winding is used for the primary and the other part is used as the secondary. It may be designed for either a step-up or a step-down transformer and the same principle as stated for regular transformers applies since the primary induces a voltage into the secondary.

A step-down autotransformer uses fewer turns of wire for the secondary than for the primary. The lower voltage secondary is tapped, or connected at the desired voltage as illustrated in Fig. 17-15. The voltage may be decreased by using fewer turns for the secondary winding or increased by using more turns for the secondary.

A step-up autotransformer uses only a portion of the single winding for the primary. The two outside leads of the entire coil are used for increasing the secondary voltage. (Fig. 17-16). Autotransformers are only used when it is not necessary to have the primary and secondary windings insulated from each other.

Variable voltage autotransformers may be made by providing numerous taps to

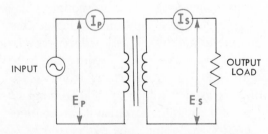

Fig. 17-14. In a transformer, the power input is found by multiplying the input current by the input voltage. The output power is found by multiplying the output current by the output voltage. These would be equal except for the losses that must be considered.

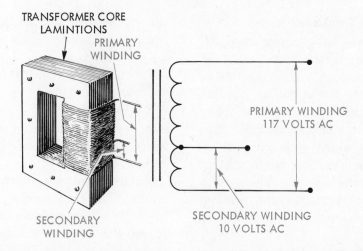

Fig. 17-15. A step-down autotransformer uses a single winding for the primary and secondary.

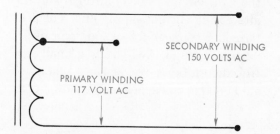

Fig. 17-16. This step-up autotransformer increases 117 volts to 150 volts.

the transformer and using a movable contact to select the desired voltage. In Fig. 17-17 a combination step-up and step-down transformer is shown. A variety of voltages may be obtained from such an arrangement. Commercially manufactured transformers with trade names such as Powerstat and Variac are variable voltage autotransformers.

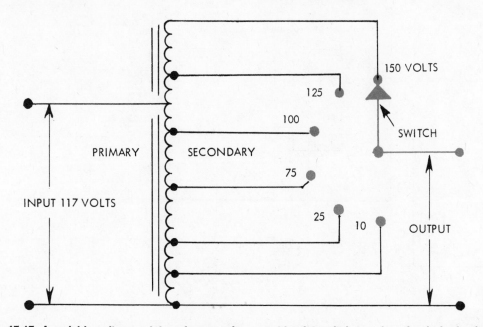

Fig. 17-17. A variable voltage autotransformer using a multi-point switch to select the desired voltage.

Other Uses of Transformers

Transformers have many uses. All types of transformers are in use in the home and in industry. It is possible to have more than one secondary winding on a transformer. For example, in many radio receivers a single transformer steps up the voltage to 300 volts with one set of windings and another winding steps the voltage down to 6 volts. The secondary can have as many different windings as necessary to step the voltage either up or down.

Train transformers used to run toy trains step down the 115 volts AC to from 5 to 25 volts. This lower voltage is connected to the train tracks and makes it safe to handle all parts of the circuit. Door chimes and door bells require a low voltage and transformers are used to step down the 115 volts to between 10 and 20 volts. Television sets use transformers in many ways. In one circuit of a television set the voltage is stepped up by a transformer to as high as 20,000 volts.

The Saturable Reactor

A device similar in construction to a transformer and known as a *saturable reactor* (Fig. 17-18) has replaced large rheostats which were formerly used to control lights in theaters and large assembly halls. The reactor consists of a three-legged laminated steel core upon which three coils are placed. The outer coils are identical and are connected in series with the light circuit to be controlled and the alternating current supply line. The center coil is connected to a source of direct current through a switch and a small control rheostat. As we learned when we studied reactance, when the outer coils

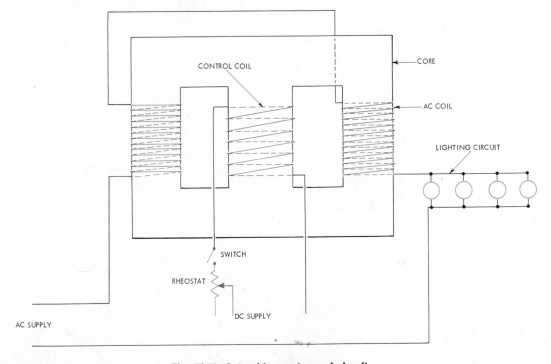

Fig. 17-18. Saturable reactor and circuit.

are connected to an alternating current supply line, the counter-emf developed opposes any increase or decrease of current, so that little current flows through the coils. At that point, the cores over which the coils are placed are said to be *saturated* with magnetic flux. If a small direct current flows through the center coil, the magnetic flux set up in the center core opposes that developed by the outer coils and reduces their counter-emf. The lower counter-emf permits more current to flow through the coils and lighting circuit. Increasing the direct current causes a corresponding increase in the lighting circuit current until the desired degree of illumination is obtained. The center coil generally consists of a large number of turns, so that it will develop a large magnetic flux with a small amount of current. In a typical saturable reactor, the control current may be as low as one-twentieth of that flowing in the lighting circuit.

INTERESTING THINGS TO DO

Making a Transformer.

Materials needed to construct the transformer (Fig. 17-19):

1 Wood base, ½" x 3" x 5"
1 Piece cardboard, fiber, or plastic tubing, 1" diameter, 1¾" long
2 Fiber or masonite washers, ⅛" thick, 1¾" outside diameter
85' Soft iron wire, 16, 18, or 20 gage (Cut approximately 200 pieces 5" long)
1 Spool magnet wire, No. 32, enamel-covered
1 Spool magnet wire, No. 24, enamel-covered
2' Stranded radio hook-up wire
1 Piece sheet steel, 20 gage, ½" x 3"
1 Piece sheet steel, 20 gage, 1¼" x 6"
2 Terminal screws

The transformer you are about to make (Fig. 17-19) has an output of 12 volts and will operate many of the projects described in this book that are intended to work on alternating current.

Make a winding form for the transformer by making holes in the center of the fiber or masonite washers large enough to make a snug fit on the ends of the 1" tubing. See Fig. 17-20.

Glue the washers to the tubing and drill a ³⁄₃₂" hole through one of the washers close to the tubing. Cut a piece of radio hook-up wire 6" long and insert one end of it through the hole in the fiber or masonite washer. Solder one end of the hook-up wire to the end of the spool of No. 32 magnet wire. Wrap the soldered joint with a piece of Scotch electrical tape and proceed to wind 1,800 turns of wire between the two washers. See Fig. 17-21. Wind the wire on the form as evenly as possible and when the winding is completed, carefully drill another ³⁄₃₂" hole through the washer, close to the winding. Cut another piece of radio hook-up wire 6" long and insert one end of it through the hole in the washer. Solder the hook-up wire to the end of the completed winding and insulate the joint with a piece of electrical tape. Wrap the wind-

Fig. 17-19. Step-down transformer.

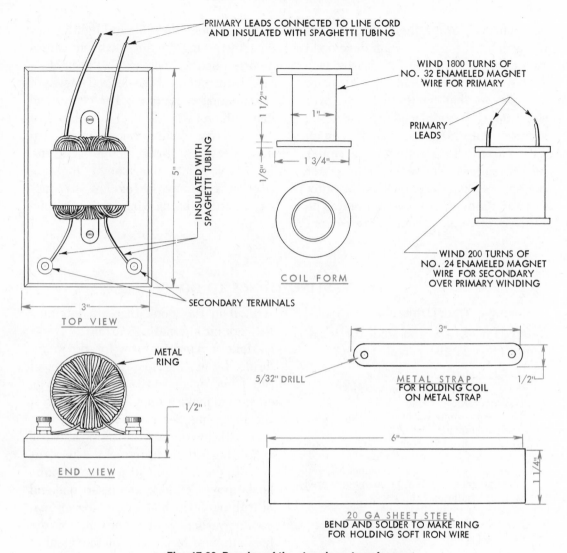

Fig. 17-20. Drawing of the step-down transformer.

ing with a layer of thin cardboard. This completes the primary winding.

Drill two $\frac{3}{32}''$ holes through the fiber or masonite washer, opposite to the ones drilled previously. One of the holes should be drilled close to the cardboard wrapping and the other near the outside edge of the washer. Cut a piece of radio hook-up wire 6″ long and insert one end of it through the inner hole in the washer. Solder the hook-up wire to the end of a spool of No. 24 magnet wire, wrap the

joint with a piece of tape and proceed to wind 200 turns of wire over the cardboard wrapping. Insert another 6″ piece of radio hook-up wire through the outer hole in the washer and solder it to the end of the No. 24 magnet wire. Insulate the joint with a piece of tape. Wrap the winding with several layers of thin cardboard. This completes the secondary winding.

Fill the center of the winding form with pieces of the 5″ soft iron wire, allow-

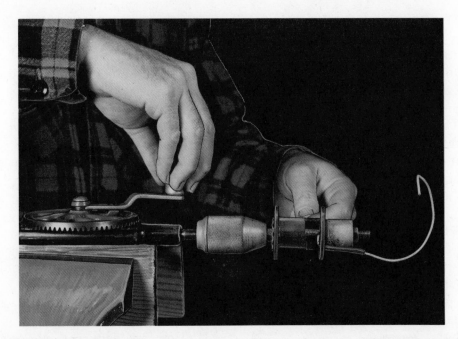

Fig. 17-21. Using a hand drill clamped in a vise to wind the transformer. A long bolt holds the coil form. One end of the bolt is tightened in the chuck of the hand drill. It is necessary to determine how many revolutions the chuck makes for each revolution of the handle. One hand of the operator feeds the wire on the form while the other hand turns the drill handle.

ing an equal amount of wire to extend from each end of the form, as shown in Fig. 17-22. Force extra pieces of wire through the center of the form, so that all of the iron wires will be held firmly in place. Bend each piece of iron around the coil form and cut the ends off so that they overlap about ½" on the outside of the form. Slip short pieces of radio spaghetti

Fig. 17-22. The wire core is placed in the center of the coil form. Ends of the wires are bent so that they touch each other.

tubing over the coil leads when the iron wires are being bent around the coil form to protect the insulated covering on the leads. Make a ring to fit snugly around the transformer with the 1¼" x 6" piece of sheet steel and force it over the steel wires surrounding the coils. Drill and shape the ½" x 3" piece of sheet steel as shown in the drawing and solder it to the metal ring. This piece will serve to secure the transformer to the wood base. Place two terminal screws at one end of the wood base and secure the transformer to the base, so that the secondary leads are at the same ends as the terminal screws. Secure the leads to the terminal screws. Connect an attachment plug cap, or a piece of lamp cord and a plug cap, to the primary terminals. The transformer is now ready for its initial tryout.

REVIEW QUESTIONS

1. How is current induced in a coil by means of a bar magnet?

2. Explain what happens to the lines of force around a coil when the current is started and stopped.

3. What is necessary to induce a current in one coil by means of current in another coil?

4. Name the two windings of a transformer.

5. What type of current is always produced in the secondary coil of a transformer?

6. What type of current is necessary in the primary winding of a transformer to induce a current in the secondary winding?

7. What is the difference between a step-up transformer and a step-down transformer?

8. If a step-up transformer has 400 turns on the primary winding and 1,200 turns on the secondary winding how much will this transformer increase the voltage?

9. Name several uses for step-down transformers.

10. What is the purpose of the iron core in a transformer?

11. How does mutual induction operate in a transformer?

12. What is a counter-emf?

13. What is meant by inductive reactance?

14. What makes up the impedance of a circuit?

15. A transformer connected to a 120 volt AC source of electricity has 400 turns on the primary winding. If we wish to obtain 10 volts from the secondary winding, how many turns of wire do we need for the secondary?

16. What are copper losses in a transformer?

17. How are eddy current losses reduced in transformer construction?

18. Why is a soft iron core used in transformers?

19. Explain why the power output of a transformer is not equal to the power input.

20. How does an autotransformer differ from a regular transformer?

21. Describe briefly how a saturable reactor operates.

UNIT 18
PROTECTING HOME ELECTRICAL CIRCUITS

Electrical Power Leads into the Home

At the local substation electricity is reduced to a fairly low voltage for distribution around the city. Voltages are usually 2,400 volts or higher on the power poles going to residential areas. Before the electricity is brought into the home the voltage must again be reduced. A transformer called a *pole transformer* usually mounted on top of a power pole is used for this purpose. The pole transformer in Fig. 18-1 provides the electricity for several homes and reduces the voltage to either 115 volts or 230 volts.

When 115 volts is brought into the home it requires two wires and is called a *two-wire service.* The use of 230-volt service in the home is becoming more common and is called a *three-wire service.* In a three-wire service one wire is called the *neutral wire.* Fig. 18-1 shows how it is possible to obtain 115 volts by

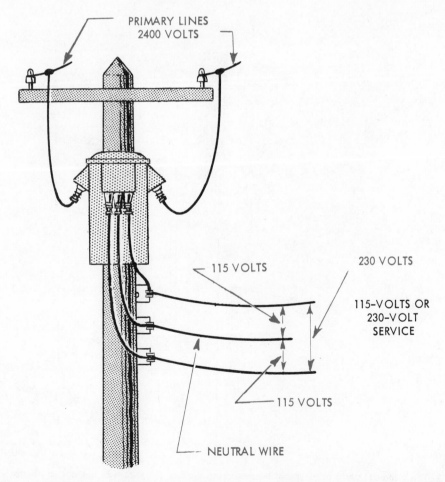

PRIMARY LINES
2400 VOLTS

115 VOLTS

230 VOLTS

115-VOLTS OR
230-VOLT
SERVICE

115 VOLTS

NEUTRAL WIRE

Fig. 18-1. A pole transformer steps down the voltage before it reaches the home. By using the two outside wires, 230 volts is available. For 115 volts, one of the outside wires and the center neutral wire are used.

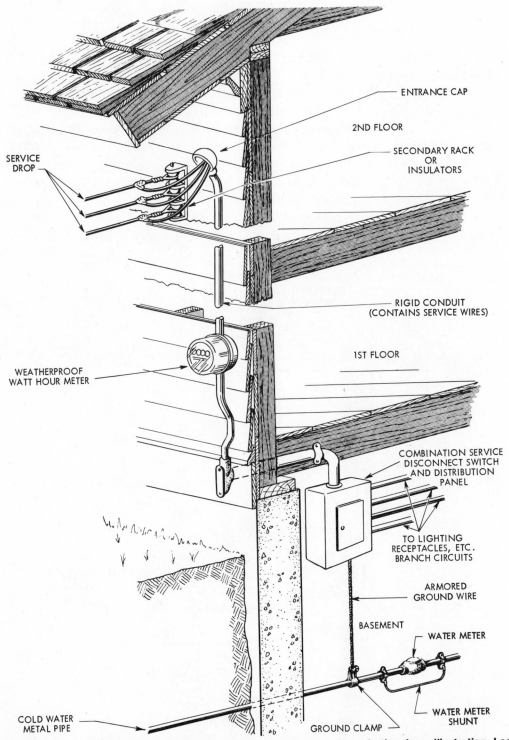

ENTRANCE CAP

2ND FLOOR

SECONDARY RACK
OR
INSULATORS

SERVICE
DROP

RIGID CONDUIT
(CONTAINS SERVICE WIRES)

1ST FLOOR

WEATHERPROOF
WATT HOUR METER

COMBINATION SERVICE
DISCONNECT SWITCH
AND DISTRIBUTION
PANEL

TO LIGHTING
RECEPTACLES, ETC.
BRANCH CIRCUITS

ARMORED
GROUND WIRE

BASEMENT

WATER METER

COLD WATER
METAL PIPE

GROUND CLAMP

WATER METER
SHUNT

Fig. 18-2. The principal parts of a typical house wiring system are shown in the above illustration. Local electrical codes may require different locations for these service connections. (From *Electrical Construction Wiring,* American Technical Society.)

connecting to the neutral wire and to either of the other wires. The 230 volts, used on water heaters and electric ranges, is available from the other two leads.

The power service leads going into the home are connected to a kilowatt-hour meter that keeps a record of the quantity of electricity used by the home. This meter was discussed in Unit 14. See Fig. 18-2.

Distributing the Electricity

After going through the meter, the electricity is connected to a *distribution panel*. This panel is a box that contains the switches used to turn off the electricity in the house and it also encloses the safety devices used to protect the various circuits in the home. Either fuses or circuit breakers are used to safeguard the electrical circuits. They open the circuit and stop the flow of electricity whenever too much current starts to flow. If too much current is allowed to flow, the wires in the house could get hot and start a fire.

These safety devices protect the circuit against "short circuits" and from overloads. Short circuits often occur when the insulation covering the wires connected to an electrical appliance such as a table lamp becomes worn. The broken insulation allows the wires to touch each other and the result is a short

circuit if the lamp is plugged into the house outlet. To prevent a fire from starting the safety device immediately opens the circuit and stops the electricity from flowing. After the cord has been repaired the fuse can be replaced or the circuit breaker reset.

If too many electrical appliances are plugged into a single electrical circuit the quantity of current needed to operate the appliances could very easily cause heating in the house wiring. This is prevented through the use of protective devices that open the circuit.

In the home there are usually from three to six branch circuits. Each branch circuit has a separate fuse or circuit breaker. When branch circuits are used, an overload or a short circuit stops the electricity from flowing in only one part of the house. The rest of the circuits may be used until the defect has been repaired.

Fuses as a Safety Device

Fuses are of two types, the *plug fuse* and the *cartridge fuse*. See Fig. 18-3. The plug fuse is the most common type of fuse found in the home where 115 volts is

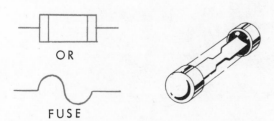

The top symbol can be used for any fusible element.

Fig. 18-3. Three of the fuses are cartridge-type fuses. The fuse on the right is a plug fuse.

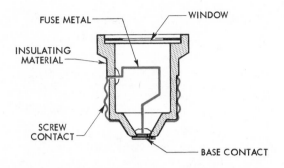

Fig. 18-4. Construction of the plug fuse that is used in homes.

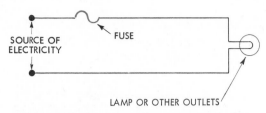

Fig. 18-7. A fuse is connected in series or in one line of the circuit the same as a switch is connected in the circuit. The entire current from the circuit flows through the fuse. If the current flow is greater than the rating of the fuse it will "blow" and the circuit is opened.

Fig. 18-5. A good fuse and a burned-out fuse. Fuses are enclosed in a case to make them safe to screw in and also to prevent the hot metal from scattering when the fuse "blows."

Fig. 18-8. Placing a fuse in the type of fuse box found in some homes.

Fig. 18-6. Cartridge-type fuses are used in this box, which has a switch that disconnects all circuits.

used. Cartridge fuses are used where heavy current is needed and on circuits using 230 volts or more.

The important part of the fuse is the thin strip of metal, usually zinc, that will melt when the current flow becomes too great (Figs. 18-4 thru 18-8). The size of the zinc strip is selected for the number of amperes of current that it will carry without melting. Each fuse is marked to indicate the amount of current it will handle before it "blows."

Most branch circuits in the home use a 15-ampere plug-type fuse. It is important to use only 15-ampere fuses in these circuits. If larger fuses are installed the wire of the circuit can be overloaded and a fire could result from the heat developed in the wire.

Using Circuit Breakers To Protect Circuits

The type of circuit protection that is commonly used in new homes is called a *circuit breaker* (Fig. 18-9). It automatically turns off the current when too many amperes flow in the circuit. The circuit breaker is a combination switch and safety device. When the switch is turned to the "on" position the circuit breaker contacts are closed. If a short or overload occurs the breaker opens the circuit. After the short has been repaired or the load cut down the breaker can be reset by turning the switch to the "off" position and then back to the "on" position.

The use of circuit breakers eliminates hunting for a fuse and also prevents a

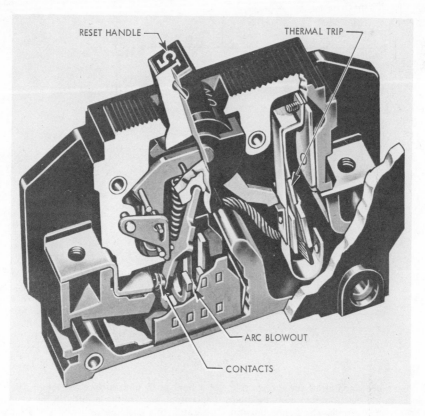

Fig. 18-9. Cutaway view of a circuit breaker unit.

careless person from installing a large fuse that could overload the circuit. Circuit breakers are labeled, as fuses, with their current-carrying capacity.

There are two types of circuit breakers—the heat strip breaker and the magnetic breaker.

Heat Strip Breaker

The *heat strip breaker* uses a strip made of two different kinds of metal either welded or riveted together. When too much current flows through the strip the metals get hot. The heat makes the metals expand but, since they are two different kinds of metal, one expands more than the other. Since the lower metal strip expands more than the upper piece, the heat strip curves upward. This bending of the heater strip allows a spring in the switch to open the contact points. See Fig. 18-10. The amount of current necessary to open the contact depends upon the design of the heater strip.

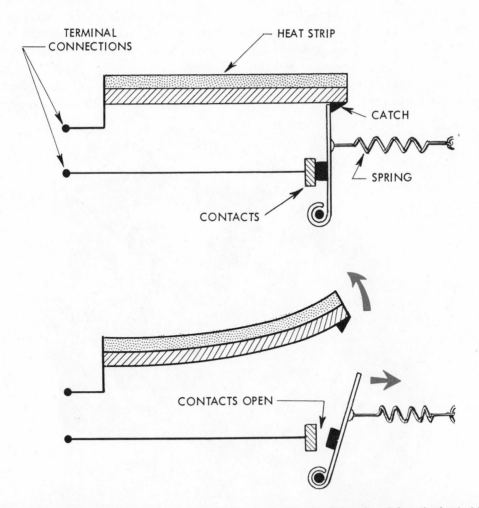

Fig. 18-10. These drawings show the construction of a heat strip circuit breaker. When the heat strip is cool, the catch holds the contact points together. If too much current flows through the terminal connections, the heat strip expands and bends upward. The catch releases the arm and the spring opens the contact points. To use the breaker again it must be reset so that the contact points are closed.

The Magnetic Circuit Breaker

The *magnetic circuit breaker* uses an electromagnetic coil to open the circuit. See Fig. 18-11. A coil is connected in series with the circuit so that all of the current must pass through it. When the current becomes too great the magnetic pull of the coil moves the metal bar called the *armature* toward the coil. As the ar-

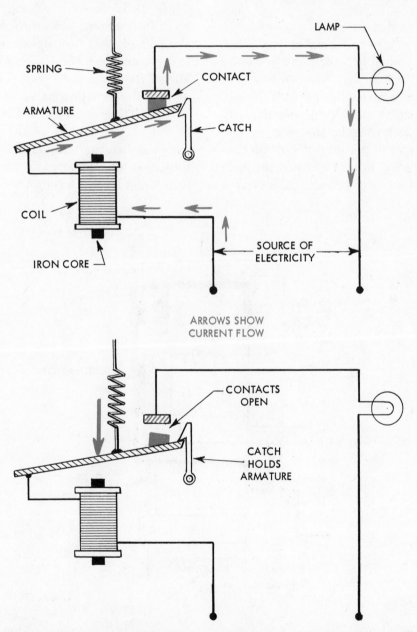

Fig. 18-11. These drawings show the construction of a magnetic circuit breaker. The coil has all of the current from the circuit flowing through it. When the breaker is set the contact points are closed and the circuit is complete. If too much current flows through the circuit, the coil pulls the iron armature down, opening the contact points. The catch holds the armature from moving upward to close the contact points again.

mature moves toward the coil it breaks the contact points and opens the circuit.

Both the heater strip breaker and the magnetic breaker must be reset by hand before the circuit is closed again.

Relays

A device that operates very much like the magnetic circuit breaker is a relay. The relay might be called an electrically operated switch that has many advantages over a manually operated switch. When opening and closing circuits with high voltages, the relay makes it possible to control these circuits without the danger of coming in contact with the high voltage. Also, circuits using high current can be much more readily controlled through the use of a relay.

The basic parts of a relay consist of a *coil*, a *magnetic core*, an *armature*, and a *set of contacts*.

Fig. 18-12 shows a normally open relay. When current flows through the coil the magnetic flux becomes strong enough to overcome the force of the spring and to attract the armature down. This movement of the armature causes the contacts to close. These contacts, which are wired to terminals A and B, of the relay, are used just like the terminals on a regular switch. If the contacts are closed, terminals A and B form a completed circuit.

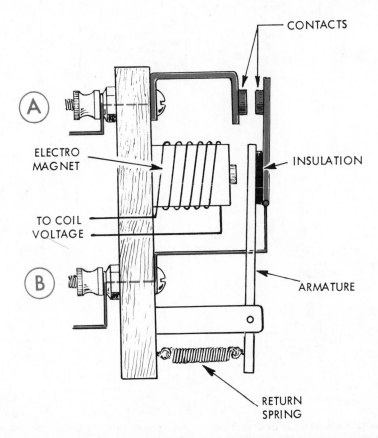

Fig. 18-12. A drawing of a normally open relay. When the coil is energized the armature is pulled toward the electromagnet, closing the contacts. The circuit from terminals A and B is completed and current flows through the colored parts of the relay.

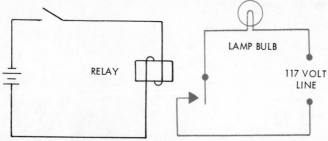

Fig. 18-13. A low voltage relay circuit being used to control a 117-volt AC circuit is shown in the photograph. The schematic with the high voltage portion in color is on the right.

Controlling High Voltage With Low Voltage

A comparatively low voltage can be used to close a relay and the contacts on the relay used to control a high voltage circuit. Relays make it possible to control circuits by remote control since the switch for operating the relay can be some distance away from the relay.

An example of a low voltage circuit controlling a high voltage circuit is shown in Fig. 18-13. The four dry cells producing six volts DC are used to close the relay contacts, which turns on the 117-volt lamp. The six-volt DC relay coil is connected to the dry cells and when the manually operated switch is closed the

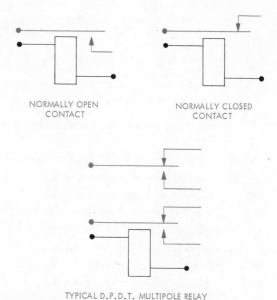

Fig. 18-14. Symbols of three different types of contacts used with relays.

relay contacts complete the circuit to the 117-volt AC lamp. When the low voltage circuit is not energized, the lamp remains off.

Just as found on different designed switches, it is possible to obtain a variety of contacts with relays. These contacts are either normally open or normally closed. Fig. 18-14 illustrates the symbol drawing for several type relays.

When using relays it is necessary to know whether the relay is a DC or AC coil relay and also to know the voltage rating of the coil. Direct current relays will chatter (vibrate) when used on alternating current.

INTERESTING THINGS TO DO

1. Making a Circuit Breaker.

Materials needed to construct the circuit breaker (Fig. 18-15):

1 Piece of soft steel rod, ⅜″ diameter, ⅛″ thick
2 Pieces wood, ¼″ x 3″ x 5″
2 Fiber or masonite washers, 1″ diameter
1 Piece fiber or cardboard tubing, ⅟₁₆″ wall, ⅜″ inside diameter, 1⅜″ long
5′ Soft iron wire, No. 18
1 Spool enamel-covered wire, No. 22
1 Piece sheet steel, ⅜″ x 2¼″, 20 gage, for contact arm
1 Piece sheet copper, ⅜″ x ⅜″, 20 gage, for contact on contact arm
1 Piece sheet steel, ⅜″ x ½″, 20 gage
1 Piece sheet copper, ⅜″ x 1¼″, 20 gage, for stationary contact
1 Piece sheet fiber, 1″ wide, 2½″ long, ⅛″ thick, for reset lever
1 Piece sheet steel or brass, 1¼″ x 3½″, 22 gage, for holding coil in place
2 Terminal screws
  Miscellaneous screws, nuts, and washers (see text)

This circuit breaker will take the place of a fuse by opening the circuit when the current exceeds the amount for which it is set. The breaker may be adjusted to operate on currents from 1 to 3 amperes and it is adjusted by moving the coil toward or away from the contact arm. As the coil is moved away from the contact arm, more current will be needed to operate the breaker. Less current will be required as the coil is moved closer to the contact arm.

Make a coil form by drilling the fiber washers so that they will fit over the fiber tubing and glue one of them at each end

Fig. 18-15. A magnetic circuit breaker.

of the tubing. Drill two small holes in one of the washers for the coil leads. Cut the piece of iron wire into short sections 1¾" long and pack them into the center of the fiber tubing, as shown in the drawing. Wind the form with six layers of No. 22 magnet wire. Solder the piece of soft iron rod to the piece of sheet steel, 1" from one end. Shape the opposite end to fit snugly around a 6–32 machine screw for the contact arm, as shown in Fig. 18-16. Bend the short piece of sheet steel and solder it to the contact arm op-

posite to the round piece of steel. This piece fits into the slot in the fiber reset lever when the arm is in the "on" position. Bend the smaller piece of sheet copper and solder it to the end of the contact arm, as shown in Fig. 18-16. Drill and shape the larger piece of sheet copper to serve as the stationary contact. Drill and shape the piece of sheet fiber for the reset lever. Secure the parts to one of the pieces of wood, as shown in the assembly drawing. The movable contact arm is held in line with the center of the coil

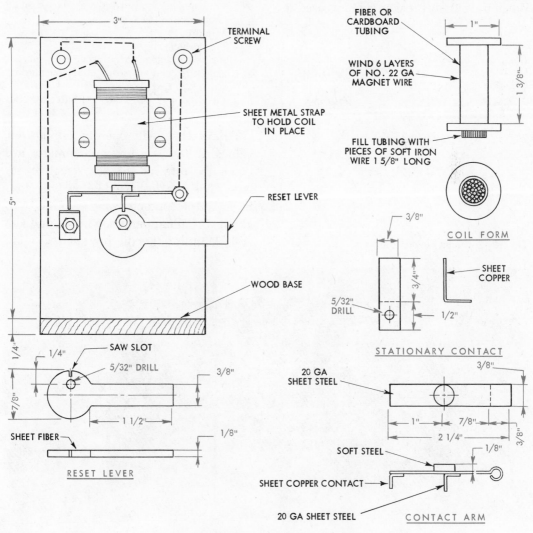

Fig. 18-16. Drawing of circuit breaker.

with a 6–32 machine screw, 1¼″ long, hexagon nuts, and brass washers. Make certain that the arm swings freely on the machine screw, otherwise the breaker will not operate properly. The strap for holding the coil should secure the coil firmly when the screws are tightened, but it should allow the coil to be adjusted when two of the screws are loosened. Wire the circuit breaker as shown by the broken lines on the drawing. Join the two pieces of wood together so that the breaker will stand in an upright position. When the circuit breaker is being used it

should be connected so that it will be in series with the lamp or device it is to control, as shown in Fig. 18-17.

While this circuit breaker was designed for low-voltage transformer or battery circuits, it will function satisfactorily on higher voltages if it is enclosed in a metal box to prevent contact with current-carrying parts.

2. Making a Sensitive Relay.

Materials needed to construct the sensitive relay (Fig. 18-18):

1 Loudspeaker output transformer, or small choke coil. (see text)
1 Wood base
4 Fahnestock clips
4 Strips sheet steel, No. 22 ga., ½″ wide, for armature, contact strips, and coil holding strip. (see text)
1 Piece copper wire, No. 14, bare, for contacts

Relays that will operate on current values as low as a few milliamperes are generally referred to as "sensitive relays." The one described below will close or make the contacts come together with about six milliamperes flowing through its coil. Winding a coil for such a relay

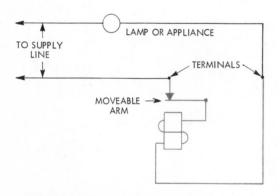

TO SUPPLY LINE

LAMP OR APPLIANCE

TERMINALS

MOVEABLE ARM

Fig. 18-17. Circuit breaker diagram.

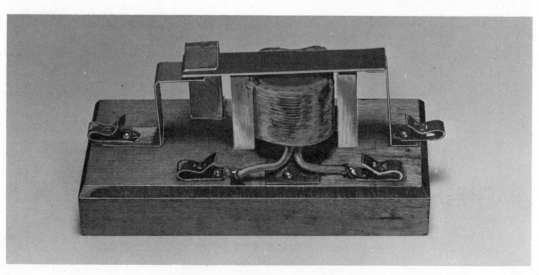

Fig. 18-18. The completed sensitive relay.

would be an extremely tedious job because of the small wire used and the large number of turns required, but an excellent substitute is available in the primary winding of the output transformer that is often discarded with a defective radio or television loudspeaker. Small choke coils such as used in radio power supplies may also be converted to sensitive relays.

Remove the top section of the transformer or choke coil core so that the ends of the core will be about even with the top of the coil. On some transformers this section is in one unit, while on others the metal laminations are interleaved so that the core will have to be taken apart and reassembled. Clean the bottom of the core and solder a strip of metal to it so that the core may be secured to the wood base. See Fig. 18-19. Since transformers and choke coils of different manufacture will vary in size, no bending dimensions are given. Both the armature strip and the contact strips should be shaped so

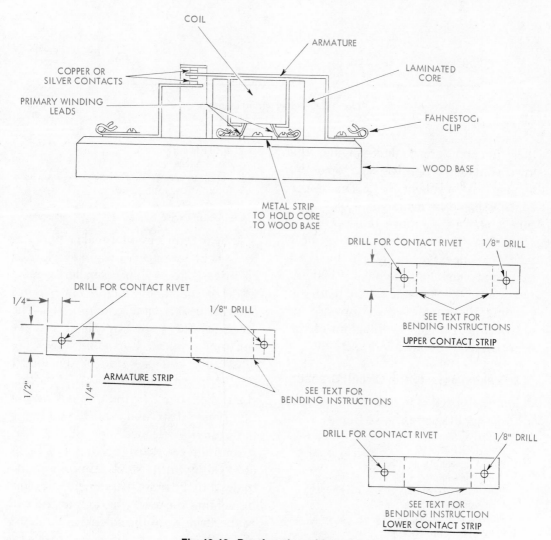

Fig. 18-19. Drawing of sensitive relay.

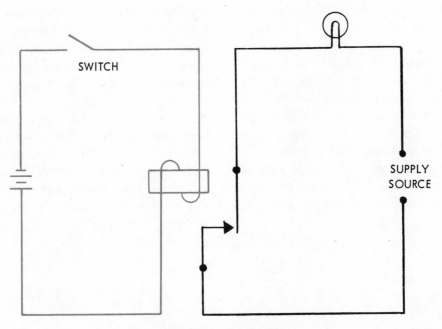

Fig. 18-20. Relay wiring diagram.

that the armature contact touches the lower contact when it clears the top of the laminations by about $\frac{1}{32}''$. The upper contact should be made when the armature is about $\frac{1}{16}''$ above the top of the core. Make the contacts by riveting short pieces of copper wire in holes in the metal strips and then filing them flat. Final adjustment of the contacts can be made by bending the contact strips upward or downward. A schematic diagram of the sensitive relay is shown in Fig. 18-20.

3. Making a Heat Strip Circuit Breaker.

Materials needed to construct the heat strip circuit breaker (Fig. 18-21):

Wood base, 3" x 5½"
1 Wood dowel, ½" x 2"
1 Wood dowel, ½" x 1"
1 Wood dowel, ½" x ¾"
1 Piece sheet steel, ¼" x 3⅝" (see text)
1 Piece sheet steel, ¼" x 1⅜"
1 Piece spring brass, ¼" x 3½", 24 or 26 ga.
1 Miniature lamp socket
1 Flashlight bulb, 2 or 3 volts

1 or 2 Flashlight cells
2 Terminal screws
1 Machine screw, R. H. brass, 4-40 x 1¼"
3 Brass M. S. nuts, 4-40
1 Spring
Connecting wire

A heat strip circuit breaker operates from heat produced by an overloaded electrical circuit. This smaller version works on the same principle but requires only the heat from a lighted match. The pieces of sheet steel specified may be cut from a tin can. Clean one side of the brass strip and one side of the longer steel strip with steel wool. Apply a thin coating of solder to the cleaned side of the brass strip and spread soldering paste on the cleaned side of the steel strip. Align the strips together on a block of wood, with the steel strip on top and solder it to the brass strip. Begin soldering by holding the soldering iron at the end of the strips until the solder on the brass melts, then press the strips together with

Fig. 18-21. Heat strip circuit breaker complete.

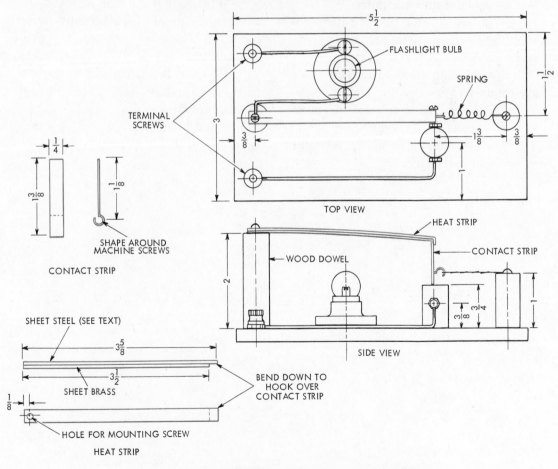

Fig. 18-22. Detail drawing of heat strip circuit breaker.

a piece of wood until the solder sets. Proceed in that manner along the strip until both pieces are securely soldered together. Drill a mounting hole in the strip and bend the opposite end of the steel strip to a right angle to serve as a catch for the contact strip. See Fig. 18-22. Shape the contact strip as shown in the drawing and solder a wire hook to it to hold the spring. Assemble the parts and mount them on the base with glue or wood screws. Connect the parts together in series and one or two flashlight cells to the terminals. To operate the breaker, hook the heat strip over the end of the contact strip to light the flashlight bulb. Pass a lighted match back and forth slowly under the heat strip a few times. Within a few seconds the heat strip will move upward, releasing the breaker strip and extinguishing the light.

REVIEW QUESTIONS

1. What is the voltage of a three-wire service brought into a home?

2. What is the purpose of safety devices used in home wiring circuits?

3. Name two types of fuses.

4. Draw a diagram showing how fuses are connected in a lighting circuit.

5. What size fuse is used in most branch circuits in the home?

6. How is a circuit breaker reset after it has opened the circuit?

7. Name two types of circuit breakers.

8. Why is it important to locate the trouble in an electrical circuit before replacing a fuse or resetting a circuit breaker?

9. How is a heat strip constructed?

10. Explain how a magnetic circuit breaker operates.

11. What is the moving part of a magnetic circuit breaker called?

UNIT 19
ELECTRICAL WIRING IN THE HOME

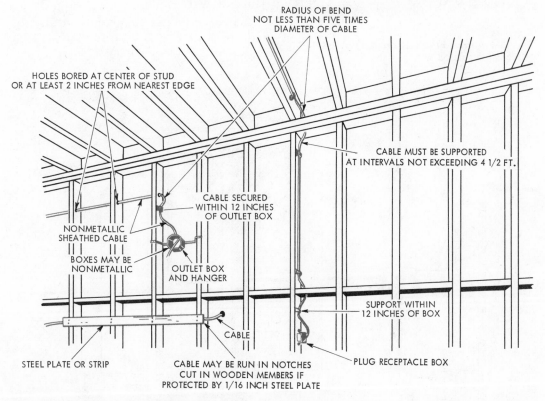

Fig. 19-1. Typical nonmetallic sheathed cable installation. (From *Interior Electrical Wiring*, American Technical Society.)

Wiring Systems

Electrical circuits in homes are connected to wall outlets, lights, and power outlets such as stoves and hot water heaters. Special protective covering as in Fig. 19-1 must be provided for the wires that are used inside the walls, in the ceiling, and under the floor. Several systems are used to safeguard the wiring in the home. The main types of wiring are (1) nonmetallic sheathed cable, Figs. 19-2 and 19-3; (2) armored cable,

Fig. 19-3. Method of fastening nonmetallic sheathed cable to floor joists and ceiling, and to switch and receptacle outlet boxes. (General Cable Co.)

Fig. 19-2. Nonmetallic sheathed cable. (Crescent Insulated Wire & Cable Co.)

Fig. 19-4. Armored cable is properly called "AC." (Crescent Insulated Wire & Cable Co.)

known as AC (also BX, which is a trade name), Fig. 19-4; and (3) electrical steel tube called conduit wiring (Fig. 19-5). Each locality has regulations regarding the type of wiring system that may be used.

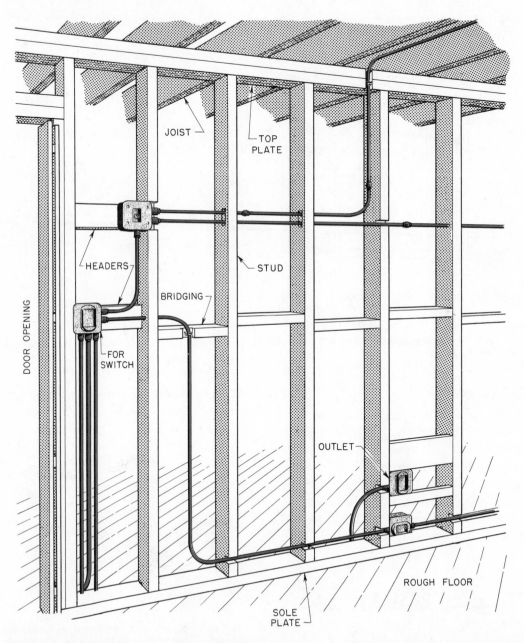

Fig. 19-5. This illustration shows the installation of thin-wall steel tubing in a wood studding partition wall. (Republic Steel Corp.)

Convenience Outlets

Wall outlets called *convenience outlets* are mounted in metal boxes called *outlet boxes*. The outlet is usually of the duplex type as shown in Fig. 19-6. Two wires carry the flow of electricity to the wall outlet. These wires start at the switch box where they are connected to

a fuse or circuit breaker. Several outlets may be connected in parallel to the same pair of wires. Number 12 wire is usually used for convenience outlets.

The third wire (Fig. 19-6), connected to the outlet, is a ground wire that goes to the water pipes in the house. On the attachment plug, sometimes a third ter-

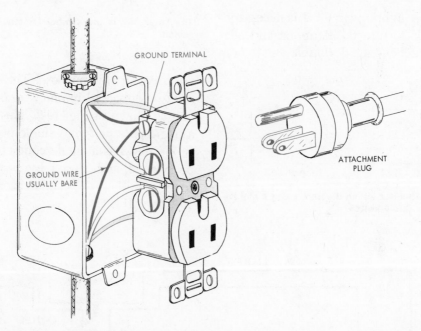

Fig. 19-6. Typical attachment plug and duplex receptacle with terminals for grounding as now required by the National Electric Code.

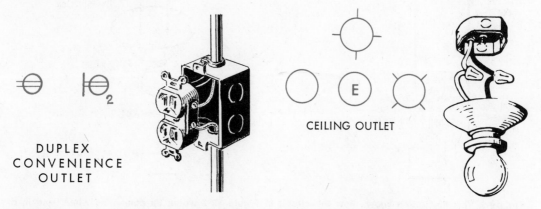

DUPLEX CONVENIENCE OUTLET

CEILING OUTLET

The duplex outlet is the standard kind and the small numeral "2" is generally not used with the symbol.

The circle at the left is the latest standard. The letter "E" may be used to prevent confusion with other kinds of symbols.

minal, a "U" ground, is available. The ground terminal is connected to a third wire that connects to the body or frame of the appliance or fixture. This wire protects someone from getting a shock in the event either of the "hot" wires become shorted to the body or frame of the appliance or fixture.

Using Single-Pole Switches

In every lighting circuit it is necessary to be able to turn the lights on and off. Wall switches called *tumbler switches*

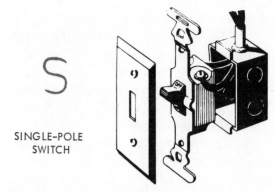

SINGLE-POLE
SWITCH

The letter "S" is the symbol for any single-pole switch.

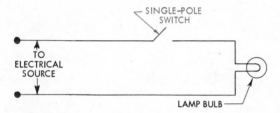

Fig. 19-7. This is a wiring diagram using a single-pole single-throw switch.

are used for this purpose. The switch is always connected in one wire of the circuit as shown in Fig. 19-7. This is called a *single-pole switch*. A single-pole switch is one that has a single contact that can be opened and closed by pushing the tumbler either up or down. See Figs. 19-8 thru 19-11.

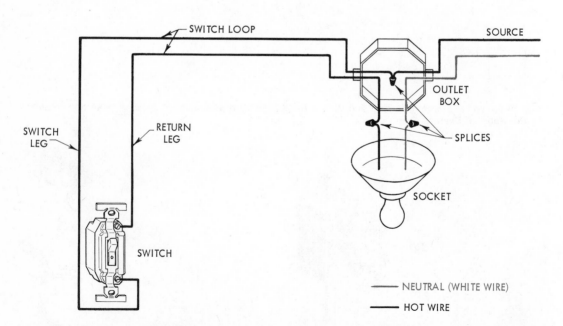

Fig. 19-8. This illustration shows how the circuit in Figure 19-7 would be connected when used in the home. All splices and connections are made inside of the boxes. Solderless connectors are used to join the wires together. The colored solid line represents the neutral wire. This wire is usually solid white in color.

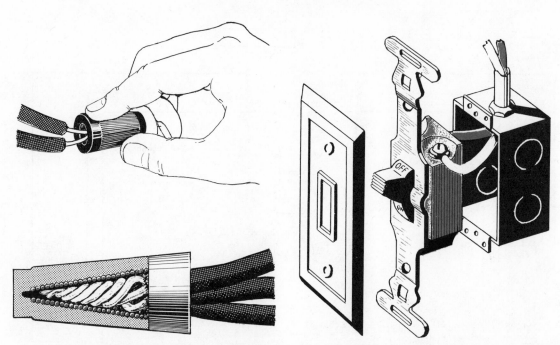

Fig. 19-9. Solderless connectors, called "wire nuts," used for splicing purposes are screwed on to the splice. The cone-shaped spiral spring inside of the molded body presses the wires together, making solder unnecessary.

Fig. 19-10. Single-pole switch. For protection the switch it is placed inside of a metal box called a switch box. The front of the switch is covered with a switch plate, usually made of a plastic material.

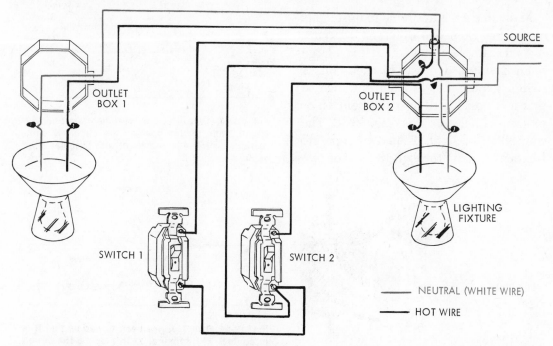

Fig. 19-11. Two single-pole switches are sometimes placed side by side in the wall so that each can control separate lights in the room. Switch No. 1 controls outlet box No. 1 and switch No. 2 controls outlet box No. 2.

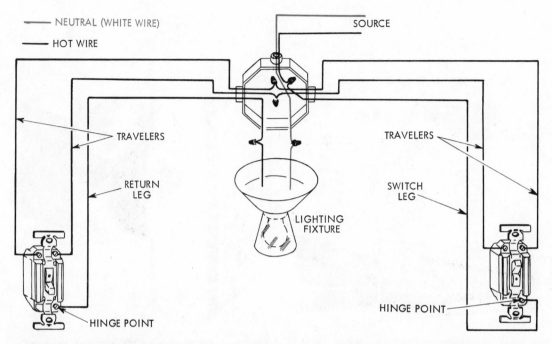

Fig. 19-12. Two three-way switches can be used to control a single light from two different locations.

Using Three-Way Switches

Many times it is desirable to turn lights on and off from two different locations. A good example of this is found in a large room having a doorway at each end. A switch is placed near each entrance so that it is possible to turn the light on or off from either door. See Fig. 19-12. The controlling of lights from two separate locations is done through the use of two

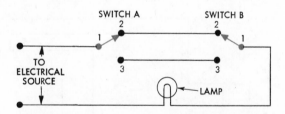

Fig. 19-13. Two three-way switches controlling a single lamp. In this position the circuit is complete as switch A is in contact with terminal 2 the same as switch B.

S_3

THREE-WAY
SWITCH

The small "3" tells that the symbol is for a three-way switch.

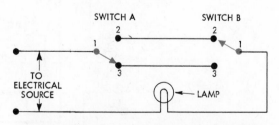

Fig. 19-14. Switch A has been turned so that it is in contact with terminal 3. This opens the circuit and the lamp is off. To turn the light on again switch B can be turned to terminal 3 or switch A must be turned back to terminal 2.

three-way switches. Three-way switches have three terminals for wire connections instead of two terminals as found on single pole switches. Figs. 19-13 and 19-14 show the principle of operation of the three-way circuit.

Mercury Switches

The most common type of switch makes or breaks the contacts through the mechanical movement of the tumbler. This switch makes a distinct "click" each time it is opened or closed as the moving blade goes in or out of the contact points. A switch that is very desirable because of its silent operation is called a *mercury*

switch. The mercury switch has a small quantity of liquid mercury that is moved against the contact points. Through the use of mercury it is possible to have a switch that does not "click" when it is turned on or off. It also eliminates radio interference during switching.

Reading Electrical Blueprints

When plans for homes are developed by an architect the placement of all of the electrical outlets, lights and other electrical connections are shown on the blueprints. Symbols are used to represent each of the electrical outlets. See Fig. 19-15.

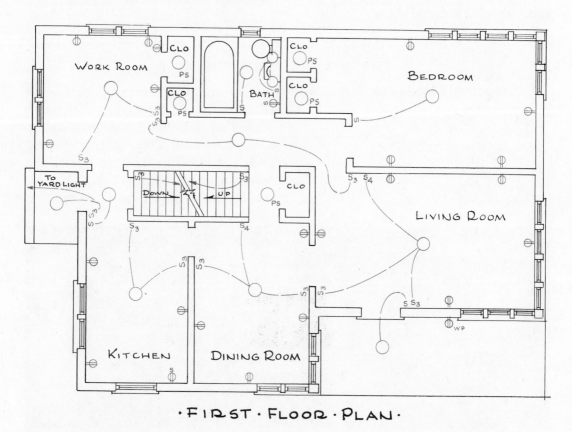

· FIRST · FLOOR · PLAN ·

Fig. 19-15. A blueprint of the first floor plan of a house showing the location of the various electrical outlets. Symbols are used for each of the outlets.

OPEN

CLOSED

SWITCHES

This is how the basic switch symbols are to be drawn.

PUSH BUTTON

This is the symbol for the common spring-return push button.

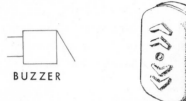

BUZZER

The buzzer may be identified by adding the abbreviation AC or DC within the square.

BELL

This symbol is used for the familiar call bell.

INTERESTING THINGS TO DO

1. Connecting a Single Pole Switch to a Light Socket.

Materials needed:

1 Light socket or receptacle
1 Fuse block
2 10-ampere fuse plugs
1 Single-pole switch
Connecting wire

Connect one terminal of the fuse block to one of the socket terminals. Connect a wire from the other socket terminal to a switch terminal. Connect the remaining switch terminal to the fuse block. The correct wiring is shown in Fig. 19-16. This is the type of circuit used to control a

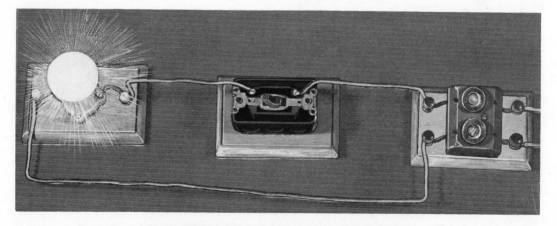

Fig. 19-16. Using a single pole switch to control a light.

light when it is necessary to turn it on or off from only one location. Whenever a home or building has been wired properly, the wiring is so arranged that the neutral or grounded side of the lighting circuit is connected to the screw or shell terminal of the socket. This is done so that if one accidentally touches the base of a lamp while removing or replacing it and while standing on a damp floor, he will not receive a shock. With the help of your instructor trace the wiring in your school shop and wire the switch circuit so that it will follow the safety procedure outlined above.

2. Connecting a Three-Way Switch.

Materials needed:

1 Light socket or receptacle
1 Fuse block
2 10-ampere fuse plugs
2 Three-way switches
Connecting wire

A three-way switch is used when it is desired to turn a light on or off from two locations, such as the ends of a hall or the bottom and top landings of a stairway. A three-way switch has a single terminal at one end of the switch and two terminals at the opposite end. The single ter-

minal is connected within the switch so that it makes contact with one of the other terminals at all times, whether the switch lever is in the up or down position.

Connect one terminal of the fuse block to one of the socket terminals. Connect the other socket terminal to the single terminal on one of the switches. Connect a wire from the remaining fuse block terminal to the single terminal on the other three-way switch. Connect the remaining two terminals on one switch to similar terminals on the other switch. These connections between the two switches are generally referred to as *travelers*. Connect the fuse block to a 115-volt circuit and if all connections have been made properly the lamp may be turned on or off from either switch. The correct wiring is shown in Fig. 19-17.

3. Connecting a Four-Way Switch.

Materials needed:

1 Light socket or receptacle
1 Fuse block
2 10-ampere fuse plugs
2 Three-way switches
1 Four-way switch
Connecting wire

Wherever it is desired to turn a light

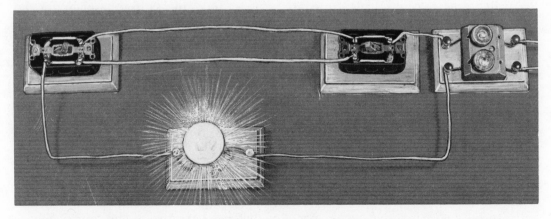

Fig. 19-17. Using two three-way switches so that a light can be controlled from two locations.

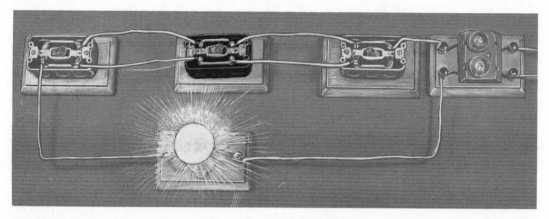

Fig. 19-18. Connecting a four-way switch circuit so that a light can be controlled from three locations.

or group of lights on or off from more than two locations, two three-way switches, together with one four-way switch for each additional control point, must be used. By adding one additional four-way switch to the circuit for each control point, the number of control points are unlimited. This type of switching circuit is very convenient for long hallways or stairways with a number of landings and makes it possible for a switch at any point to work independently of the other switches.

A four-way switch has two terminals at each end which are connected within the switch so that at either position of the switch arm, two terminals are connected directly across to the opposite terminals, or diagonally across to the opposite terminals. When you have finished wiring your circuit you may trace the path of current through the switch connections and see just how each switch can control the light independently of the other switches. In wiring the four-way circuit the procedure for wiring the three-way circuit is followed, with the exception that a four-way switch is connected between the two wires that would nor-

mally connect the two three-way switches together. Connect the fuse block to a 115-volt circuit and if all connections have been made properly the lamp may be turned on or off with any of the switches. The correct wiring is shown in Fig. 19-18.

4. Making a Home Lighting Dimmer.

Materials needed:

1 Dual lighting switch, S. P. S. T.
1 Dual switch plate
1 Silicon rectifier, 6 amperes, 400 volts

Means for controlling brightness is becoming an attractive feature for home lighting. Subdued lighting is not only desirable for TV viewing, but it also creates a more pleasant atmosphere for the enjoyment of music or just meeting with friends.

The dimmer you are about to make is a simple arrangement of a silicon rectifier and a dual switch. Dual switches consist of two single pole switches combined in one unit and arranged to operate horizontally, so that they can replace a switch of the regular type.

Attach the rectifier to two of the switch terminals as shown in Fig. 19-19. Some switches have two of the terminals con-

Fig. 19-19. The completed dimmer switch. The silicon rectifier is connected to two terminals of the dual switch.

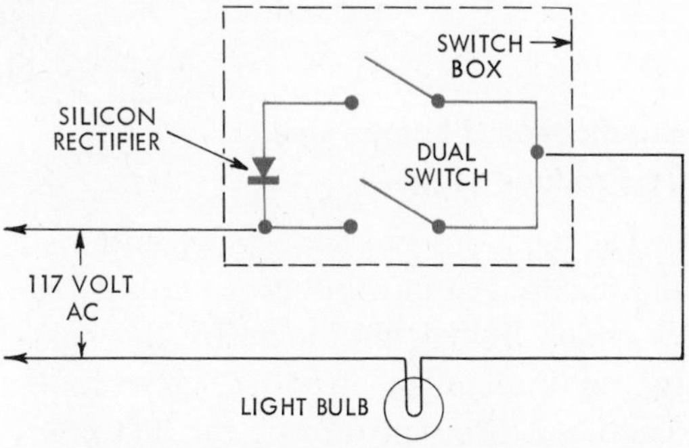

SWITCH BOX

SILICON RECTIFIER

DUAL SWITCH

117 VOLT AC

LIGHT BULB

Fig. 19-20. Wiring diagram for light dimmer. Each switch may be operated independently.

nected together inside the switch body, so, if that type switch is used the rectifier should be connected across the two separate terminals. Wire the dual switch to the circuit as shown in the diagram, Fig. 19-20. The current and voltage ratings for the rectifier were purposely specified at high values to permit it to operate at normal temperatures. Rectifiers of this type are subject to damage when overheated.

In operation the rectifier passes only one-half cycle of the alternating current supply, which has an effect similar to reducing the current flowing through the lamp by approximately one half.

REVIEW QUESTIONS

1. Name three types of wiring systems.

2. Why are protective coverings necessary for house wiring?

3. Give the common name used for wall outlets.

4. What size wire is usually used for wall outlets?

5. Draw a wiring diagram showing how a switch is connected in a circuit to turn a light off and on.

6. Why are convenience outlets and wall switches placed in metal boxes?

7. Draw a wiring diagram showing how two three-way switches are used to turn lights on and off from two locations.

8. Why are mercury switches used in some homes?

9. Draw a diagram of a room in your home, using symbols to show the location of convenience outlets, lights, and switches.

UNIT 20
TYPES OF LIGHTING

Incandescent Lamps Used To Produce Light

The incandescent lamp was mentioned in Unit 12. An incandescent lamp is one in which light is produced by the heating of a filament inside a glass bulb. Thomas Edison introduced the first practical incandescent lamp in 1879. Edison's lamp bulb contained a carbon filament sealed inside of an evacuated glass bulb (Fig. 20-1). All of the air had to be removed from the bulb to keep the carbon from burning up.

The modern incandescent lamp contains a spiral tungsten filament that will withstand very high temperatures. To prevent the tungsten from burning up, the oxygen is pumped out of the glass bulb. A small amount of argon and nitrogen gas is then put inside the bulb. This gas increases the light-producing ability of the bulb. Most incandescent lamps are designed to burn from 750 to 1,000 hours.

Shapes and Sizes of Incandescent Lamps

Incandescent lamps come in many shapes and sizes. The general-service type lamps used in the home range from 25 to 300 watts. The larger the wattage the greater the amount of electricity needed for operation of the lamp and the greater the output of light. These bulbs use what is known as a *medium screw-type base*. The glass may be either clear or inside-frosted. Inside-frosted is widely used as it reduces glare. Small lamps used for night lights and Christmas tree lights have either an *intermediate screw-type*

Fig. 20-1. Edison's first electric lamp appeared in 1879.

INCANDESCENT
LIGHT

This symbol is used for all incandescent-filament lights.

Fig. 20-2. Shown in this photograph are four sizes of screw-base type lamps commonly found in the home.

base or a *candelabra base.* Lamps from 300 watts to 1,500 watts use a large base called a *mogul base.* See Fig. 20-2.

Three-Way Incandescent Lamps

Many table and floor lamps use a *three-way lamp.* This means that the lamp can

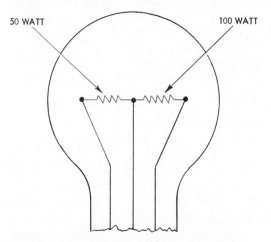

Fig. 20-3. A three-light lamp contains two filaments. The switch is used to select either filament or both can be used at the same time.

produce three different amounts of light. They contain two filaments wired so that either may be used independently or the two filaments used in parallel so that both are on at the same time. See Fig. 20-3. These three-way lamps are usually 50-100-150–watt or 100-200-300–watt lamps. A three-way socket is used for these lamps and special three-way type switches are required to turn on each of the filaments. For example, in the 50-100-150 bulb the switch in the first position turns on the 50-watt filament, in the second position it turns on the 100-watt filament, and in the third position both filaments are in use.

Fluorescent Lamps Used To Produce Light

Fluorescent lamps have become very popular as a means of lighting. This popularity is due to their ability to produce more light with less electricity than incandescent lamps and also fluorescent lamps will last a lot longer without burning out.

The fluorescent lamp gives off light from an "electric discharge," or arc. An electric discharge can give off light just as lightning produces light when it discharges between the sky and the ground. In the fluorescent lamp an electric discharge is made to occur between the two ends of the sealed glass tube.

Construction of the Fluorescent Lamp

A fluorescent lamp is made of a large glass tube that has had all of the air removed from it (Fig. 20-4). After the air

trons produces enough heat to vaporize the mercury. When current flows through a mercury vapor it produces a light called *ultraviolet light*. This ultraviolet is called *violet radiation* and is not a very bright light.

The inside of the fluorescent glass tube is coated with a very thin layer of powdered chemicals called *phosphors*. When the ultraviolet radiation from the mercury vapor hits the coating of phosphors it bursts into a brilliant glow of fluorescent light. The color of the light given off by the fluorescent coating depends upon the type of powder used. If a tube is broken,

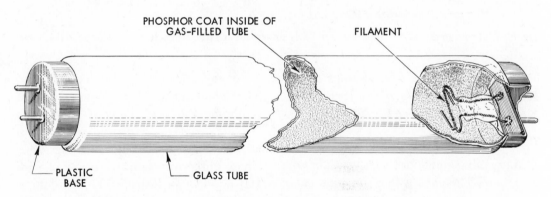

Fig. 20-4. Fluorescent lamps last longer than incandescent lamps and produce more light with less electricity.

has been removed a small amount of gas, such as argon gas, and a very small amount of mercury are placed inside of the tube. At each end of the glass tube is a small lamp filament that is called an *electrode*. These filaments are not intended to produce light but are made so that when they get hot they will throw off electrons. A special coating is placed on the filaments to give off the electrons. The electrons that are thrown off the filaments will flow through the argon gas from one electrode to the other. This flow of elec-

extreme care must be taken to avoid inhaling the phosphorus or getting it into any cuts you might have.

The Starter Switch

The filaments at each end of the fluorescent tube are not needed once the flow of electrons has been started in the tube. After the arc between the two electrodes is started the current will continue to flow—as long as the circuit is completed. The filaments can be disconnected from the circuit as soon as the arc starts.

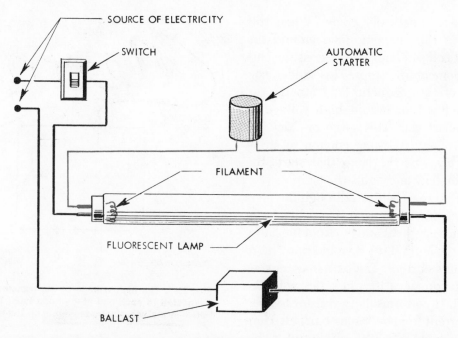

Fig. 20-5. The automatic starter is connected in series with the filaments of a fluorescent-tube circuit. As soon as the arc starts through the tube the starter automatically opens the filament circuit and the filaments are turned off.

A switch called a *starter switch* is connected in series with the filaments as shown in Fig. 20-5. As soon as the filaments become hot enough to give off electrons the starter switch is made to automatically open the filament circuit. These automatic starter switches are usually made of some type of bimetal strip that will open once the filaments become hot. The starter switch is mounted near one end of the tube so that it can easily be replaced if it becomes defective.

The Ballast

The arc in a fluorescent lamp will not start a flow of electrons unless there is a sudden high voltage produced between the two electrodes. It is necessary to get an electric arc to jump from the electrode at one end of the lamp to the electrode at the other end. To obtain this sudden

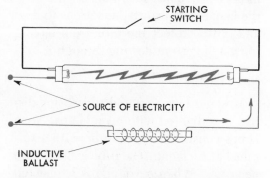

Fig. 20-6. When the starting switch is opened the ballast produces a high-voltage surge that strikes the arc in the fluorescent tube.

high voltage a coil called a *ballast* is connected in series with the circuit, as shown in Fig. 20-6. The ballast is a coil of wire wound around an iron core.

When the fluorescent lamp is first turned on the hot filaments give off electrons. At this time current is flowing through the ballast coil. Then the starting switch automatically opens. When this happens the magnetic field around the ballast coil suddenly collapses as the current momentarily stops. This sudden collapse of the magnetic field around the coil induces an instant high voltage in the ballast coil. This surge or "kick" of high voltage is strong enough to strike the arc across the lamp that starts the electron flow and lights the lamp.

The flow of electrons through the mercury vapor and the argon gas could easily become very great and burn out the lamp. Once the lamp starts it would draw more and more current. The ballast again goes into action since it is in series with the circuit. It performs like a resistor to keep the current from becoming too high. Here the ballast acts like a control valve and limits the amount of current flowing through the tube.

From this we can see that the ballast has two functions (1) to start the arc once the filament has started electrons to flow and (2) to protect the tube from having too much current flowing through it.

Neon Lamps

Most outdoor signs and advertising displays are lighted with neon lamps. Neon lamps consist of a glass tube with a terminal at each end. The tube is filled with neon gas. When a voltage is connected between the two terminals an electrical arc occurs, giving off a colored light. Pure neon gas gives off an orange color. To obtain additional colors other gases are added to the neon gas. Colors such as blue, green, red, yellow, and white are very common.

Some small neon tubes can be ignited with 115 volts. When large signs require longer neon tubes a higher voltage is necessary to light the tube. A step-up trans-

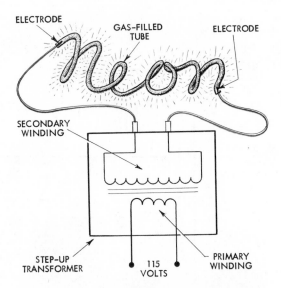

Fig. 20-7. The high voltage of the transformer is connected to each end of the neon tube. The arc between the two electrodes lights up the sign.

former is used to increase the voltage for the tube. See Fig. 20-7.

The longer the tube the higher the voltage must be stepped up. Step-up transformers with secondary voltages anywhere from 1,500 to 15,000 volts are used on neon signs. Since the neon lamp uses very little current, small wire can be used on the primary and secondary windings of the transformers. Because of the high voltages required for the operation of neon signs, it is extremely dangerous to work on these circuits unless the source of power is turned off.

Plastic Fiber Optics Light Guides

Recently developed *light guides,* shown in Fig. 20-8, will conduct light in circles or around sharp corners with no loss of the light passing through them. The guides are made up of a bundle of 0.01" diameter fibers enclosed in a lightproof plastic tube. Each fiber acts as a separate conductor, with the light follow-

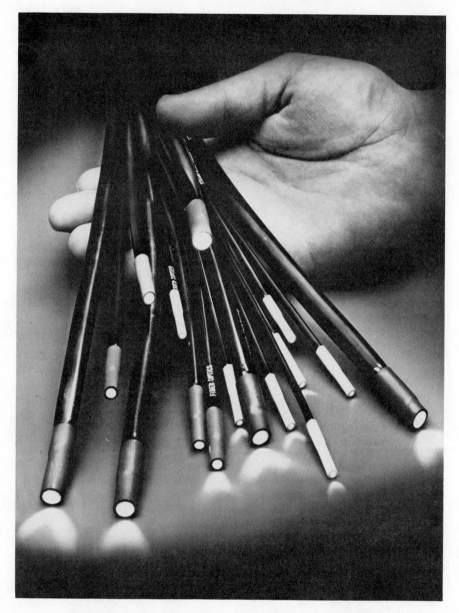

Fig. 20-8. Plastic optics light guides. (American Optical Corp.)

ing a zig-zag path from one end to the other. Some of the many applications of the light guides include illuminating inaccessible areas for inspection, actuating photocell controls from a distance, or providing intriguing home decorations. When a few inches of the outer covering is removed, the ends will spread out like the branches of a small tree. If the guide is illuminated from below with a colored light, the glowing fibers form a cascading fountain of light that is certain to enhance the attractiveness of most modern homes. Sharp corners and curves present no barriers to light passing through the plastic light guides shown in Fig. 20-8.

INTERESTING THINGS TO DO

1. Making an Experimental Plastic Fiber Optics Light Guide.

Materials needed to construct the plastic fiber optics light guide (Figs. 20-9 and 20-10):

1 Piece plastic fiber optics light guide 0.130″ diameter (see text)
1 Flexible test clip insulator, Mueller No. 49
1 Flashlight, penlight type
Masking tape, ½″ wide

Insert end of flashlight in large end of test clip insulator. Insert an end of the light conductor fibers through the small end of the test clip insulator and push it forward until it reaches the tip of the bulb in the flashlight. Mark the end of the light conductor fibers with a pencil where they enter the small end of the test clip insulator. Remove the insulator from the

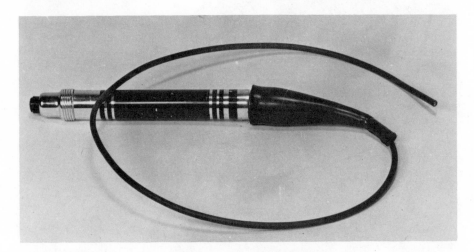

Fig. 20-9. Fiber optics light guides.

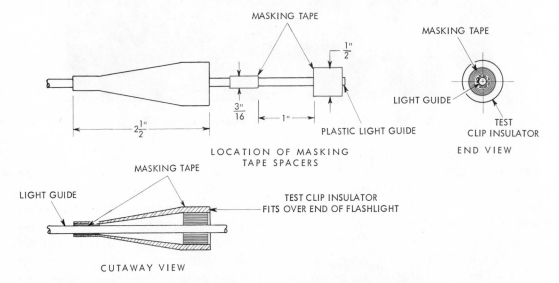

Fig. 20-10. Fiber optics light guide attached to a flashlight.

flashlight and push the light conductor through the insulator until the pencil mark is visible. Wrap the light conductor with masking tape as shown in the drawing. The purpose of the masking tape spacers is to keep the light conductor centered. They should be slightly larger than the inside diameters of the ends of the insulator, so that when withdrawn within the insulator, they will hold in place. The distance between the spacers may vary slightly from that shown, depending upon the make of the flashlight used. Plastic fiber light guide material is available in lengths of two feet or longer from Edmund Scientific Company, Barrington, New Jersey, and Poly Paks, Lynnfield, Massachusetts.

2. Making a Table Lamp.

Materials needed to construct the table lamp (Fig. 20-11):

1 Piece wood, 1″ x 5″ x 8″
1 Piece wood, 1½″ x 3½″ x 8″
1 Threaded nipple, brass or steel, ⅛″ pipe size, 1″ long
1 Socket, brass, pull-chain, threaded cap
6′ Lamp cord, parallel, No. 18
1 Attachment plug cap.

Make a ¼″ bevel along the upper edge of the piece of wood that is to be used for the lamp base. Starting at the center of one end of the base, drill a 5⁄16″ hole lengthwise halfway through it. Drill another 5⁄16″ hole through the base at a right angle to the first hole at the center, so

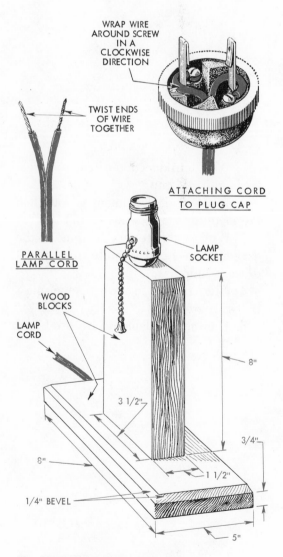

WRAP WIRE AROUND SCREW IN A CLOCKWISE DIRECTION

TWIST ENDS OF WIRE TOGETHER

ATTACHING CORD TO PLUG CAP

PARALLEL LAMP CORD

LAMP SOCKET

WOOD BLOCKS

LAMP CORD

8″

3 1/2″

3/4″

8″

1 1/2″

1/4″ BEVEL

5″

Fig. 20-12. Table lamp assembly.

Fig. 20-11. Table lamp.

230 ELECTRICITY AND ELECTRONICS—BASIC

that the two holes will meet. Beginning at the center of one end of the piece of wood that is to be used for the upright section, drill a $^{11}/_{32}''$ hole lengthwise, half-way through it. Drill another $^{11}/_{32}''$ hole through the other end of the wood block, so that the two holes meet. Screw the pipe nipple into one end of the block so that only $^{1}/_{4}''$ extends above the wood. Secure the upright piece to the base with glue

or wood screws as shown in Fig. 20-12. Insert the cord through the wood base and stand. Screw the socket cap to the nipple and connect the socket to the cord. Attach a plug cap to the other end of the lamp cord.

The lamp may be finished natural with clear shellac or lacquer, or painted to match any color scheme.

REVIEW QUESTIONS

1. Who introduced the first practical incandescent lamp?

2. What kind of filament is found in the modern incandescent lamp?

3. Why is it necessary to remove the oxygen from the glass bulb in an incandescent lamp?

4. Give the reason why some glass bulbs are frosted.

5. How many filaments are used in a three-way incandescent lamp?

6. What is the purpose of the filament in a fluorescent lamp?

7. What material is used to coat the inside of a fluorescent lamp?

8. What is the purpose of the starter switch in a fluorescent lamp circuit?

9. Name several uses for the plastic light guide other than those mentioned in the text.

UNIT 21
HEATING WITH ELECTRICITY

Heating Houses With Electricity

The heating of homes and commercial buildings with electricity has shown remarkable growth, and indications are that it will continue to expand. This progress has been made because of the availability of electric power at favorable rates and because of the development of new and effective heating equipment.

A variety of methods are being used to provide indoor heating and comfort through electricity. These heater units are made in a number of types and styles and can be classified by mounting or location as follows:

1. Portable heaters
2. Wall mounted heaters
3. Ceiling heaters
4. Baseboard heaters
5. Floor or slab heaters
6. Central heating systems

The elements used in almost all heaters include a wire with a high resistance. Nickel and chromium is used in most heating elements with iron and manganese sometimes added to the metal alloy. Most systems use a thermostat to turn the electricity going to the element on or off automatically to maintain the desired temperature.

Types of Heaters

Some portable heaters use a metal reflector to direct the heat since radiant heat can be reflected the same as light. Other portable type heaters use a fan or blower inside the cabinet to blow the air over the heating element and distribute heat into the room. Wall mounted heaters are very similar to portable heaters except that they are permanently installed. Fig. 21-1 illustrates air circulation from both the radiant and the blower type heaters.

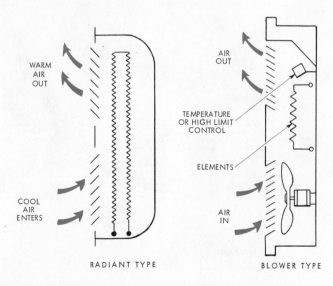

WARM AIR OUT

COOL AIR ENTERS

RADIANT TYPE

AIR OUT

TEMPERATURE OR HIGH LIMIT CONTROL

ELEMENTS

AIR IN

BLOWER TYPE

Fig. 21-1. Wall mounted heaters have the heater element located so that the air will circulate past the element and be distributed into the room.

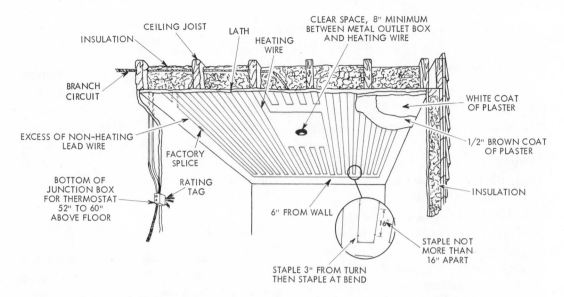

Fig. 21-2. This figure shows the materials used in the construction of a ceiling radiant heating system. (General Electric)

Fig. 21-3. Installing electric radiant heating panels before completing the ceiling. (Electrical Products Div., 3M Co.)

Ceiling heaters are embedded cable (Fig. 21-2) or radiant panels (Fig. 21-3). The embedded ceiling heating system is installed during building construction. The heater cable, a continuous length of insulated resistance wire, is precut by the manufacturer to a specific output (wattage). Radiant heating panels are available in a variety of sizes and heat output. One common method of construction uses a heat producing grid made of stamped sheet of resistance metal laminated between two layers of glass. Panels may be obtained for 120 or 240 volts.

Baseboard heaters are installed at the floor level, usually on an outside wall under windows, as in Fig. 21-4. These units usually have a completely encased heater element with heat dissipating fins as shown in Fig. 21-5.

Fig. 21-4. This figure shows a baseboard heater unit located against the wall at floor level and under the windows. (Bryant Electric Co.)

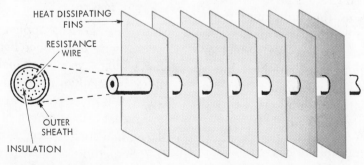

Fig. 21-5. This figure shows the construction of an enclosed heater element that uses fins to dissipate the heat to the surrounding air.

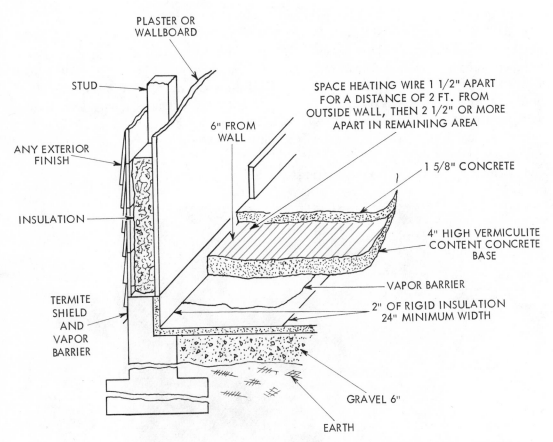

Fig. 21-6. This figure shows the construction of a concrete floor heating system. (General Electric)

Fig. 21-6 shows how a concrete floor heating system has the heating wire placed in the concrete. The heater element comes in the form of mats or cables which are placed slightly below the surface when the concrete is laid.

In addition to the individual room heaters, central heating systems are also available. These systems use a duct or a piping system to distribute heat. Electric furnaces or heat pumps are the main source of heat. Heat pumps can be used for either heating or cooling.

**Types of Heating Appliances
for the Home**

Many types of heating appliances are used around the home. Some of these are:

Toasters
Waffle irons
Electric flat irons
Water heaters
Laundry dryers
Electric wall heaters
Electric ironers

Portable electric
heaters
Electric blankets
Heating pads
Coffee makers
Electric ranges

All of these heating appliances use a resistance wire to produce heat. *Nichrome wire*, which is an alloy of nickel and chromium, is usually used as the heater wire. The wire is often wound in the form of a coil so that a long length of wire can be placed in a small space, as shown in Fig. 21-7. Sometimes a flat wire called *ribbon nichrome wire* (Fig. 21-8) is used for elements. All elements must be mounted in

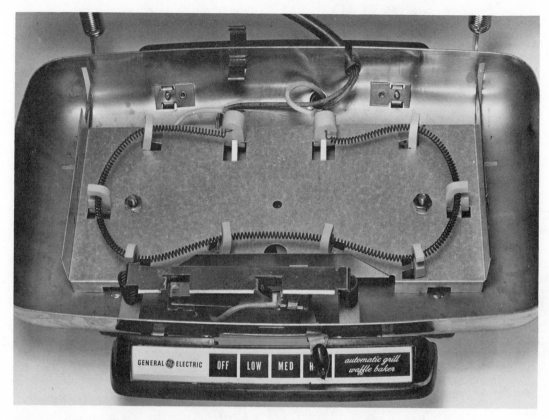

Fig. 21-7. A spiral type heating coil is used in this electric waffle iron.

Fig. 21-8. Flat wire called *ribbon nichrome* wire is usually used as the elements in electric toasters.

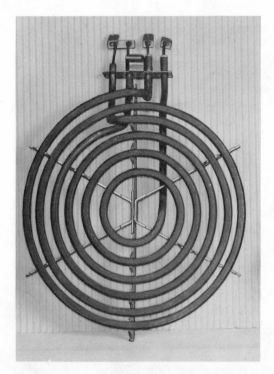

Fig. 21-9. A heating element used in an electric stove. This unit has an element called a *calrod* inside of the spiral metal tube.

or on some type of insulating material. When the element is out in the open, such as in toasters and wall heaters, ceramic forms or mica sheets are used as the insulating material.

In addition to the open elements some elements called *calrod elements* are enclosed in a metal tube. See Fig. 21-9. The heating element is placed in the center of the hollow metal tube and an insulating material is packed in around it.

The element extends out each end of the tube and the ends of the tube are sealed so that air or moisture cannot get to the element. After the tube is sealed it is formed to the needed shape such as the spiral found in some electric ranges. In flat irons the calrod element is sometimes cast into the base of the iron (Figs. 21-10 and 21-11).

A hotter element can be produced by the calrod method since the element is placed much closer to where the heat is needed. Also there is no problem with air and moisture damaging the elements.

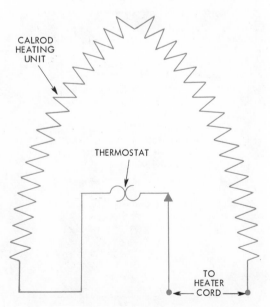

Fig. 21-10. Automatic electric iron with temperature control. Heating element is cast in the base of the iron.

Fig. 21-11. This is a wiring diagram of an electric iron.

Regulating the Heat

Appliances such as electric blankets, electric dryers, waffle irons, and flat irons use automatic heat regulators. These heat regulations, called *thermostats*, open and close the electrical circuit according to the selected temperature. Thermostats are usually made of bimetal strips that are placed inside of the heating unit. They operate like an automatic switch and are connected in series with the heater element.

As the element gets hot it gives off heat that warms the thermostat. Since the thermostat is made of a bimetal strip, the heat makes the strip expand and bend upward. When the temperature is great enough the strip opens the contact and opens the circuit. As the heater cools the temperature becomes lower and the bimetal strip bends back, closing the circuit so that the element again gives off heat.

Testing Heating Appliances

A simply constructed device consisting of a cord with attachment plug connected so that a 117-volt light bulb is in series with a pair of test leads may be used to check heating appliances. This is called a *continuity tester* and is used in many commercial electric repair shops. However, since there is a possibility of an inexperienced person getting a shock from exposed terminals of the lamp socket, this type of continuity tester is not recommended for student use. The easily built tester shown in Figs. 21-16 and 21-17, page 240, is suggested in its place. Various applications of the commercial type continuity tester are shown in Figs 21-12 through 21-15 inclusive.

The attachment plug is plugged into a convenience outlet and when the two test leads are touched together this completes the circuit and the lamp lights. To test a heater appliance, one lead of the tester is placed on one prong of the appliance attachment plug and the other lead is placed on the other prong, as shown in Fig. 21-12.

It is important that the two test leads do not touch each other. If the lamp does not light this shows that there is an open circuit and either the element is burned out or that there is a break in the heater

Fig. 21-12. An electric iron can be tested with a continuity tester to determine whether the heating unit is good.

cord. If the lamp lights, this would indicate a complete circuit and that the heating unit is good.

Testing for Shorts to the Frame

When one of the electric wires comes in contact with the appliance frame this makes the appliance a dangerous piece of equipment to use. Anyone touching the appliance could easily get an electrical shock. The continuity tester can be used for testing for shorts to the frame. One lead of the tester is placed on the prongs of the appliance plug and the other lead is touched to the frame of the appliance. See Fig. 21-13.

If the lamp lights this shows that there is a complete circuit from the electric wiring to the frame. A complete circuit from the element or from any part of the electric wiring to the frame is often called a *ground*. All grounds must be repaired before the appliance can be used safely.

Checking the Heater Cord

After testing the appliance with the continuity tester and finding either a short or an open circuit, it is then necessary to locate the trouble. Most failures in portable equipment such as flat irons, toasters, waffle irons, and portable heaters occur in the heater cord. See Fig. 21-14. The constant bending of these cords breaks the wires. The heater cord should be disconnected from the appliance and the continuity tester used to find out if the cord is at fault. Both wires must be tested to find out if there is continuity or a break in the wires. Also a check must be made to see if the wires are shorted together. If either a short or a break in the cord is located it is probably best to replace the cord with a new one.

Checking the Heater Element

With the cord removed from the appliance, place the tester leads across the

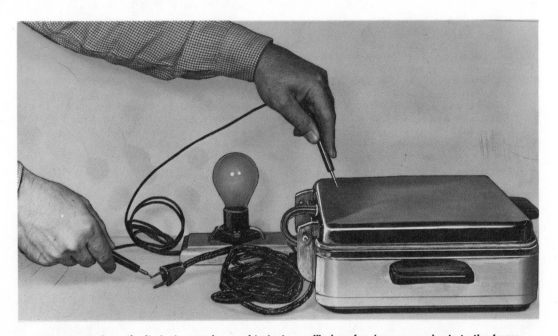

Fig. 21-13. A continuity tester can be used to test a waffle iron for dangerous shorts to the frame.

Fig. 21-14. A continuity tester is used like this to test the cord of an electric appliance for failure.

two terminals of the heater element as shown in Fig. 21-15. If the light fails to come on this shows that the element is burned out. In most appliances the burned-out element cannot be rewound and the old unit, including the heater wire and the insulating material, must be removed and a new unit installed.

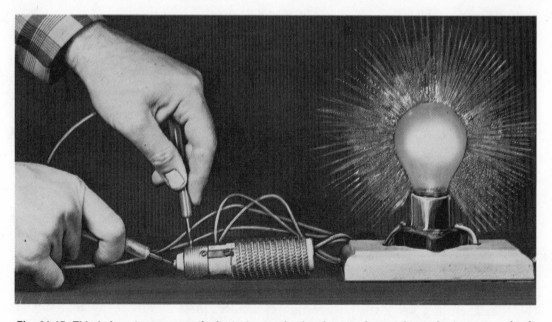

Fig. 21-15. This is how to use a continuity tester to check a heater element for a short or open circuit.

INTERESTING THINGS TO DO

Making a Continuity Tester.

Materials needed (Fig. 21-16):

1 Small plastic box (see text)
1 Neon lamp, NE-2
1 Rubber grommet, ⅜″
1 Fixed capacitor, 0.1 Mfd., 200 volts
2 Insulated pin jacks
2 Insulated pin plugs
3′ Test lead wire
6′ Lamp cord, parallel, No. 18
1 Attachment plug cap
2 Insulated test prods

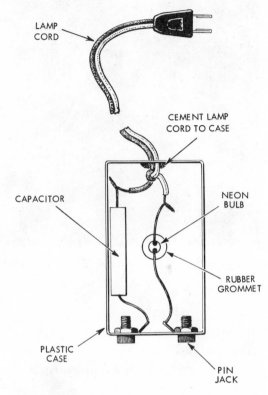

Fig. 21-17. Bottom view of continuity tester with cover removed.

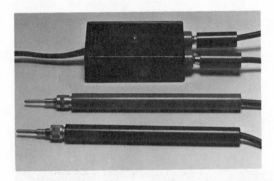

Fig. 21-16. The completed continuity tester.

The compact, completely enclosed continuity tester described below is designed for student use. Besides its small size it has another advantage in that it can be used to test continuity in circuits and electronic components with resistance as high as 200,000 ohms.

The plastic box need be large enough only to hold the capacitor and pin jacks, as shown in Fig. 21-17. The box shown in the photograph measured ⅝″ × 1¼″ × 2½″. Drill a ⅜″ hole in the top of the box for the rubber grommet. Drill ¼″ holes at opposite ends of the box for the lamp cord and the pin jacks. Insert the grommet in the hole in the box and gently press the neon lamp through the center of the grommet so that its end extends about ⅛″ above the box. Place the pin jacks and the lamp cord in proper holes and secure the lamp cord to the box with glue or cement. Make connections as shown in Fig. 21-16. The test prods may be obtained from an electronic supply house, or made with fiber rods and nails. Secure the pin plugs to one end of the test leads and the test prods to the other end. Plug the tester into a 117-volt AC circuit and touch the ends of the test prods together. If the neon lamp lights up brilliantly, the tester is ready to test your circuits.

REVIEW QUESTIONS

1. List four types of electric heating systems used in the home.

2. What is the purpose of the fins on heater elements that have been encased in a metal tube?

3. Name several types of home appliances that use a heating element.

4. What kind of wire is used in heating elements?

5. Why are calrod heating elements considered a good type of heating element?

6. What is the heat regulator on most electrical appliances called?

7. Explain how a heat regulator used on home appliances operates.

8. Draw a circuit for a continuity tester like the one you learned about.

9. How is a continuity tester used to find if a heating element is burned out?

10. Explain how a continuity tester is used to determine whether or not there is a ground in a heater appliance.

11. Where do most failures occur in portable heater appliances?

12. Why is it usually necessary to replace most heater elements with new factory-built units?

UNIT 22
THE ELECTRIC MOTOR

Purpose of Electric Motors

The construction of electric motors is very similar to that of electric generators. Just as the generator has a field and an armature so does the electric motor. Generators are used to produce electricity and need to be rotated. The electric motor uses the electricity developed by a generator or a battery to produce motion. Electric motors are used in such devices as fans, refrigerators, sewing machines, vacuum cleaners, washing machines, lathes, circular saws, and motion picture projectors.

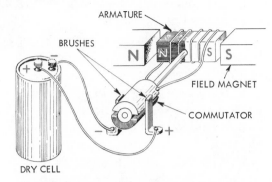

Fig. 22-1. Armature will start to rotate as poles on the armature repel like poles in the field magnet.

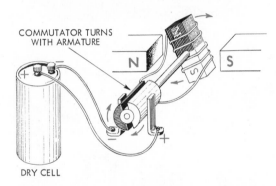

Fig. 22-2. The armature has rotated so that unlike poles now attract each other.

The letters show that the machine is a motor.

Fundamentals of a Simple DC Motor

Motors and generators look very much alike and in some cases generators may be used for motors and some motors can be used for generators. In Units 8 and 16 we learned that a generator produced electricity if a coil was rotated in a magnetic field. The simple generator can be made into a motor to produce motion by connecting a battery to the brushes as in Fig. 22-1. The armature has a current flowing through the coils and that makes it an electromagnet. All electromagnets have a north and a south pole so the armature has a north and south pole. The

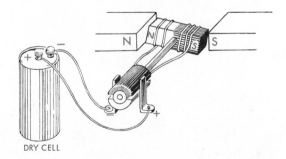

Fig. 22-3. The armature polarity is now changed by the commutator so that again like poles repel each other.

permanent field magnet also has a north and a south pole.

The brush on the left-hand side is connected to the negative terminal of the battery and current flow is such that this side of the armature becomes a north pole. The brush on the right-hand side is connected to the positive terminal and that side of the armature becomes a south pole. Thus the armature has a north pole next to the north pole of the magnet and a south pole next to the south pole of the magnet. Like poles repel each other so both poles of the armature try to push away from the poles of the magnet.

This repelling of like poles makes the armature rotate. As the armature rotates, the north pole of the armature is attracted toward the south pole of the magnet. Just before the two poles come together by their attraction for each other the polarity of the armature is changed by the commutator. Again the two like poles repel each other and the armature continues to rotate. See Figs. 22-2 and 22-3. The direction that a current carrying conductor will move in a magnetic field is shown by the *Right Hand Rule*, Fig. 22-4.

Motors with Electromagnetic Field Coils

An electromagnet can be used to produce the magnetic field instead of a permanent magnet. The electromagnet called a *field coil* consists of insulated wire wound around a steel core. The battery is used to produce the magnetic field for the field coil as well as to provide the current for the armature. Figs. 22-5 and

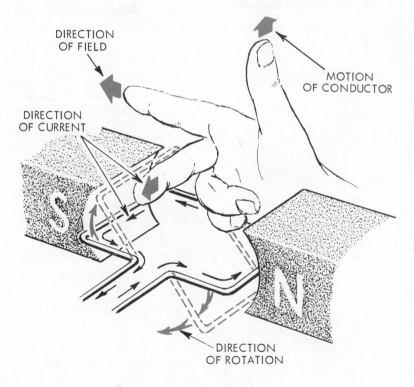

RIGHT HAND MOTOR RULE

Fig. 22-4. The right hand motor rule. In the drawing, the thumb indicates the direction a current carrying conductor will move in a magnetic field.

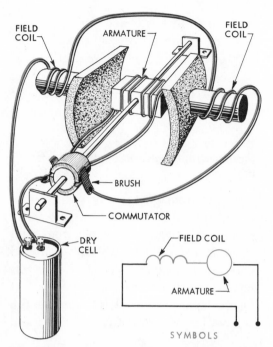

Fig. 22-5. Electric motor with field coil connected in series with the armature coil.

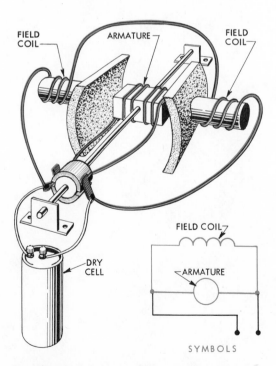

Fig. 22-6. Electric motor with field coil connected in parallel with armature coil.

22-6 show how field coils may be connected in series or in parallel with the armature.

Armatures with Several Coils

To improve the operating efficiency of commercial motors several sets of coils are used in the armature. See Fig. 22-7. By using several sets of coils it is necessary to have a commutator with a number of different segments to connect each of the coils to. In this way the brushes are always in contact with a set of coils that are directly across from the field poles. Using a number of coils in the armature produces a much smoother running motor.

Using Alternating Current on Motors

Some motors may be used on either direct current or alternating current. Motors using an electromagnetic field with a commutator may be operated from AC or DC. When alternating current is connected to these motors, the magnetic field is continually changing in both the armature winding and in the field coil winding. Since the currents in both the armature and the field coil are changing together, the polarity of each is changed at the same time. When one pole of the field coil is the north pole the armature pole nearest it is also a north pole and they repel each other. When the direction of current flow changes and this same field pole becomes a south pole, the armature pole is also changed to a south pole and they continue to repel each other. The commutator is the device that makes the rotation of the motor possible.

Universal Motor Repairs

Small motors designed to operate on either alternating or direct current are

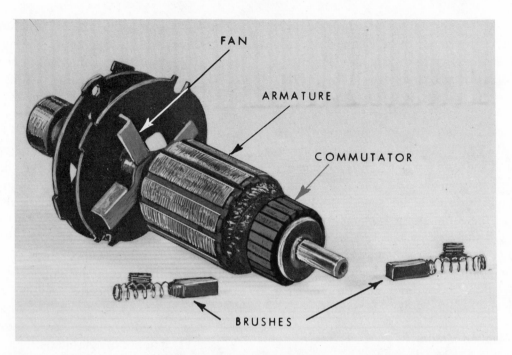

Fig. 22-7. The armature of an electric motor showing the commutator segments. The segments are insulated from each other and are connected to different sets of coils in the armature.

called *universal* motors. These motors have the field coil connected in series with the armature coil as in Fig. 22-5. This type of small motor is found in vacuum cleaners, fans, sewing machines, electric mixers, and similar household appliances.

The carbon brushes on universal motors sometimes become worn and must be replaced. When replacing brushes it is important to disconnect the appliance from the electric circuit before starting to work.

The new brushes should be the same type and size as those used by the manufacturer. The old brushes can be removed by unscrewing the brush-holder screws found on each side of the motor, as shown in Fig. 22-8. Screws in the end of the brush holders press against a small spring that keeps the brush in contact with the commutator.

Fig. 22-8. Removing the brushes from an electric motor used on a sewing machine.

The commutator on these motors sometimes needs to be cleaned. Usually it is necessary to disassemble the motor to clean the commutator. When taking the motor apart it is advisable to take out the brushes so that they won't become damaged when removing the armature. Use a very fine sandpaper and sand the commutator lightly. When the copper segments on the commutator shine this should be a good indication that the commutator is clean.

Oil should only be used on the bearings of an electric motor. Some motors have cups where the oil is to be placed. Use oil very sparingly and do not get it on the brushes or the commutator.

Induction Motors

The most common type of electric motor used on alternating current is the *induction* motor (Fig. 22-9). Induction motors are used on refrigerators, garbage disposals, blowers, washing machines, and on many types of machinery. It can be used only on alternating current and does not require a commutator or brushes.

The induction motor consists of two main parts—the *stator*, which is the stationary set of coils wound in the frame of the motor, and the *rotor*, which is the rotating part of the motor. See Fig. 22-10. The rotor is made of laminated steel with slots cut in it to hold copper bars. The copper bars that are in the slots of the steel core are all connected together at the end by two rings of copper. This type of rotor is called a *squirrel cage* rotor (Fig. 22-11). The stator acts like a primary of a transformer and induces a current in the rotor.

Fig. 22-9. Electric motors are made in many sizes and are specially designed to meet particular requirements.

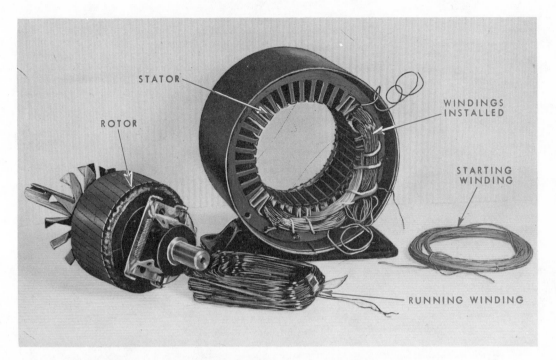

Fig. 22-10. An induction motor operates on alternating current and has no commutator or brushes.

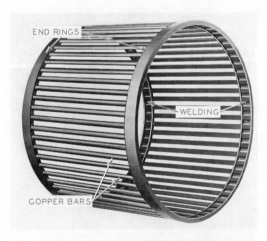

Fig. 22-11. A squirrel cage rotor as it would appear when removed from the slots of the laminated sheet steel rotor core and reassembled. (General Electric Co.)

When the magnetic field of the stator induces a current in the copper bars, the rotor becomes an electromagnet. The field of the stator repels the rotor and

pushes it around. This pushing of the rotor by the stator is what makes the motor run. The main advantage of the induction-type motor is that there are no brushes and commutators that must be connected in the circuit. Elimination of any direct connection between the stator and the rotor produces a fairly trouble-free motor.

Starting the Induction Motor

Most induction motors require a start to get the rotor moving. The usual method of starting an induction motor is to use two stator windings. One winding is called the *running winding* and the other is called the *starting winding*. See Fig. 22-12. The starting winding helps to start the rotor moving and is disconnected after the motor has reached running speed. When the starting winding is cut out of the circuit the running wind-

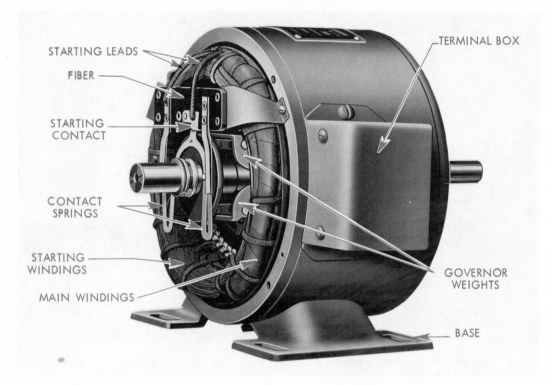

STARTING LEADS

FIBER

STARTING CONTACT

CONTACT SPRINGS

STARTING WINDINGS

MAIN WINDINGS

TERMINAL BOX

GOVERNOR WEIGHTS

BASE

Fig. 22-12. This is an alternating current motor with one end removed, showing the arrangement of the starting switch. (General Electric Co.)

ing keeps the motor going. An automatic cut-out switch is arranged so that as the speed of the motor picks up it will open and disconnect the starting winding from the circuit. When the motor stops the switch automatically closes and the starting winding is again in the circuit.

INTERESTING THINGS TO DO

1. Tin Can Motor.

Materials needed to construct the tin can motor (Fig. 22-13):

- 2 Pieces tin, ½" x 5¼" (cut from a tin can)
- 2 Pieces tin, ½" x 1⅞"
- 1 Piece steel rod, 1/16" x 2½"
- 2 Pieces sheet brass, ⅜" x 1¼", 16 gage
- 2 Pieces spring brass, ¼" x 1⅛", 26 gage
- 1 Piece brass tubing, ¼" inside diameter, ½" long, 22 gage
- 1 Piece fiber rod, round, ¼" diameter, ½" long
- 1 Piece wood, ½" x 2½" x 3"
- 1 Piece wood, ⅜" x ½" x ¾"
- 2 Terminal screws, 6-32, 1" long
- 1 Spool magnet wire, No. 24, cotton- or enamel-covered

Fig. 22-13. A tin can motor.

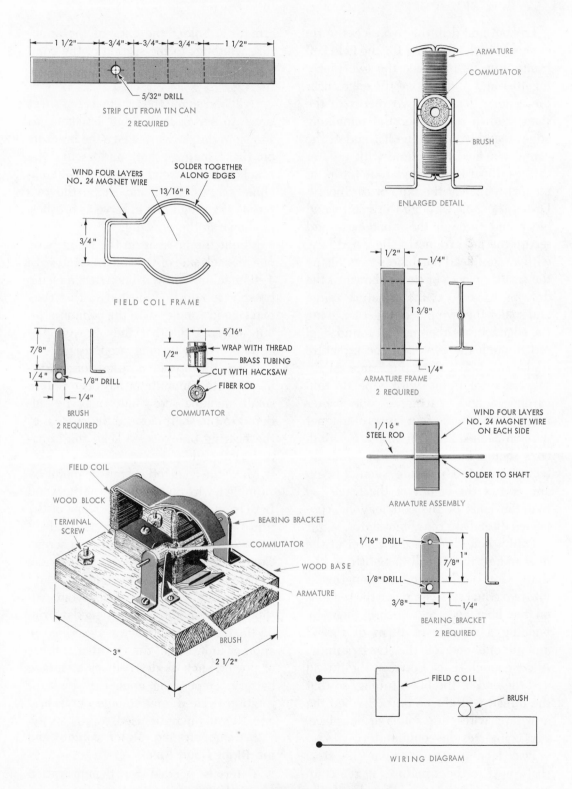

Fig. 22-14. Tin can motor parts and assembly.

Lay out and drill the two pieces of tin as shown in the drawing for the field coil frame, Fig. 22-14. Place the two pieces together and solder along the edges near the center. Bend the two pieces to the shape shown and solder the remaining edges together. Wrap the flat end of the completed field coil frame with tape or thin cardboard and wind four layers of magnet wire over the tape or cardboard. Drill a $\frac{5}{32}''$ hole through the small wood block and through the wood base and secure the field frame to the wood base with a roundhead machine screw. Shape the smaller pieces of tin as shown in the drawing to serve as the armature frame and solder the two pieces together along the edges. Insert the piece of round steel rod through the center of the armature frame and solder it to the frame. Wrap the armature frame with tape or thin cardboard and, starting at the center near the shaft, wind four layers of magnet wire on each side of the armature. Both coils should be wound in the same direction and the winding should begin and end at the center of the frame, so that the ends of the coil may be connected directly to the commutator.

Drill a hole through the center of the fiber rod, so that it will fit tightly on the shaft. Cut the brass tubing lengthwise into two equal sections, place the sections on the fiber rod, and secure them by winding a number of turns of thread around one end of the brass tubing. Allow enough space between the thread and the end of the brass tubing, so that the thread will not be burned when the armature wires are soldered in place. This completes the commutator.

Place the commutator on the steel shaft, next to the armature, so the commutator slots are on each side of the armature. Solder the ends of the armature windings to the section of the commutator that is on the same side of the shaft.

Drill and shape the two pieces of sheet brass to serve as bearing brackets, as shown in the drawing. Place the brackets on the armature shaft and secure the brackets to the wood base with 4–40 machine screws. Drill and shape the two pieces of spring brass to serve as brushes, as shown in the drawing.

Mount the brushes on the wood base, one on each side of the commutator, with 4–40 machine screws. The tension of the brushes should be adjusted so that they make good contact with the commutator, but not so tight that they prevent the armature from turning properly.

When the proper position for the armature and commutator has been found, small machine screw nuts may be soldered to the shaft close to the outside of the bearing brackets, to keep the armature centered.

Make the connections for the motor by running a wire on the bottom of the wood base from a terminal screw to one of the brush screws. Connect one of the field coil wires to the remaining brush screw. Connect the other field coil lead to the remaining terminal. The motor should now be ready for its initial tryout. Although the motor was designed to run on the transformer that was described in another unit, it will run on other sources of power, such as dry cells or a storage battery. Depending upon the speed of rotation desired, any voltage between 4 and 10 volts may be used.

2. Demonstrating Motor Action and the Right Hand Rule.

Materials needed for demonstration motor (Fig. 22-15):

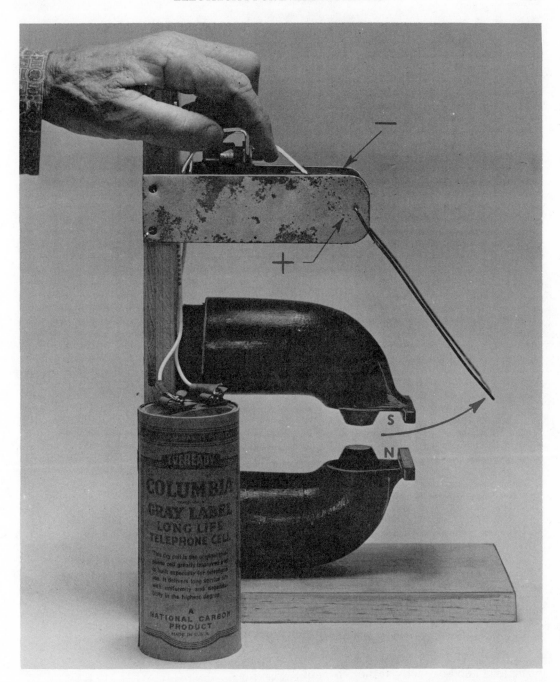

Fig. 22-15. The completed unit for showing motor action. With polarities of the magnet as shown, the wire loop will move to the right when the switch is pressed. Use the right hand rule and determine the direction the current must be flowing through the wire loop.

1 Horseshoe shape magnet
1 Dry cell
1 Switch, momentary contact
18″ Copper wire, No. 10 or 12.

Wood and sheet metal for mounting magnet and wire loop.

A dramatic demonstration of motor ac-

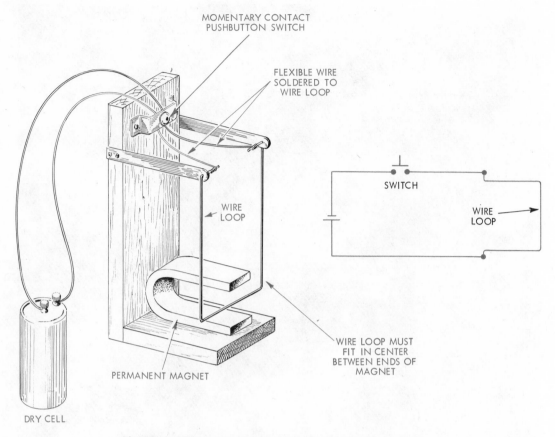

Fig. 22-16. Construction details for demonstrating motor action.

tion can be made with a magnet, dry cell, switch, and loop of wire, as shown in Fig. 22-16. Any horseshoe shape magnet may be used, but the stronger it is the greater will be the effect.

Mount the magnet so that one pole or end is directly above the other. Bend the piece of wire into a U shape and mount it with metal brackets so that it will swing freely between the pole pieces of the magnet and be exactly at the center of the poles when it is at rest. Connect the free ends of the heavy wire in series with the switch and dry cell with flexible wire. When all connections have been made, close the switch momentarily. Which way did the wire swing? If the polarity of the magnet is not marked, try to de-

termine the position of its north and south poles by means of the right hand rule shown in Fig. 22-4.

3. Piston Type Motor.

Materials required to construct the piston type motor (Fig. 22-17):

2 Fiber washers, $\frac{1}{8}''$ thick, $1\frac{1}{8}''$ diameter
1 Piece wood dowel, $\frac{3}{8}'' \times 2''$
1 Piece soft steel, round, $\frac{1}{4}''$ diameter, $2\frac{1}{4}''$ long
1 Piece steel, round, $\frac{1}{8}''$ diameter, $3\frac{1}{4}''$ long
1 Piece sheet brass, $\frac{1}{16}''$ thick, $\frac{1}{4}'' \times 1\frac{1}{2}''$
2 Pieces sheet steel, 18 gage, $1\frac{1}{2}'' \times 2\frac{1}{2}''$
1 Piece brass rod, round, $\frac{1}{2}''$ diameter, $\frac{3}{16}''$ long
1 Piece spring brass, 26 gage, $\frac{3}{16}'' \times 2\frac{3}{4}''$
1 Piece wood, $\frac{3}{4}'' \times 1\frac{1}{2}'' \times 2''$
1 Piece wood, $\frac{1}{2}'' \times 4'' \times 6''$
2 Terminal screws
100' Magnet wire, No. 22, enam.
1 Flywheel (see text)

Fig. 22-17. Piston type motor.

This type motor has an action somewhat like a steam engine in that the power is supplied to the flywheel by a piston moving back and forth. Make a coil form by drilling a $^{17}/_{64}''$ hole through the piece of wood dowel and place a fiber washer at each end of the dowel. Drill two small holes in one washer for the coil leads and wind eight layers of No. 22 magnet wire on the form (Fig. 22-18). Shape one end of the wood block to match the curve of the coil and glue the coil to the block. Secure the coil mount to the wood base with screws or glue in the approximate position shown in the assembly view. Shape and drill the piece of sheet brass to serve as the connecting rod.

File away one end of the piston rod so that the end of the connecting rod will fit against it and drill and tap the end of the rod as shown on the drawing for the piston. Secure the connecting rod to the piston with a 6-32 machine screw. Tighten the screw so that the connecting rod can move freely, then solder the end of the machine screw to the piston. The flywheel may be turned from wood with a piece of pipe serving as a rim to give it weight, or it may be made by casting plaster of Paris in a jar lid, as was done with the motor shown in the photograph. Bend the piece of steel rod as shown in the drawing to serve as the crankshaft. Drill, shape, and bend the two pieces of sheet steel for the bearing stands, as shown in the drawing.

Assemble the crankshaft, flywheel, and bearing stands by first placing a 6-32 machine screw nut that has been drilled out to $^{1}/_{8}''$ over the straight end of the shaft. Next place a bearing stand on the shaft, then the flywheel, and finally, the other bearing stand and another drilled out machine screw nut. Place the whole assembly on the wood base and insert the end of the crankshaft through the hole in the connecting rod. Line up all of the parts so that the moving parts work freely, then secure the bearing stands to the base with wood screws. Secure the flywheel to the shaft so that it will be centered between the bearings. Solder the machine screw nuts to the shaft to keep the flywheel centered.

Shape the piece of round brass rod to provide a cam approximately 160 degrees wide as shown in the drawing and place it on the end of the shaft. Drill and shape the piece of spring brass to serve as the brush, as shown in the drawing, and secure it to the wood base so that its end will rest against the contact cam. Adjust the cam so that it makes contact with the brush slightly after the piston begins its backward stroke and breaks contact

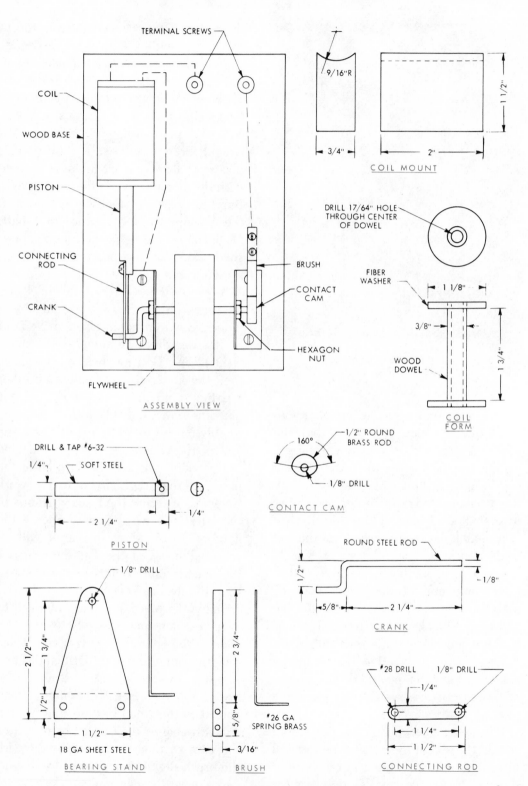

Fig. 22-18. Details of piston type motor.

with the brush just before the piston begins its forward stroke. In some instances the edges of the cam may need further dressing with a file to provide maximum operating results. Solder the cam to the shaft when it has been adjusted to the correct position. Wire the motor as shown in the assembly view and the motor will be ready to run. Direct current from 3 to 8 volts will operate the motor satisfactorily.

REVIEW QUESTIONS

1. Name several uses for electrical motors.

2. What is the purpose of the commutator on a simple motor?

3. Draw a diagram of a simple motor using an electromagnetic field.

4. Why do motor armatures sometimes have several sets of coils?

5. Why can some motors be used on both direct current and alternating current? What are the motors called?

6. How are commutators cleaned?

7. What is the name of the rotating part and what is the name of the stationary coils in an induction type motor?

8. What is one of the main advantages of an induction motor?

9. Explain the construction of a squirrel cage rotor.

10. What happens in the circuit of the starter winding, in an induction motor, after the motor is in rotation?

UNIT 23
THE AUTOMOBILE ELECTRICAL SYSTEM

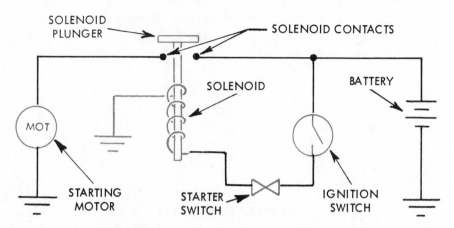

Fig. 23-1. Drawing of the basic circuit used for the starting motor. (Delco-Remy Div., General Motors Corp.)

The modern automobile uses electricity in many ways. Electricity is used to (1) crank the engine (Fig. 23-1), (2) provide lights for night driving, (3) ignite the fuel that gives power to the engine, (4) operate instruments such as fuel gage, temperature gage, and oil pressure gage, (5) light signaling devices such as stop lights and turning lights, and (6) operate many accessories such as radios, horns, heaters, and windows. The complete wiring for the automobile requires many circuits as shown in Fig. 23-2.

The Storage Battery

We learned about the storage battery in Unit 7. It is a very good source of electricity because it can deliver large amounts of current and can be recharged when run down. Each cell of a storage battery delivers 2 volts. To obtain 12 volts from a storage battery it is necessary to have six cells connected in series. A 6-volt storage battery has three cells con-

nected in series. Automobiles use either 6-volt or 12-volt storage batteries.

To reduce the number of wires used for the electrical circuits in the automobile the steel frame of the chassis is used as one wire in the circuit. This is possible because the low voltage of the battery is not dangerous. Some automobile manufacturers design their engines to have the negative terminal of the battery connected to the frame and others connect the positive terminal to the frame. The battery terminal connected to the frame is said to be *grounded* to the frame. A heavy flexible cable called a *ground cable* is used for this purpose.

The Starting Motor

The automobile uses a direct current motor to crank the engine and get it started. Modern engines are difficult to turn over and the motor called the *starting motor* must be very powerful. The principle of the direct current motor was

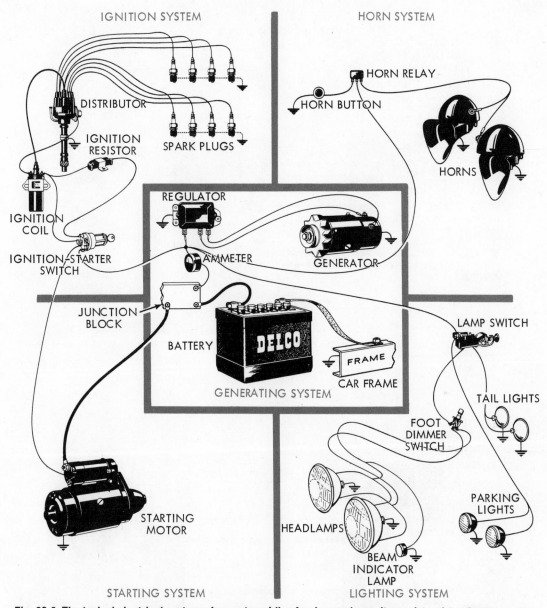

Fig. 23-2. The typical electrical system of an automobile. As shown above, it consists of 5 subsystems, the generating system being necessary to the operation of the other four systems. (Delco-Remy Div., General Motors Corp.)

discussed in Unit 22. Fig. 23-3 shows the construction of a starting motor.

The battery provides the current necessary to rotate the engine. When the starter switch is pushed down this completes the circuit and the engine starts. The starting motor shaft is coupled to the engine flywheel and as it rotates it turns the engine over.

In cranking the engine the starting motor draws a large amount of current from the storage battery. The amount of current varies from 150 to 500 amperes, depending upon the design of the motor.

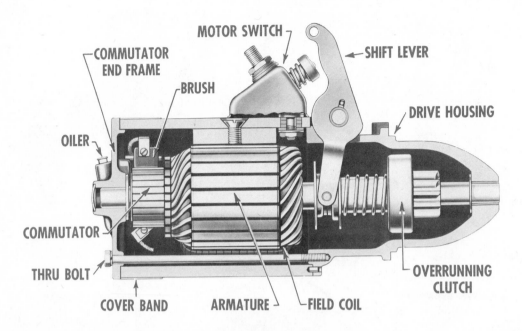

Fig. 23-3. This illustration shows the construction of a direct current motor used to start an automobile. (Delco-Remy Div., General Motors Corp.)

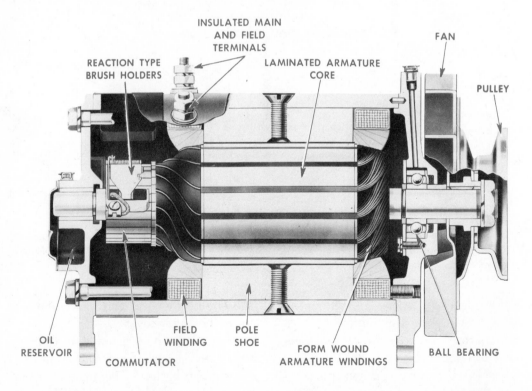

Fig. 23-4. The construction of a two-brush automobile generator is shown in this illustration. (Delco-Remy Div., General Motors Corp.)

Because of the very heavy current flow necessary to operate the starting motor, most engines use a solenoid switch. As shown in Fig. 23-1, the solenoid is controlled by turning on the ignition and closing the starting switch. When the coil of the solenoid is energized, it pulls the plunger down and the contacts form a complete circuit from the battery to the starting motor. These contacts are made to carry the very large amounts of current necessary to run the starting motor which in turn cranks the engine. Once the engine is running, the starting switch is turned off so that the solenoid coil loses its magnestism and a spring forces the plunger to open the solenoid contacts.

The Generator

The storage battery can supply the electrical needs of the automobile for only a short time. A generator (Fig. 23-4) is needed to charge the battery and to help provide current for the rest of the electrical system. The generator is usually driven by a belt that is coupled to the engine.

The direct current generator was discussed in Unit 8. To generate electricity an armature coil is rotated in a magnetic field. The brushes collect the direct current from the commutator and this current is used throughout the automobile.

After the engine has been started by the starting motor, the generator is ro-

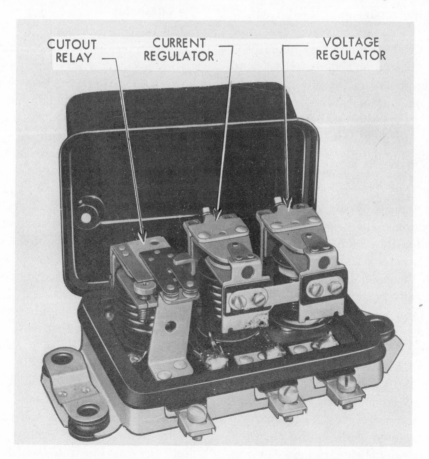

Fig. 23-5.Generator regulators control the voltage supplied by an automobile generator.

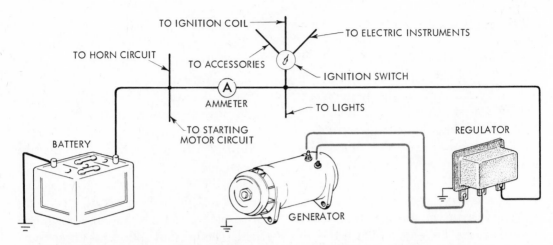

Fig. 23-6. This basic wiring circuit for an automobile shows the generator and the regulator, which maintains constant voltage. (From *Automotive Fuel and Ignition Systems,* American Technical Society.)

tated by the engine and it begins generating direct current. As the generator builds up voltage it charges the battery. This is indicated on the ammeter found on the dashboard of the automobile. In some automobiles a warning red light on the dashboard indicates that the generator is not charging. When the generator is charging the light goes out.

A special device called a *generator regulator* (Fig. 23-5) is used to keep the voltage supplied by the generator from going too high. The generator regulator, often called the *voltage regulator,* provides an automatic control on the voltage output of the generator. The voltage regulator usually prevents the voltage from the generator from going higher than 7.2 to 7.4 volts in a 6-volt system. On a 12-volt system the voltage is regulated from 14.0 to 14.2 volts. A voltage slightly higher than the battery voltage is needed for the generator to charge the battery. Through the use of this generator regulator the voltage of the entire electrical system remains fairly constant. See Fig. 23-6.

The Alternator

The increased demands for electrical accessories on automobiles such as power windows, power seats, and two way radio systems, has made a very heavy load on the direct current generating systems. Many of the accessories are used when the automobile is going at low speed and this is when the direct-current generator develops very little voltage.

One method of overcoming some of the problems found in the direct-current generator is to use an alternating-current generator and rectifier system. This system provides good voltage output at low speeds and also has excellent efficiency at high speeds.

The alternating-current generator is called an alternator, Figs. 23-7 and 23-8, and consists primarily of a rotor and a stator. The rotor includes a field coil which is connected to slip rings. The field coil draws only about 2 amperes of current and is connected to the battery by brushes which are in contact with the slip rings, as illustrated in Fig. 23-9. When the rotor is turning the magnetic

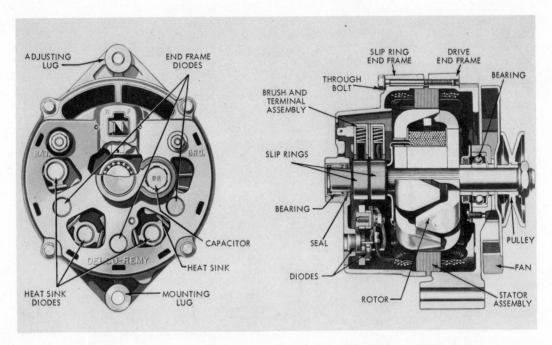

Fig. 23-7. Cutaway view of an alternator. (Cadillac Motor Div., General Motors Corp.)

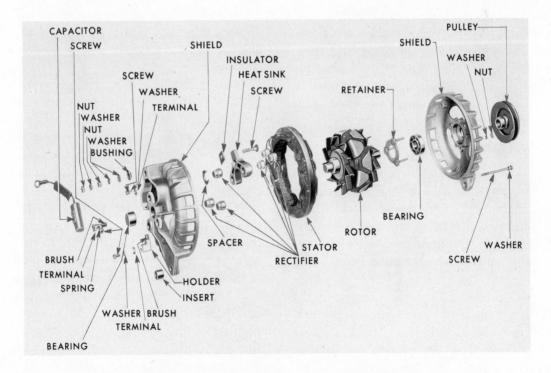

Fig. 23-8. An exploded view of the complete alternator. (Plymouth Div., Chrysler Corp.)

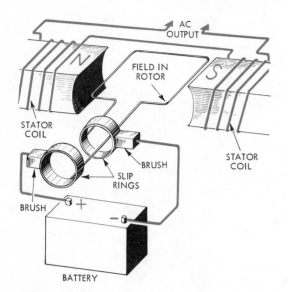

Fig. 23-9. Drawing of basic parts used in rotating field alternator.

Fig. 23-10. Construction of a spark plug. The spark from the ignition coil jumps across the gap to ignite the fuel. (General Motors Corp.)

lines of force in the rotor field coils cut across the coil windings located in the stator. An alternating-current is generated in the stator windings.

In order to have a direct-current for charging the battery, the alternating-current produced by the alternator is passed through a rectifier. The rectifier, which is usually made of either silicon diodes or selenium diodes, changes the alternating current into direct current.

The Ignition System

Automotive engines operate through the explosion of a mixture of gasoline and air in the engine cylinders which produces power to drive the crankshaft. The purpose of the ignition system is to develop and deliver a high voltage arc of electricity to spark plugs (Fig. 23-10) in the cylinders to fire the mixture at the right time. The basic ignition circuit is shown in Fig. 23-11.

A very high voltage is needed to jump the gap of the spark plug. Since the battery will deliver only 12 volts (6 volts in some cars), a step-up transformer must be used to obtain the high voltage required by the spark plugs. This is accomplished by the ignition coil, Fig. 23-12. This coil has a primary winding with 200 to 300 turns of heavy wire wrapped around a steel core. The secondary coil consists of 16,000 to 23,000 turns of fine magnet wire wrapped on the same steel core as the primary winding. This type of transformer is able to step up the voltage to over 20,000 volts.

Since both the battery and generator produce direct current it is necessary to start and stop the current in the primary winding in order to induce a current in the secondary winding. This is the function of the distributor. The distributor contains a breaker cam which is rotated by the engine to open and close the breaker points and make or break the primary circuit. Also, attached to the breaker cam is a rotor, which is connected to the high voltage secondary of the ignition coil. The rotor turns with the cam and makes contact with each of the spark plug wires one at a time. This connects the high voltage to each of the spark plugs so that the air-fuel mixture will be ignited at the proper time.

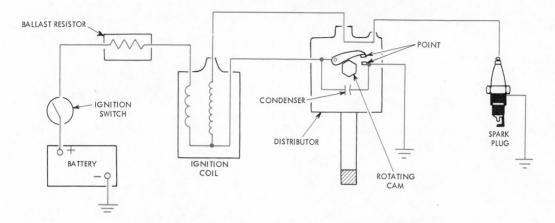

Fig. 23-11. These are the basic parts of automobile ignition system.

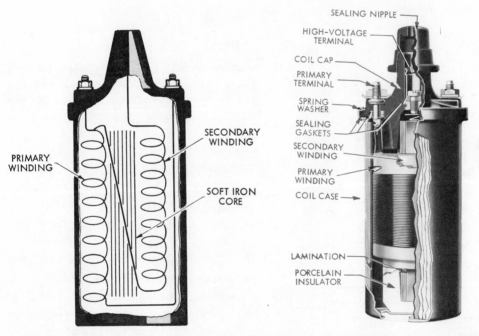

Fig. 23-12. Cutaway view (left) and internal wiring (right) of a typical ignition coil. (Delco-Remy Div., General Motors Corp.)

The system in operation is illustrated in Fig. 23-13. When the points are closed, current flows through the primary circuit (indicated by solid arrows) building up a large magnetic field in the primary winding of the coil. When the points open, the field collapses, inducing a large surge of high voltage in both the primary and secondary of the coil. This high voltage in the secondary is routed through the rotor to the spark plugs where it arcs across the gap to ignite the fuel, (dashed arrows). The collapse of the magnetic field in the coil also induces a large current in the primary. Since the points are open at this time, the current has no com-

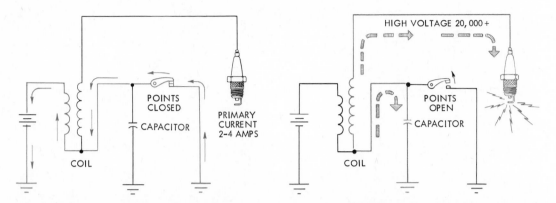

Fig. 23-13. These simplified drawings show the operation of the ignition system. In the drawing at the left, colored lines and arrows show the path of primary current when points are closed and the magnetic field is building up in the primary of the coil. The drawing at the right shows what happens when the points open: the primary field collapses, inducing a surge of high voltage in the secondary circuit to the plugs and through the condenser.

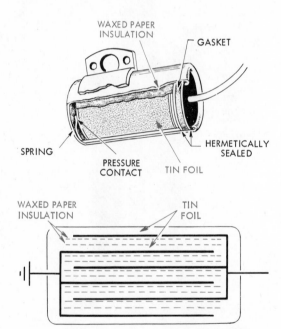

Fig. 23-14. Cutaway view of a capacitor (top) and a diagram of capacitor construction (bottom).

plete path and will jump across the points. This current is so high that the points would be burned up unless some means were used to reduce the arcing. This is done by the use of a *condenser* (Fig. 23-14) across the points. (In elec-

tronics work, the term *condenser* has been replaced by *capacitor*.) When the field of the coil collapses, most of the high current will be bypassed through the condenser.

Transistor Ignition

The conventional ignition system was invented more than fifty years ago by Charles Kettering, and is sometimes called the "Kettering system." While it has been modified and improved to some degree during the fifty years of its existence, there has been no basic change to make it keep pace with the developments made in the automobile. The needs of the automobile of today have gone beyond the conventional system's ability to supply them. Transistor ignition is one of the developments which may replace it.

The larger horsepower engines require more voltage at high speeds for efficient ignition of the fuel. In the conventional system, the points make and break the primary circuit slower or faster depending on the speed of the engine. If the engine is going very fast, the points will

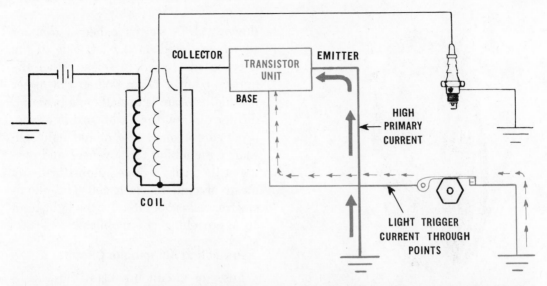

Fig. 23-15. A schematic of a transistor ignition system. The "Transistor Unit" shown in the drawing also has a circuit containing resistors and diodes in addition to the transistor. It has been simplified for clarity. In this system only a small amount of current goes through the points to "switch" the transistor which then carries the heavy primary current. Because of the higher primary current that is handled by the transistor a special coil is required for this system.

open and close quickly and the primary of the coil will not have time to build up to a very high voltage. So, at higher speeds the voltage will decrease making the engine less efficient.

In order to get a higher voltage, more current could be used to build a stronger magnetic field in the coil, but the points can handle only so much current without burning. The limitations of the present systems are due mostly to the inability of the points to handle the large amounts of current that are needed to raise the voltage. Other defects found in the conventional system are limited life of the points, and condenser, along with the maintenance necessary to keep these units in working condition.

The transistorized ignition system, Fig. 23-15, eliminates these defects and provides far more dependable service than could be obtained from the older system. The transistor is capable of handling large amounts of current and its function in the circuit is to "switch" the primary circuit on and off so that the points carry only a very small current. Since the points now carry such a minute portion of the total current, arcing between them is eliminated and a capacitor such as used in the conventional system is not required. However, a special coil with a higher turns ratio and current rating must be used.

Automobile Lights

Good lights are very important requirements for the safe use of an automobile. The laws of most states require that the headlights must provide enough light to enable one to see objects at least 350' ahead. In addition tail lights, stop lights, and license plate lights are all required by law.

Headlights are of the sealed-beam type (Fig. 23-16). Since the entire unit is

Fig. 23-16. A sealed beam headlamp. (Chevrolet Motor Div., General Motors Corp.)

sealed against dirt, moisture, and corrosion, there is little loss in the amount of light produced by the sealed beam throughout its life. These sealed units include the bulb (Fig. 23-17), which consists of two filaments, the glass lens, and the reflector.

The bulbs are an incandescent type that will operate off the low voltage produced by the battery or the generator. The sealed-beam headlight has two filaments. One filament produces the light for the upper beam used in country driving. The other filament produces the passing beam light, which is focused

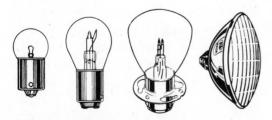

Fig. 23-17. Illustrated here are types of bulbs used in automobiles. (General Electric Co.)

downward. A switch called a *dimmer switch* mounted on the left side of the floor board is used to select either the upper or lower beam. When the upper headlights beam is turned on, a beam indicator bulb on the dashboard lights up, producing a small spot of red light. On some automobiles this lowering and raising of the beam is done automatically by means of a photoelectric cell. This photoelectric cell is operated by the light from an approaching automobile.

Protecting Automobile Circuits

Fuses or circuit breakers (Figs. 23-18 and 23-19) are used to protect the lighting and accessory circuits in the automo-

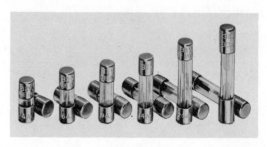

Fig. 23-18. These are typical fuses used in automotive vehicles. (Littelfuse Inc.)

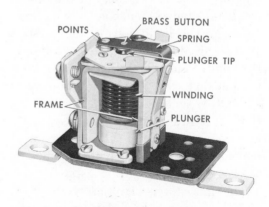

Fig. 23-19. A circuit breaker used in automobiles. If too much current flows through the coil the plunger forces the armature upward and opens the contact points. (From *Automotive Fuel and Ignition Systems*, American Technical Society)

bile. These protective devices are used to prevent the wires from becoming damaged if a short circuit occurs. If either a fuse "blows out" or the circuit breakers open the circuit, it is important to locate the trouble and repair it before turning the switch on again.

Directional Signal Lights

Directional signal lights that indicate whether the driver is going to turn right or left have become a very useful accessory on automobiles. The lights mounted on the front and rear of the automobile flash on and off at the rate of almost 90 times per minute. When the switch lever mounted on the steering column is turned on, an indicator bulb on the dashboard also flashes. This indicator bulb shows a small arrow of light to indicate to the driver the direction which the outside lights are flashing. See Figs. 23-20 and 23-21.

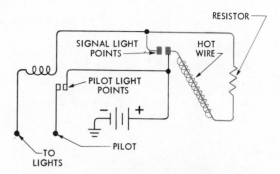

Fig. 23-21. The basic circuit of the flasher switch used on directional signal lights. When the switch is turned on, current flows through the "hot wire" and resistor. The resistor in the circuit prevents the bulb from lighting. The "hot wire" has current flowing through it, making it expand. As it expands, the signal light points come together and the bulb lights, because the resistor is shorted out of the circuit. The coil near the pilot light points has enough current flowing through it to pull the points closed and light the arrow on the dashboard. As soon as the current stops flowing through the hot wire, it cools, contracts and opens the signal light points. The bulb is turned off but as the "hot wire" heats again the points are closed and again the bulb lights. This heating and cooling of the "hot wire" is what makes the bulb flash off and on. (From *Fuel and Ignition Systems,* American Technical Society)

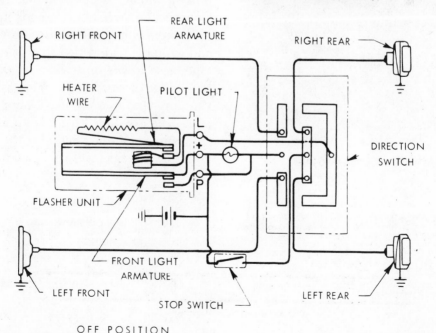

OFF POSITION

Fig. 23-20. Typical directional signal wiring diagram. (From *Automotive Electrical Systems,* American Technical Society.)

INTERESTING THINGS TO DO

Ignition and Spark Plug Tester.

Materials needed to construct the ignition and spark plug tester (Fig. 23-22):

- 1 Piece fiber tubing, ½" outside diameter, 1/16" wall, 7" long
- 2 Pieces wood dowel, 3/8" diameter, ½" long
- 1 Radio resistor, 4.7 megohms, ½-watt
- 1 Neon lamp, 1/25-watt, type NE-2
- 3' Stranded radio hook-up wire
- 1 Battery clip
- 1 Box nail, 6-penny

This handy tester (Fig. 23-23) will help locate trouble in your automobile ignition system. When the clip is attached to some metal part of the frame or engine and the pointed end of the tester is placed in contact with the top of the spark plug, the neon lamp will light up brilliantly if the spark plug and distributor are operating properly. If the neon lamp lights up dimly or fails to light at all, either the spark plug or distributor is at fault. With a defective distributor the neon lamp will show reduced light on all of the spark plugs. When little or no light shows at only one or two spark plugs, the trouble can usually be traced to defective plugs.

File a section of the fiber tubing at the center with a rat-tail file, so that the electrodes of the neon lamp will be visible. Drill a hole through one of the sections of wood dowel slightly smaller than the box nail and press the nail through the hole. Solder one end of the radio resistor to the head of the nail. Connect the other end of the resistor to one of the neon lamp leads. The resistor and neon lamp should be spaced and connected, so that the neon lamp will be at the center hole in the fiber tubing when they are inserted into the tubing, as shown in the drawing. Connect the piece of radio hook-up wire to the remaining lead on the neon lamp and wrap the wire with a strip of friction tape close to where it will pass through the section of wood dowel. This will prevent any strain on the neon lamp leads. Insert the assembled neon lamp and resistor into the tubing and glue the wood dowel with the nail in place. Drill

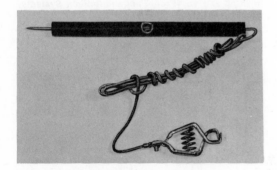

Fig. 23-22. Ignition and spark plug tester.

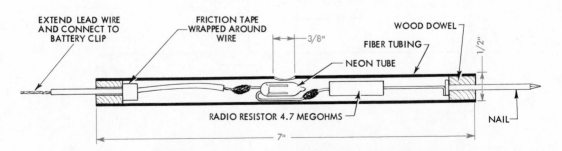

Fig. 23-23. Drawing of ignition and spark plug tester.

a ⅛″ hole through the remaining piece of wood dowel, pass the hook-up wire through it, and glue it in the end of the fiber tubing. Attach a battery clip to the end of the hook-up wire and the tester is ready to use.

REVIEW QUESTIONS

1. Name several uses for electricity in the automobile.

2. How many cells are used in a 12-volt storage battery?

3. How is the chassis of the automobile used as part of the electrical circuit?

4. Why does the storage battery need to be in excellent condition to start an engine?

5. What is the purpose of a generator in an automobile?

6. Why is a voltage regulator necessary?

7. Explain the purpose of an ignition coil.

8. How is the distributor used in the automobile ignition circuit?

9. What is the purpose of the spark plugs?

10. Why are sealed-beam lights used?

11. What methods are used to protect automobile electrical circuits?

Using

Electronics

for Communication

The modern telephone, Fig. 24-1, is one of the most frequently used electrical devices. It can change sound into a flow of electric current that can be sent over long distances and then change the current back into sound. The telephone was

Fig. 24-1. The illustration shows how interior parts of a modern dial telephone are arranged.

invented by Alexander Graham Bell, who sent the first message over a telephone circuit on March 10, 1876.

Sound Waves

Sound is made by a movement of air. This movement of air is called *air vibrations.* When someone speaks, air is set into waves of vibrations, Fig. 24-2. These vibrations hit a human eardrum and sound is heard. Each sound has a different number of vibrations per second. The number of vibrations per second is called the *frequency.*

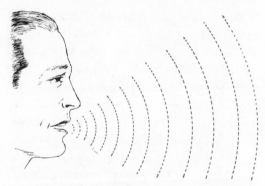

Fig. 24-2. When someone speaks air is set into vibrations. These vibrations are called *sound waves.*

Vibrating frequencies that can be heard by the human ear range from 20 hertz (cycles per second) to about 20,-000 hertz (c.p.s.). They are called *audio frequencies* because they are audible to the human ear. A frequency of 15,000

hertz (c.p.s.) is a very high-pitched vibration that very few people can hear. Vibrating frequencies are often drawn in picture form as shown in Fig. 24-3.

The Telephone Transmitter

The part of the telephone into which you speak is the telephone transmitter, called a *microphone.* A simple microphone consists of a round, thin, flexible diaphragm connected to a small cup that holds some grains of carbon. See Fig. 24-4. These grains of carbon are called *carbon granules;* they are made of roasted coal. The granules are held in the cup of a round disk that can move back and forth in the cup. This disk is connected to the diaphragm by a small rod. When voice waves hit the diaphragm it moves with the sound vibrations. The vibration of the diaphragm makes the small disk move inside of the cup of carbon. As the diaphragm is moved back and forth the

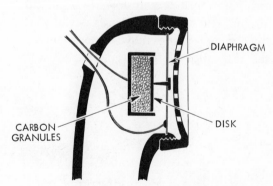

Fig. 24-4. Construction of a telephone microphone.

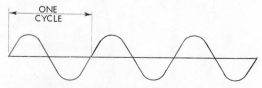

Fig. 24-3. This is the kind of picture used to show a waveform.

MICROPHONE

The microphone symbol is simple to draw.

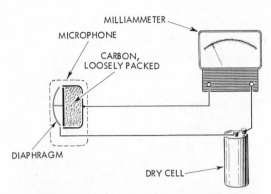

Fig. 24-5. Carbon granules of a microphone are loosely packed and provide a resistance to the current flow. The milliammeter shows that some current is flowing in the circuit.

carbon grains are packed more closely and then less closely.

If a battery is connected across the cup as shown in Fig. 24-5, a current would flow through the carbon, since it is a conductor of electricity. The carbon acts like a resistor connected across the battery. When the diaphragm moves as in Fig. 24-6, the carbon is packed closer together and more current will flow through the circuit. The current increases because as the carbon granules move closer together the resistance of the circuit is reduced.

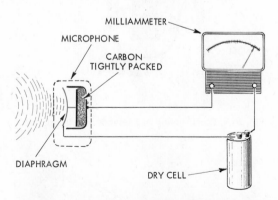

Fig. 24-6. Sound wave pushes diaphragm back and packs carbon granules together; when granules are closer together the resistance of the cup of granules is lowered. Current flow, as shown by the milliammeter, is increased as resistance is reduced.

We know that more resistance reduces the flow of electricity and less resistance increases the flow of electricity. When the diaphragm moves back the carbon grains become loosely packed and the current is reduced because the resistance in the circuit is increased.

The current flowing through the circuit will vary with the vibrations of the air waves that hit the diaphragm. The microphone produces a changing electric current that is varied with the sound waves.

The Telephone Receiver

The part of the telephone that is held to the ear is called a *receiver*. The telephone receiver must be able to change the electric current produced by the microphone back into sound waves. A simple receiver consists of a permanent magnet with a coil of wire wound around it and a thin flexible iron diaphragm mounted in front of the magnet and coil. See Fig. 24-7. The permanent magnet at-

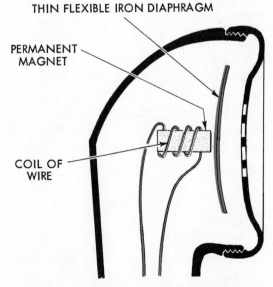

Fig. 24-7. A telephone receiver construction is shown here.

tracts the iron diaphragm and pulls it in slightly. When a current flows through the coil it becomes an electromagnet. The diaphragm has two magnets working on it—the permanent magnet and the electromagnet. If the current through the coil is changing, it will either increase the pull on the diaphragm or reduce the pull on the diaphragm. The current in the electromagnet moves the diaphragm back and forth. This movement of the diaphragm pushes the air back and forth in front of it. The movement of air in front of the diaphragm produces sound that can be heard by the human ear.

A Simple Telephone Circuit

To connect a telephone transmitter to a telephone receiver, it is usually neces-sary to use a step-up transformer. The step-up transformer is used to step up the small voltage produced by the microphone so that a much greater voltage is available for the receiver. See Fig. 24-8. The primary of the transformer is connected to the microphone and the secondary is connected to the receiver. The varying direct current produced by the movement of the carbon granules in the microphone induces an alternating current in the secondary of the transformer. The stepped-up secondary voltage is used to move the diaphragm of the receiver.

A Two-Way Telephone Circuit

To have a two-way telephone circuit (Fig. 24-9) it is necessary to have a receiver and a transmitter at each end of

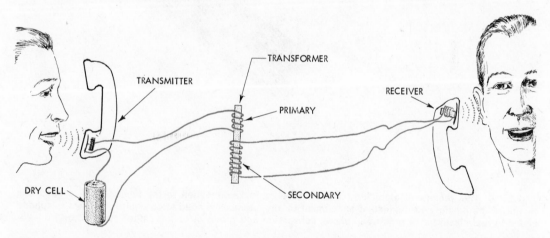

Fig. 24-8. A simple telephone circuit using a step-up transformer to couple the transmitter to the receiver.

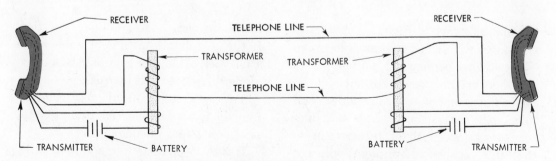

Fig. 24-9. This is how the connections for a two-way telephone circuit are made.

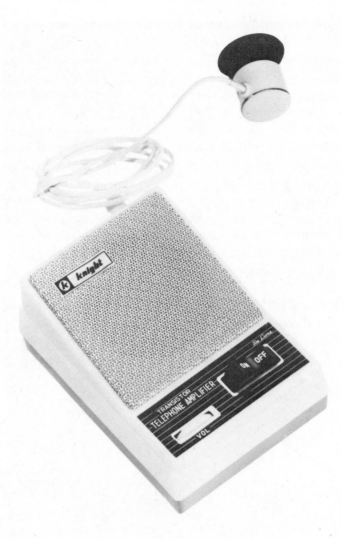

Fig. 24-10. This telephone amplifier requires no electrical connection to the telephone. A suction cup mount on the pickup permits instant attachment to any phone. The solid state circuit amplifies telephone sound to room level for "hands free" phone conversion and group listening. (Allied Radio Corp.)

the line, as shown in Fig. 24-9. A step-up transformer is also used at each location. The two lines connecting the telephones together may be some distance apart. When the phones must be located several miles apart the resistance of the wire lines reduces the strength of the current so that the receiver diaphragm will not move. To increase the strength of such

telephone circuits an amplifier is needed. If the telephones are many miles apart a number of different amplifiers located along the route must be used.

Transistor room amplifiers (Fig. 24-10) may be easily connected to individual telephones for convenience.

It is even possible to communicate by phone from one's automobile (Fig. 24-11).

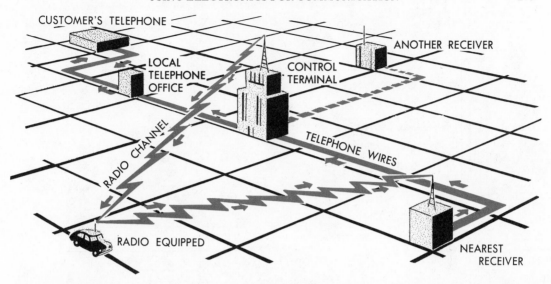

Fig. 24-11. The mobile radiotelephone service in cities makes it possible to place and receive telephone calls in an automobile. (Bell Systems.)

INTERESTING THINGS TO DO

Making a Carbon Microphone.

Materials needed to construct the carbon microphone (Fig. 24-12):

1 Piece wood, ½″ x 2″ x 3″
1 Piece sheet steel or brass, ½″ x 9½″, 24 gage
1 Metal bottle cap, approximately 1¼″ diameter
1 Felt washer, outside diameter to fit inside of bottle cap
1 Piece sheet brass, circular, diameter ⅛″ less than inside of bottle cap
1 Piece thin cardboard, circular, 3⅛″ diameter
2 Machine screws, FH, brass, 6-32, ¾″ long
5 Machine screw nuts, hexagon, brass, 6-32
1 Machine screw, RH, brass, 4-40, ¼″ long
2 Machine screw nuts, hexagon, brass, 4-40
1 Machine screw, RH, steel, 6-32, ½″ long
1 Piece carbon rod (removed from an old dry cell)

Fig. 24-12. The carbon microphone.

Drill the strip of sheet metal as shown in Fig. 24-13 and bend it to form a ring 3″ in diameter. Solder the two ends together where they overlap. Drill ⅛″ holes through the center of the brass disk and the circular piece of cardboard. Secure the brass disk to the cardboard with the 4–40 machine screw and hexagon nut. Glue the felt washer to the brass disk so that the head of the brass ma-

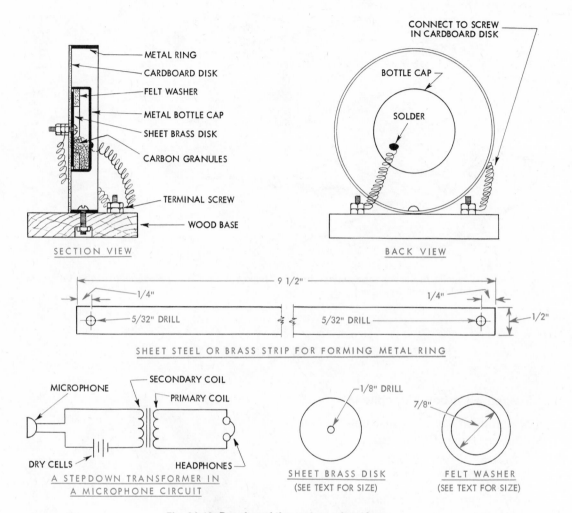

Fig. 24-13. Drawing of the carbon microphone.

chine screw is exactly in the center of the washer.

Crush the carbon rod into small pieces about $\frac{1}{16}$″ in diameter. For best results the broken pieces of carbon should be screened through a piece of window screen. Fill the bottle cap about three-fourths full with the carbon granules. Cement the cardboard circle to the bottle cap, making certain that the felt washer fits snugly inside the bottle cap. Cement the cardboard circle containing the bottle cap to the metal ring. Trim the

cardboard to the same size as the metal ring after the cement has set.

Drill a $\frac{5}{32}$″ hole through the center of the wood base and secure the metal ring to it with a 6–32 machine screw. Drill two $\frac{5}{32}$″ holes in the wood base and place flathead machine screws in them to serve as terminals. Solder a piece of No. 30 magnet wire to the back of the bottle cap and connect the opposite end to one of the terminal screws. Connect another piece of No. 30 wire to the screw in the center of the cardboard and con-

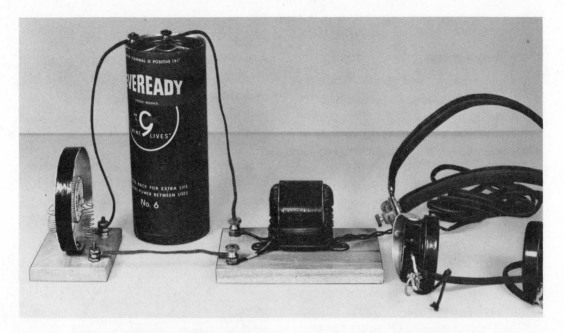

Fig. 24-14. The microphone connected to a transformer and a pair of earphones.

nect the opposite end to the remaining terminal screw. The microphone is now ready to operate.

A simple circuit for a microphone may be made by connecting the microphone in series with two dry cells and a pair of headphones. A much improved circuit, shown in Fig. 24-14, may be made by using the transformer which is described in Unit 17. This circuit makes the transformer step up the varying voltages caused by the microphone, so the sound in the headphones is increased many times. With two microphones and two sets of headphones a complete telephone system may be connected together.

REVIEW QUESTIONS

1. Who invented the telephone?
2. How is sound transmitted?
3. What are audio frequencies?
4. Name the principal parts of a telephone transmitter.
5. Explain how the carbon granules in a microphone produce a varying electric current.
6. Name the principal parts of a modern handset telephone receiver.
7. Explain how the diaphragm of a telephone receiver produces sound.
8. Draw a simple telephone circuit showing the receiver and transmitter.
9. Why is the transformer used?
10. When two telephones are a long distance apart, what must be used to increase the signal strength?

UNIT 25
RECEIVING RADIO WAVES

Radio Frequencies

A radio receiver is a standard article in almost every home. In addition to its use in the home, it is also used to provide communication between ships at sea, to control airplanes, to guide air missiles, and for many other purposes. Radio signals cannot be seen but are being sent out in every direction by many types of radio stations. These radio signals are called *radio waves.*

Radio waves are produced by alternating current that is changing directions of flow very rapidly. We learned that audio frequencies range from 20 hertz (c.p.s.) to 20,000 hertz (c.p.s.). These are the frequencies that are used to produce sound. Radio waves are made up of alternating current that has a frequency that is greater than 20,000 hertz (c.p.s.). There are a great many radio waves; some have a frequency as high as 300 million hertz (c.p.s.) or more. Radio broadcasting stations that are received by a standard broadcast receiver have frequencies from 535,000 hertz (c.p.s.) to 1,605,000 hertz (c.p.s.).

Because radio frequencies have such a large number of cycles per second it is usual to express the frequency in *kilohertz* (kc.p.s.). *Kilo* means one thousand.

A broadcast station that states that it is operating on a frequency of 600 kilohertz means that its frequency is 600,000 hertz (c.p.s.).

Sending Out Radio Waves

When very rapid alternating currents, called *radio frequencies,* flow through a wire they tend to leave the wire and to start traveling through space. They go out in every direction.

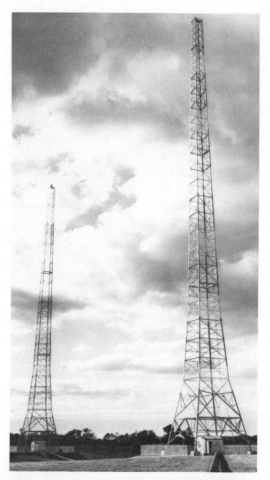

Fig. 25-1. These are the transmitting towers of the NBC 50,000-watt station WRCA, Port Washington, Long Island. (National Broadcasting Co.)

ANTENNA

This is the general symbol for an antenna.

At a broadcast station a large transmitter is used to generate radio-frequency waves (Fig. 25-1). The transmitter is connected to a tower called an *antenna*. The radio waves flow up the antenna and leave it to go out into the air. See Fig. 25-2.

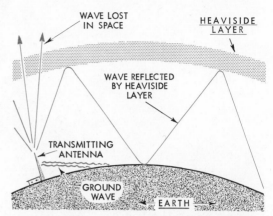

Fig. 25-3. Radio waves go out from the transmitter in all directions. Ground waves follow the ground. Some sky waves are lost in space. Other sky waves hit the Heaviside layer and are reflected back to earth. Waves may be reflected back and forth between the Heaviside layer and the earth so that they sometimes travel very long distances.

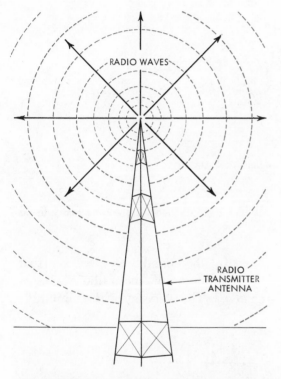

Fig. 25-2. Radio waves leave the transmitting antenna going out in every direction.

Some waves follow the ground and are called *ground waves*. The ground waves do not go very far and soon become too weak to be received. Some radio waves go up into the sky; they are called *sky waves*. The sky waves may go straight out into space and become lost. Other waves hit a layer of electrified particles called the *Heaviside layer*. The Heaviside layer acts like a mirror reflecting the waves back to the earth. See Fig. 25-3. It

is because of the Heaviside layer that radio signals can be received many thousands of miles away from the transmitter. The Heaviside layer varies in height above the earth from 50 to 200 miles.

Radio waves travel at the speed of light, 186,000 miles per second. At this speed, signals are received almost instantly after being sent out.

Putting the Sound with the Radio Waves

When we tune a radio receiver to a broadcast station we hear the sound of the announcer or music. The sound could not be heard very far if the radio waves were not used to carry it through the air.

A microphone similar to the telephone microphone is used in the broadcast station to pick up the sound of the announcer's voice or the music. This voice or music is the audio frequency that we hear when we turn on a radio receiver.

The microphone changes the sound vibrations into a varying electric current. An amplifier is then used to increase the

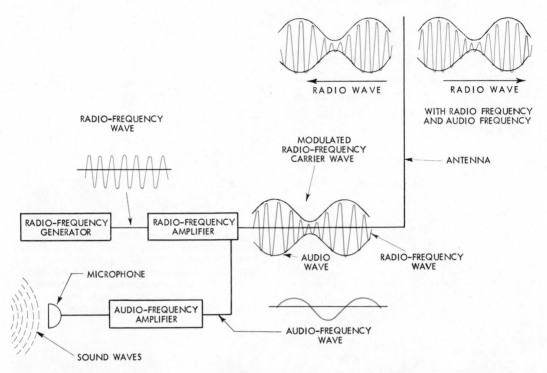

Fig. 25-4. This block diagram of a transmitter shows how the audio frequencies are combined with the radio-frequency carrier wave.

strength of the sound frequencies. After the amplifier makes the audio waves stronger they are combined with the radio waves by the transmitter. The radio-frequency wave being produced by the transmitter is called a *carrier wave* because it carries the audio frequencies with it. Fig. 25-4 shows what happens when the sound waves are combined with the radio waves. When the audio-frequency waves combine with the radio-frequency wave, at the transmitter, the radio-frequency wave is said to be *modulated*. The purpose of a radio receiver is to tune in on the radio waves and then separate the sound so that it can be heard through the loudspeaker.

Amplitude Modulation

If the voltage or current of the radio frequency waves are varied when modu-

lated by the sound wave, we say that the amplitude of the radio waves is changed. This varying of the amplitude

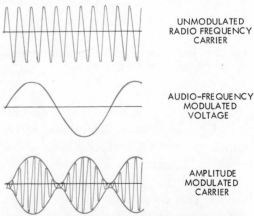

Fig. 25-5. Graphic representation of Amplitude Modulation. At top is the carrier wave of the transmitter. The audio wave from a microphone is imposed on the carrier and the two combine to produce the modulated carrier wave shown at the bottom.

of the radio frequency is called *amplitude modulation* as illustrated by the modulated radio frequency wave in Fig. 25-5. Amplitude modulation is often abbreviated as *AM* and it is the type of modulation used for standard broadcasting stations.

Frequency Modulation

One other method of modulation called frequency modulation (*FM*) is used for broadcasting the audio portion of a television signal and also on FM broadcast stations. In frequency modulation the audio or sound is superimposed on the carrier by varying the frequency of the carrier. When the modulated signal is applied to the carrier wave, the frequency of the carrier is increased during one half cycle of the modulated signal and decreased during the other half cycle of the opposite polarity, Fig. 25-6. The amplitude of the carrier remains the same during modulation and the sound or audio is represented by the change in frequency of the carrier. One advantage of FM broadcasting is that static or noises do not affect the carrier and thus do not interfere with the signal.

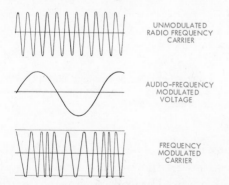

UNMODULATED RADIO FREQUENCY CARRIER

AUDIO-FREQUENCY MODULATED VOLTAGE

FREQUENCY MODULATED CARRIER

Fig. 25-6. Graphic representation of Frequency Modulation. When the audio frequency modulating signal is imposed on the carrier, the frequency of the carrier signal increases or decreases according to the amplitude and polarity of the audio wave.

Receiving Radio Waves

To receive radio waves it is necessary to have a radio receiver that will tune in the desired stations. Radio receivers use either an outside antenna wire or a wire inside of the cabinet for the antenna. If the receiver is a long distance from the transmitter, an outside wire antenna that has been raised above the housetops will help bring in the waves.

When the radio waves hit the receiver antenna a very weak current will begin to flow in the antenna wire. Since there are a great many stations all sending out radio signals, a number of different radio-frequency currents can be coming in contact with the receiving antenna at the same time. It then becomes necessary to be able to select only one station at a time. A *tuner* is used in the receiver to tune in each of the different stations. When we turn the dial of a radio receiver, we are adjusting the tuner to the station that we wish to hear.

The Ground System

The tuner of a radio receiver is connected to the antenna and also to the ground. The ground may be a wire connected to a water pipe or sometimes to the metal frame of the radio receiver. Every electrical circuit requires two paths for the current to flow through. In a radio signal the air is one path, and the ground is the other path.

Tuning with a Coil

The purpose of the tuner is to select the station that is sending out radio waves on a fixed frequency. The tuner must select one frequency and not permit any of the other signals to be heard in the receiver.

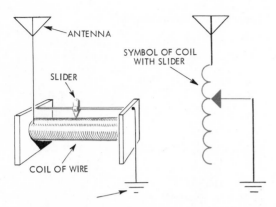

Fig. 25-7. A coil with a slider may be used to tune a radio receiver.

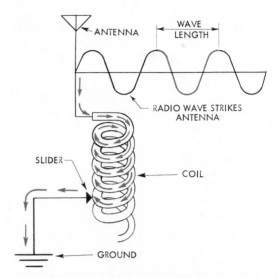

Fig. 25-8. Radio waves hit the antenna and start electrons flowing through the coil to ground.

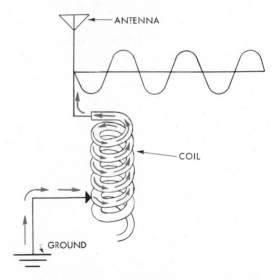

Fig. 25-9. When the alternating current of the radio waves changes direction the electrons flow from ground to antenna.

One method of making a tuner is to use a coil of wire with a slider that comes in contact with each of the turns on the coil, as shown in Fig. 25-7. One end of the coil is connected to the antenna, and the ground is connected to the slider. By moving the slider, the length of the coil of wire between the antenna and ground can be changed. When the radio waves strike the antenna a current starts to flow down the antenna and through the coil to ground. The alternating current of the radio waves will flow first in one direction and then in the other direction, as shown in Figs. 25-8 and 25-9. This current is a flow of electrons in the coil, and the more turns of wire used on the coil the longer it will take the electrons to flow through the coil.

When the slider is moved so that only a few turns of wire are connected between the antenna and ground, the electrons can flow through the coil in one direction and then back in the other direction in a very short time.

After the electrons flow through the coil and back again another radio wave strikes the antenna. If this radio wave is in step with the current flowing in the coil, the second wave will start more elec-trons flowing at the same time that the electrons in the coil are ready to start back again. The coil of wires is then in tune with the radio wave.

The other radio waves that strike the antenna will not be in step with the elec-tron flow in the coil, and they will not be able to flow in the coil. These unwanted radio signals are not accepted by the tuner.

A large number of turns of wire will

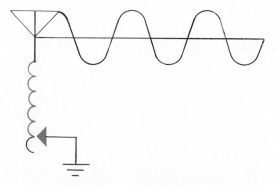

Fig. 25-10. The tuner receives low-frequency stations when there are many turns of wire in the coil between the antenna and ground.

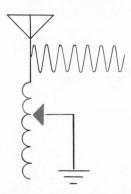

Fig. 25-11. The tuner receives higher frequency stations when there are very few turns between the antenna and ground.

tune to a low frequency because it takes longer for the electrons to flow through the coil. A small number of turns of wire tune to a high frequency. See Figs. 25-10 and 25-11. When the coil is tuned to a particular frequency it is said to be in *resonance* with that frequency.

Tuning with a Variable Capacitor

Another method of tuning a radio receiver is to use a coil of wire with a *variable capacitor* connected across each end of the coil. (*Capacitors* were formerly called *condensers* and the term is still sometimes used.) A variable capacitor consists of a group of metal plates all joined together, called the *stator* plates, and another group of plates all joined together by a shaft so that they can be rotated, called the *rotor* plates. See Fig. 25-12. The rotor plates slide inside the stator plates without touching each other.

VARIABLE
CAPACITOR

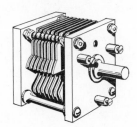

The curved line represents the moving element of a variable capacitor.

Fig. 25-12. Three kinds of variable capacitors are shown here. They were formerly called condensers.

Air separates the rotor plates from the stator plates. The variable capacitor has the same effect in tuning the circuit as changing the number of turns on a coil. See Figs. 25-13 thru 25-15.

The capacitor acts like a storage place for electrons. It can store either a few electrons or many electrons. When the rotor is turned so that all of the plates are inside of the stator plates the capacitor is able to store more electrons than when it is opened.

When the capacitor is closed and stores lots of electrons, the circuit acts like a coil with many turns of wire. It then tunes to a low frequency. See Fig. 25-14.

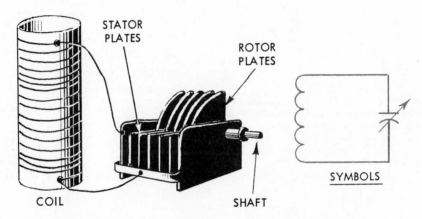

Fig. 25-13. Coil and variable capacitor that are used as a radio tuner.

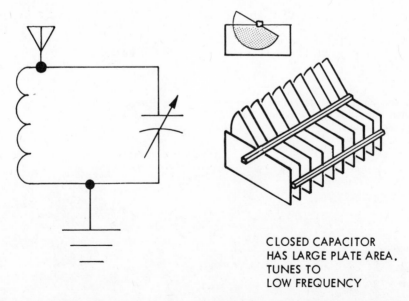

CLOSED CAPACITOR HAS LARGE PLATE AREA. TUNES TO LOW FREQUENCY

Fig. 25-14. When the variable capacitor is almost closed it stores lots of electrons and tunes to a low frequency. The frequency is determined by the time it takes for all of the electrons to flow from one side of the capacitor through the coil to the other side of the capacitor and then back again.

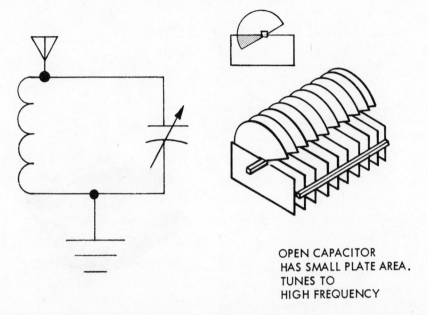

OPEN CAPACITOR
HAS SMALL PLATE AREA.
TUNES TO
HIGH FREQUENCY

Fig. 25-15. When the capacitor is opened it stores few electrons. This circuit tunes to a higher frequency.

If the capacitor is opened and the plates are separated, very few electrons are stored. The tuner will now receive higher frequency signals because there will not be as many electrons to flow through the circuit. See Fig. 25-15. Each movement of the capacitor tunes the coil to a new frequency.

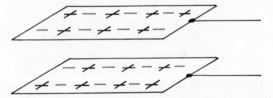

Fig. 25-16. An uncharged capacitor has an equal amount of positive and negative charges on each plate. The plates are separated by an air dielectric.

Construction of a Capacitor

We have briefly discussed the use of variable capacitors in tuning circuits, but since capacitors are so very important in all phases of electronics, a more complete discussion is given. A capacitor consists of two or more metal plates which have been placed close to each other as shown in Fig. 25-16. The plates do not touch each other, and they are separated by air or some other insulating material called the "dielectric". If a battery is connected across the plates as in Fig. 25-17 electrons will flow onto plate "A" which is con- nected to the negative terminal of the

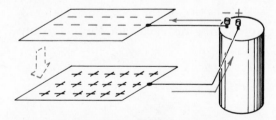

Fig. 25-17. When the capacitor is charged, plate A has a surplus of electrons. Plate B is positive since it has a deficiency of electrons.

battery. The electrons on plate "B" will be repelled by the electrons on plate "A". Thus the electrons on plate "B" will flow toward the positive terminal of the bat-

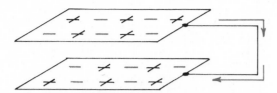

Fig. 25-18. If the plates are connected by a wire, electrons will flow from plate A to plate B until the charge is equal.

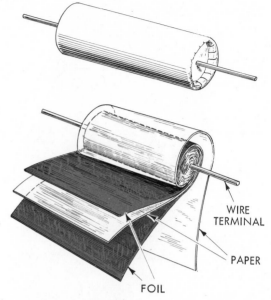

tery. This electrons movement will stop when the charge or electromotive force between the plates is equal to the electromotive force of the battery.

Now if the battery is disconnected plate "A" has a negative charge and plate "B" with a shortage of electrons will have a positive charge. If the wires from the two plates are touched together the electrons on plate "A" will flow to plate "B" until both plates have an equal number of electrons. See Fig. 25-18. The plates are said to be neutral and the capacitor is then discharged.

WIRE TERMINAL

PAPER

FOIL

Fig. 25-19. Paper capacitors are made of alternate layers of paper and foil.

Determining the Capacitance of a Capacitor

We have learned that a capacitor can store electricity. Its storing capacity depends upon (1) the area of the plates, (2) the dielectric of the insulating material, and (3) the distance that the plates are apart.

In capacitors using paper as a dielectric, two sheets of metal foil are rolled together with the paper placed between the metal plates as in Fig. 25-19. The longer and the wider the metal foil the greater the area of the two plates. By having a large area for the plates they will be able to store more electrons and thus produce a capacitor with ability to hold more electrons. See Fig. 25-20.

The insulating material such as the paper has what is known as a dielectric con-

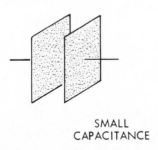

SMALL
CAPACITANCE

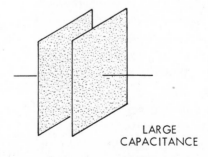

LARGE
CAPACITANCE

Fig. 25-20. If the area of the plates of a capacitor is increased, the capacitance is increased, providing the dielectric and distance between the plates remain the same.

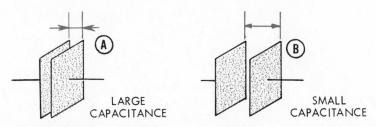

Fig. 25-21. The closer the surface of the plates are in a capacitor, the greater the capacitance, if the plate area and the dielectric are the same.

stant. Air is said to have a dielectric constant of 1 and other materials are compared with air. For example, paper has a dielectric constant of about 3 depending upon the type and the thickness of the paper. A capacitor with paper as a dielectric will then have 3 times more capacitance than a capacitor with air as the dielectric. Of course, this is assuming that the distance between the plates of the paper capacitor and the air capacitor were exactly the same.

The closer the plates are to each other, the more effect the charge on one plate will have on the other plate, Fig. 25-21. This means that the closer the plates are together the greater the capacitance of the capacitor.

The Unit of Capacitance

The fundamental unit of capacitance is the *farad*. For most practical purposes

the farad is too large a unit, so that, usually capacitors are measured in *microfarads* or *picafarads,* formerly called micromicrofarads. Microfarad means one millionth of a farad and it is abbreviated μf. Picafarad means one millionth of a microfarad and it is abbreviated pf.

Types of Capacitors

Capacitors are called either fixed (Fig. 25-22) or variable capacitors. A variable capacitor used to tune broadcast receivers is usually a .00035 microfarad. This same capacitor in picafarads would be a 350 picafarad capacitor. This means when the rotor plates are completely inside of a stator plate it has a capacitance of 350 picafarads. When the rotor plates are turned so that they are all out of the stator plates, the capacitance should be about zero.

Fixed ceramic capacitors using titan-

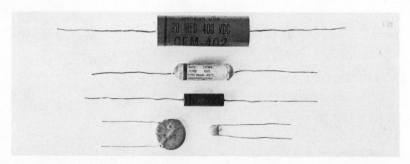

Fig. 25-22. Fixed capacitors come in various sizes and voltage ratings. The two capacitors shown on the bottom are of the ceramic disc type. The top and third are tubular types with different capacity and voltage ratings. The capacitor between the tubulars is a molded plastic type.

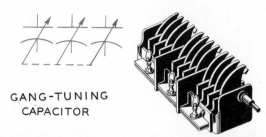

GANG-TUNING
CAPACITOR

A dash line is used to indicate that there is a mechanical connection.

FIXED
CAPACITOR

The curved line indicates the outside electrode in fixed paper or ceramic capacitors and the negative electrode of an electrolytic capacitor.

ium dioxide for the dielectric are fast becoming one of the most popular type capacitors because they are small and are not easily affected by temperature changes. Mica also is a very useful dielectric and mica capacitors are usually molded in a plastic case.

Electrolytic Capacitors

A very common capacitor used in electronic circuits is the electrolytic capacitor. See Fig. 25-23. Electrolytic capacitors provide a very large capacitance in a small container. It is possible to have a 500 microfarad electrolytic capacitor in a can only one inch in diameter and two inches long. These capacitors may be either of the wet or dry type.

It is extremely important to observe the polarity markings of electrolytic capacitors when wiring them in circuits. If the capacitor is connected backwards

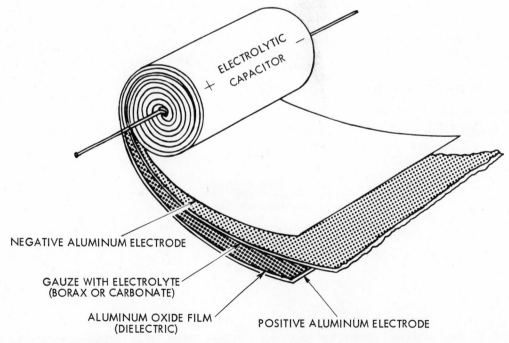

NEGATIVE ALUMINUM ELECTRODE

GAUZE WITH ELECTROLYTE
(BORAX OR CARBONATE)

ALUMINUM OXIDE FILM
(DIELECTRIC)

POSITIVE ALUMINUM ELECTRODE

Fig. 25-23. Electrolytic capacitors are desirable where a large capacity is needed for a small space.

so that the polarity is reversed the capacitor will be ruined and the circuit will be shorted.

Breakdown Voltage

Capacitors are made to withstand certain voltages. To exceed this voltage rating ruins the capacitor. This voltage rating, called the *working voltage,* is marked on the capacitor or is shown in the color coding.

Testing Capacitors

The most common failure of a capacitor occurs when there is a short in the capacitor. When a capacitor is shorted, there is an internal breakdown in the dielectric. The break in the dielectric permits the two plates to touch each other or it carbonizes so that there is a low resistance between the plates. A shorted or leaky capacitor can be tested through the use of an ohmmeter.

When testing for a shorted capacitor,

in a circuit, it is usually desirable to disconnect one lead of the capacitor from the circuit. By disconnecting the capacitor from the circuit, it is possible to test only the capacitor and not other parts of the circuit. Place the ohmmeter leads across the capacitor as shown in Fig. 25-24. If the capacitor is shorted, the resistance will be very low and the ohmmeter will read a low resistance. Any capacitor of 0.1 microfarad or more will produce a kick of the ohmmeter needle when first connected. This is due to the charging of the capacitor by the battery of the ohmmeter. If a paper, mica, or ceramic capacitor registers less than about 10 megohms after a second or two, it may be considered to be leaking or shorted.

An electrolytic capacitor will read low resistance the first instant it is tested but should register more than 100,000 ohms after a few seconds. When an electrolytic capacitor is tested with the ohmmeter leads reversed, a different resistance

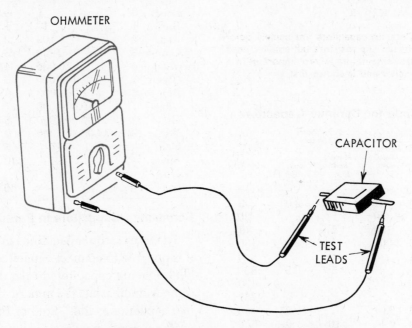

OHMMETER

CAPACITOR

TEST LEADS

Fig. 25-24. Testing a capacitor for a short using an ohmmeter.

value will be registered. A leaking or shorted capacitor should be replaced.

To determine whether or not a capacitor has the correct capacitance, it is necessary to use a capacitor tester. Some capacitor testers may be applied without disconnecting the capacitor from the circuit, but, for the beginner, it is advisable to disconnect the capacitor before testing.

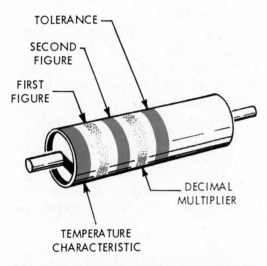

Fig. 25-25. Ceramic capacitors are usually color coded with bands like resistors but smaller ones may use dots. Temperature is very important in a ceramic capacitor and is shown first.

Color Coding Capacitors

Paper and electrolytic capacitors are usually labeled to indicate their capacitance. Mica and ceramic capacitors use either a labeled marking or a color coding. The color code gives the capacitance in picafarads. Ceramic capacitors use a band marking system as in Fig. 25-25. Mica capacitors use a six dot system as in Fig. 25-26.

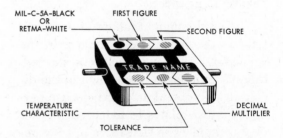

Fig. 25-26. The color code on mica capacitors shows the information indicated.

Capacitor Color Code

Color	Significant Figure	Decimal Multiplier	Tolerance (%)	Voltage Rating
Black	0	1	—	—
Brown	1	10	1	100
Red	2	100	2	200
Orange	3	1000	3	300
Yellow	4	10,000	4	400
Green	5	100,000	5	500
Blue	6	1,000,000	6	600
Violet	7	10,000,000	7	700
Gray	8	100,000,000	8	800
White	9	1,000,000,000	9	900
Gold	—	0.1	5	1000
Silver	—	0.01	10	2000
No color	—	—	20	500

Color Code for Ceramic Capacitors

Color	Significant Figure	Decimal Multiplier	Capacitance Tolerance More than 10pf (in %)	Capacitance Tolerance Less than 10pf (in pf)	Temp. Coeff. deg. C.
Black	0	1	±20	2.0	0
Brown	1	10	±1		−30
Red	2	100	±2		−80
Orange	3	1000			−150
Yellow	4				−220
Green	5		±5	0.5	−330
Blue	6				−470
Violet	7				−750
Gray	8	0.01		0.25	30
White	9	0.1	±10	1.0	500

Connecting Capacitors in Parallel

To increase the capacitance in a circuit, it is possible to connect capacitors in parallel. Placing capacitors in parallel is the same as increasing the area of the plates in a capacitor as illustrated in Fig. 25-27.

If a circuit needs additional capaci-

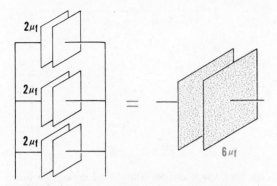

Fig. 25-27. When capacitors are connected in parallel it has the effect of increasing the plate area and the total capacitance is increased.

tance, several capacitors may be connected in parallel. For example, when two capacitors of 10 microfarads and 12 microfarads are connected in parallel, the total capacitance is 22 microfarads.

The formula for capacitances connected in parallel is:

$$C_{\text{TOTAL}} = C_1 + C_2 + C_3 + \text{etc.}$$

Connecting Capacitors in Series

When capacitors are connected in series, the total capacitance in the circuit is decreased. Capacitors connected in series provide the same effect as increasing the spacing between the plates of the capacitor as shown in Fig. 25-28.

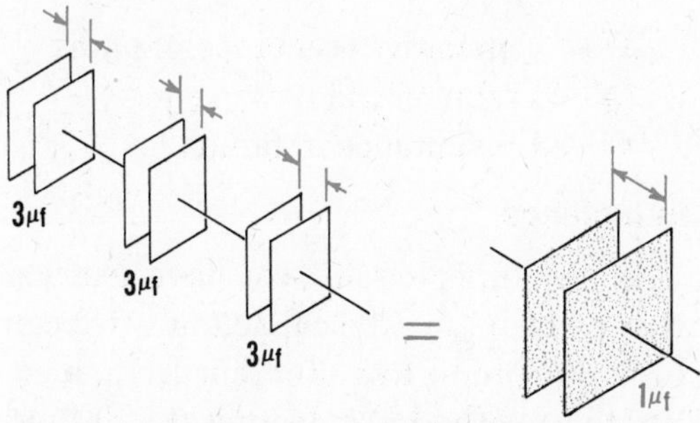

Fig. 25-28. Capacitors connected in series have the same effect as increasing the distance between the plates and capacitance is decreased.

The formula for capacitances in series is:

$$\frac{1}{C_{\text{TOTAL}}} = \frac{1}{C_1} + \frac{1}{C_2} + \frac{1}{C_3} + \text{etc.}$$

$$C_{\text{TOTAL}} = \frac{1}{\dfrac{1}{C_1} + \dfrac{1}{C_2} + \dfrac{1}{C_3} + \text{etc.}}$$

If two capacitors of the same capacitance are connected in series, the total capacitance in the circuit is cut in half. When two 10 microfarad capacitors are in series, the total capacitance is then equal to 5 microfarads.

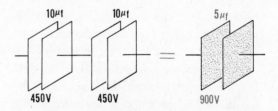

Fig. 25-29. When capacitors are connected in series the voltage rating is equal to the sum of the working voltages of the capacitors.

Many times in high voltage circuits the voltage ratings of the capacitors are not great enough for the circuit. In such instances it is possible to place capacitors in series to obtain the necessary voltage rating. For example, if the output voltage of a circuit is 700 volts and if a 10 microfarad capacitor having a voltage rating of 450 volts is available, it could not be used in the circuit. Two such capacitors could, however, be connected in series so that the voltage rating would be increased to 900 volts. The total capacitance in the circuit with the two 10 microfarad capacitors in series would then be 5 microfarads, Fig. 25-29.

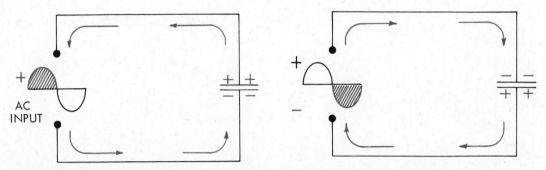

Fig. 25-30. When alternating current is applied to a capacitor, the capacitor will charge during the first half cycle as shown in the top drawing. When the current reverses and the next half cycle flows, the capacitor discharges and is recharged to the opposite polarity as shown in the bottom drawing. This charging and discharging continues as long as AC is applied.

The Effect of Alternating Current on a Capacitor

When a direct current is applied to a capacitor, current stops flowing when the plates of the capacitor become fully charged. Since the dielectric material is an insulator it prevents further current from flowing through the circuit. If instead of DC we apply an alternating current to the plates of a capacitor, current will flow in the circuit. With AC the electrons flow first in one direction and then reverse and flow in the opposite direction. Fig. 25-30 shows that electrons flow toward one plate of the capacitor during one-half of the alternating current cycle and then when the current reverses they flow toward the other plate of the capacitor. Thus, electrons go back and forth in the circuit even though they do not flow directly through the capacitor. As a result of this current flow, it is customary, when using alternating current, to say that current flows through the capacitor.

Capacitive Reactance

When a capacitor is placed in an AC circuit it offers opposition to the current flow much like a resistor. The capaci-

tor creates a counter electromotive force that opposes the flow of current in the circuit. A small capacitance will have much more opposition to current flow than a large capacitance. Also, when a low frequency is applied to a capacitor it will have a greater opposition than when a high frequency is used. Thus, both the value of the capacitor and the frequency determine the amount of current that flows in the circuit.

This opposition to current flow is called capacitive reactance and it is stated in ohms. The amount of capacitive reactance depends upon the value of the capacitor and the frequency of the circuit. The formula for capacitive reactance is:

$$X_c = \frac{1}{2\pi f C}$$

$X_c =$ Capacitive reactance in ohms

$f =$ Frequency in hertz (c.p.s.)

$C =$ Capacitance in farads

Inductance

In the tuner circuit we have learned that by changing the capacitance we can tune the circuit to a different frequency. Another method of selecting the desired frequency would be to change the number of turns on the coil. By changing the turns on the coil we can change its inductance. This is often done with switches or sliders which make contact with turns on the coil. Many of the coils used in tuning electronic circuits are called "*air core coils*" because they have no magnetic material in their centers. Another coil called a "*slug tuned*" type has a metal core which is moved in and out to vary its inductance. The term *inductance* may be defined as the property of a circuit which opposes a change of current through it. The inductance of coils used for tuning radio circuits is usually expressed in terms of *millihenrys*, or *microhenrys. Milli* means one thousandth and *micro* means one millionth. The inductance of the larger coils called "choke coils" that are usually used in power supplies is generally expressed in henrys. The inductance of a coil is determined by:

(1) the diameter of the coil
(2) the length of the coil
(3) the number of turns of wire
(4) the core.

Inductive Reactance

The opposition to current flow through a coil is called inductive reactance and is measured in ohms. The amount of reactance is directly proportional to the frequency and the size of the coil. That is, the higher the frequency, or the larger the coil, the more reactance there will be in the circuit. The formula for inductive reactance is:

$$X_L = 2\pi fL$$

$X_L =$ Inductive reactance in ohms
$f =$ Frequency in hertz (c.p.s.)
$L =$ Inductance in henrys

Impedance

When we speak of the *impedance* of a circuit we mean its total resistance to the flow of alternating current. This can consist of the resistance of the coil and its inductive reactance or a circuit containing capacitive reactance supplied by a capacitor.

When a coil is connected to a source of alternating current, the counter electromotive force developed within the coil prevents the current from reaching its maximum value instantly. The current is said to "lag" behind the voltage, as shown in Fig. 25-31. When a capacitor is connected to an alternating current supply, an opposite effect occurs. Here the counter electromotive force developed in the capacitor by the charging current prevents the source voltage from reaching its maximum value until the capacitor is fully charged. The current is then said to "lead" the voltage, as shown in Fig. 25-32. Since the effects of lagging and leading currents tend to neutralize each other when they are equal, they must be considered when determining the total im-

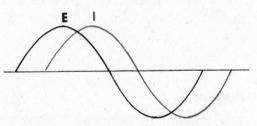

Fig. 25-31. An alternating current cycle showing the current lagging behind the voltage.

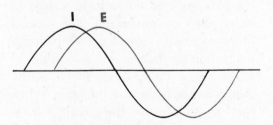

Fig. 25-32. Alternating current cycle showing the current leading the voltage.

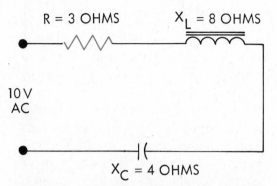

Fig. 25-33. A coil and capacitor connected to form an impedance circuit. The resistance of the coil, R, is always shown as a separate unit in series with the coil.

pedance of a circuit. For example, in the circuit shown in Fig. 25-33, a coil and capacitor are connected in series. The coil has a resistance of three ohms and an inductive reactance of eight ohms. The capacitor has a capacitive reactance of four ohms, which will cancel four ohms of the inductive reactance and leave a total of four ohms as the effective reactance of the circuit. Substituting the above values in the impedance formula, we find that the total impedance of the circuit is:

$$Z = \sqrt{R^2 + X^2_L}$$
$$= \sqrt{3^2 + 4^2} = \sqrt{25} = 5 \text{ ohms}$$

Resonance

When an inductance and a capacitor are adjusted so that their reactances are equal, they are said to be in resonance to the frequency of the voltage source to which they are connected. The process of tuning a radio signal from a broadcasting station means that we have adjusted either a capacitance or an inductance so that their reactances are the same. When they are so adjusted the circuit will respond to one frequency and reject all others.

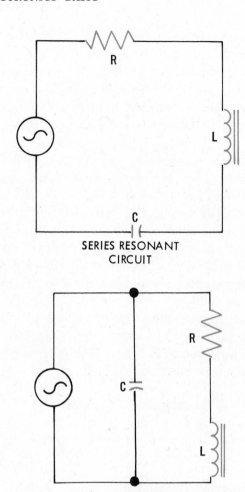

SERIES RESONANT CIRCUIT

PARALLEL RESONANT CIRCUIT

Fig. 25-34. Resonant circuits may be either series or parallel. The frequency at which they are resonant is determined by the amount of inductance of the coil and the capacitance. Large inductances and capacitances make the circuit resonant at low frequencies. Small inductances and capacitances tune to high frequencies.

A series resonant circuit and a parallel resonant circuit are shown in Fig. 25-34.

Calculating Resonant Frequency

The frequency of the supply line to which a coil and capacitor will become resonant is governed by the inductance of the coil and the capacitance of the capacitor. This frequency may be calculated by the following formula:

$$F = \frac{1}{6.28 \times \sqrt{LC}}$$

F = Frequency in hertz (c.p.s.)
L = Inductance in henrys
C = Capacity in farads

Resonant circuits present one of the most interesting phases of our study of electronics, because many of the principles under which they function appear to run contrary to what we have learned about current flow in series and parallel circuits. For example, in Fig. 25-33 the combination of inductance, capacitance, and resistance was calculated to have an impedance of five ohms. Assuming a supply of 10 volts, AC, and substituting Z for R in the Ohm's law formula, $I = E/Z$, we find that two amperes would flow in the circuit. Now let us assume that we have replaced the capacitor with one having a reactance of eight ohms.

On first thought we might conclude that adding the additional reactance to the circuit would reduce the current flow through it, but if we measured the current flow with an ammeter we would find that rather than decreasing, the current flow has increased to 3.3 amperes. When we increased the capacitive reactance to eight ohms we made it equal to the reactance of the coil. Since both units had the same reactance their effects were cancelled, leaving only the three ohm resistance of the coil to determine the current flow.

Resonance experiments at the high frequencies used in radio are often difficult to perform, owing to the lack of adequate measuring equipment. Since the principles of resonance are the same regardless of the frequencies used, we can perform experiments with 60-cycle alternating current which will provide a thorough understanding of what takes place in resonant circuits. To conduct these ex-

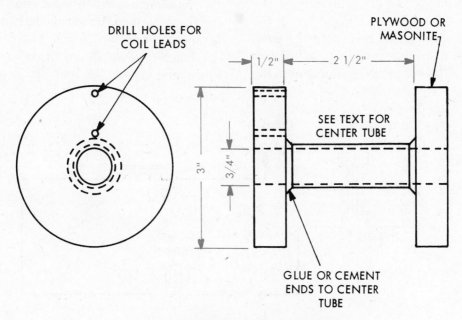

Fig. 25-35. Details for making coil form.

periments we will need the following materials:

- 1 24-volt door chime transformer
- 1 S.P.S.T. toggle switch
- 1 Rheostat, wire wound, 25 to 50 ohms
- 1 Capacitor, non-electrolytic, 10 mfd, 250 volts or higher
- 3 Miniature lamp receptacles
- 3 Pilot lamps, 6-8 volts
- 2 Lbs. magnet wire, 24 ga., enameled covered
- 20 Pieces iron wire, 16 or 18 ga., five inches long
- 1 Coil form (see Figure 25-35)

The center of the coil form may be made from a piece of one inch wood dowel, drilled out to ¾″, or a piece of micarta or brass tubing. If brass tubing is used it should be slotted its full length on one side to prevent eddy currents from being set up in the tube when magnetic lines pass through it.

Series Resonance

Connect the parts as shown in Fig. 25-36. Adjust the rheostat to about its center position, connect the transformer to a 117-volt AC supply and turn on the switch. Place pieces of iron wire in the core center, one by one, until the lamp reaches maximum brilliancy. When further addition of pieces of iron wire to the

coil center causes the lamp to get dimmer, the point of resonance will have been reached. The purpose of the rheostat is to prevent excessive voltage from burning out the lamps. It should be adjusted as needed to keep the lamp voltage within safe limits. By moving the iron wires in a group toward and away from the point of resonance we will be duplicating the action of tuning a high frequency radio signal with a slug-tuned coil, just as it is done in tuning a typical broadcast receiver.

If we connect a 150-volt AC voltmeter across the terminals of the capacitor, it will indicate about 132 volts (Fig. 25-37). The voltmeter placed across the terminals of the coil will show the same reading. At this point we may wonder how it is possible to get such high voltage readings when the input voltage is only 24 volts. The explanation lies in the fact that the high voltage readings do not represent the line voltage but are due to counter electromotive force developed in the coil and capacitor by the current flowing through them. If we calculate the reactance of the 10 μf capacitor with the reactance formula shown in the section on capacitors, we will find that it has a

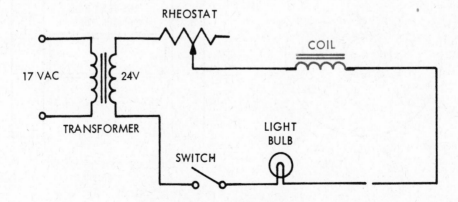

Fig. 25-36. Series resonant circuit.

Fig. 25-37. In a series-resonant circuit, resonance is indicated by high voltage across the terminals of the capacitor and the inductance. As shown above these voltages rise to 132 volts with a line voltage of only 24 volts.

reactance of approximately 265 ohms at 60 cycles. By measuring the resistance of the coil with an ohmmeter, or calculating it from the amount of wire used, we will get a value of about 52 ohms. We learned that when a circuit is resonant the capacitive reactance and the inductive reactance cancel their effects and leave only the resistance of the circuit to control the amount of current flow. Since we know that the resistance of the coil is 52 ohms and the applied voltage is 24, we can quickly determine by the use of Ohm's law that the current flowing in the circuit will be approximately one-half ampere.

Now, here is where we can account for the high voltage. The reactance of the capacitor has been calculated to be 265 ohms and since at resonance capacitive resistance and inductive reactance are equal, the coil will also have a reactance of 265 ohms. Using Ohm's law again and solving for E, ($E = 265 \times 0.5 = 132.5$ volts) we find that a current of 0.5 ampere flowing through a reactance of 265 ohms will produce a counter electromotive force of 132.5 volts. This corresponds very closely to the voltmeter measurement of 132 volts.

If we place separate voltmeters across the coil and capacitor, both would indicate the maximum voltage simultaneously. Actually, if the meter pointer could respond to the rise and fall of the voltage and our eyes could follow the meter pointer, we would see each meter register maximum voltage alternately while the other meter showed zero voltage. Although the separate coil and capacitor units show high voltage, their combined effect on the voltage of the circuit is zero. This can be shown by connecting a voltmeter across coil and capacitor and noting the reading. The meter will indicate not the combined voltage of the two units, 264 volts, but only the supply line voltage of 24 volts.

Series resonant circuits should be handled with caution, not only for personal safety, but for the safety of equipment as well. Even moderate voltages such as 117 can rise to the dangerously high levels of 600 to 700 volts under certain conditions of series resonance.

Parallel Resonance

Connect the parts as shown in Fig. 25-38. Adjust the rheostat so that all of the resistance will be in the circuit. This can be adjusted later to provide a safe operating voltage for the light bulbs. Connect the transformer to a 117-volt AC supply and turn on the switch. The light bulb, L_1, and either L_2 or L_3 should now light fairly brightly. Place pieces of iron wire in the coil center until L_1 goes out and L_2 and L_3 reach maximum brilliancy (Fig. 25-39). At this point it may be necessary to readjust the rheostat. When further addition of pieces of iron wire to the coil center causes L_1 and either L_2 or L_3 to get brighter the point of resonance will have been reached. By

moving the iron wires in a group toward and away from the point of resonance, we can duplicate the action of tuning a radio signal as we did in the series resonance experiment.

Unlike a series resonant circuit, the voltage across the coil and capacitor remains constant in a parallel resonant circuit. As we observed when adjusting the parallel circuit, the current from the supply line as indicated by L_1 decreased materially when resonance was reached; yet the current flowing within the circuit increased by a similar ratio. Like the series resonant voltage that is many times greater than the supply line voltage, the large current that flows in a parallel resonant circuit with little assistance from the supply line may be easily accounted for.

With the circuit in a resonant condition, we will assume that current from the charged capacitor is beginning to flow around the parallel circuit and through the coil, as shown in Fig. 25-40. As the current from the capacitor con-

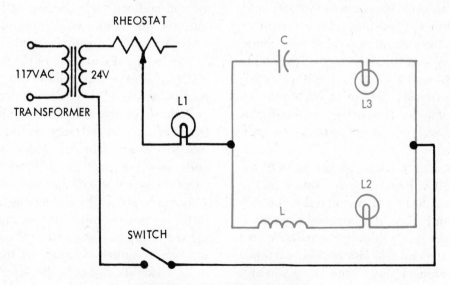

Fig. 25-38. Parallel resonant circuit.

Fig. 25-39. In parallel-resonant circuit, resonance is indicated by a high current flow within the circuit and a small current flow in the supply line. The lamps within the circuit above light up to nearly full brilliancy; yet no visible glow appears in the lamp connected in the supply line.

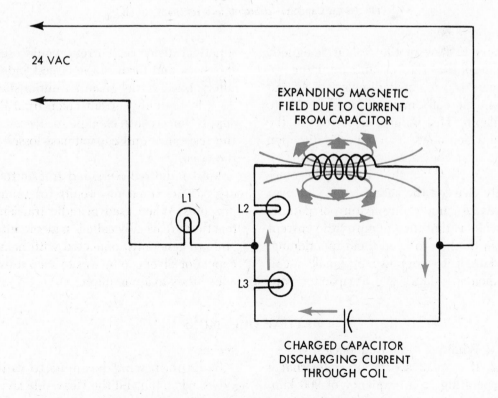

Fig. 25-40. Capacitor discharge in a resonant circuit.

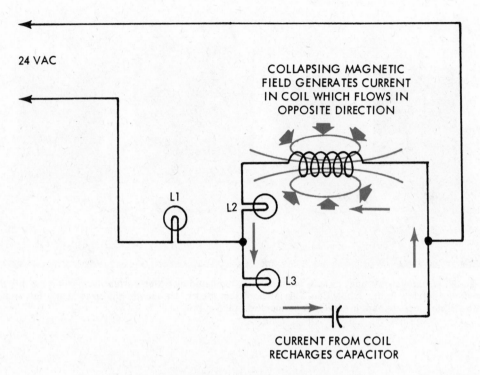

Fig. 25-41. Capacitor charging in a resonant circuit.

tinues to flow in the coil, its magnetic field continues to expand until the capacitor is completely discharged. At that point the coil's magnetic field begins to collapse. This induces a current in the coil which flows in an opposite direction to charge the capacitor again, as shown in Fig. 25-41. As the capacitor becomes fully charged the action begins all over again. An interesting feature of parallel circuits is that they require little current from the line to keep them functioning. In fact, if it were possible to make a coil without resistance and a capacitor with a perfect dielectric, current would oscillate back and forth in the circuit indefinitely, once it was given an initial start. As it is, the only current taken from the supply line is just enough to overcome the resistance and capacitance losses in the circuit.

Most radio receivers and transmitters use parallel resonant circuits for tuning purposes. When used in radio transmitters they are usually called "tank circuits" and are generally connected with heavy copper or silver conductors to keep resistance losses to a minimum.

REVIEW QUESTIONS

1. What are radio frequencies?

2. If a broadcast station states that it is operating on a frequency of 900 kilohertz, what is its frequency in hertz per second?

3. Explain what happens to radio waves when they hit the Heaviside layer.

4. What is the speed of radio waves?

5. Why is a radio-frequency wave sent out by a transmitter called a carrier wave?

6. What is the purpose of a tuner in a radio receiver?

7. Why will a coil with many turns of wire tune to a lower frequency than a coil with a few turns of wire?

8. What separates the rotor plates and the stator plates in a variable capacitor?

9. Why does a variable capacitor that has been closed, so that all of the rotor plates are inside of the stator plates, tune to a lower frequency?

10. What is the unit of measure that is used to indicate the capacitance of capacitors?

11. Why are radio-frequency transformers sometimes used in the tuner circuit?

12. Using radio symbols, draw a diagram showing a radio tuner. The radio tuner should be connected to an antenna and a ground. A variable capacitor should be used to tune the circuit.

13. What is the difference between AM modulations and FM modulations?

14. What is the dielectric in a capacitor?

15. List the factors that determine the capacitance of a capacitor.

16. What is the unit of capacitance?

17. Change .0001 microfarads into picafarads.

18. List several different types of capacitors.

19. What is meant by "working voltage" of a capacitor?

20. If capacitors of 1 microfarad, .5 microfarad and .25 microfarad are connected in parallel, what would the total capacitance be?

21. If two capacitors of 4 microfarads are connected in series, what is the total capacitance?

22. What determines the inductance of a coil?

23. How can you increase the resonant frequency in a circuit with an inductance and a capacitance?

UNIT 26
HEARING THE RADIO SIGNALS

The Purpose of a Radio Receiver

The radio wave sent out by a broadcast station is a high-frequency wave called a carrier wave because it is carrying the voice frequencies with it. These radio-frequency waves are being changed in strength, or modulated, by the audio waves. If we were to connect a pair of earphones across a radio tuner and try to listen to a broadcast station, we could not hear anything. The alternating current of the radio waves is so rapid that they could not be heard. The diaphragm of the earphone could not vibrate at all because the current would be changing directions so rapidly. Some method must be used to change the radio waves into sound waves.

The purpose of a radio receiver is (1) to tune in a radio station, (2) to separate the audio frequencies from the radio frequencies, and (3) to change the electrical audio vibrations into sound vibrations. See Fig. 26-1.

Using a Semiconductor As a Detector

In listening to standard broadcast signals it is necessary to select the desired radio frequency signal and to change the amplitude modulated radio waves back into sound waves. A device that removes the modulation or audio from the radio frequency signal is called a *detector*. One of the simplest detectors is a semiconductor made of germanium or silicon called a crystal diode. An explanation of the theory of semiconductors is included in the unit on semiconductors. Fig. 26-2

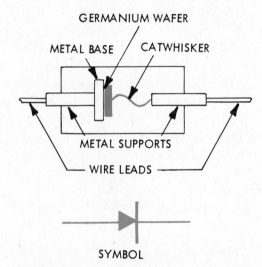

Fig. 26-2. Construction of a germanium point-contact diode. The diode will permit alternating current to flow through it in one direction but not in the opposite direction.

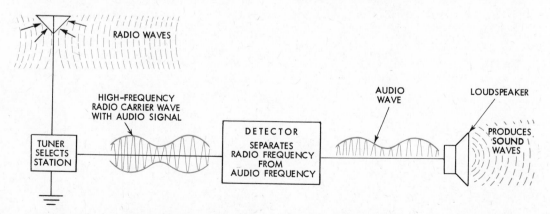

Fig. 26-1. In this block diagram are illustrated the basic principles of radio receiver functioning.

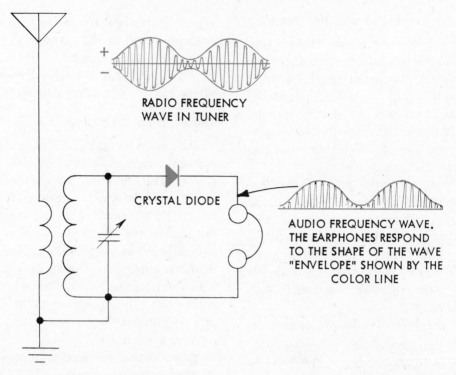

+
−

RADIO FREQUENCY
WAVE IN TUNER

CRYSTAL DIODE

AUDIO FREQUENCY WAVE.
THE EARPHONES RESPOND
TO THE SHAPE OF THE WAVE
"ENVELOPE" SHOWN BY THE
COLOR LINE

Fig. 26-3. A simple radio receiver using a diode as a detector. The detector permits the audio signal to be separated from the radio frequency signal.

shows the construction of a germanium-point-contact diode. Such a diode acts like a one-way valve that will permit current to flow freely through it in one direction but will allow very little current to flow in the opposite direction.

In Fig. 26-3 a tuner consisting of an antenna coil and a variable capacitor are used to select the desired signal. Connected across the tuner is a crystal diode and a pair of earphones. When the modulated radio frequency signal in the tuner circuit is applied to the diode, the diode will permit the alternating current to flow in one direction but not in the other direction. Since the current flow is only in one direction, we now have a varying direct current flowing through the earphones. In an amplitude modulated sig-

nal the variation in amplitude appears in both the positive and negative portion of the alternating current radio frequency signal. With the diode in the circuit, half of the radio frequency cycle is permitted to flow and as shown in Fig. 26-3 the audio is still with the signal. It is this audio signal that we wish to hear.

HEADPHONES

This symbol is the one to use for a double headset.

Using the Earphones with the Diode

The earphones are constructed very much like the telephone receiver. See Fig. 26-4. A permanent magnet is used to provide a pull on the thin metal diaphragm. Two sets of electromagnetic coils are connected so that when a varying current flows through them they can make the diaphragm vibrate.

Without the diode the earphone diaphragm would not be able to react to the very rapid high frequency radio currents. Now that the diode is in the circuit a varying direct current flows through the earphone coils and this current is always flowing in the same direction even though it is pulsating.

The earphone diaphragm cannot vibrate at the speed of the radio frequency portion of the signal but it can react to the variations in amplitude of the signal. As the amplitude of the signal varies, the current in the earphone coils varies caus-

ing the diaphragm to vibrate. The vibrations produced by the earphones are the same as the audio signal which was made by the sound waves hitting the microphone in the radio broadcasting station.

The Electron Tube Diode

The electron tube, often called a vacuum tube, may also be used as a detector. The simplest electron tube is called a diode which means that it has two basic elements. The two elements, one called the filament and the other called the plate, are sealed in a glass bulb or metal container. The air and gas are removed from the tube to form a vacuum within the tube. The vacuum is necessary to prevent the filament from burning out, when heated, and also to remove all gases so that the electron flow is not affected.

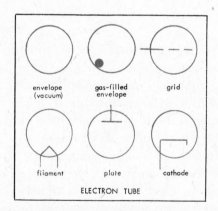

ELECTRON TUBE

These elements are combined to form the symbol for any electron tube.

Thermionic Emission

The filament is made of a thin wire of such material as oxide coated nickel, tungsten, or thoriated tungsten. If a source of electricity is connected to the filament terminals, Fig. 26-5, the filament

Fig. 26-4. This cross-section view shows the construction of an earphone.

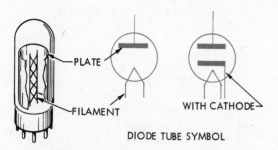

Fig. 26-5. A diode electron tube consists of a cathode and a plate. The cathode is often referred to as the filament.

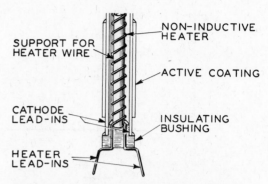

Fig. 26-6. Illustration showing the construction of a heater-type filament and cathode.

will become hot and will turn red in color. The red-hot filament releases free electrons which boil off its surface. This releasing of free electrons from the hot surface of the filament is called *thermionic emission*. These electrons leave the filament to form a cloud of electrons around the filament. This is called a "space charge."

The voltage used to heat the filament may be AC or DC. The AC voltage is usually obtained by using a transformer which steps down the AC line voltage to the smaller amount needed by the filament. Direct current for the filament may be supplied from batteries or a power supply. If batteries are used, they are called "A" batteries. Common voltages for the filament are 1.5, 6.3, and 12.6 volts.

Electron Tubes with a Cathode

When using direct current on the filament of a tube the filament will produce a constant emission of electrons, but if alternating current is connected to the filament, the electron emission would change with the alternating current. In tubes that are to be used with alternating current on the filaments, an oxide coated sleeve is placed over the filament. See

Fig. 26-6. This covering over the filament is called the cathode.

In tubes with a cathode the filament is called a heater because it heats the cathode. When the cathode gets hot, it starts throwing off electrons and since it is quite massive, the temperature of the cathode does not change with the alternating current. Thus the heater heats the cathode and the cathode emits a steady flow of electrons. The cathode is not considered an additional element in the tube as it does the work of the filament. A lead from the cathode must also be made to one of the prongs in the tube base.

The Diode Electron Tube Detector

The diode electron tube operates much the same as the semiconductor diode in that it rectifies or changes the radio frequency signal into pulsating direct current. Fig. 26-7 illustrates a schematic diagram of a basic circuit using the electron tube as a diode detector. The filament is connected to a low voltage alternating current which heats the cathode and the cathode emits a constant flow of electrons. When the signal in the tuning circuit produces a positive charge on the plate it pulls the negatively

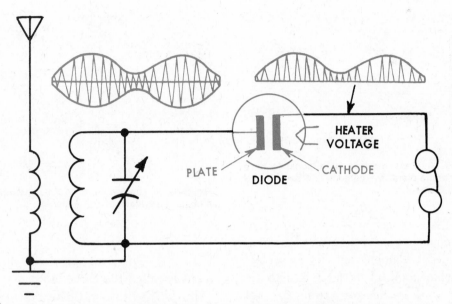

Fig. 26-7. Schematic diagram of a diode electron tube detector.

charged electrons from the cathode to the plate. These electrons flow through the tuning circuit and return to the cathode through the earphones. When the radio frequency signal in the tuner produces a negative charge on the plate, the plate repels the electrons emitted by the cathode, and no current flows through the earphones. Each time the plate is positive, current flows through the earphones and each time the plate is negative, no current flows through the earphones.

From this explanation we can see that the diode tube operates much the same as the semiconductor diode by allowing the current to flow in but one direction through the earphones. The earphones react to the amplitude variations of the pulsating direct current flowing through them. This amplitude change includes the modulation produced at the broadcasting station and thus sound is heard in the earphones.

One disadvantage of the electron tube diode and the semiconductor detectors is that they cannot increase the strength of the signal. If the signal is not very strong they cannot produce sound through the earphones. The electron tube can be used as a detector, and it also can be used to increase or amplify the strength of the signal. It is often referred to as a valve or control device that enables a very small voltage change to be amplified many times. To provide the power needed for an electron tube to operate as an amplifier, it is necessary to use an outside source of voltage such as a battery or a power supply that will provide direct current. Voltage applied to the plate is called the "B" supply or the "B" battery.

Plate Current Flow

If we can give the plate a positive charge by connecting it to the positive side of a battery as in Fig. 26-8 the elec-

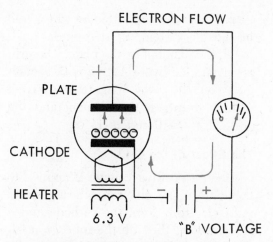

ELECTRON FLOW

PLATE

CATHODE

HEATER

6.3 V

"B" VOLTAGE

Fig. 26-8. When the plate is positive, electrons flow from the cathode to the plate.

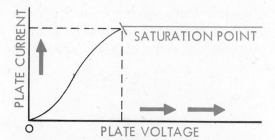

Fig. 26-9. A curve showing how the plate current increases as the voltage on the plate is increased. When the plate current will not increase, even though the voltage is increased, the tube has reached its saturation point.

trons boiling off the cathode will be attracted to the plate. Since the electrons have a negative charge and the plate has a positive charge, a current will flow through the vacuum tube.

Should the battery polarity connected to the plate be reversed so that the plate has a negative charge no current will flow in the tube. When the plate has a negative charge, it will repel the electrons from the cathode. Thus, the vacuum tube will conduct current only when the plate is positive with respect to the cathode. The vacuum tube can conduct current only in one direction and only when the plate has a positive charge. If the plate voltage is increased, the plate current will also be increased until the cathode can give up no electrons. When the plate current will not increase, even though the plate voltage is increased, the tube has reached its saturation point. See Fig. 26-9.

It should be noted that the negative side of the battery is connected to the cathode and the positive side is connected to the plate. By having the nega-

tive terminal of the battery connected to the cathode the circuit is complete. Electrons flow from the cathode through the tube to the plate and return to the cathode. Should any of these connections be disconnected, the current will stop flowing. In tubes which do not have a cathode the electron return is to the filament.

Construction of a Triode

A simple three-element electron tube is called a *triode*. The triode consists of a filament, a grid, and a plate. See Fig. 26-10. The filament, located in the center of the tube, is made of a thin wire of

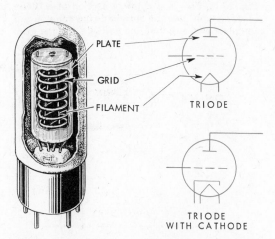

Fig. 26-10. A triode tube has a filament, grid, and plate.

tungsten that contains a small amount of thorium. Next to the filament is a fine wire in the shape of a coil called the

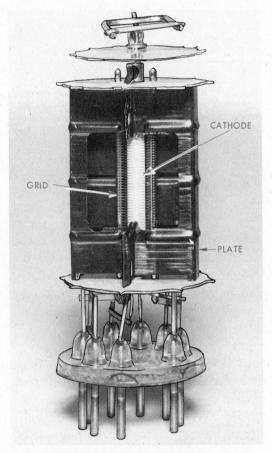

Fig. 26-11. This is a cutaway section of a triode electron tube. The grid surrounds the cathode and the plate encloses both the cathode and the grid.

grid. The grid is supported by wires, held in the glass stem, so that it does not touch the filament or the plate. The grid is surrounded by a sheet of metal rectangle called the *plate.* Some triodes have a cathode between the filament and the grid, Figs. 26-10 and 26-11.

The Effect of the Grid

When a positive voltage is applied to the plate of an electron tube the plate pulls electrons from the cathode and a current flows through the tube. In a triode tube, the grid is placed between the cathode and the plate so that the electrons must pass through the grid to get to the plate. The spaces between the turns of the wire on the grid are so wide that there is practically a free passage of electrons from the cathode to the plate.

If a small negative voltage is placed on the grid, it will repel some of the electrons going to the plate so that the plate current is reduced as illustrated in Fig. 26-12. Since the plate has a fairly large positive charge most of the electrons will be pulled through the spiral grid, but some of them will be repelled by the negative charge on the grid. Should a larger negative charge be placed on the grid it will repel more of the electrons

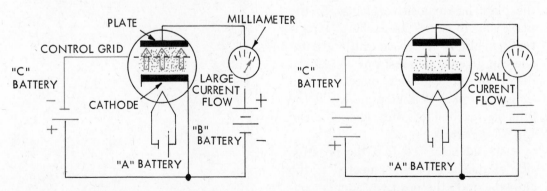

Fig. 26-12. The control-grid controls the plate current flow. The greater the negative charge on the grid, the smaller the plate current flow through the tube.

flowing toward the plate, and the plate current will be further reduced. It is usually necessary to keep a negative voltage on the grid. When batteries are used to place a voltage on the grid they are called "C" batteries, and the voltage is called *grid bias*.

The Electron Tube Amplifies a Signal

When an alternating current is applied to the grid of the tube, the grid voltage will vary and produce a changing plate current in the plate circuit. The plate current wave form is identical to the alternating current wave form applied to the grid and is also amplified because the plate current is many times larger than the grid current. See Fig. 26-13.

To use the electron tube as an amplifier it is necessary to connect the plate circuit or the output circuit to a load. This load may be a pair of earphones, a resistor, or a transformer, Fig. 26-13.

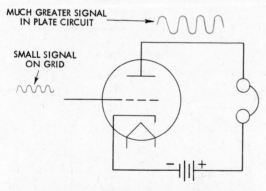

Fig. 26-13. A radio tube amplifies the signal. A very small signal on the grid will produce a large change in plate current.

A Grid Bias Detector

If the grid were connected directly to the tuner circuit, the alternating current in the tuner would flow onto the grid. The plate current would change very rap-

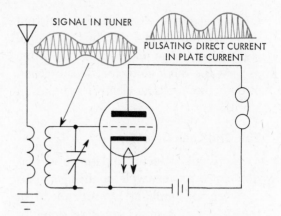

Fig. 26-14. The "C" battery in this grid bias detector prevents the current from flowing during the negative cycle of the signal.

idly with alternating current on the grid and this change in the plate current would be so fast that the earphones would not operate. It is necessary to have the tube work like a detector, so that the earphone diaphragm can be made to vibrate with the audio waves.

One method of using a triode tube as a detector is called grid bias detection. In such a detector a "C" battery is connected in the grid circuit as shown in Fig. 26-14. The battery is connected so that the grid has a negative charge and this grid voltage is called "C" bias. Just enough negative voltage is placed on the grid so that, when no signal is coming through, very little plate current will flow. As a signal is applied to the tuning circuit, the charge applied to the grid will also vary. During the positive portion of the signal the grid will become less negative and current will flow in the plate circuit. The adding of the positive voltage of the signal to the negative voltage of the "C" battery produces a less negative voltage on the grid.

As the signal changes to the negative portion of the cycle, the grid gets an increased negative charge and no current flows in the plate circuit. Thus the signal is detected in the plate circuit the same as with the diode detector. This method of detection uses the electron tube as an amplifier.

The Grid Leak Detector

The diode detector and the grid bias detector work very well for strong signals or when an amplifier is used ahead of the detector. A more sensitive detector that gives better results for weak signals is called a grid leak detector. Such a de- tector uses a capacitor and a resistor con- nected in parallel, in the grid circuit, as shown in Fig. 26-15. The plate or B volt-

age for the grid leak detector is from 45 volts to 150 volts, depending upon the type of tube used.

The Purpose of the Grid Capacitor

The capacitor in the grid circuit has a very small capacitance. Its capacitance is 250 picafarads or .00025 microfarads. When the negative half cycle of the signal in the tuning circuit reaches side A of the capacitor in Fig. 26-16, the electrons that were on side B are repelled. These electrons leave side B and flow on to the grid giving the grid a negative charge. Since the grid is cold there is no way that the electrons can leave the grid.

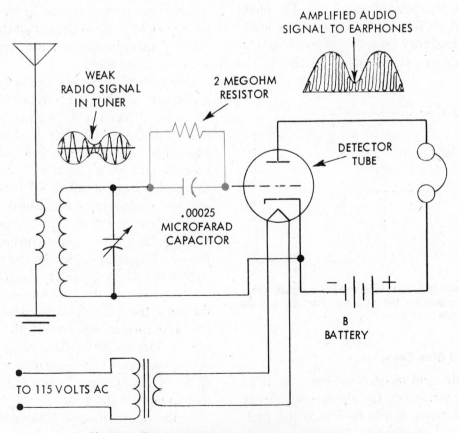

Fig. 26-15. This is a grid leak and capacitor detector.

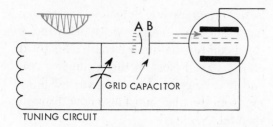

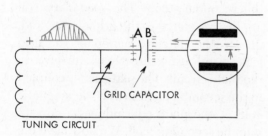

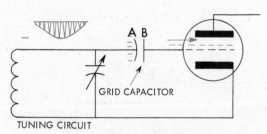

Fig. 26-16. These three drawings illustrate how the grid capacitor affects the electron charge on the grid. During the signal's negative cycle, the electrons on side B are forced onto the grid. When the positive cycle is on side A, the grid collects a few electrons from the cathode.

During the next half cycle of the signal, side A of the capacitor receives a positive charge causing the electrons on the grid to flow back toward side B. With the electrons leaving the grid, the grid does not have a negative charge; the electrons emitted by the cathode are free to flow toward the positively charged plate. Some of the electrons that flow toward the plate strike the grid and remain on the grid since it has a small positive charge.

As this process continues, the grid gets a greater and greater negative charge, and could become large enough to stop the entire flow of current from the cathode to the plate.

The Purpose of the Grid Resistor

The grid resistor, called the grid leak, has a quite high resistance. Usually a resistor of about two million ohms is used. This is a 2 megohm resistor, since *meg* means million. The purpose of the grid leak resistor is to allow some of the electrons that are accumulated on the grid to leak off. By doing this the current flow from the cathode to the plate will continue, but only when permitted by the control grid.

As was stated before, if only the capacitor remains in the circuit, the electrons trapped on the grid would soon stop the current flow in the tube. With the large resistance placed across the capacitor a path is provided so that the electrons can "leak" off and flow away from the grid. See Fig. 26-17. When side *A* of the capacitor has a positive charge, the resistance permits a few electrons from side *B* to flow through.

With the combination of the capacitor and resistor in the circuit we now have a detector in operation. When the grid has a negative charge no current flows in the plate circuit; when the grid has a

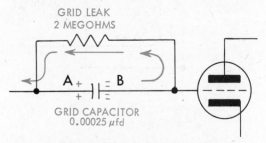

Fig. 26-17. The high resistance grid leak permits some of the electrons on the grid to leak off.

positive charge, current flows to the plate and through the earphones. The grid leak and capacitor have provided a detector action that makes it possible for the earphones to react to the amplitude of the pulsating direct current. This amplitude variation of the signal contains the audio portion of this signal which we want to hear.

The Regenerative Receiver

The grid leak detector may be made even more sensitive through the use of a plate coil, called a tickler coil. A receiver using a plate coil is said to be a regenerative receiver and this regeneration helps in amplifying the signal.

Fig. 26-18 is a schematic drawing of a basic regenerative detector circuit. To make such a receiver we must wind a third coil for the tuner circuit. This third coil is placed close to the secondary coil and it is connected so that current flowing from the plate must also flow through the coil.

When a radio frequency signal flows in the primary coil, a current is induced into the secondary coil. The secondary coil applies the signal to the grid circuit, and, due to the detector action of the grid leak, a pulsating direct current flows in the plate circuit. The plate coil is coupled to the secondary coil so that the magnetic field of the plate coil induces a current into the secondary coil. We now have the energy of the plate circuit fed back into

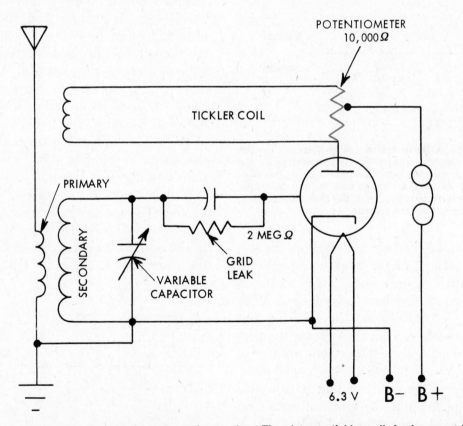

Fig. 26-18. A schematic diagram of a regenerative receiver. The plate, or tickler coil, feeds energy back into the secondary coil. Regeneration is controlled with the potentiometer.

the tuning circuit. Since the variations in the plate circuit are the same as those in the secondary coil, the two currents are in step with one another. Thus, the energy fed back into the secondary coil is increased, and the signal is made stronger.

Controlling the Regeneration

When the energy of the plate circuit is coupled back into the grid circuit, the electron flow may be built up to such an extent that the receiver becomes a transmitter. We call this regenerative circuit an oscillator, as it is oscillating or generating, a radio wave. The signal may be picked up and heard on other receivers. These signals sound like a whistle or howl in the receiver.

In the regenerative receiver such oscillations can be heard in the earphones.

These whistles and howls interfere with the ability to hear the desired audio signal and, therefore, must be controlled.

One method of controlling the regeneration, or feed back, is to connect a potentiometer across the plate coil as in Fig. 26-18. Now the current flow has two paths to follow. Part of the current flows through the plate coil, and part of the current flows through the resistor. By adjusting the potentiometer so that just the correct amount flows through the coil, regeneration is controlled.

For best results with a regenerative receiver, the potentiometer should be turned until the signal is loudest and just before a whistle is heard in the phones. When the set starts to oscillate and the whistle is heard, turn the potentiometer back until only the signal can be heard.

INTERESTING THINGS TO DO

1. Making a Crystal Diode Radio Receiver.

Materials required to construct the crystal diode radio receiver (Fig. 26-19):

1 Piece wood, ½" x 4½" x 4½"
1 Piece wood, ½" x 1" x 3½"
1 Spool wire, enamel-covered, No. 24
1 Piece spring brass, ⅜" x 4⅜", 26 gage
1 Piece tubing, brass, ¼" outside diameter (OD), ¾" long
3 Spring clips, Fahnestock, ¾" long
3 Wood screws, RH, steel, ⅜"–6
1 Wood screw, RH, steel, 1¼"–6
1 Washer, brass, No. 6
1 Crystal diode, germanium

Drill a small hole partly through the small wood block ¼" from one end and

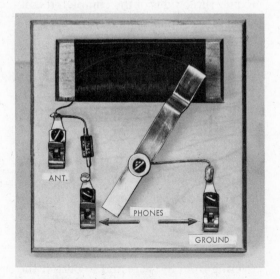

Fig. 26-19. Crystal diode radio receiver.

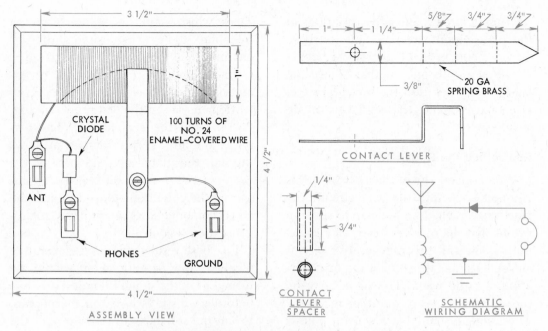

Fig. 26-20. Drawing of crystal diode radio receiver.

insert one end of the spool of wire in the hole to hold it in place. Wind 100 turns of wire on the block and secure the other end of the wire by drilling a small hole through the edge of the wood block and passing the wire through it. Shellac or lacquer three sides of the completed coil, but do not lacquer the side on which the slider is to bear. Glue the coil to the wood base.

Lay out and drill the piece of spring brass as shown in Fig. 26-20 and bend it to the shape shown to serve as the contact lever. Secure the contact lever to the wood base with the piece of brass tubing, washer, and long wood screw so that the pointed end will make an arc across the flat side of the coil. Bear down slightly on the pointed end of the contact lever and move it back and forth across the coil several times to remove the enamel covering from the wire and to permit the lever to make contact with the wire. Se-

cure the Fahnestock clips to the wood base with wood screws and make the connections shown on the drawing. Connect the crystal diode between the antenna clip and one of the phone clips, as shown on the drawing.

Connect a pair of headphones and antenna and ground leads to the proper clips and you should be able to tune in a nearby broadcasting station by moving the contact lever across the coil. A ground connection is usually made by attaching a piece of copper wire to a water pipe and connecting the other end to the "ground" connection on the receiver. The best length of antenna can be determined by trial. A long antenna will permit the receiver to pick up more stations, but they will be difficult to separate. Choose a length for the antenna that will permit you to receive the largest number of radio stations with little or no interference between them.

2. Capacitor-Tuned Diode Detector.

Materials required to construct the capacitor-tuned diode detector (Fig. 26-21):

1 Piece wood, 3″ x 5″
1 Variable capacitor, .000365 μf
1 Spool magnet wire, enamel-covered, No. 28
1 Cardboard form, 1″ diameter, 3″ long
1 Crystal diode
4 Fahnestock clips

Drill four $\frac{1}{16}$″ holes about $\frac{1}{4}$″ apart and $\frac{1}{4}$″ from one end of the tubing, as shown in Fig. 26-22. Drill another $\frac{1}{16}$″ hole $\frac{1}{2}$″ from the same end of the tubing and insert one end of the magnet wire through the hole and out through one of the lower holes to hold the wire

firmly in place. Wind 100 turns of wire on the cardboard tubing. Drill a $\frac{1}{16}$″ hole close to the winding, pass the end of the winding through the hole, and secure it to one of the holes at the end of the tubing. Drill another $\frac{1}{16}$″ hole $\frac{1}{8}$″ above the first winding and wind 30 turns of wire on the form to serve as the primary winding.

Wind the primary winding in the same direction as the larger coil was wound. Secure the end of the coil in the same manner as the end of the first coil was secured. Cut a circle of wood so that it will fit into the terminal end of the coil and glue it in place. Secure the coil to the wood base with a wood screw. Secure

Fig. 26-21. Capacitor-tuned diode detector.

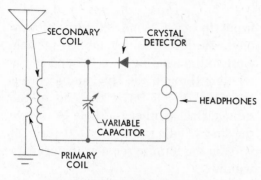

WIRING DIAGRAM

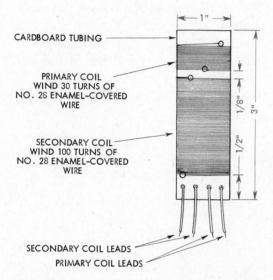

Fig. 26-22. Drawing for capacitor-tuned diode detector.

Fig. 26-23. One-tube regenerative receiver.

6 Fahnestock clips
1 Fixed capacitor, mica, .00025 μf (C_2)
1 Resistor, 2,000,000 ohms, $\frac{1}{2}$-watt (R_1)
1 Potientiometer, 10,000 ohms (R_2)
1 6J5 tube
1 Octal tube socket
1 Piece sheet steel, 4" x 7", 20 gage
1 Piece masonite, $\frac{1}{8}$" x 1" x 4"
1 Rubber grommet, $\frac{1}{4}$"
1 Rubber grommet, $\frac{3}{8}$"
2 Pointer knobs

the Fahnestock clips to the wood base and connect the parts together as shown in the schematic diagram, Fig. 26-22. Instructions on the proper antenna and ground to use with a crystal receiver are given in the section describing the diode detector set.

3. One-Tube Regenerative Receiver.

Materials required to construct the one-tube regenerative receiver (Fig. 26-23):

1 Antenna coil (see construction details in tuned crystal receiver, Fig. 26-22)
1 Variable capacitor, .000365 μf (C_1)

Lay out the piece of sheet steel and drill holes where shown in Fig. 26-24. Bend the two ends of the sheet metal to a 90° angle to form the ends of the chassis. Secure the capacitor and coil to the top of the chassis in the approximate positions shown. Starting at the bottom end of the coil, count 30 turns of wire upward

POTENTIOMETER

The potentiometer symbol shows three terminals.

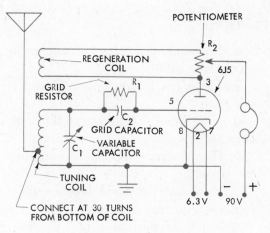

POTENTIOMETER

R_2

REGENERATION COIL

6J5

GRID RESISTOR

R_1

3

5

C_2

GRID CAPACITOR

8

2

7

C_1

VARIABLE CAPACITOR

TUNING COIL

6.3 V

90 V

CONNECT AT 30 TURNS FROM BOTTOM OF COIL

WIRING DIAGRAM

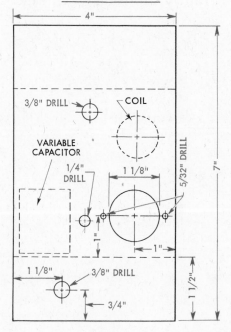

4"

3/8" DRILL

COIL

VARIABLE CAPACITOR

1/4" DRILL

1 1/8"

5/32" DRILL

7"

1"

1"

1 1/8"

3/8" DRILL

3/4"

1 1/2"

CHASSIS LAYOUT

Fig. 26-24. Drawing of one-tube regenerative receiver.

and solder a connection for the antenna. Secure the potentiometer in the 3/8" hole in the front end of the chassis. Make a

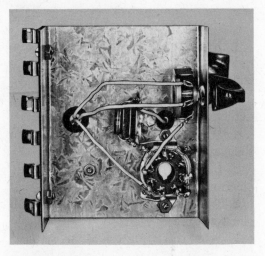

Fig. 26-25. Wiring underneath the chassis of the one-tube receiver.

terminal strip with a piece of masonite and Fahnestock clips and secure it to the back of the chassis. Wire the receiver as shown in Figs. 26-24 and 26-25.

When operating the receiver the potentiometer control knob is turned so the receiver is at the most sensitive point without distorting the signals. If the knob is turned too far the music or speech will become unintelligible and a high-pitched squeal will be heard in the headphones. The best operating point is where the receiver is the most sensitive, yet the music or speech is understood clearly. If the receiver fails to produce a high-pitched squeal at any position of the potentiometer knob, the connections between the primary coil and the potentiometer should be reversed.

This receiver will work satisfactorily with batteries or with either of the power supplies described in Unit 29.

Review Questions on following page.

REVIEW QUESTIONS

1. Name the three main purposes of a radio receiver.

2. What is a detector?

3. What is the function of a diode in a detector circuit?

4. What kind of current flows through the earphones of a detector circuit?

5. List the two elements in a diode electron tube.

6. Why is a vacuum necessary in an electron tube?

7. What is the purpose of the getter?

8. Explain how a cathode functions in an electron tube.

9. Name the three elements in a triode tube.

10. How does the grid control the plate current?

11. How does an electron tube amplify the signal?

12. How does the diode detector differ from the grid bias detector?

13. Name the purpose of the following: "A" battery, "B" battery, "C" battery.

UNIT 27
ELECTRON TUBE AMPLIFIERS

The Electron Tube as an Amplifier

The most important advantage of an electron tube is its ability to make radio signals stronger. Diode semiconductors such as germanium and silicon, as well as diode electron tubes, may be used as detectors but they will not amplify the signal.

In the electron tube, a very weak signal coming into the control grid can produce a much larger variation of the plate current.

Resistance-Coupled Audio Amplifiers

The signals produced by a detector are not very strong. Usually we like to use a loudspeaker, instead of earphones, so that several people can listen to the receiver at the same time. The audio-frequency signal can be made stronger through the use of another electron tube called an *audio-frequency amplifier*. See Fig. 27-1.

One method of coupling the detector to an audio amplifier is to use a resistance and capacitor combination known as a *resistance-coupling*. Another method of coupling uses a transformer between the detector and the amplifying tube, but it has been almost entirely replaced by resistance coupling. While resistance coupling does not increase signal strength as transformer coupling does, it has the advantages of providing very good quality audio signals and of being much cheaper to construct. A typical amplifier resistance-coupled to a detector and using a pentode tube is shown in Fig. 27-2. A pentode tube has five elements

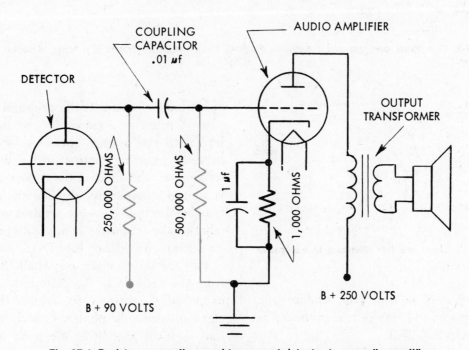

Fig. 27-1. Resistance coupling used to connect detector to an audio amplifier.

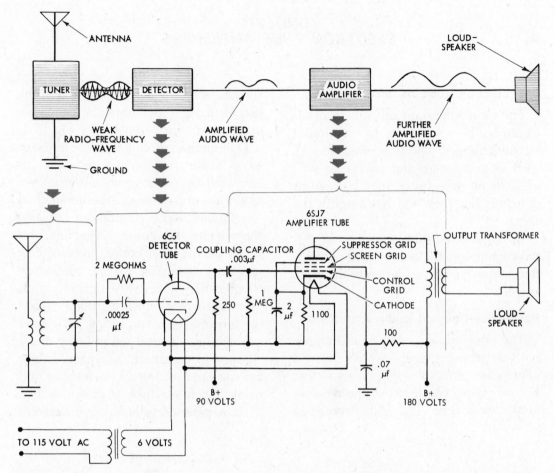

Fig. 27-2. This block diagram and schematic diagram show the arrangement of a tuner, detector, and amplifier.

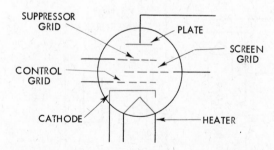

Fig. 27-3. There are five elements in a pentode tube.

consisting of *control grid, screen grid, suppressor grid, plate,* and *cathode,* as shown in Fig. 27-3.

One of the undesirable characteristics

of a triode tube is that the grid and the plate can act as a capacitor and interfere with the normal operation of the tube. By inserting another grid, called a *screen grid,* the effect of the capacitance is almost completely eliminated. This beneficial action, however, is offset somewhat by the action of *secondary emission* on the screen grid. See Fig. 27-4.

The stream of electrons which flows from the cathode to the plate is known as *primary emission.* Sometimes these electrons strike the plate with such force that they dislodge other electrons from it. These electrons moving away from the

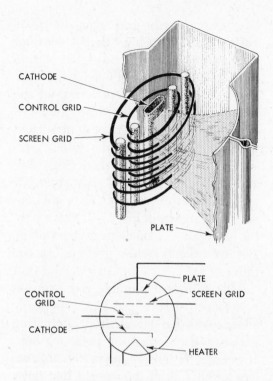

Fig. 27-4. The tetrode tube has four elements.

plate are known as "secondary emission." Since a screen grid has a positive charge it tends to attract some of the secondary-emission electrons. This reduces the normal flow of electrons in the plate circuit. By inserting another grid, known as a *suppressor grid*, the undesirable effects of secondary emission are overcome. Since the suppressor grid is connected to the cathode, which gives it a negative charge, it opposes the flow of electrons from the plate to the screen grid. This additional grid provides a tube that is very stable in operation and capable of amplifying a signal many times.

We have learned how a varying voltage on the grid of an electron tube can cause a varying current to flow in its plate circuit. In a resistance-coupled amplifier the varying current flows through a resistor called a *plate-resistor*. See Fig. 27-5. This produces a voltage drop across

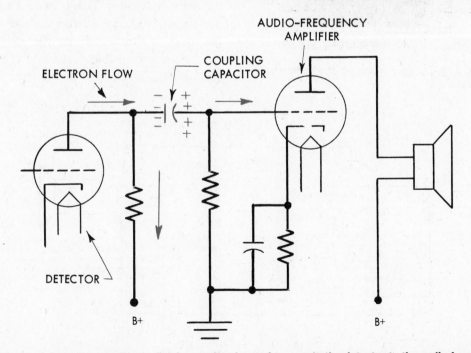

Fig. 27-5. In resistance coupling, a fixed capacitor is used to couple the detector to the audio-frequency amplifier. Changes in electron-flow from the detector plate provide a variation in electron-flow to the coupling capacitor. The grid of the amplifier tube receives its signal through the coupling capacitor.

the resistor. The reactance of the coupling capacitor is so low that a large portion of the voltage drop will appear across the grid-resistor. Since the grid and the grid resistor are in series, the varying voltage across the grid resistor will cause the voltage on the grid to vary, which in turn will cause similar changes in the output circuit of the tube.

Preventing Distortion of the Signal

The signal from the detector can provide a very strong alternating current to the grid of the amplifier tube. With such

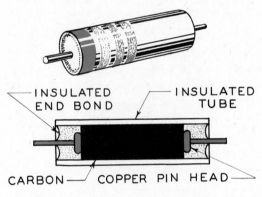

Fig. 27-6. This is a cross-section of a carbon fixed resistor.

large variations of grid signal the plate current can be so high that it does not vary exactly like the grid signal. A true signal would not be produced in the loudspeaker. This is called *distortion* of the signal. To prevent this distortion, it is necessary to limit the amount of current that can flow through the tube. A resistor called a *cathode resistor* (Fig. 27-6) and a capacitor called a *bypass capacitor* are used for this purpose. They are connected as shown in Fig. 27-7. This makes the grid have a small negative voltage and it is called placing "grid bias" on the tube.

Although most portable receivers use batteries to supply grid bias, practically all receivers that operate from alternating current use a method known as *self-bias*. If we refer to the diagram in Fig. 27-7, we can see that all of the current that flows in the plate circuit also flows through the cathode resistor. This produces a voltage drop across the resistor and because the grid is connected to the cathode through the coupling resistor, the same voltage will be present at the grid. This

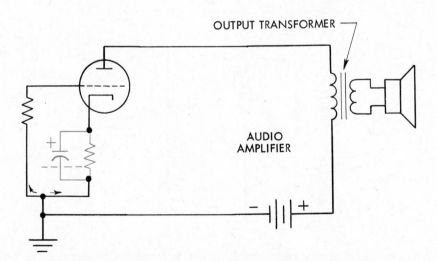

Fig. 27-7. Using a cathode resistor and capacitor to place a small negative voltage on the amplifier grid; this prevents distortion of the signal.

is the grid bias, or bias voltage. The method used to supply this voltage is known as "self-bias" because it is produced by the current flowing through the plate circuit of the tube. It should be noted that where a cathode resistor is used, the cathode has a positive polarity only in relation to the polarity of the grid, which is negative. In the cathode-plate circuit the cathode is negative. The capacitor across the cathode resistor acts as a filter to bypass any alternating current that might be present so that only direct current will go through the resistor, giving a uniform current flow to the cathode.

Loudspeakers

Loudspeakers are used so that the sound may be heard some distance away from the radio receiver. A cone is used in the loudspeaker to produce sound waves. As the cone moves back and forth, it moves the air in front and in back of it. This movement of air is what makes the sound waves that we hear.

One of the common types of loudspeakers, called a *permanent magnet speaker,* is shown in Fig. 27-8. A small coil of wire wound on a hollow tube is glued to the bottom of the cone. This is called the *voice coil.* The coil is placed so that it can move freely over the pole of a very strong alnico magnet.

A transformer, called an *output transformer,* is used to couple the tube to the speaker (Fig. 27-9). Audio frequency signals flowing from the plate of the amplifier tube induce a voltage in the secondary of the transformer (Fig. 27-10). These current variations flow through the

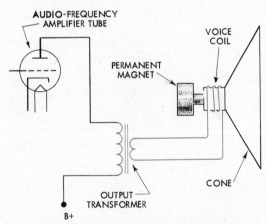

Fig. 27-9. Connecting an output transformer to a permanent-magnet speaker. The secondary of the transformer connects to the voice coil; audio frequency current flowing through the voice coil makes the cone move in and out, producing sound vibrations.

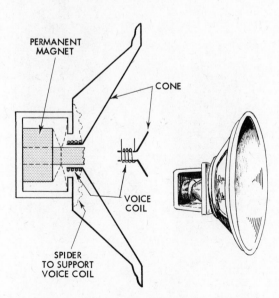

Fig. 27-8. This is how a permanent-magnet (PM) loudspeaker is constructed.

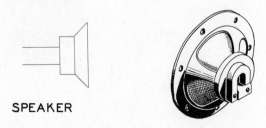

SPEAKER

Letter symbols may be added to identify the kind of speaker.

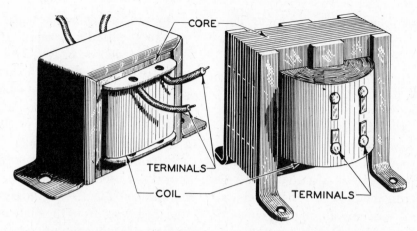

Fig. 27-10. A step-up transformer makes the audio signal stronger.

voice coil. The magnetic field created by the voice coil pulls the cone in out of the permanent field of the magnet. As the voice coil moves it also causes the cone to move.

Uses for Audio Amplifiers

Audio amplifiers have many uses other than in radio receivers. They are used for such purposes as intercommunicating systems, telephone amplifiers, public address systems, and for reproducing high quality music from tape and transcription recorders in the home. For these uses a number of electron tubes may be coupled together to produce the required volume of sound. See Fig. 27-11.

Fig. 27-11. Several kinds of electron tubes are shown here; they are designated to serve a variety of special purposes.

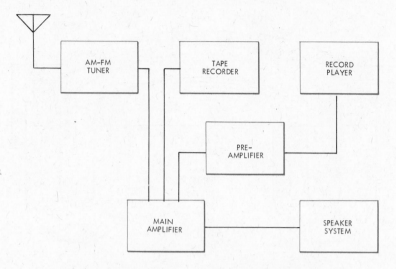

Fig. 27-12. Block diagram of a high fidelity sound system.

High Fidelity Amplifiers

The audible range of sound extends from 20 to 20,000 hertz. True high fidelity would require amplifying equipment capable of reproducing faithfully any sound between the lower and upper limits of the audible range. The term *high fidelity*, commonly known as *hi-fi*, is accepted to mean the output from any high quality sound equipment. As shown in the block diagram, Fig. 27-12,

Fig. 27-13. A modern audio amplifying system for the home consisting of a combined receiver and amplifier, turntable, and two high fidelity speakers. Speakers may be separated to produce stereo effect. (Radio Shack)

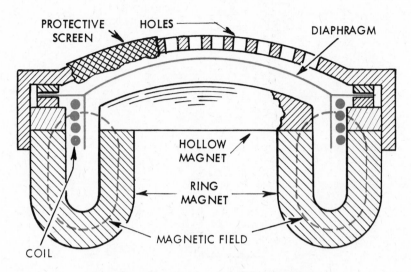

PROTECTIVE SCREEN   HOLES   DIAPHRAGM

HOLLOW MAGNET

RING MAGNET

MAGNETIC FIELD

COIL

Fig. 27-14. Cross-section of dynamic microphone.

a hi-fi system is made up of a number of units. Since the output of the whole system can be no better than that of the individual components, each part is usually selected for the greatest possible frequency response. See Fig. 27-13.

The radio receiver in a hi-fi system generally includes an FM and an AM tuner. Tape recordings are often made from the tuners, either directly or through a microphone. The microphone is usually a *crystal, ceramic,* or *dynamic* type. We learned how a crystal microphone works in an earlier chapter. The principle of a ceramic microphone is somewhat similar to that of a crystal microphone in that stresses produced by sound waves on a ceramic material cause a voltage to be generated between its contact strips. A cross sectional view of a dynamic microphone is shown in Fig. 27-14. The moving coil is attached to the microphone diaphragm. Sound waves striking the diaphragm cause the coil to move in a magnetic field. This induces a current in the coil which then flows to an amplifier input through a suitable coupling device.

Loudspeaker Systems

To have a quality amplifier system requires a good loudspeaker system. The range of audio frequencies to which a loudspeaker will respond efficiently is determined to a large extent by the size and construction of its cone. Since a single speaker will not deliver a satisfactory output from a full range of audio frequencies, three speakers with overlapping ranges are usually used with hi-fi equipment. The speaker which handles the high frequencies is called a *tweeter.* A speaker called a *woofer* reproduces the low frequencies, and a *mid-range* speaker takes care of the frequencies in between. Filters made up of capacitors, choke coils, and resistors, called *cross-over networks,* separate the frequencies and send them to the proper speaker. Three speaker units are often combined in one frame, with two smaller speakers nesting inside the larger cone. This arrangement is known as a *triaxial* speaker, Fig. 27-15. Although a triaxial speaker has the advantage of economy, the method of mounting each speaker separately, as

Fig. 27-15. A triaxial speaker. (University Loudspeakers Inc.)

shown in Fig. 27-16, is considered to be better for quality reproduction.

The box surrounding a loudspeaker, known as a *baffle*, plays an important part in its proper operation. You can prove this to yourself by holding an uncovered speaker in your hands while it is playing and noting the harsh, tinny sound it delivers. Next place a temporary baffle with an opening in front of the speaker and you will sense immediately the change to pleasant listening. The purpose of a baffle is to prevent the sound waves from the front of the speaker from canceling those projected from the back of the speaker. This is accomplished by extending the distance of the sound path between the front and back of the speaker by means of a panel or enclosure.

Fig. 27-16. A high-fidelity speaker system showing placement of the high, middle, and low range speakers. (Fisher Radio)

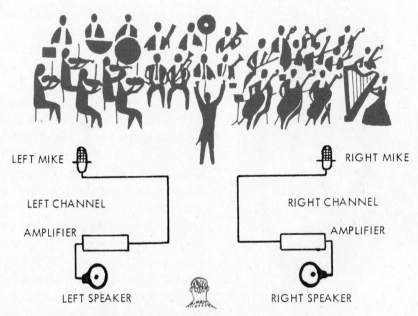

LEFT MIKE   RIGHT MIKE

LEFT CHANNEL   RIGHT CHANNEL

AMPLIFIER   AMPLIFIER

LEFT SPEAKER   RIGHT SPEAKER

Fig. 27-17. A block diagram of a basic stereo system.

Stereophonic Reproduction

Stereophonic reproduction, usually abbreviated stereo, is a system of sound reproduction which attempts to retain the feeling of space and location which is lost when sound is transmitted on a single channel. To obtain quality sound from a stereophonic reproduction system two high fidelity sound systems are necessary. See Fig. 27-17.

Stereo reproduces sound with such realism that the listener has the feeling of being right in the studio or concert hall with the performers. Since it creates the feeling of listening with two ears it is often referred to as *binaural* reproduction. The sounds reaching the ears from two separate speakers are timed slightly different to produce this effect.

A basic stereo system includes two hi-fidelity amplifiers and two high quality loudspeakers, Fig. 27-18. For best results the speakers should be placed 6 to 8 feet apart.

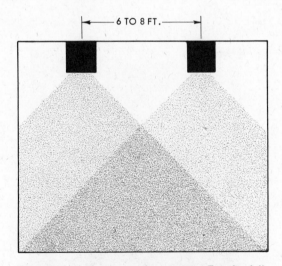

6 TO 8 FT.

Fig. 27-18. A stereo speaker system. For the full stereo effect speakers should be placed from 6 to 8 feet apart with the listener in the darker area.

Turntables

Turntables (Fig. 27-19) for playing records and transcriptions are usually capable of running at speeds of 16⅔, 33⅓, 45, and 78 rpm and are available with

Fig. 27-19. A typical turntable. (Garrard Div., Plessey Consumer Products)

Fig. 27-20. Stereophonic pick-up cartridge. (Allied Radio Corp.)

Fig. 27-20. Unlike microphones, which operate from pressure of sound on a diaphragm, the force which actuates a pick-up is supplied by a needle which travels in a groove on a record. The output of a pick-up cartridge is frequently very low, so an amplifier called a *preamplifier* is often connected between it and the main amplifier to bring the signal up to a higher level.

The pick-up cartridge of a stereo record player usually has a needle which rides in a V-shaped groove on the record. The sides of the groove have smaller grooves that were cut by a stylus needle at the time the record was made. Each side of the V-shaped groove represents a separate channel. Although stereo pick-ups vary in size and shape, most of them use the basic principle shown in Fig. 27-21. In operation the needle of a stereo

variations in speed as little as 0.2 percent. A phonograph pick-up or cartridge for reproducing sound from a record is generally of a ceramic, crystal, or magnetic type and operates similarly to microphones using the same elements. See

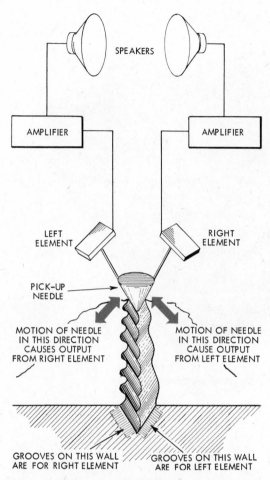

SPEAKERS

AMPLIFIER

AMPLIFIER

LEFT
ELEMENT

RIGHT
ELEMENT

PICK-UP
NEEDLE

MOTION OF NEEDLE
IN THIS DIRECTION
CAUSES OUTPUT
FROM RIGHT ELEMENT

MOTION OF NEEDLE
IN THIS DIRECTION
CAUSE OUTPUT
FROM LEFT ELEMENT

GROOVES ON THIS WALL
ARE FOR RIGHT ELEMENT

GROOVES ON THIS WALL
ARE FOR LEFT ELEMENT

Fig. 27-21. Diagram showing basic principles of a stereo record pick-up. Signals are recorded on opposite sides of groove with slight time lag between the two signals.

pick-up follows the cuttings on the side. The action of the needle is the same as in regular pick-ups. Its movement sets up a small voltage in the crystal, ceramic, or magnetic unit that is being used, from which it goes to a pre-amplifier. Separate input channels are required on stereo amplifiers to handle the output from dual tape recorders and phonograph pick-ups.

Tape Recorders

A basic diagram of a tape recorder is shown in Fig. 27-22. The tape used in a recorder consists of a thin plastic strip with a coating of small magnetic particles. The tape passes in front of the poles of an electromagnet known as a *recording head,* which is connected to an amplifier. In an unmagnetized state the magnetic particles on the tape point in random directions. When a signal from an amplifier energizes the recording head, the magnetic particles are aligned in the direction of the tape travel and magnetized to varying degrees by the audio signal from the amplifier. The bias signal from the oscillator that is in series with the recording head helps to reduce distortion and tape noise.

Tape recorders generally use a head for playback that is similar in construction to the recording head but operates in a different manner. When recording, the recording head magnetizes the tape by induction with an audio signal from an amplifier. When the tape is played back, a reverse action takes place. The magnetized tape now induces a signal in the reproducing head as it passes in front of it. This signal is in turn amplified in the same manner as the original recorded signal. Hi-fi tape recorders use separate recording and reproducing heads, but in hand-held tape recorders that are used mainly for voice, one head usually serves both purposes. A tape recorder is equipped with an erasing head energized by a high frequency oscillator, which serves to remove unwanted recordings by demagnetizing the tape.

Tape recorders are designed so that they can use the entire width of the tape for recording or they may be designed for two, four, or eight tracks on a single tape. See Fig. 27-23. Having more than one track on a tape increases the playing time

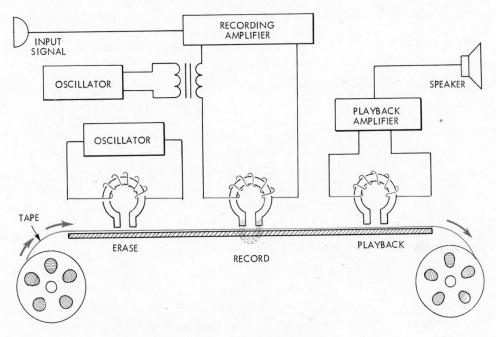

Fig. 27-22. Basic diagram of a tape recorder.

Fig. 27-23. Tape cassette recorders use a cartridge that provides the convenience of quick loading and removal of the tape.

from a single tape but the output level of the recorder is reduced when multi-tracks are used. Fig. 27-24 illustrates the position of tracks on a single-, twin-, and four-track system.

Recorders are arranged to move the tape from left to right so that the recording head in a two-track system records track one as shown in Fig. 27-25. By turning the tape over, track two is then used. In a four-track system, tracks one and three are recorded when the tape is placed with track one on the top. Tracks two and four are recorded when the tape is placed so that track four is on the top.

When recording on a two-track stereo system, both tracks are recorded simultaneously. In a four-track stereo system, tracks one and three are used for one recording and tracks two and four for the other recording. Tape recorders often have variable speeds. The most common

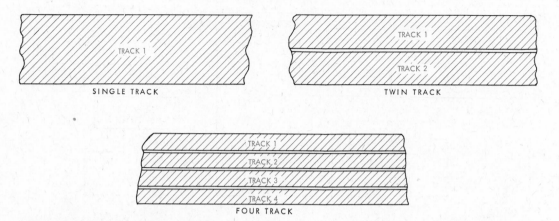

Fig. 27-24. Position of tracks for a single-, twin-, and four-track system. A strip of unmagnetized tape provides a separation between each track.

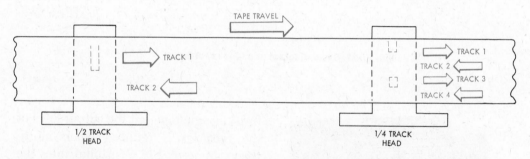

Fig. 27-25. Drawing of the location of the recording heads and the direction of tape travel in a two- and four-track system.

system provides three speeds, 7½ inches per second, 3¾ inches per second, and 1⅞ inches per second.

Radio-Frequency Amplifiers

To increase the radio signals before they reach the detector, an amplifier called a *radio-frequency amplifier* is used. It operates very much like the audio-frequency amplifier except that it amplifies the high-frequency radio signals instead of the low-frequency audio signals. See Fig. 27-26.

Transformer coupling is usually used to couple the radio-frequency amplifiers together. These transformers are coils like the coils used for the tuner of the detector.

One of the important uses for radio-frequency amplifiers is to improve the tuning of the set. Each radio-frequency amplifier can have its own tuner. A variable capacitor is used to tune the circuit.

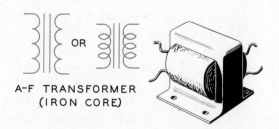

A-F TRANSFORMER
(IRON CORE)

A transformer with a magnetic core is represented like this.

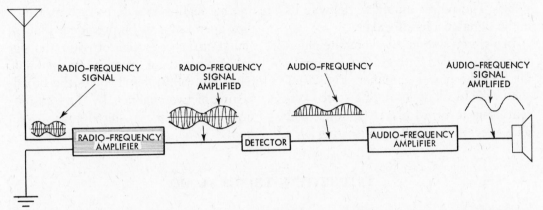

Fig. 27-26. This block diagram shows where a radio-frequency amplifier is used in a receiver circuit.

By tuning the amplifier, the receiver can be made to separate the broadcast stations better. Improving the set so that it can easily separate the stations is called making the set more *selective*.

Usually the variable capacitors are connected together so that the radio-frequency amplifiers and the detector are all tuned at the same time. Variable capacitors that are connected together are called *ganged capacitors*.

AM and FM Tuners

Many radio receivers and stereo systems have AM and FM tuners. By using the selector switch it is possible to select either AM or FM radio signals. The tuners are radio frequency amplifiers which are designed to tune in either AM or FM broadcasting stations. Often the tuners are connected to a pre-amplifier system which is then connected to a power am-

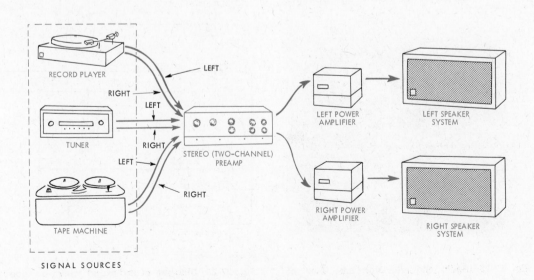

Fig. 27-27. Components in a stereo system.

plifier. The power amplifier delivers its audio signal to a loudspeaker.

In a stereo system, two separate channels are provided for both the pre-amplifier and the power amplifier. Fig. 27-27 shows the block diagram of a stereo system using a record player, a tuner, and a tape recorder. Stereo broadcasting adds another feature to a stereo system. Multiplex operation can be provided to allow simultaneous reception of two radio signals necessary to provide stereophonic reception. Multiplex involves the broadcasting of two channels by the transmitting FM station. A stereo tuner is required to separate the two channels.

INTERESTING THINGS TO DO

Radio and Television Tube Filament Tester.

Materials needed to construct the radio and television tube filament tester (Fig. 27-28):

1 Piece sheet steel, 20 gage, 5½" x 6"
1 Resistor, 100,000 ohms
1 Neon lamp, NE-51
2 Octal sockets
2 Miniature sockets, 7 pin
1 Miniature socket, 9 pin
1 Rubber grommet, ¼"
1 Rubber grommet, ⅜"
6' Lamp cord
1 Attachment plug

One of the frequent causes of a radio or television receiver failing to operate is the burning out of one or more tube filaments. With this filament tester you can locate such tubes quickly and accu-

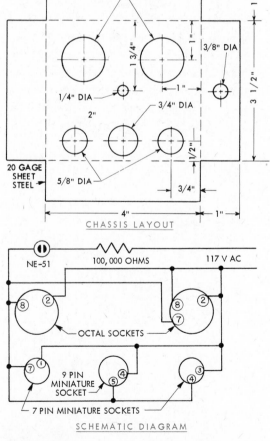

Fig. 27-28. Radio and television tube filament tester.

Fig. 27-29. Diagram of radio and television tube filament tester.

rately. Tube manufacturers use different combinations as filament terminals for octal sockets and seven pin miniature sockets. Thus, two sockets of each type are provided to handle all present-day filament terminal arrangements. Since nine pin miniature tubes have only one filament terminal arrangement at present, only one such type tube socket is required.

Lay out, shape, and drill the piece of sheet steel as shown in Fig. 27-29. Bend the sides and ends of the chassis along the dotted lines and solder the corners together. Attach the tube sockets to the chassis in the holes provided. Secure a rubber grommet in the hole in the top of the chassis and press the neon lamp into the grommet with the terminals inside the chassis. Wire the tester according to the schematic diagram and attach the line cord after passing it through a rubber grommet in the end of the chassis. When testing either an octal base or a seven pin miniature tube, first place the tube in the socket on the left side, then in the socket on the right side. If the neon lamp lights in either case, the tube filament is good. If the neon lamp fails to light, the filament is defective. To test a nine pin miniature tube, place it in the socket and observe the neon lamp as directed above.

REVIEW QUESTIONS

1. Why are audio-frequency amplifiers used?

2. What kind of a transformer is used in a transformer-coupled audio amplifier?

3. Explain why it is important that an electron tube produce a radio signal without distortion.

4. What are the advantages of a resistance-coupled amplifier over the transformer-coupled amplifier?

5. Explain the purpose of the voice coil in a loudspeaker.

6. What is the purpose of the cone in a loudspeaker?

7. What is used to connect the loudspeaker to an electron tube?

8. Name several uses for audio amplifiers.

9. What are electron tubes with more than three elements called?

10. What are the two main purposes of a radio-frequency amplifier?

11. What is a baffle used for in a loudspeaker system?

12. Explain the meaning of stereophonic reproduction.

13. Explain how a tape for a tape recorder obtains a recorded signal.

14. How many recording heads are required for a stereo tape recorder?

15. Draw a block diagram of a stereo system using a tuner.

UNIT 28
TRANSISTOR FUNDAMENTALS

The Transistor

One of the newest additions to the field of electronics has been the development of the *transistor* (Fig. 28-1). Transistors can be used as amplifiers just like electron tubes. They are now being used in radio receivers, television sets, hearing aids, Geiger counters, transmitters, and in many other places.

The transistor has several advantages over the electron tube. (1) It is very small and takes little space. (2) It does not require a large power supply like the electron tube. Small flashlight cells will last a long time with transistor circuits. (3) It does not have a heater like the electron tube, so practically no heat is produced. (4) The transistor can take rough handling and not become noisy as some tubes do.

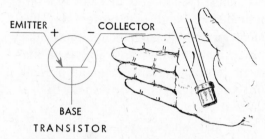

The elements of a transistor are shown this way in a symbol.

N-Type Semiconductors

Transistors are made from materials called semiconductors. A semiconductor is a substance that is not as good a conductor of electricity as metal, but is a better conductor than an insulator. There are a number of semiconductor materials, but the two most often used in the manufacture of transistors are germanium and silicon. Transistors require semiconductors with special electrical properties.

Germanium, in its very purest form, is very much like an insulator as it has few electrons which are free to move about. By adding very small quantities of impurities to the germanium, it can be made

Fig. 28-1. Comparing the size of a transistor and an electronic tube.

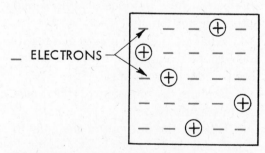

Fig. 28-2. An N-type semiconductor has a number of free electrons.

to conduct electricity. The addition of such impurities as antimony or arsenic to the germanium will increase the number of electrons which are free to move about in the germanium crystal. See Fig. 28-2. When a germanium crystal has an excess of "free" electrons, it is called an N-type semiconductor.

P-Type Semiconductors

A second method of making a semiconductor is by the addition of aluminum or gallium to germanium. When the aluminum or gallium is added to the germanium, a shortage of electrons is produced in the crystal. Such a semiconductor is called a P-type semiconductor, and its usage brings into being a new concept in electricity. This new concept states that a shortage of electrons produces a hole in the semiconductor. This hole is free to move about much the same as free electrons are in the N-type material. See Fig. 28-3.

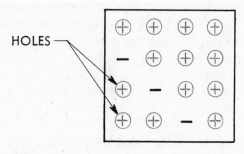

Fig. 28-3. A P-type semiconductor has a number of free holes.

If a battery is placed across the ends of a P-type semiconductor, a current will flow as shown in Fig. 28-4. The side of the semiconductor connected to the positive terminal of the battery will repel the holes in the semiconductor. The holes which have a positive charge will

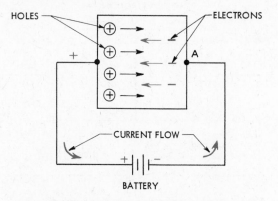

Fig. 28-4. When a battery is connected across a P-type semiconductor, current will flow through the material. The holes move toward point A and the electrons move in the opposite direction.

move toward the negative side of the semiconductor. The electrons from the negative terminal of the battery flow to the semiconductor and combine with the positive holes at point A of the semiconductor. When a hole and an electron come together, they combine and neutralize each other. New holes are then formed in the P-type material and these new holes move toward point A. As these holes are formed, they release electrons in the semiconductor and these electrons flow toward the positive terminal of the battery. Thus, a current flows through the semiconductor.

Forming an N-P Junction

When an N-type and a P-type material are joined together, as in Fig. 28-5, an area formed between the two semiconductors is called a junction. If a voltage is applied across the two materials so that the negative terminal of a battery is connected to the N-type semiconductor and the positive terminal of the battery is connected to the P-type semiconductor, a current will flow through the circuit.

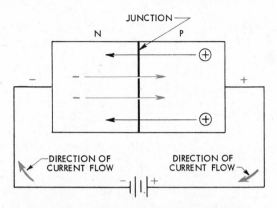

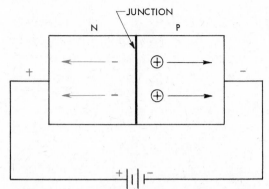

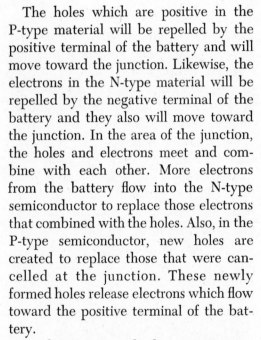

Fig. 28-5. When a negative charge is applied to the N-type material and a positive charge to the P-type material, a current will flow through the N-P junction.

Fig. 28-6. When a positive charge is applied to the N-type semiconductor and a negative charge to the P-type semiconductor, practically no current flows through the N-P junction.

The holes which are positive in the P-type material will be repelled by the positive terminal of the battery and will move toward the junction. Likewise, the electrons in the N-type material will be repelled by the negative terminal of the battery and they also will move toward the junction. In the area of the junction, the holes and electrons meet and combine with each other. More electrons from the battery flow into the N-type semiconductor to replace those electrons that combined with the holes. Also, in the P-type semiconductor, new holes are created to replace those that were cancelled at the junction. These newly formed holes release electrons which flow toward the positive terminal of the battery.

In the circuit with the negative terminal of the battery connected to the N-type material and the positive terminal connected to the P-type material, current flows through the circuit. Such a circuit produces a current flow that is called *forward bias*.

Reverse Bias on the N-P Junction

Should the battery polarity be reversed

as in Fig. 28-6, no current will flow through the circuit. The electrons in the N-type material will be attracted to the positive terminal of the battery, and the holes in the P-type material will be attracted to the negative battery terminal. Since both electrons and holes move away from the junction, there is very little opportunity for the holes and electrons to combine. Practically no current will flow in the circuit. When the polarity placed on an N-P junction is such that the N-type material is connected to a positive charge and the P-type material is connected to a negative charge, current will not flow, and this is called *reverse bias*.

The N-P Junction is a Detector

The N-P junction semiconductor will permit current to flow in one direction, but when the polarity across the junction is reversed, current will not flow. If an alternating current is applied to a semiconductor junction, the output from the semiconductor will change the AC into pulsating direct current.

When discussing radio receiver detectors, we learned that both the semi-

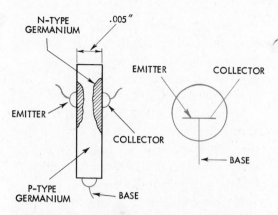

Fig. 28-7. This illustration shows the construction of a transistor with the diagram of a transistor symbol.

conductor diode and the diode vacuum tube were used to change the alternating radio frequency waves into pulsating direct current. This pulsating direct current made the earphones function to form the sound waves. Many modern transistor radio receivers use germanium crystals called junction diodes as detectors. See Fig. 28-7.

The Tunnel Diode

The *tunnel* diode is a recent development which, because of its small size and unusual characteristics, is expected to play a large part in the development of devices for new electronic applications. In a regular junction diode the junction, or barrier, between the *N* and *P* elements prevents current from flowing in the reverse direction, but by making the barrier only one-millionth of an inch thick, electrons are able to tunnel through it at a pressure of only a fraction of one volt. One of a tunnel diode's unusual characteristics is that it can be made to oscillate, switch, or amplify like a transistor or multi-element electronic tube. Some of

the advantages claimed for tunnel diodes are:

1. Withstanding operating temperatures up to 650°F.
2. Electrical charges move through it at the speed of light, making it ideal for use at frequencies above 2,000 megahertz.
3. Its small size makes possible the construction of miniaturized electronic equipment such as a complete radio transmitter in a space no larger than a fifty-cent piece.

Forming a Junction Transistor

Junction transistors are formed by using three layers of semiconductor materials placed together like a sandwich as shown in Fig. 28-8. This is called an N-P-N junction. The two outside semiconductors are of N-type material, and the center semiconductor is of P-type material. The center P-type material is called the base. The base is extremely thin and is usually less than .001 inch wide. The N-type material on one side of the base is called the emitter, and the N-type material on the opposite side is called the collector. Leads coming from the transistor are identified as the emit-

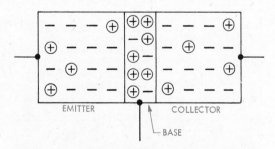

Fig. 28-8. An N-P-N transistor consists of an N-type emitter, an N-type collector, and a P-type base.

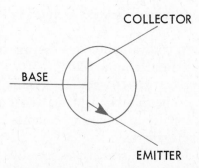

Fig. 28-9. A symbol for an N-P-N transistor. The arrow for the emitter points away from the base.

ter, the collector, and the base, as shown in Fig. 28-9.

A second type transistor called the P-N-P transistor is similar to the N-P-N except that the base semiconductor is of the N-type and the emitter and collector are of the P-type.

N-P-N Transistor Action

To understand the fundamental operation of a transistor, we can assume that external batteries are connected to the transistor leads so that current will flow through the transistor. The battery marked X in Fig. 28-10 is connected between the emitter and the base. Since

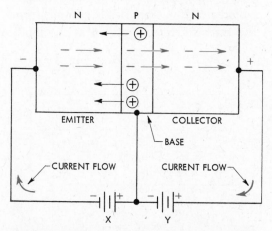

Fig. 28-10. When the proper voltage is applied to the emitter, base, and collector of an N-P-N transistor, current flows through the entire transistor.

the polarity across the junction is such that N-type material has a negative charge and the P-type material has a positive charge, this is forward bias, and current flows through the junction.

If Battery Y in Fig. 28-10 is connected across the collector and the base so that the negative terminal goes to the collector and the positive terminal goes to the base, no current flows.

If the collector is connected to the positive terminal of Battery Y, Fig. 28-10, electrons come through the base and are attracted toward this positive charge and will flow right on through the collector. Because the base is so thin, the electrons which flow from the emitter toward the base actually tend to flow right through it toward the collector. Thus, current flows through the entire transistor.

Applying a Signal to the Emitter

To learn how a transistor functions, we need to apply a signal to the emitter circuit. In Fig. 28-11 a microphone transformer has been placed in the circuit of the emitter and the base. When someone speaks into the microphone, an alternating current appears in the secondary of the transformer. The pure direct current produced by the battery in the emitter circuit is now varied by the AC signal. Since the AC signal is first positive and then negative, the voltage in the circuit is either increased or decreased.

When the signal is positive, it subtracts from the voltage of battery X, and the electron flow through the emitter is reduced. The current flow through the output transformer connected in the collector circuit will also be reduced because electrons from the emitter flow into the base and through the collector. When the input signal becomes negative, the

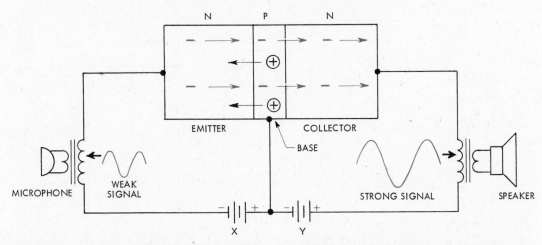

Fig. 28-11. A weak signal applied to the emitter circuit through the microphone is amplified by the transistor.

emitter will have an increased voltage, as the negative signal will add to the voltage of battery X. Increasing the current flow in the emitter will also increase the current flow through the output transformer of the collector circuit.

From this we can see that a signal applied to the emitter circuit produces a similar signal in the collector circuit. Thus, the emitter controls the collector current. This action is similar to that found in the vacuum tube where the grid controls the plate current.

The P-N-P Transistor

A P-N-P transistor can be used for an amplifier the same as the N-P-N. When using the P-N-P transistor (Fig. 28-12), the voltage polarities are opposite to those used on the N-P-N transistor. Fig. 28-13 illustrates how the polarities are connected for the P-N-P transistor.

When wiring transistors in circuits, it is extremely important to know whether P-N-P or N-P-N is to be used. By using the wrong battery polarities on transistors, they can easily be damaged.

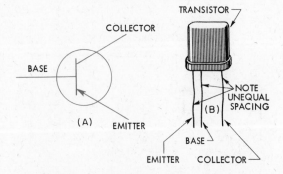

Fig. 28-12. A symbol for a P-N-P transistor. The arrow for the emitter points toward the base.

Amplification in a Transistor

Because the battery polarity produces forward bias in the emitter circuit, current flows very readily. Since current flows easily, there is very little resistance in the circuit. In the collector and base circuit reverse bias is applied so that very little current flows in this part of the circuit. The collector-base has a fairly high resistance.

When a signal is applied to the emitter, current will flow through the output circuit of the collector. This current will flow even though a very large resistance

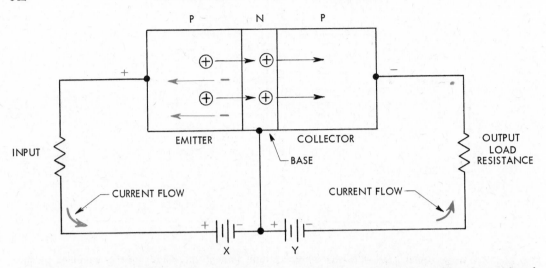

P   N   P

INPUT   EMITTER   COLLECTOR   OUTPUT
                                                              LOAD
                                    BASE   RESISTANCE

CURRENT FLOW   CURRENT FLOW

X   Y

Fig. 28-13. In a P-N-P transistor the positive holes in the emitter are repelled by the positive charge placed on the emitter by battery X. The holes flow through the thin base and into the collector. In the collector they combine with the electrons produced by the negative terminal of battery Y. Electrons in the emitter are attracted toward the positive terminal of battery X and new holes are then formed in the emitter.

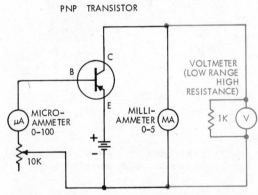

PNP   TRANSISTOR

Fig. 28-14. Circuit for demonstrating how a transistor amplifies.

is placed in the collector circuit. A very small change in emitter voltage will produce a current change in the collector circuit. This changing current is flowing through a large output load resistor. A small current of only a very few milliamperes, when flowing through a large load resistor, can produce a large voltage drop. Using Ohm's law, we know that Voltage = Current times Resistance ($E = I \times R$). A transistor amplifies be-

cause a small voltage change applied to the emitter circuit will cause a large voltage change in the collector output circuit.

The ability of a transistor to amplify can be shown with a microammeter, milliammeter, transistor, potentiometer, and dry cells, connected as shown in Fig. 28-14. Adjust the potentiometer so that readings of both meters will be on the low side and within the range of the meters, as shown in Fig. 28-15. Readjust the potentiometer, so that both meters will show increased readings. Make this adjustment carefully so that you do not exceed the current rating of the transistor collector circuit. In the example shown in Fig. 28-16, the new meter readings are 26 microamperes and 1 milliampere. Referring back to Fig. 28-15, we can see that a current change of 11 microamperes in the *base-emitter* circuit has caused a change of nearly 500 microamperes, or 0.5 milliampere, in the *collector-base* circuit. Since the *base-emitter* circuit repre-

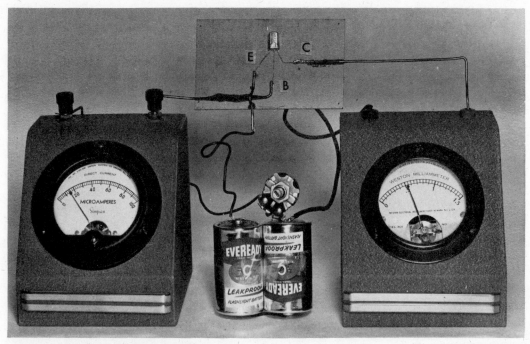

Fig. 28-15. The base-emitter circuit on the left and the collector-emitter circuit on the right have been adjusted to show a low current reading.

Fig. 28-16. By increasing the base-emitter current by a few microamperes an increase of nearly one hundred percent is produced in the collector current.

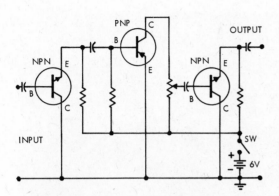

Fig. 28-17. A transistor audio amplifier using a common collector for stage one and three and a common emitter for the second stage.

sents the input circuit and the *collector-base* circuit the output circuit, we can see how the transistor amplifies. The output of the transistor may be shown in terms of voltage change rather than current by replacing the milliammeter with a 1,000 ohm resistor and connecting a low range voltmeter across it.

Transistors may be coupled together to raise a signal to any desired level, and like electronic tubes they may be connected in several different ways. A diagram of a typical resistance-coupled

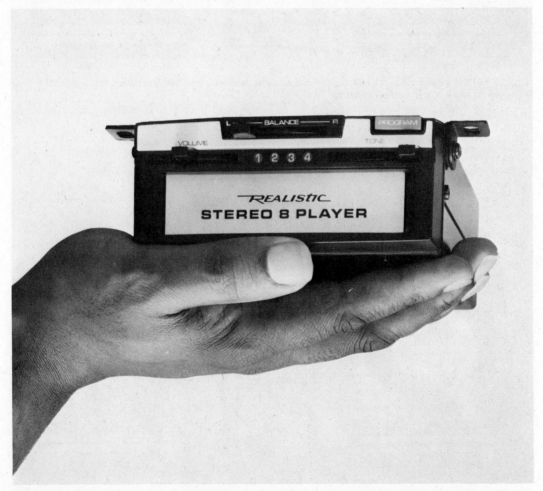

Fig. 28-18. Stereo tape player for automobiles and trucks. Use of diodes and transistors makes small size possible. (Radio Shack)

amplifier using three transistors is shown in Fig. 28-17. Multi-unit transistor amplifiers for hi-fi and stereo with frequency response and output equal to tube amplifiers are now available, with the added advantage of requiring much less space. Small tape players, Fig. 28-18, use a combination of diodes and transistors. Fig. 28-19 shows a transistor amplifier and an electronic tube amplifier.

Transistor Circuits

Transistors (Fig. 28-20) may be connected in any one of three ways. These

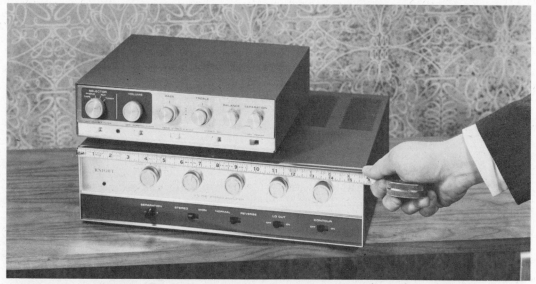

Fig. 28-19. An electronic tube stereo amplifier (bottom) and a transistor amplifier (top) compared for size. Both have similar frequency response and output of 50 watts. (Allied Radio Corp.)

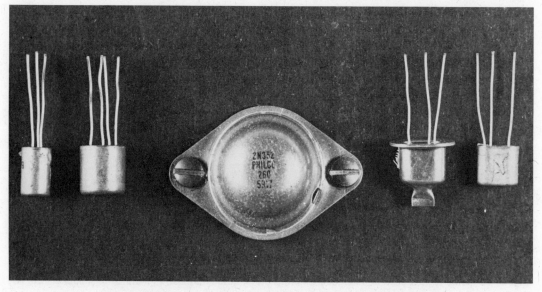

Fig. 28-20. Several types of transistors used in electronic circuits.

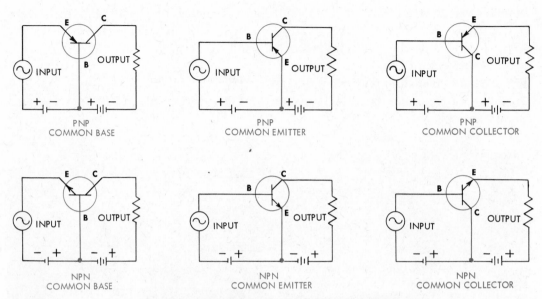

Fig. 28-21. The basic circuits for transistor amplifiers.

hook-ups, called configurations, are named common-base, common-emitter, and common-collector. In each circuit one of the electrodes is common to both the input and output circuit.

The basic hook-ups for transistor amplifier circuits are shown in Fig. 28-21. You can determine the type of a transistor amplifier circuit by noting which electrode provides a common connection for one of the input and one of the out-

put terminals. For example, in the common base drawings in Fig. 28-22, the base provides that connection. If you apply the same reasoning to the other diagrams you will see how they are so-named.

Semiconductor Photocells

Practically all semiconductors show sensitivity to light rays, some to a higher degree than others. Of the many available semiconductors, silicon and germa-

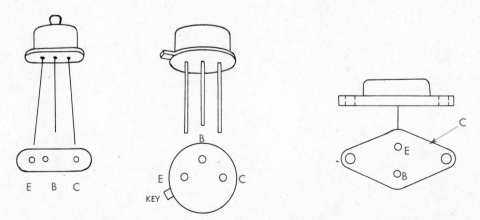

Fig. 28-22. Some typical base connections for transistors. In most industrial installations, sockets are not used.

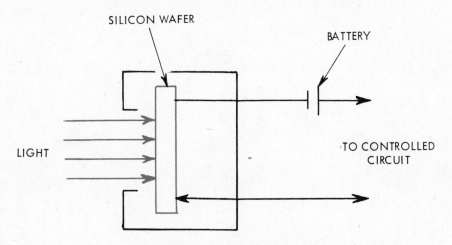

Fig. 28-23. Point contact photodiode.

nium are generally preferred in industry for photocells because their active areas need be only a fraction of an inch across. This permits grouping the cells closely together for such applications as punched card and tape readouts for computers and alarm systems. One type of semiconductor photocell known as a *point contact photodiode* is shown in Fig. 28-23.

Another type of semiconductor photocell, shown in Fig. 28-24, is made in the form of a *PNP transistor*. Current flow in the collector circuit is governed by the

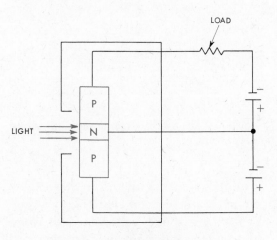

Fig. 28-24. Transistor photodiode.

intensity of the light striking the N or *barrier* area. This type of photocell has the advantage over a photodiode in that it provides amplification.

Integrated Circuits

A recent development that has revolutionized the manufacture of electronic communication devices is the *integrated circuit*, generally abbreviated *IC*. With the use of IC's miniaturization, electronic equipment has progressed to a degree never thought possible when they were first introduced a few years back. For example, computers which once required the space of a large office file may now be reproduced in a case barely larger than a typewriter. This is understandable when we consider that 25 or more of the components used in electronic circuits such as transistors, resistors, capacitors, and diodes may be produced in an IC in a container less than one-half inch in diameter. For servicemen repairing radio receivers, television receivers or stereo equipment, the replacement of a defective IC circuit becomes as simple an operation as inserting a transistor in its socket. See Fig. 28-25.

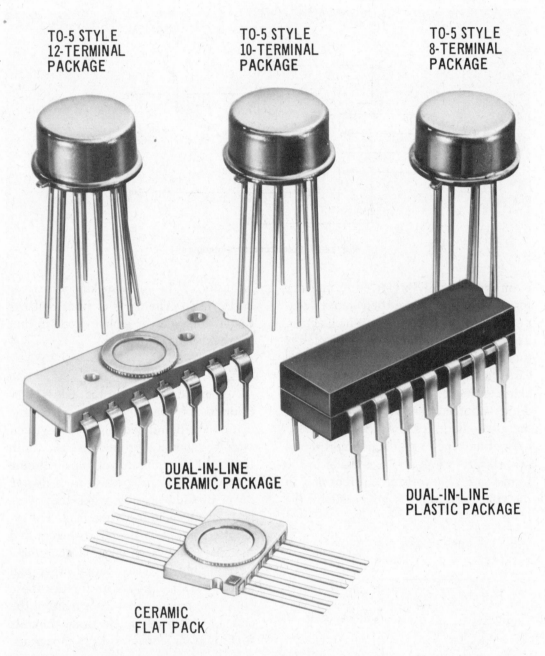

TO-5 STYLE
12-TERMINAL
PACKAGE

TO-5 STYLE
10-TERMINAL
PACKAGE

TO-5 STYLE
8-TERMINAL
PACKAGE

DUAL-IN-LINE
CERAMIC PACKAGE

DUAL-IN-LINE
PLASTIC PACKAGE

CERAMIC
FLAT PACK

Fig. 28-25. A few of the many kinds of integrated circuit containers. All types have tabs or reference marks from which circuit terminals may be located. (Radio Corp. of America.)

In manufacturing an IC, a large pattern of the desired circuit is reduced photographically on the light sensitized surface of a silicon *chip* to produce the required miniaturization. The chip is then etched by chemical or electrical means to provide the diode, capacitor, transistor, and resistor action required for the par-

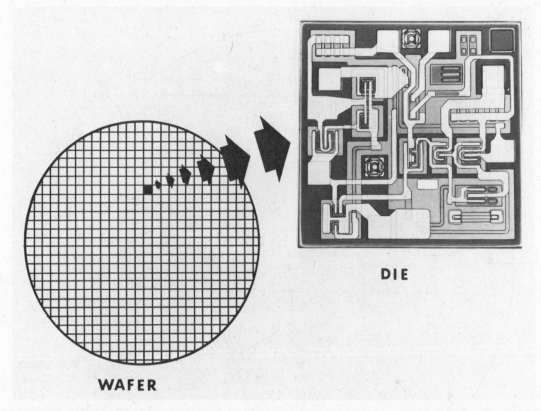

WAFER

DIE

Fig. 28-26. Hundreds of integrated chips or dies are fabricated from a silicon wafer. If we think of the silicon wafer as having a flat surface area equivalent to that of a half-dollar, we can get an idea of the actual size of the integrated circuit shown in the figure. (Motorola Semiconductor Products, Inc.)

ticular circuit. After the chip is etched, leads are attached for outside circuit connections; then the completed IC is hermetically sealed in a suitable container. See Fig. 28-26.

Using Integrated Circuits in Electronic Projects

Of the many types of integrated circuits that are available, one that is particularly suited for electronic project construction is the Fairchild, type UL 914. Its cost is low and with the addition of a few external components it may be combined into 40 or more different circuits.

The UL 914 IC consists of four transistors and six resistors, enclosed in a $5/16''$ diameter epoxy case. The leads from the circuit are brought out in a way that one or more transistors may be used by merely shorting the unwanted transistors, base to emitter. For example, if only transistors Q_1 and Q_2, Fig. 28-27, are needed, transistors Q_3 and Q_4, can be eliminated from the circuit by connecting the B and E leads of Q_3 and Q_4 together.

Printed Circuits

Printed circuitry, a method of electronic circuit wiring in which thin strips of copper foil, bonded to an insulating panel, serve as conductors, is widely used

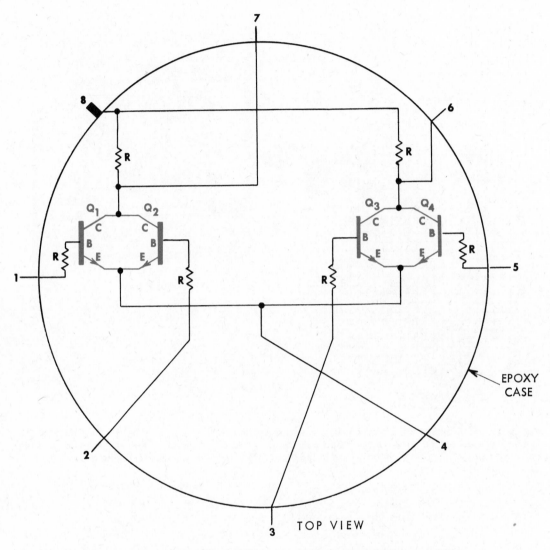

Fig. 28-27. Interior connections of Fairchild integrated circuit UL914.

in the manufacture of radio and television equipment, computers, industrial controls, and in many other electronic applications where saving of time and space is a factor (Fig. 28-28). It makes possible the lowering of production costs over the older hand-wiring methods and facilititates circuit tracing should it become necessary. Basically, the process of making a printed circuit begins with outlining a desired circuit on a copper-clad

panel with material known as *resist*. The resist may be a liquid, a stick-on tape, or a dry transfer. After the resist is applied, the panel is placed in an etching solution where the areas of copper not protected by the resist is etched away, leaving only the copper circuit lines. In one method of making printed circuits, the surface of the copper is coated with a light-sensitive solution, then exposed to light through a negative of the required circuit

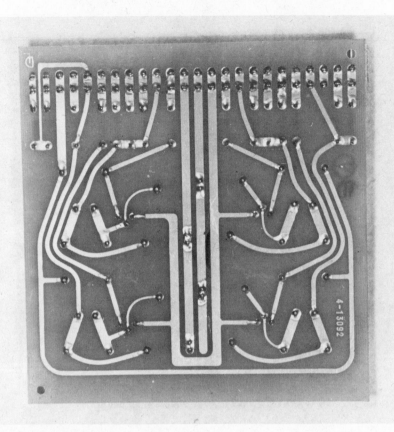

Fig. 28-28. A printed circuit from a data processing machine is shown here. On the opposite side are mounted 4 transistors, 4 capacitors, and 31 resistors, all within a 5″ × 5″ area.

that was taken with a camera. The sensitized panel is then developed and placed in a dye for a short period, after which it is etched in the usual manner.

Electronic Computers

The modern computer affects our lives in so many ways that the present area is frequently referred to as the *Computer Age*. Computers are used in scientific and industrial laboratories. They are used by stores and banks for making out statements for their customers. Checks for wages and salaries are made out by computers. And successful landings on the moon would not have been possible without the aid of computers.

Essentially, a computer is a device for making calculations with extreme rapidity. It can multiply a number like 12185 by 585 in the few seconds required to jot the figures down on paper, and it can divide a ten-figure number by a six-figure number in a like space of time. However, computers are not limited to solving mathematical problems. They can also assemble and evaluate information supplied by measuring devices and provide a solution to a problem.

Computers are divided into two basic types: analog and digital, according to the purposes for which they are to be used. Although both types are completely electronic, digital computers are more

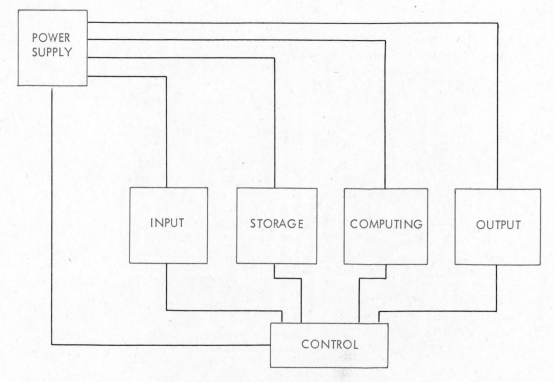

Fig. 28-29. Block diagram of digital computer.

generally employed because of flexibility, and because of greater accuracy resulting from the nature of the information supplied to the computer. A block diagram of the units which make up a digital computer is shown in Fig. 28-29.

The information coming out of a computer can be no more accurate than the information fed into it, and for that reason computer operators must be trained specifically for the job. The operators or programmers, as they are known, convert ordinary information into forms which can be used by the machine. This generally includes perforating tapes with a special typewriter, so that they will produce proper responses when placed in the computer. The tape passes into a slot in the *input* section where contacts extend through the perforations and close cir-

cuits which create electrical pulses as the tape moves along.

The *storage* section contains either electronic or magnetic devices for retaining information supplied by the input section. When a new sequence of operations is being inserted into the unit, all of it usually goes to the storage section until fully assembled, after which instructions are issued to the control section and portions are removed from the storage section as needed. In office computers, reels of magnetic tape, in cabinets, hold data indefinitely until called for by the control unit.

In the *computing* section, mathematical operations are made from procedures supplied earlier by the input section. Problems in higher mathematics can be solved if the necessary steps involving

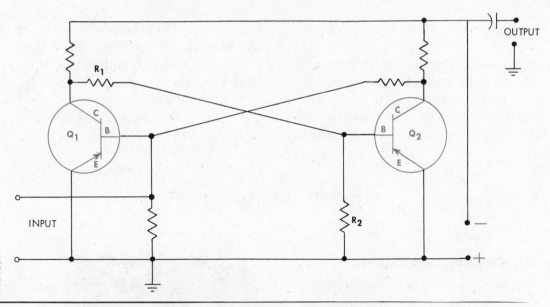

Fig. 28-30. Bistable of flip-flop computer circuit.

simplified routines of addition, subtraction, multiplication, and division have been provided.

The *output* section supplies information called for by the input section, delivering it by typed replies, printed tapes, punched cards, or an arrangement of lighted lamps on a wall panel.

The *control* section is the heart of the computer. It uses electrical circuits to perform switching operations that will carry out the instructions given by the input section. Pulse signals which carry information from one section of the computer to another originate here. The control section extracts data from the storage section and transfers it to the computing section, takes it from the computing section and returns it to the storage section, or turns it over to the output section, as the occasion requires.

Although electronic tubes were used in early models of computers, modern computers generally use transistors. Their smaller size permits making more compact units than with tubes, and maintenance costs are reduced considerably when transistors are used.

A computer circuit which is usually used in the storage section is shown in Fig. 28-30. This is known as a *bistable* circuit because it has two stable states, either Q_1 conducting and Q_2 OFF, or Q_1 OFF and Q_2 conducting. A pulse from an external source will cause a rapid shift from one state to the other and for that reason it is known also as a *flip-flop* circuit. Two pulses are required to return the circuit to its original state.

Assuming that Q_1 is ON and Q_2 is OFF, a positive pulse to the base of Q_1 will cause a reverse bias voltage at Q_1 and cause it to cut off. R_1 and R_4 now become a bias voltage divider for Q_2. The increased current flow through the voltage divider causes the base of Q_2 to become more negative which turns Q_2 ON. A negative pulse to the base of Q_1 will turn Q_1 ON and Q_2 OFF.

The control section accomplishes its

work within the computer largely by operations known as *gating*. A gate is a switch that permits an output signal only when certain conditions have been satisfied. There are two kinds of gates, *AND* and *OR*. An *AND* pulse is let through only after a series of requirements have been met. An *OR* pulse results when any one of multiple conditions have been carried out. The *AND* gate may be represented by a number of switches in series, an *OR* gate by switches in parallel. Control circuits are made up of networks of both *AND* and *OR* sub-circuits.

INTERESTING THINGS TO DO

1. Transistor Radio Receiver.

Materials needed to construct the transistor radio receiver (Figs. 28-31 and 28-32):

1 Antenna coil (see text)
1 Variable capacitor, .000365 μf (see text) (C_1)
1 Crystal diode, general purpose, G.E. or Sylvania 1N64
1 Fixed capacitor, .02 μf (C_2)
1 Resistor, 220,000 ohms, ½-watt (R)
1 Transistor, Raytheon 722 or G.E. 2N107
2 Pen light cells

This radio receiver may be built by placing the parts on a wood base and using the standard-size parts described with the crystal set in Unit 26. If you want to build a very small set that you can carry in your pocket, miniature parts

Fig. 28-32. A soap dish was used to hold this transistor radio receiver. A shaft has been soldered to the padder-type capacitor that is used to tune the receiver.

to work with transistors may be obtained from radio mail order companies and wholesale radio houses. Using miniature parts makes it possible to build the complete receiver shown in Fig. 28-33 in a plastic box 1″ deep, 2″ wide, and 3″ long.

To build the receiver in a small space use a Transistor Loop Antenna instead of a standard-size antenna coil. For the standard variable capacitor use a 365 pf Super-Midget variable capacitor. The only other substitution will be a miniature-type fixed capacitor for the capacitor, C_2. Wire set according to the schematic diagram. Phone tip jacks may be provided for the headphones if it is not desired to have them permanently attached to the set.

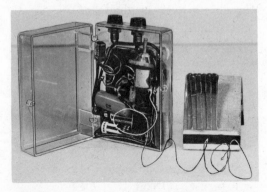

Fig. 28-31. A transistor radio receiver built in a small plastic case. A match folder is next to the receiver.

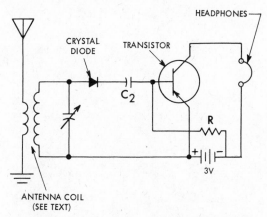

Fig. 28-33. Schematic diagram of transistor radio receiver.

1 Piece brass rod, round, $\frac{1}{16}$" diameter, $3\frac{1}{2}$" long
2 Small magnets (see text)
1 Ball, styrofoam or balsa wood, 2" diameter
1 Wood base, $\frac{1}{2}$" x 6" x 8"
1 Piece spring brass, 24 ga., $\frac{5}{16}$" x $1\frac{3}{4}$"
1 Piece spring brass, $\frac{5}{16}$" x $\frac{5}{8}$"
1 Piece sheet brass, 20 ga., $\frac{1}{2}$" x $\frac{3}{4}$"
1 Transistor (see text)
1 Transistor socket (optional)
2 Flashlight cells, 1.5 volt
1 Potentiometer, 5,000 ohms
2 Fahnestock clips

This motor operates on a new principle. It has no brushes or commutator. The current changing action of those items is supplied by a transistor.

The placement of parts as shown in the photograph may be followed, or they may be arranged to suit the builder's fancy.

Begin the motor by making a winding form for the coil, Fig. 28-35. The slots should extend into the center wood block

2. A Brushless Direct Current Motor.

Materials needed to construct the brushless direct current motor (Fig. 28-34):

1 Spool magnet wire, enamel covered, 26 to 30 ga. (see text)

Fig. 28-34. Completed brushless direct-current motor.

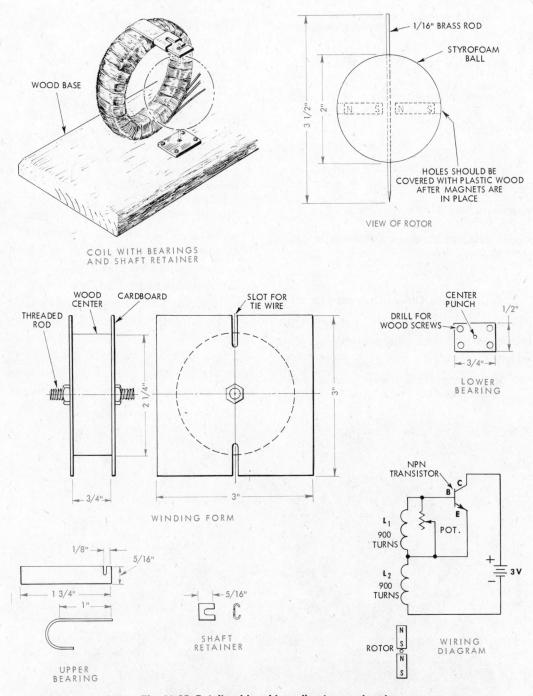

WOOD BASE

COIL WITH BEARINGS
AND SHAFT RETAINER

1/16" BRASS ROD

STYROFOAM
BALL

N S N S

HOLES SHOULD BE
COVERED WITH PLASTIC WOOD
AFTER MAGNETS ARE
IN PLACE

VIEW OF ROTOR

WOOD CENTER   CARDBOARD   SLOT FOR TIE WIRE

THREADED ROD

CENTER PUNCH

DRILL FOR WOOD SCREWS

1/2"

3/4"

LOWER BEARING

2 1/4"

3/4"

3"

3"

WINDING FORM

1/8"

5/16"

1 3/4"

1"

5/16"

SHAFT RETAINER

UPPER BEARING

NPN TRANSISTOR

C
B
E

L₁
900 TURNS

POT.

+
3V

L₂
900 TURNS

ROTOR

N
S
N
S

WIRING DIAGRAM

Fig. 28-35. Details of brushless direct-current motor.

so that pieces of wire may be passed under and around the completed coil to
hold it together temporarily. Wind a few
turns of thin cardboard around the cen-

ter wood block, then wind 900 turns of
magnet wire on the form. Any size wire
from 26 to 30 may be used, and since
the amount of wire required may vary, it

is better to wind the form directly from a spool, rather than try to estimate the exact amount. After 900 turns have been wound, make a loop of wire about eight inches long, twist it together, then wind another 900 turns on the form in the same direction. The wire may be wound by placing the form in a hand-drill or lathe. Place tie wires around the coil and remove it from the form. Wrap the completed coil with tape, removing the tie wires as you proceed with the wrapping. Drill holes through the wood base for the coil leads and secure the coil to the base with glue or cement.

Sharpen one end of the round brass rod to a point. Drill a $\frac{1}{16}''$ hole through the center of the rotor ball. Drill another hole through the ball that is perpendicular to the first hole and large enough to hold the small magnets. The magnets are the small type usually obtainable from hardware and novelty stores. Drill and center punch the piece of brass for the lower bearing. Shape the upper bearing and shaft retainer as shown in the drawing. Clamp the bearing to the top of the coil, place the rotor ball on the shaft and locate the bottom bearing so that the rotor will revolve in the center of the coil. After the rotor has been properly aligned it should be cemented to the brass rod. The upper bearing may also be cemented to the coil. The sliding retainer holds the rotor shaft in place, yet permits the rotor assembly to be removed easily.

Mount the potentiometer, transistor, and Fahnestock clips on the wood base and connect the parts together as shown in the wiring diagram. Although connections may be made directly to the transistor leads, a transistor socket is recommended if you wish to experiment with different types of transistors. The wiring diagram shows an NPN transistor, but a PNP will work equally well if the flashlight cell connections are reversed so that the transistor collector connection, "C", goes to the negative terminal of the cell. This change is important, otherwise the transistor may be damaged.

When all connections are complete the motor is ready for its initial tryout. First, make certain that the rotor spins freely. Then turn the potentiometer shaft to about its center position and connect the flashlight cells. Start the rotor and it should quickly reach a high speed on its own power. Further adjustment of the potentiometer will determine its best operating position.

The transistor circuit used in the motor is a common-emitter type. We learned that a bias voltage is necessary for the proper operation of that type of circuit and it is the varying of that voltage that makes the rotor spin around. When the rotor magnets are at a right angle to the coil the bias voltage is obtained from the three-volt supply through the coil L_1.

In order to understand the operation of the motor, let us assume that the north pole of one of the rotor magnets is near coil L_2, and that the current flowing through the collector-base circuit and through the coil is in a direction to create a magnetic field that will attract the magnet. As the magnet approaches the coil it induces a voltage in coil L_1 which reenforces the bias voltage between the emitter and the base. The increased bias causes a corresponding increase in the collector current, which increases the pull on the magnet until the momentum of the rotor carries the magnet away from the coil. As the rotor continues to revolve the south pole of the magnet approaches coil L_2. Due to the changed polarity a voltage is induced in coil L_1 which opposes the bias voltage. This reduces the collector current and makes the transistor inactive until a north pole of the magnet again approaches coil L_2, where the action begins all over again. The function of the potentiometer is to adjust the bias voltage for maximum speed of the rotor.

3. Transistor Amplifier.

Materials needed to construct the transistor amplifier (Fig. 28-36):

1 Piece wood, ½″ x 3″ x 3″
1 Transistor, Raytheon CK 722
1 Fixed capacitor, electrolytic, 10 μf, 25 volts
1 Resistor (see text) R_1
1 Resistor, 220,000 ohms, R_2
2 Penlight cells
4 Fahnestock clips

This transistor amplifier will provide more volume for either the crystal diode receiver or the transistor receiver which are described elsewhere in this book. Mount the parts in the approximate position on the wood base as shown in Fig. 28-36. Wire the set according to Fig. 28-37. Two of the Fahnestock clips should be marked *input* and two should be marked *output*. For best results the value of resistor R_1 should be about 470 ohms

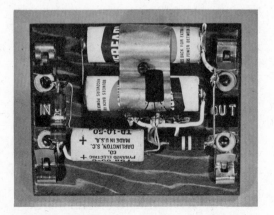

Fig. 28-36. Transistor amplifier.

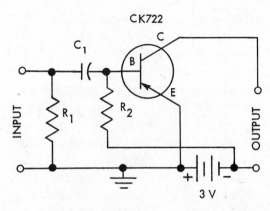

Fig. 28-37. Wiring diagram of transistor amplifier.

when the amplifier is used with the transistor receiver and about 47,000 ohms when it is used with the crystal diode receiver. To reduce current drain from the pen light cells, the headphones or speaker should be disconnected from the output side of the amplifier when it is not in use.

4. Making a Photocell Amplifier.

Materials needed to construct the photocell amplifier Fig. 28-38):

Wood base, 4½″ x 6″
1 Transistor, PNP audio type
1 Photocell, Gen. Elect., GE-X6
1 Sensitive relay (see text)
1 Potentiometer, 100,000 ohms, R_2 (see text)
1 Resistor, 4,700 ohms, ½ watt, R_1
1 Transistor battery, 9 V
1 Battery clip for transistor battery
2 Flashlight cells, 1.5 volt
1 Flashlight bulb, 3 V
1 Miniature lamp socket
1 Cardboard tube, 1″ x 4″
Flexible hook-up wire for photocell housing
1 Three-lug terminal strip

This project will provide some fascinating experiments in the control of electrical devices with a beam of light. The project as described shows not only the control of a flashlight bulb, but a buzzer, bell, or small motor may be connected easily in its place.

Fig. 28-38. Photocell amplifier.

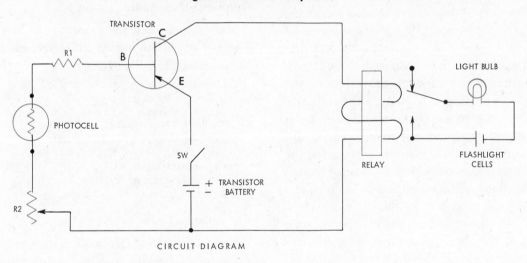

CIRCUIT DIAGRAM

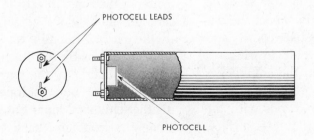

CUTAWAY VIEW OF PHOTOCELL HOUSING

Fig. 28-39. Photocell amplifier details.

Mount the parts on the wood base and connect them as shown in the circuit diagram, Fig. 28-39. Mount the transistor on the three-lug terminal strip and hold the transistor leads next to transistor case with long nose pliers while soldering, to prevent heat damaging the transistor. The switch shown in the transistor emitter circuit is mounted on the back of the potentiometer. If a separate switch is desired, it should be included in the parts list. The sensitive relay for which construction details are given in Unit 18 will work very well with the amplifier, since it may be adjusted to operate with a few milliamperes of current. If a relay is purchased, it should function on not more than five milliamperes. Make a housing for the photocell by cutting a circle of heavy cardboard equal to the outside diameter of the cardboard. Mount two terminal screws near the edge of the cardboard circle so that their heads will clear the inside of the cardboard tube. Mount the photocell on the cardboard circle by drilling two small holes for the photocell leads. Insert the leads through the holes and secure them to the terminal screws as shown in the cutaway view. Coat the inside of the cardboard tube with flat black paint. Glue the cardboard circle with the photocell to an end of the cardboard tube. Attach flexible leads to the terminal screws and connect the opposite ends of the leads between R_1 and R_2, as shown in the circuit drawing.

The photocell used in the amplifier is a cadmium sulfide photoresistive type, the resistance of which varies with the intensity of the light striking its surface. Its resistance is highest in total darkness. When the photocell is exposed to light such as a flashlight beam, its resistance

drops and current flows in the base-emitter circuit of the transistor. As we learned in our study of transistors, a small increase of current in the base-emitter circuit will cause a large increase of current in the collector circuit. If the current is sufficient to operate the relay, the relay contacts will close and turn on the light bulb or whatever device is connected to them. The sensitivity of the amplifier may be controlled by the potentiometer. The 4,700 ohm resistor connected to the transistor base serves to protect the transistor by limiting the maximum current through it to a safe value.

5. Integrated Circuit High-Gain Audio Frequency Amplifier.

Materials needed to construct the integrated circuit high-gain audio frequency amplifier (Fig. 28-40):

1 Mounting base, $1/8$" x $2\frac{5}{8}$" x $2\frac{5}{8}$", hardboard, plywood, or plastic
1 Integrated circuit (IC), Fairchild, UL 914
1 Socket for IC, UL 914
3 Electrolytic capacitors, miniature, Sprague, 6 V., 15 μf, C1, C2, C3
1 Ceramic capacitor, .001 μf, C4
1 Ceramic capacitor, .002 μf, C5
2 Resistors, carbon, 27,000 ohms, $\frac{1}{2}$ watt, R_1, R_2
6 Fahnestock clips, $\frac{3}{4}$" long

Drill a hole slightly smaller than the diameter of the IC socket through the center of the base. Insert the socket leads through the hole and cement the socket to the base. Although the IC may be connected directly to the components, a socket will simplify the wiring and permit the IC to be withdrawn and used in other circuits. Mount Fahnestock clips along the front and back edges of the base to serve as input, output, and battery terminals. Mount the capacitors and resistors by extending their leads through

Fig. 28-40. Since integrated circuit leads need to be inserted into a socket only a fraction of an inch, the unit is usually mounted on its socket as shown in the high-gain amplifier above. However, the leads may be shortened if extreme care is used.

small holes in the base and bending them at a sharp angle against the bottom of the base. Cover the component leads where they cross with small plastic tubing. See schematic drawing, Fig. 28-41.

Following customary practice, the IC is shown from a top view with its terminals numbered in a counter-clockwise direction. When viewed from the bottom for connecting, the leads should be considered as numbered in a clockwise direction. A small ridge extending vertically on the socket marks the location of the key terminal, No. 8. Because the IC socket terminals are close together, use a fine-pointed soldering pencil when soldering component leads to them. Secure spacers on the bottom of the base at the corners to provide clearance for the IC socket and connections. A battery

switch is not included in the circuit shown, but if one is desired a subminiature toggle switch may be mounted in the area at the left side of the base.

Use extreme care when placing the IC in its socket. Make certain that each lead is perfectly straight, then insert them, one at a time, in the socket terminal holes. A toothpick will help guide the leads into place. When all leads are aligned correctly, press the IC gently into its socket.

6. Integrated Circuit Wide Range Audio Oscillator.

Materials needed to construct the integrated circuit wide range audio oscillator:

1 Mounting base, ⅛" x 2⅝" x 2⅝"
1 Integrated circuit, Fairchild, UL 914
1 Socket for IC Fairchild, UL 914

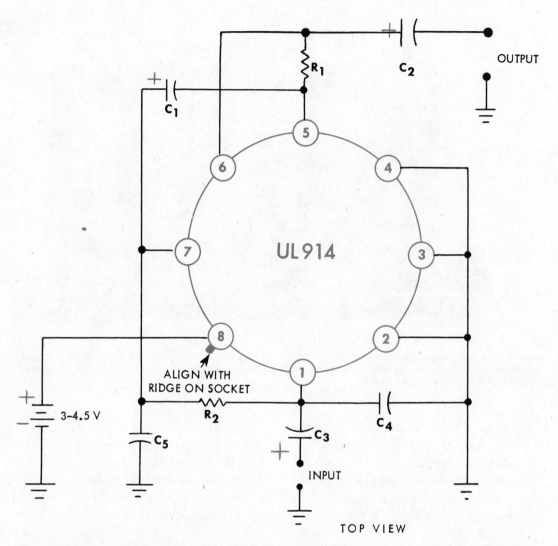

Fig. 28-41. Integrated circuit high-gain audio frequency amplifier. Ground symbols shown indicate just a common connection to the negative side of the power supply.

1 Midget volume control, 3,000 ohms, R_6
4 Carbon resistors, 5,600 ohms, R_1, R_3, R_4, R_5
1 Carbon resistor, 120 ohms, R_2
1 Electrolytic capacitor, miniature, Sprague, 6 V , 15 μf, C_1
1 Ceramic capacitor, .1 μf, C_2 (see text)
2 Fahnestock clips, ¾" long

This wide-range audio oscillator is only one of the many additional projects which may be built with the UL 914 IC.

With the exception of some component substitution, its construction is very similar to that of the high-gain audio frequency amplifier, Fig. 28-41. With the circuit shown, Fig. 28-42, the range of audio frequencies will be approximately 3,000 Hz to 15,000 Hz. By substituting C_2 for a 1 μf capacitor, the range may be lowered to 150 Hz to 3,000 Hz. A .02 μf capacitor will increase the range to approximately 12,000 Hz to 40,000 Hz.

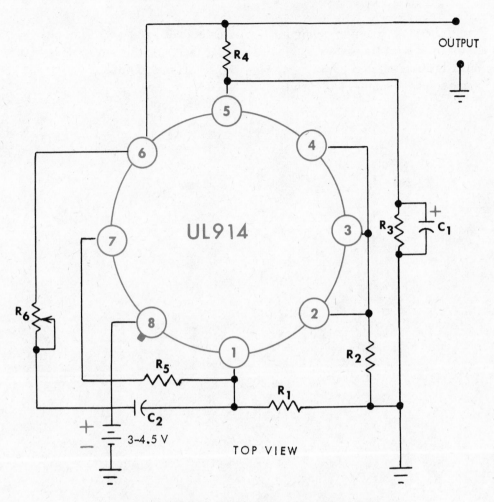

Fig. 28-42. Integrated circuit wide range audio oscillator.

REVIEW QUESTIONS

1. What is meant by the term semi-conductor?

2. Explain the difference between an N-type and a P-type semiconductor.

3. How does a free hole differ from a free electron?

4. If current is to flow through an N-P junction, how must the battery polarity be connected to the junction?

5. What is an important use made of the junction diode?

6. Name the three principal parts of a junction transistor.

7. In a complete transistor circuit, what happens in the collector circuit when an AC signal is applied to the emitter?

8. What is the basic difference between an N-P-N and a P-N-P transistor?

9. Why is it extremely important to observe the battery polarities when connecting transistor circuits?

10. Name the most common configuration circuit used with transistors.

11. What is an integrated circuit?

12. Name some advantages of printed circuits over hand-wired circuits.

13. What are the advantages of using transistors in computers?

UNIT 29
POWER SUPPLIES

Silicon Rectifiers

One of the very common type rectifiers uses silicon diodes. Silicon rectifiers (Fig. 29-1), like other semiconductor diodes, are essentially cells with a simple P-N junction. As a result, they have a very low resistance to current flow in one direction, but high resistance to current flow in the opposite direction.

The P-N junction of the silicon diode is much like that used in a transistor. The P-type material has small amounts of aluminum added to the silicon and the N-type material has phosphorous added to the silicon. When an alternating current is applied to the diode, current will flow in one direction through the diode but

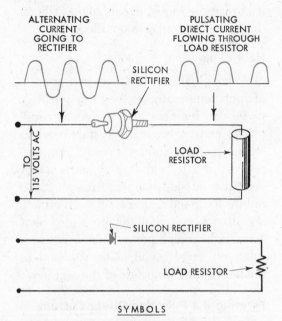

Fig. 29-2. Circuit using a silicon rectifier as a half-wave rectifier. Alternating current is rectified so that current through the resistor is a pulsating direct current. Current flows half of each cycle.

will not flow in the opposite direction.

Fig. 29-2 shows how the silicon rectifier is connected in an alternating current circuit. Since it will permit the current to flow in one direction and not in the other direction, a pulsating direct current will flow through the resistor. This type of rectifier is a *half-wave* rectifier as it produces a direct current during half of the alternating current cycle. No current flows during the other half of the cycle.

The silicon rectifiers have many advantages over other type rectifiers, and because of these advantages they are being used to replace old type rectifiers. These advantages include having a very high operating efficiency with little voltage loss, and being so small that they are

Fig. 29-1. The small silicon rectifier on the left will handle as much current as the vacuum tube rectifier on the right.

often used in places where space is an important factor. In addition, their ability to handle high currents makes silicon diodes very popular as rectifiers.

Heat Sinks

Although silicon rectifiers can operate at high temperatures, they are sensitive to sudden temperature changes because of the extremely small crystals used in their structure. Sudden rises in temperature caused by either high currents or excessive outside temperature can cause failure. To avoid damage, silicon rectifiers are often mounted on devices called *heat sinks*. A heat sink generally consists of a relatively large metal plate attached to the heat-conducting side of the rectifier.

Filtering the Pulsating Direct Current

The pulsating direct current coming out of the rectifier would not work on the plate of an electron tube. The plate current would change with each of the pulses. Constant DC without any variations is necessary for the electron tube power supply.

It is necessary to smooth out the pulsating direct current and make it a pure direct current. This is done through the use of a *filter*.

The filter consists of two fixed capacitors and a resistor connected as in Fig. 29-3. These capacitors are very large ones having a capacitance of 20 microfarads or more. When the current flows through the filter, the capacitors become charged and store large quantities of electrons. As soon as the current stops flowing from the rectifier the capacitors furnish electrons to the circuit. Thus the capacitors tend to provide a constant flow of electrons to the radio receiver.

Each time the current flows through

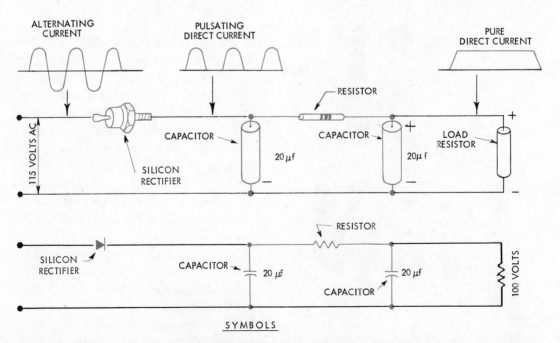

Fig. 29-3. Half-wave silicon rectifier and filter circuit. Capacitors and resistor filter pulsating direct current so that a pure direct current is available at the output.

the rectifier a surge of electrons flows through the filter. The resistor is used to try to stop these sudden surges of elec-

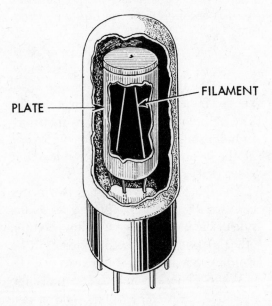

Fig. 29-4. A diode is a two-element electron tube.

trons. Through the use of the resistor and the capacitors, a constant direct current is made available for the radio receiver.

Diode Electron Tube Rectifiers

Two-element electron tubes called *diodes* (Fig. 29-4) are used as half-wave rectifiers. The diode consists of a filament and a plate. A transformer is used to step up the voltage for the high-voltage supply, to provide filament voltage for the rectifier tube, and, also, to supply the heater voltage for the radio receiver tubes. See Fig. 29-5.

Alternating current flows through the secondary windings. When the plate of the diode tube is positive, it attracts the electrons being thrown off by the filament. Electrons flow through the tube from the filament to the plate and through the transformer. These electrons return to the filament through the load

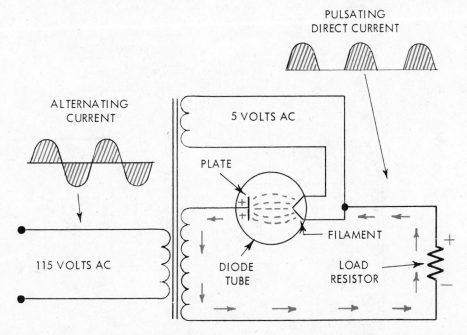

Fig. 29-5. Half-wave rectifier using a diode electron tube. When plate is positive it pulls electrons from the filament and current flows through the tube. No current flows when plate is negative.

resistor. The filament is then the positive terminal for the power supply, and the high-voltage transformer lead is the negative terminal.

As the alternating current changes the direction of electron flow, the plate becomes negative and no current flows through the tube. Since current flows through the tube during only half of the alternating current cycle, the diode produces a pulsating direct current. Pulsating direct current from the half-wave rectifier cannot be used to operate a receiver until it has been filtered.

Full-Wave Electron-Tube Rectifiers

Half-wave rectified current is hard to smooth out because one-half of the time no current is flowing. The filter must be able to provide current during the time when the rectifier is not in operation. Rectifiers that rectify both of the alternating current cycles so that a more constant flow of current is available are often used. These rectifiers are *full-wave* rectifiers.

An electron tube for full-wave rectifiers uses two diodes in one glass envelope. Usually 250 volts or more are needed for a radio receiver power supply. The high-voltage secondary of the transformer is tapped in the center. Each side of the center connection produces 250 volts.

The double-diode tube has two plates and two filaments. One plate goes to one side of the high-voltage winding, and the other plate goes to the other side of the winding. See Figs. 29-6 and 29-7.

When plate 1 is positive it pulls the

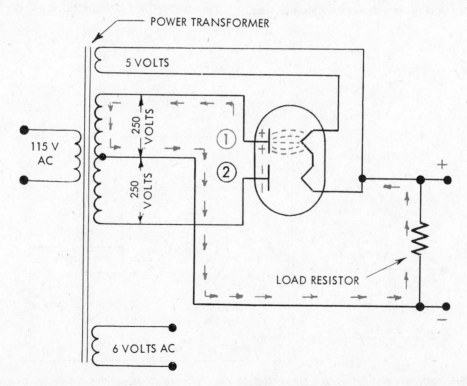

Fig. 29-6. When plate 1 is positive, plate 2 is negative. Electrons flow from filament to plate 1 and out through the center tap of the transformer.

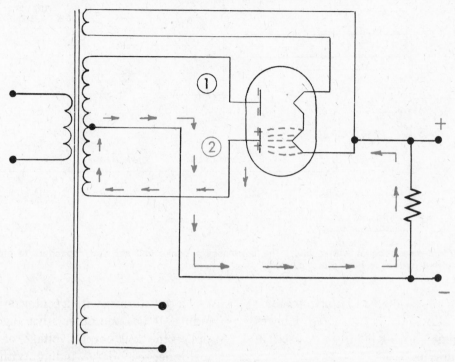

Fig. 29-7. When plate 2 is positive electrons are pulled to it. Electrons flow out through the center tap of the transformer. Both cycles of alternating current are rectified.

electrons from the filament and current flows through that part of the tube. As the alternating current starts to flow in the other direction, plate 1 becomes negative and plate 2 becomes positive. Now current flows through plate 2 out through the center tap. The electron flow through the center tap is always in the same direction. The direct current pulses flowing through the load resistor look like Fig. 29-8. Current is flowing almost all of the time, but it is still necessary to have a filter system.

Filters with a Choke Coil

A much improved filter system can be made using a *choke coil* (Fig. 29-9) instead of a resistor. Many power supplies use a choke. The choke is very much like one winding of a transformer since it is made of many turns of wire wrapped around a laminated iron core. The choke is better than the resistor because it provides better filtering and does not cut down the voltage as much as the resistor does.

The choke coil tries to keep a steady current flowing. It can be compared to a flywheel in an engine that keeps the engine turning over at a constant speed. The choke helps in smoothing out the pulsating direct current. A choke coil,

ALTERNATING CURRENT
ON PRIMARY OF
TRANSFORMER

PULSATING
DIRECT CURRENT
THROUGH FULL-WAVE
RECTIFIER

Fig. 29-8. Illustration showing full-wave rectifier current flow.

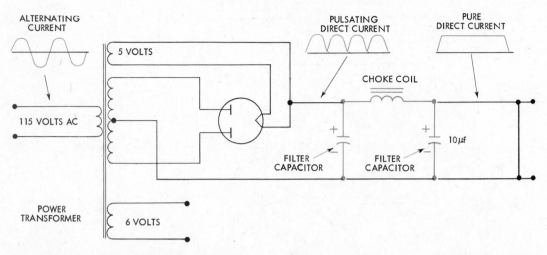

Fig. 29-9. Full-wave rectifier with a filter. The filter uses a choke coil and two capacitors to change pulsating direct current to pure direct current.

like any coil, is called an *inductance*. The unit of inductance is the *henry*. Chokes with from 4 to 30 henrys are used in power supplies.

A full-wave rectifier does not require as much filter as a half-wave rectifier. Smaller filter capacitors can be used. Capacitors with a capacitance of about 10 microfarads are most common.

Full-Wave Bridge Rectifier

A full-wave bridge rectifier circuit uses four rectifiers and does not require the use of a transformer with a center tapped winding. It has one other advantage; it supplies the full output voltage of the transformer secondary winding. With the relative small size of silicon diodes, a bridge circuit with four diodes can be constructed in a limited space compared to the space that would be required for four vacuum tubes.

Fig. 29-10 is a schematic diagram of a full-wave bridge circuit. When the secondary of the transformer at point *A* is positive, point *B* is negative. This permits

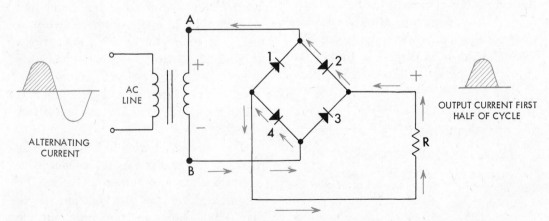

Fig. 29-10. Electron flow in a full-wave bridge rectifier during first half of cycle.

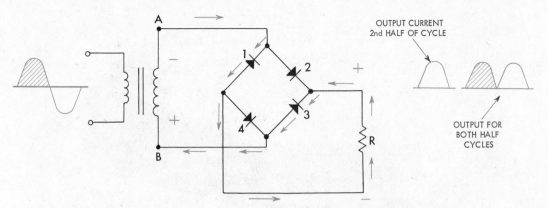

Fig. 29-11. Electron flow in a full wave bridge rectifier during second half of cycle.

the electrons at point B to flow through diode 4, through the load resistor R, and through diode 2 to the positive point A of the transformer. Diodes 1 and 3 have a high resistance to electron flow during this part of the alternating current cycle and will not conduct current. This flow of current produces a half-wave pulse in the output circuit.

When the alternating current cycle reverses (Fig. 29-11) point A is negative and point B is positive. Now electrons from point A flow through diode 1,

through the load resistor R and back to point B through diode 3. Diodes 2 and 4 cannot conduct current during this part of the cycle. Thus, the current through the resistor R continues to flow in the same direction as during the first half cycle. The output current consists of two pulses of direct current for each cycle of alternating current which is induced into the secondary of the transformer. To provide pure direct current, it is necessary to connect a filter system to the output of the rectifier.

INTERESTING THINGS TO DO

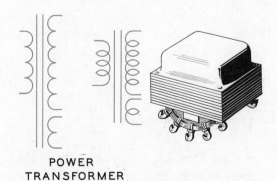

POWER
TRANSFORMER

The symbol shows how a power transformer may supply different voltages.

1. Making a Half-Wave Transistor-Battery Charger.

Materials needed to construct the half-wave transistor-battery charger (Fig. 29-12):

1 Silicon rectifier, 400 V , 500 MA
1 Resistor, wire wound, 4,000 ohms, 8 or 10 watts, R_2
1 Resistor, 50,000 ohms, ½ watt, R_1
1 Neon lamp, 1/25 watt, NL
1 Plastic case with cover (see text)
1 Pair battery terminals
1 Attachment plug
1 Piece lamp cord

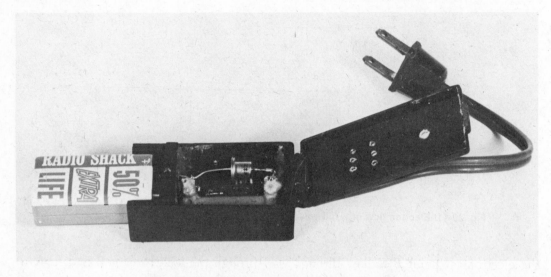

Fig. 29-12. Half-wave transistor battery charger.

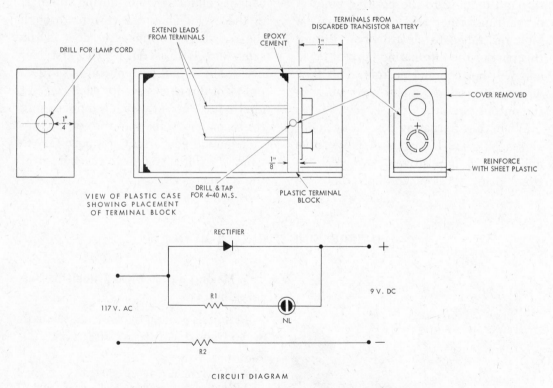

Fig. 29-13. Half-wave transistor battery charger circuit diagram.

Although the carbon-zinc type cell is considered to be a primary cell and not capable of being recharged, experiments with a modern cell have shown that if its electrolyte has not become dry, or its zinc element eaten away, it may be recharged many times. The charger described here will add extra life to your

9-volt transistor batteries and also re-charge storage type transistor batteries, such as nickel-cadmium.

The circuit consists of a single silicon rectifier, which, as we learned when we studied power supplies, will permit current to flow only in one direction, and a resistor to reduce the supply to about 12 volts. A neon lamp, with a resistor, is included in the circuit, to indicate when the charger is operating.

Mount the parts in a small plastic case which may be obtained from hobby stores or electronic supply houses. Do not use a metal case. Since the size of the 4,000 ohm resistor may vary with the brand, the dimensions of the plastic case will be governed by those of the resistor. Cut an opening for a 9-volt battery in one end of the plastic case, as shown in Fig. 29-13. Cut a piece of ⅛″ plastic for a terminal block and cement a pair of battery terminals to it. Extend lead wires from the terminals through the terminal block before cementing the terminals in place. Cement the terminal block in the open end of the plastic case so that it will be recessed ½″. This will prevent the terminals being accidentally short-circuited. If the plastic case is made of thin plastic, it should be reinforced with pieces of sheet plastic, as shown in the drawing. Drill small holes through the cover and sides of the plastic case for ventilation purposes. Connect the parts as shown in the circuit diagram. After the lamp cord and plug are connected, secure the cord to the inside of the case with epoxy cement to prevent strain on the parts to which the cord is connected. Drill and tap the terminal block as shown in Fig. 29-13. Drill a hole through the plastic cover and fasten it to the case with a 4-40 machine screw.

The open circuit voltage at the charging terminals will be about 22 volts. When charging, the voltage will vary between 9 and 12 volts, depending upon the condition of the battery.

2. Full-Wave Rectifier.

Materials needed to construct the full-wave rectifier (Figs. 29-14 and 29-15):

Fig. 29-14. A full-wave power supply using a power transformer and rectifier tube.

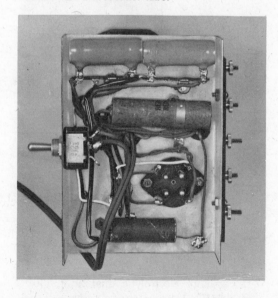

Fig. 29-15. Wiring underneath the chassis of the power supply.

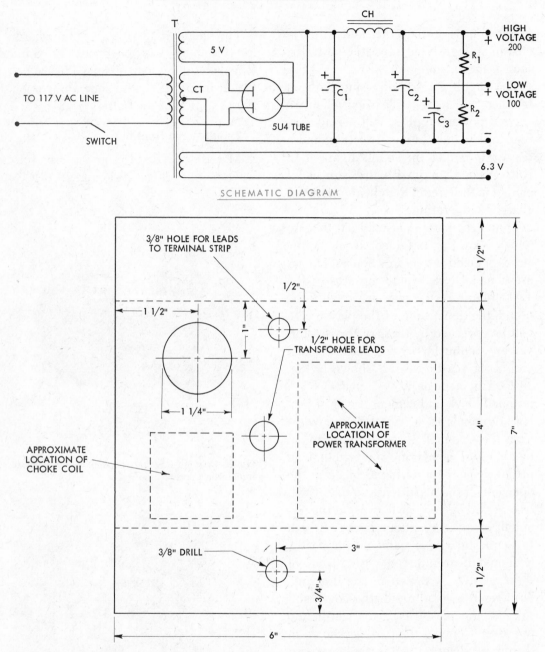

SCHEMATIC DIAGRAM

CHASSIS LAYOUT

Fig. 29-16. Drawing of full-wave power supply.

1 Power transformer, 450 volts, CT, 50 MA, 5-6.3—volts (T)
1 Choke coil, 6-henry, 50 MA
1 Capacitor, electrolytic, dual 20 μf, 450 volts (C_1, C_2)
1 Capacitor, electrolytic, 4 μf, 450 volts (C_3)

2 Resistors, 20,000 ohms, 10-watt
1 Rectifier tube, 5U4
1 Tube socket
1 Toggle switch, single-pole
1 Rubber grommet, 3/8"
1 Rubber grommet, 1/2"

1 Piece masonite, ⅛" x 2" x 5"
5 Fahnestock clips
1 Line cord and plug cap
1 Piece sheet steel, 6" x 7", 20 gage

Lay out and drill the piece of sheet steel as shown in Fig. 29-16. Bend the ends along the broken lines to an angle of 90°. Mount the choke coil and the power transformer on the top of the chassis in the approximate positions shown on the drawing. Place the toggle switch in the ⅜" hole in the front end of the chassis. Make a terminal strip with the piece of masonite and Fahnestock clips and secure it to the back end of the chassis. Secure the electrolytic capacitors and the two resistors underneath the chassis.

Wire the power supply as shown in the schematic diagram. The two resistors connected in series serve to keep the high voltage of the power supply at a constant value and to provide a means of getting an additional lower voltage. The voltage across the output of the power supply will be approximately 200 volts, and since the two resistors connected across the output have the same resistance, the voltage between the point where they are connected together and the negative terminal will be approximately 100 volts. Mark the terminals on the terminal strip so that the output voltages may be easily identified.

3. Making a Printed Circuit 6-Volt Power Supply.

Materials needed to construct the printed circuit 6-volt power supply (Fig. 29-17):

4 Silicon rectifiers, 500 MA, 400 PIV, D_1, D_2, D_3, D_4
1 Filament transformer, 6.3 volts, T_1

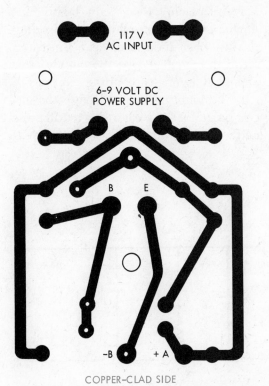

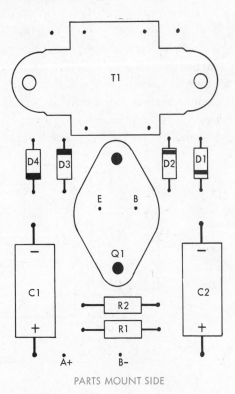

Fig. 29-17. Printed circuit 6-volt power supply card.

2 Electrolytic capacitors, 500 μf, 15 volts, C_1, C_2
1 Resistor, 1500 ohms, ½ watt, R_1
1 Resistor, 470 ohms, ½ watt, R_2
1 PNP power transistor, 1,000 MA, 40 volts, Q_1
1 Piece copper clad printed circuit board 3″ x 4″

The negative required for a printed circuit may be made by photographing a diagram of an existing circuit against a white background, or by painting a desired circuit on a sheet of clear thin acetate and photographing it as directed.

Cut the circuit board to the required size and smooth off any burrs along the edges. Clean the board with a greaseless abrasive such as Ajax or Comet cleanser. Rub its copper surface with a paper towel but do not touch it with your hand or fingers. Skin oil deposits will prevent the photo-resist from penetrating the copper surface.

Dip a *clean* cotton Q-tip into the photo-resist solution and apply it to the copper surface, moving up and down the board. Since the photo-resist solution makes the copper surface light sensitive, it should be applied under subdued lighting. Allow the photo-resist to dry in a well ventilated

place for five minutes. Apply another coating of photo-resist to the circuit board in a crosswise direction. When the circuit board is completely dry, place the negative on it with the emulsion side against the copper surface. Expose the negative and board to direct sunlight for 10 minutes.

Remove the negative and place the circuit board in the developer. Agitate for three minutes, then rinse the board in cold water. Place the developed board in the dye solution for one minute. Rinse again in cold water. Place the board in the etching solution and agitate the solution until the etching is completed. A 9″ x 9″ Pyrex dish containing a heaping tablespoon of ammonium persulfate crystals in one-half inch of water will etch several power supply circuit boards. The etching time may be reduced considerably by placing the circuit board face down in the etching solution and holding the dish over a source of heat. Rinse and scrub the circuit board thoroughly after etching to remove any of the solution.

Drill mounting holes through the circuit board for the parts, using a drill press and wood back-up block. Clean the areas

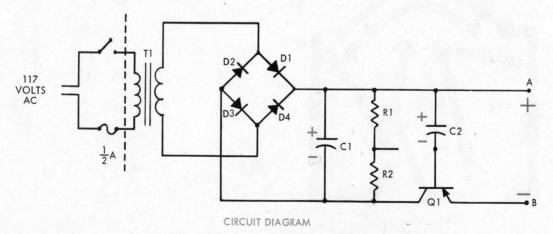

CIRCUIT DIAGRAM

Fig. 29-18. Printed circuit 6-volt power supply circuit diagram.

around the holes on the copper side with steel wool to provide a good contact for solder. Mount the parts on the circuit board and solder their terminals to the copper foil. See schematic diagram Fig. 29-18. Test the circuit for proper operation, and if no changes are required, spray a protective coating of plastic over the copper surface. Mount the completed circuit board in a suitable metal cabinet.

The foregoing instructions are based upon the use of Kepro printed circuit materials, which may be obtained from local or mail order electronic supply houses.

REVIEW QUESTIONS

1. Why is direct current needed for radio receivers?

2. What kind of current is produced by a half-wave rectifier?

3. Explain the purpose of a filter.

4. What does the capacitor do in a filter system?

5. Why are electrolytic capacitors used in filter systems?

6. What are the elements found in a diode electron tube?

7. When a single diode is used, what is that kind of rectifier called?

8. Explain the advantages of a full-wave rectifier.

9. How many diodes are needed in a full-wave rectifier that uses a transformer with a center tapped secondary winding?

10. What is the purpose of a choke in a filter?

11. How many diodes are used in a full-wave bridge rectifier?

12. What would be the advantage of using semiconductors instead of vacuum tubes in a full-wave bridge rectifier?

UNIT 30
TRANSMITTING RADIO WAVES

Radio Frequency Signals

We have studied the basic principles of receiving radio signals. Now we will learn about the transmitting of radio waves. A fundamental transmitter consists of a *radio frequency generator,* a *power supply* for the generator, and the *antenna.* As illustrated in Fig. 30-1, the radio frequency generator is connected to the antenna which sends the signal out through space. A radio frequency generator is called an *oscillator.* Frequencies above 15,000 hertz (c.p.s.) (15 kilohertz) are called radio frequencies because they are useful in radio transmission.

Because of the very wide range of radio frequencies, they have been divided into different classifications as shown below.

FREQUENCY	CLASSIFICATION	ABBREV.
15 to 30 kHz	Very-low frequencies	v.l.f.
30 to 300 kHz	Low frequencies	l.f.
300 to 3000 kHz	Medium frequencies	m.f.
3 to 30 MHz	High frequencies	h.f.
30 to 300 MHz	Very-high freq.	v.h.f.
300 to 3000 MHz	Ultra-high freq.	u.h.f.
3000 to 30,000 MHz	Superhigh freq.	s.h.f.

Basically, all radio frequency signals are used to establish communications.

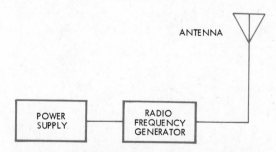

Fig. 30-1. A block diagram illustrating that the basic requirements for a transmitter are a power supply, radio frequency generator, and antenna.

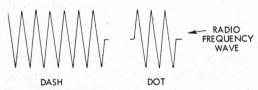

Fig. 30-2. A continuous radio frequency wave is interrupted to produce dots and dashes for International Morse code signals.

Different kinds of radio signals are used to carry the desired information. We have already learned about amplitude modulated signals and frequency modulated signals that are used to carry audio frequencies. Another method of sending information is through the use of the international Morse code. Here the signal is interrupted by a key so that the radio frequency waves are started and stopped at regular intervals, as shown in Fig. 30-2. These signals are called *continuous wave telegraphy,* often abbreviated as *c.w.* Television and facsimile are two other kinds of signals used to send information.

Oscillation

One of the requirements of a transmitter is to generate a radio frequency wave with the use of an oscillator. A basic oscillator circuit includes an inductance L and a capacitance C connected as in Fig. 30-3. If we charge the capacitance, it will start to discharge by having an electron flow through the coil, toward the positive plate of the capacitor, setting up a magnetic field about the coil. As the electron flow starts to die down the magnetic field about the coil collapses and this collapsing of the field induces a back electromotive force into the coil. The back electromotive force, induced by the col-

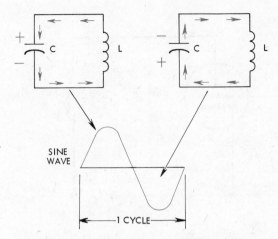

Fig. 30-3. In a parallel L-C circuit the charging and discharging of the capacitor produces a sine wave.

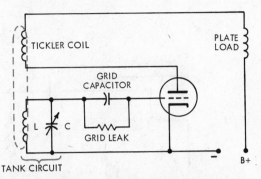

Fig. 30-4. A basic regenerative oscillator circuit. The frequency of the circuit is determined by the value of *L* and *C*. This circuit is known as the Armstrong oscillator.

lapsing of the magnetic field, recharges the capacitor. When the capacitor is recharged, it will have an opposite polarity. Energy is again stored in the capacitor and again the capacitor will discharge through the coil.

The back and forth flow of electrons produces an oscillation in the *LC* circuit. The frequency of oscillation is determined by the value of the capacitance and the inductance. We have already learned that the formula for this is:

$$F = \frac{1}{2\pi\sqrt{LC}}$$

These oscillations in the *LC* circuit would continue if it were not for the resistance that is in the circuit. Since every circuit has some resistance, the signal would soon die out; therefore, it is necessary to use some device to keep the circuit oscillating.

The Regenerative Oscillator

The regenerative circuit in Fig. 30-4 uses an electron tube to produce a con-

tinuous wave oscillation. Energy from the tickler coil is fed back into the grid circuit, and oscillation takes place in the *LC* circuit. This *LC* circuit is called the *tank circuit*.

When the circuit is first turned on, the rush of plate current produces a magnetic field in the plate or tickler coil. This magnetic field induces a current into the grid coil. The feeding of energy from the plate back into the grid starts the circuit into oscillation. To get regeneration or oscillation, it is important that the output of the plate coil be correctly coupled to the grid coil. The feedback must be in step with the oscillations occurring in the grid circuit. If the circuit fails to oscillate, it may be necessary to reverse the connections to one of the coils.

The grid leak plays a very important part in the operation of the oscillator. It is used to obtain "self" grid bias for the electron tube and provides for efficient operation of the tube.

The Hartley Oscillator

There are many different types of electron tube oscillators. For the most part, the variations in circuits depend upon the method used for feedback. Fig. 30-5

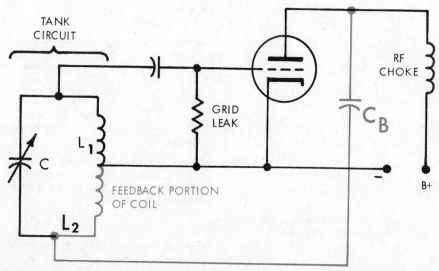

Fig. 30-5. The Hartley oscillator circuit. Feedback is obtained by coupling some of the plate energy back into the grid circuit by means of an inductance. The feedback circuit is shown in color. L_1 and C_1 make up the basic oscillator and L_2 is the portion of the coil which couples the plate feedback into the grid circuit. C_8 is a blocking capacitor which keeps the B+ voltage from reaching the oscillator.

illustrates another type of oscillator called the *Hartley oscillator*. It differs from the plate coil regenerative oscillator in that only one coil is used. The single coil is tapped for the cathode connection. The oscillating frequency of the Hartley oscillator is determined by the value of L and C.

We must remember that the current flowing in the plate circuit is also flowing in the cathode circuit. Electrons leaving the plate must flow through the cathode coil to get back to the cathode. Thus, the section of the coil shown below the cathode tap in Fig. 30-5 induces a current into the grid circuit and provides the necessary feedback.

The transistor can also be used as an oscillator. A Hartley transistor oscillator is illustrated in Fig. 30-6. The *LC* circuit is the same as for the electron tube. Voltage from the collector circuit is developed across a portion of the coil, in-

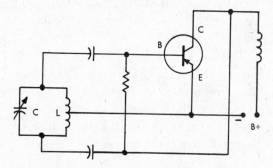

Fig. 30-6. A transistorized Hartley oscillator.

ducing a current of the proper phase into the base circuit, in order to maintain oscillation.

The Crystal Oscillator

In the unit on *Producing Electricity* the piezoelectric effect of crystals was studied. We learned that if a voltage is applied across the opposite sides of a crystal, a vibration will be set up in the crystal. These vibrations become very strong when the frequency of the applied voltage is the same as the mechanical resonant frequency of the crystal. When properly connected with an electron tube or transistor these crystals can be used in oscillator circuits. They provide very excellent frequency stability, and, in circuits where just one frequency is needed, they are very desirable.

The method of cutting the quartz and the thickness of the material determines the frequency at which it will vibrate, and this is called its *fundamental frequency*. A quartz crystal may be about one half inch square, and several thousandths of an inch thick. It is placed between two metal plates in a crystal holder as in Fig. 30-7. The plates called electrodes, just touch each side of the crystal so that it is free to vibrate. Each plate is connected to a terminal or prong of the holder, so that these two connections provide contact with the crystal.

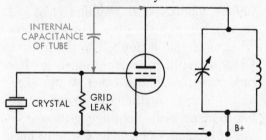

Fig. 30-7. A crystal is placed between two metal plates. The frequency depends on the thickness of the crystal. Thick crystals vibrate slowly, thin crystals vibrate rapidly.

A crystal oscillator circuit is shown in Fig. 30-8. The crystal represents an *LC* circuit in the grid circuit. If the plate circuit composed of L_1 and C_1 is tuned to the same frequency as the crystal, energy from the plate is fed back to the grid through the capacitance in the tube elements. This is possible because there is a

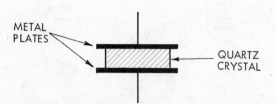

Fig. 30-8. A basic crystal oscillator circuit. Feedback is obtained through the inter-electrode capacitance of the tube.

capacitive effect between the plate and grid that acts as a coupling capacitor from the plate to the grid circuit; this is called the inter-electrode tube capacitance. Because the energy from the plate is fed back into the grid at the same resonant frequency as the crystal, the crystal is set into vibration. The frequency of the oscillation is determined by the crystal. Because of the crystal, the oscillator has very good frequency stability.

Radio Frequency Amplifiers

Since oscillators usually do not provide a great deal of power output, they are coupled to radio frequency amplifiers. The amplifier is used to increase the power output of the signal so that it can be received at a much greater distance. Then the amplifier is connected to a transmitting antenna (Fig. 30-9). If additional power is necessary, more than one amplifier stage may be used. The oscillator is coupled to the radio frequency amplifier either by inductive coupling (Fig. 30-10) or capacitive coupling (Fig. 30-11).

To obtain high efficiency from power amplifiers, operated at radio frequencies, it is desirable to use an amplifier called a *Class C* amplifier. Amplifiers are divided into classifications such as *Class A, Class*

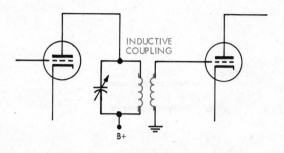

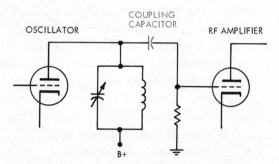

Fig. 30-11. The capacitor, in capacitive coupling, provides a low impedance path for the radio frequency signal. It also keeps the DC voltage of the oscillator plate from being applied to the amplifier grid.

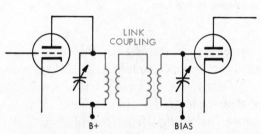

Fig. 30-9. A block diagram of a transmitter using an oscillator and a radio frequency amplifier coupled to an antenna.

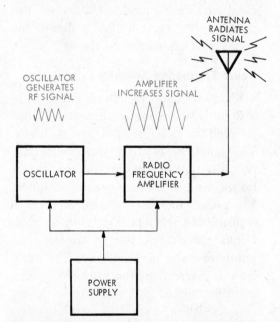

Fig. 30-10. The top drawing illustrates inductive coupling using the plate tank coil of the oscillator as the primary of a radio frequency transformer and the grid coil of the amplifier as the secondary. The bottom drawing shows inductive coupling through the use of a link. Link coupling permits the oscillator and the amplifier to be located some distance apart.

B and *Class C*. These classifications are made according to the operating conditions under which the tube works. In Class A amplifiers the grid bias is such that plate current flows at all times. Because of their excellent frequency response, Class A amplifiers are used in radio receivers and in high fidelity amplifiers. The Class B amplifier is biased so that very little plate current flows when no signal is applied to the grid. A Class B amplifier provides much greater power output than a Class A amplifier, and it is used for the final power amplifier in many audio amplifier systems.

The efficiency of a Class C circuit may be as high as 80%. In a Class C operation, the plate current flows for less than one half of the radio frequency cycle. Since the plate is drawing current for only a portion of the time this increases the efficiency of the tube. Stated in another way, the plate consumes power for just a fraction of the time required for the entire cycle.

The Class C Grid Circuit

To see how a Class C amplifier functions we must first review the grid cir-

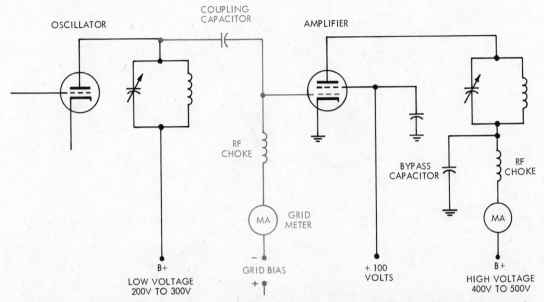

OSCILLATOR COUPLING CAPACITOR AMPLIFIER

RF CHOKE

BYPASS CAPACITOR

RF CHOKE

MA GRID METER

MA

B+
LOW VOLTAGE
200V TO 300V

GRID BIAS

+ 100
VOLTS

B+
HIGH VOLTAGE
400V TO 500V

Fig. 30-12. An oscillator and a Class C amplifier circuit using capacitive coupling. The grid and coupling circuits are shown in colored lines. Bias for the grid of the amplifier is supplied through an RF choke which also prevents the signal from the oscillator from flowing to ground. Milliammeters measure current flow and may be used for tuning the circuit.

cuit. Grid bias is placed on the grid of the tube as illustrated in Fig. 30-12. This bias is usually about twice cutoff. By this we mean that if a —20 volts of bias, on the grid, will stop the plate current from flowing for a particular tube we must use a —40 volts for Class C operation.

With no signal applied to the grid no current flows in the plate circuit. Now we must couple the oscillator to the grid of the amplifier so that a signal is applied to the grid. In this particular circuit capacitive coupling is used. The capacitor must have a low reactance to the frequency applied, and capacitors of about 100µf are frequently used. The signal, called the drive, from the preceding amplifier or oscillator must be strong enough to overcome the negative bias of the tube and drive the grid positive.

A radio frequency choke is used to keep the radio frequency applied to the

grid. This choke has a high impedance to the applied signal so that it will keep the signal from flowing toward the ground. A 2.5 millihenry choke is often used for this purpose.

When the grid becomes positive, electrons will flow from the cathode to the grid and current will flow in the grid circuit. This grid current can be shown through the use of a milliammeter connected in the circuit. The graph of the current flow in a Class C amplifier is shown in Fig. 30-13. At the bottom of the drawing we can see the effect of the input signal on the grid.

The Class C Plate Circuit

The plate circuit shown in Fig. 30-12 consists of the inductance and capacitance, called the tank; the radio frequency choke; the bypass capacitor; and the plate voltage. The tank circuit must

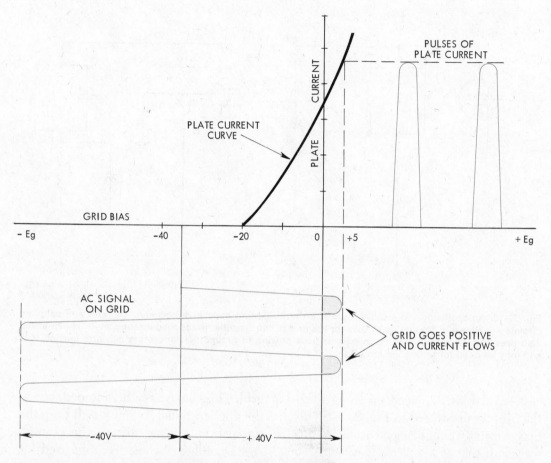

Fig. 30-13. A graph showing the effect of the applied grid signal on the plate current of a Class C amplifier. The horizontal waveform on the left represents the signal on the grid. When this signal causes the grid to go positive as shown by the solid color portion of the signal then current flows as indicated by the plate current pulses in the drawing.

tune to the resonant frequency of the applied signal. The radio frequency choke and bypass capacitor are used to keep any radio frequency from flowing back to the power supply. The plate voltage is determined by the type of tube used. Some Class *C* amplifiers use up to 3,000 volts on the plate.

With the grid biased to twice cutoff, no current will flow in the plate circuit until a signal is applied to the grid. As a strong signal is applied to the grid, the grid voltage varies with the signal. This variation of grid voltage produces pulses of plate current as shown in Fig. 30-13.

To reproduce the applied grid signal in the plate circuit, we must tune the tank to resonance. When this circuit is in resonance, the pulses of plate current flow through the coil and capacitor. The charging and discharging of the capacitor, through the inductance must be at the same rate as the pulses of plate current. Thus, the fly wheel effect of the tank circuit produces a continuous wave signal at the desired frequency.

It is extremely important to have the tank tuned to resonance to avoid burning up the electron tube. The milliammeter, shown in Fig. 30-12, is used to indicate the current flow, and it also can be used to show when the circuit is tuned to resonance. The plate tank is a parallel resonant circuit and when tuned to resonance it presents a maximum impedance. At resonance the high impedance of the circuit results in a reduction of plate current. Thus, when tuning an amplifier to resonance we can watch the plate milliammeter and observe a drop in the plate current. Before resonance the plate current will be extremely high, but at resonance a very definite dip will show on the milliammeter.

Preventing Amplifier Self-Oscillation

Power amplifiers are used to amplify the signal of the oscillator; therefore, it is not desirable that they generate their own signal. Because of the interelectrode capacitance in an electron tube, it is very easy for the energy from the plate to feedback into the grid. When this occurs the tube starts oscillating and generates a new signal. To avoid self-oscillation, it is necessary to neutralize the amplifier.

One method of neutralization is through the use of screen grid tubes. Tubes with a screen grid help eliminate feedback because the screen grid is placed between the grid and plate inside of the tube. The screen grid reduces the coupling between the plate and grid and thus tends to prevent self-oscillation.

The Dipole Antenna

If a radio frequency amplifier is to send out a signal for communication purposes, we must connect the transmitter to an antenna. The antenna is a wire

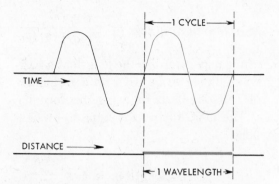

Fig. 30-14. One wavelength is the distance that the radiated energy will cover, traveling at the speed of light, during one cycle of the radiated energy.

that takes the energy from the transmitter and radiates it into space in the form of electromagnetic waves. See Fig. 30-14. To operate efficiently, the antenna must be resonant with the signal from the transmitter.

A fundamental radio transmitting antenna is called a *half-wave dipole*. A dipole is a length of wire that is equal to one half the wave length of the radio frequency signal. This wire acts like a resonant circuit. The wire includes inductance, capacitance, and resistance just like a regular tuned circuit. We can calculate the length of wire needed, providing we know the operating frequency.

The formula for determining one wavelength is:

$$\frac{Wavelength}{in\ meters} = \frac{300}{Freq.\ in\ Megahertz}$$
$$A\ meter = 39.29\ inches$$

This formula is not quite accurate for an actual wire. These formulas apply to a wave traveling in space. Because of the resistance in a wire a practical half-wave antenna is actually about 5% shorter. Thus an average formula for a resonant length of wire would be:

$$\frac{1}{2} \text{ wavelength in feet} = \frac{468}{Freq. \text{ in } MHz.}$$

We may calculate the length of a half-wave dipole to be used on a frequency of 7,000 kilohertz by using this formula.

The 7,000 kilohertz is equal to 7 megahertz.

$$\frac{1}{2} \text{ wavelength in feet} = \frac{468}{7}$$

Length of half wave dipole = 66.85

Transmission Lines

To get the energy from the radio frequency amplifier to the antenna we need to use a transmission line. A transmission line consists of two parallel lengths of wire that are spaced an equal distance

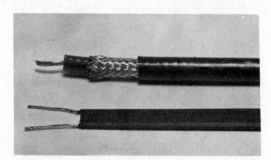

Fig. 30-15. Transmission lines used to carry power to the antenna usually consist of a coaxial cable shown at top, or a twin lead line, shown at the bottom of the photograph.

apart from each other. These two wires have an impedance to current flow since they include capacitance, inductance and resistance. There are a number of different transmission lines available. One of the most common types is *coaxial cable*. Coaxial cable includes an inner conductor centered within an outer shield. A polyethylene insulator is used to insulate the inner conductor from the outer shield as illustrated in Fig. 30-15. Another type of transmission line is the *twin* or *ribbon lead* also illustrated in Fig. 30-15.

When an antenna is connected to a transmission line, it is important that all of the energy going from the output of the amplifier through the transmission line be transferred to the antenna. A maximum transfer of energy occurs when the transmission line impedance equals the antenna impedance.

The half-wave dipole usually has the transmission line connected in the center, Fig. 30-16. Such an antenna has an impedance of about 73 ohms. Therefore, to get a maximum transfer of energy from the transmission line to the half-wave dipole, the transmission line must also have an impedance of about 73 ohms. Both the coaxial cable and the twin lead may be obtained with 73 to 75 ohms

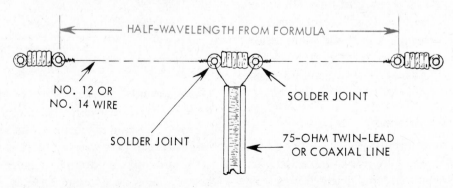

HALF-WAVELENGTH FROM FORMULA

NO. 12 OR
NO. 14 WIRE

SOLDER JOINT

SOLDER JOINT

75-OHM TWIN-LEAD
OR COAXIAL LINE

Fig. 30-16. Construction of a half-wave dipole fed with a 75-ohm twin-lead transmission line.

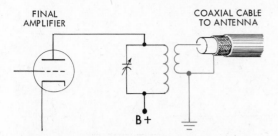

FINAL AMPLIFIER

COAXIAL CABLE TO ANTENNA

B+

Fig. 30-17. A coaxial cable transmission line inductively coupled to the output of the final amplifier.

impedance. The antenna impedance depends on the design of the antenna. Each type of antenna requires that the transmission line be made to match the impedance of the antenna.

The transmission line may be coupled to the output of the power amplifier using inductive coupling as shown in Fig. 30-17.

Frequency Multipliers

Oscillators are far more stable at low frequencies than at high frequencies. Since transmitter stability is very essential the oscillator is often placed in operation at a lower frequency than the final amplifier. To increase the frequency

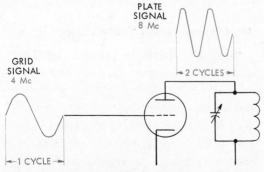

PLATE SIGNAL 8 Mc

GRID SIGNAL 4 Mc

2 CYCLES

1 CYCLE

Fig. 30-18. The frequency multiplier stage of a transmitter. The plate circuit is tuned to twice the frequency of the grid, so that for each cycle on the grid, two are produced in the plate circuit.

of a signal it is possible to use a frequency multiplier. The frequency multiplier stage operates on a harmonic of the lowest frequency called the fundamental frequency. The fundamental frequency is called the *first harmonic* and the second harmonic is twice the fundamental frequency. Thus, the third harmonic would be three times the fundamental frequency. If a fundamental oscillator frequency is 4 megahertz, the fourth harmonic would be 16 megahertz.

A frequency multiplier circuit is very similar to a regular Class C amplifier. In the regular amplifier the plate signal is tuned to the same frequency as the input or grid signal. The multiplier stage tunes the plate circuit to a harmonic or a multiple of the grid circuit signal. To double the frequency of a 4 megahertz oscillator, the output of the frequency multiplier stage must be tuned to 8 megahertz, Fig. 30-18.

To act as a doubler, the plate circuit must be tuned to twice the input frequency. The multiplier is able to multiply the frequency because of the flywheel action of the tank circuit. A signal on the grid produces a pulse of plate current in the tank circuit. Since the tank circuit is tuned to twice the frequency of the input signal the circulating current in the tank will produce two complete cycles of current before the next pulse of plate current. These pulses of plate current keep the tank circuit oscillating. The action of a multiplier to triple or quadruple the frequency is the same.

It should be pointed out that each time the frequency is increased the efficiency of the output is decreased. Therefore when the harmonic frequency is several times that of the fundamental frequency it may be necessary to use

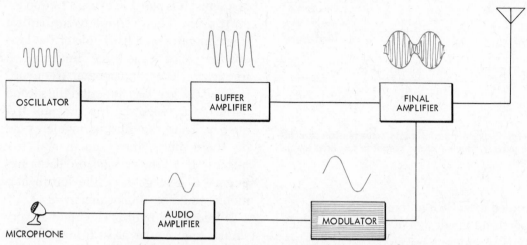

Fig. 30-19. Block diagram of an amplitude modulated transmitter.

several stages of amplification to make up for the loss in signal strength.

If the oscillator and the frequency multiplier do not provide enough driving power for the final amplifier, another stage of radio frequency amplification may be used. Such an amplifier is often called a *buffer*. A buffer may also be used between the oscillator and the final amplifier to prevent the amplifier from changing the operating frequency of the oscillator. See Fig. 30-19.

Keying the Transmitter

If we wish to operate a transmitter using the international Morse code, we must have some method of stopping and starting the carrier. Code transmitters, called c.w. transmitters use a telegraphy key to turn the carrier off and on in the form of dots and dashes. There are a number of methods used to key a transmitter. One of the most popular methods uses a key to open and close the cathode circuit, Fig. 30-20. When the key is closed, current flows in the tube. If the key is open, no current flows. In Fig. 30-

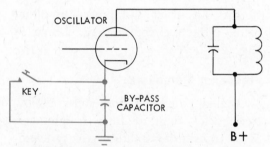

Fig. 30-20. Placing the telegraph key in the cathode circuit permits the plate current to be turned on and off.

21, the cathodes are opened in both the oscillator and final amplifier stages.

Modulating the AM Transmitter

In an amplitude modulated signal, the audio signal is used to vary the amplitude of the carrier. When the audio signal or modulating voltage is "positive," the carrier amplitude is increased; when the modulating voltage is negative, the carrier amplitude is decreased. To modulate a carrier it is necessary to apply the audio wave to the carrier so that the amplitude is varied in accordance with the

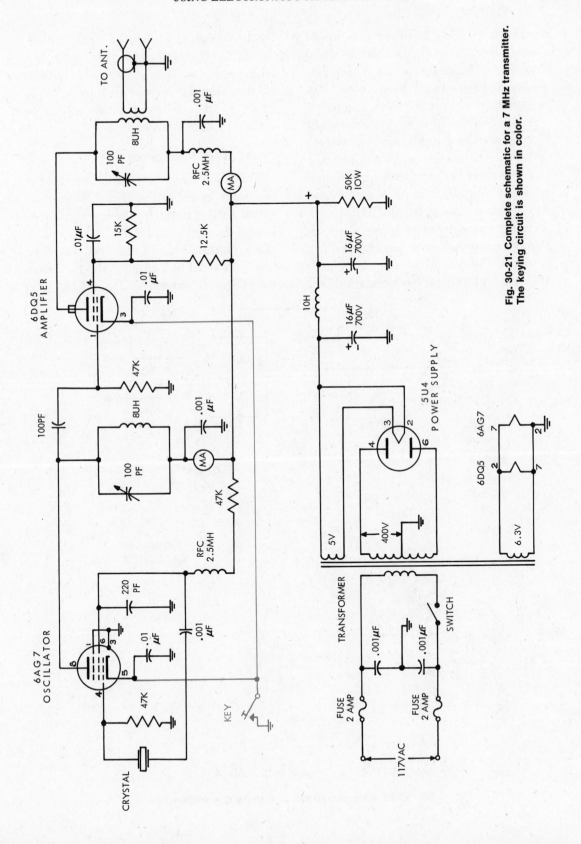

Fig. 30-21. Complete schematic for a 7 MHz transmitter. The keying circuit is shown in color.

sound waves. This requires the use of a modulator. A modulator is an audio amplifier connected to the radio frequency amplifier so the audio signal can be superimposed on the carrier signal.

A complete modulator system might be compared to a public address system that is used to amplify audio frequencies. First, we must have a microphone that is used to change the audio waves into a very weak pulsating current. The weak pulsating current produced by a microphone is connected to a speech amplifier to increase or amplify the audio signal. After the audio signal has been amplified

by the speech amplifier, the signal is then applied to the modulator or output tube. In a public address system, the output of the amplifier is coupled to a loudspeaker; in a modulator the output is coupled to the RF amplifier.

Types of AM Modulators

There are a number of different methods used to apply the audio frequency signal to the radio frequency amplifier. One of the very popular methods is called plate modulation. In this system, two tubes are used in a circuit called a *push-pull Class B amplifier*, Fig. 30-22. The

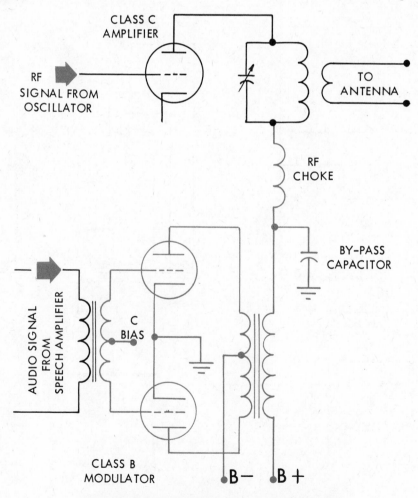

Fig. 30-22. Plate modulation of a Class C amplifier.

output of the modulator is coupled to the final radio frequency amplifier through the secondary of a modulation transformer. The audio signal from the modulator is induced into the secondary of the transformer and this voltage is applied to the plate voltage of the radio frequency amplifier. Thus, the audio signal adds or subtracts from the DC plate voltage. The principal disadvantage of plate modulation is that a considerable amount

of audio power is necessary. Large audio amplifiers are very expensive to build.

Another modulation system that requires less audio is called grid modulation. In grid modulation the audio signal is applied to the grid of the radio frequency amplifier as shown in Fig. 30-23. A serious disadvantage of grid modulation is the reduction in carrier output.

Screen grid modulation is another method used to apply the audio signal

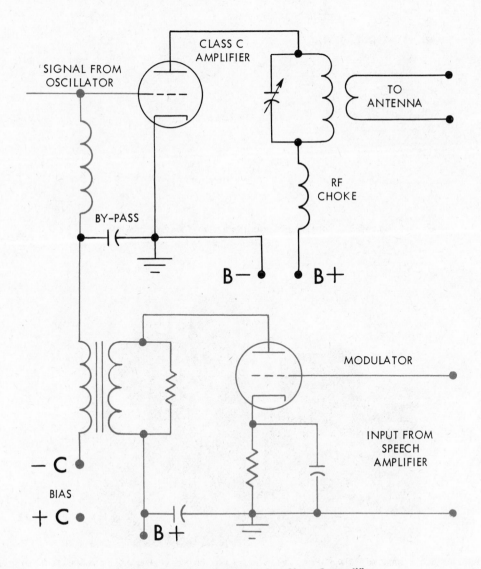

Fig. 30-23. Grid modulation of a Class C amplifier.

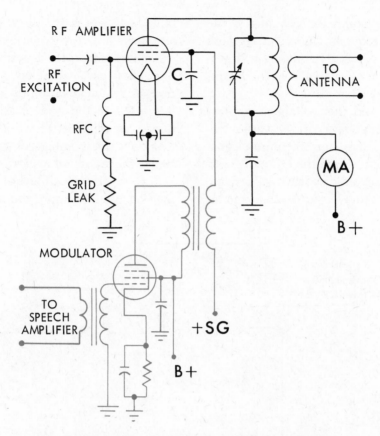

Fig. 30-24. Screen grid modulation of Class C amplifier.

Fig. 30-25. A modern amateur radio station. The receiver and the transmitter are combined in a single unit to make what is known as a *tranceiver.*

to the radio frequency signal. Fig. 30-24 illustrates how the audio is applied to the screen grid through the use of a transformer. The carrier output of screen grid modulation is only about one fourth to one third of that obtainable from the same radio frequency amplifier with plate modulation.

A combination radio receiver and transmitter is shown in Fig. 30-25.

INTERESTING THINGS TO DO

1. Making a Short Range Voice and Code Transmitter.

Materials needed to construct the short range voice and code transmitter (Fig. 30-26):

1 Variable capacitor, midget broadcast type, 400pf C_3
1 Fixed capacitor, 0.05μf, 450 volts, C_1
1 Trimmer capacitor, 100pf C_2
1 RF choke coil, L_1 (see text)
1 Antenna coil, broadcast type, L_2 (see text)
1 Potentiometer, 250,000 ohms, R
1 Transistor, PNP, 2N107 or equivalent
1 Toggle switch, S. P. S. T.
1 Transistor battery, 9 volts
1 Base, sheet metal, 3½" x 3½"

This transmitter will permit you to send voice or code signals to your home radio receiver. Since its range is limited to about 50 feet there is little possibility that it will interfere with other radio receivers outside your home.

All of the parts are mounted on a metal base to reduce the effect of body capacity when you adjust the set. The coil, L_2, may be purchased or made by winding 160 turns of No. 32 enameled wire on a piece of wood dowel, ¾" × 2¼". The choke coil, L_1, has an inductance of 2.5 mH and may be purchased

Fig. 30-26. The completed transmitter. The homemade choke coil is shown at the left of the tuning capacitor.

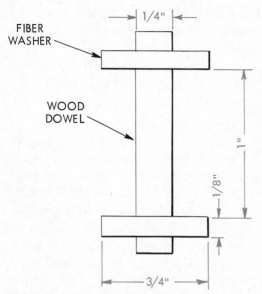

Fig. 30-27. Form for winding choke coil, L_1.

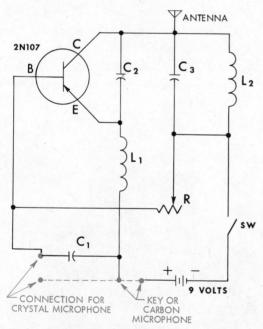

Fig. 30-28. Short-range voice or code transmitter.

piece of wire across the key terminals and connect the microphone as shown by the dashed line. The length of the antenna, which is a piece of flexible wire, should not be longer than 10 feet.

When we studied radio transmitters we learned that a circuit must be in an oscillating condition before it can generate a radio frequency signal. In this circuit oscillation is maintained by feeding back energy from the collector to the emitter by means of capacitor C_1. To adjust the transmitter, place it close to a radio receiver that is tuned to a point on the dial where no station can be heard, preferably in the 900 to 1600 kHz range. Adjust capacitor C_3 on your transmitter until a signal is heard on the radio receiver. Next, adjust capacitor, C_2, until oscillation occurs. This will be indicated by a high pitched squeal from the radio. If you retune the radio receiver carefully you will find a point on the tuning dial where the oscillation signal fades out and then builds up again as the tuning dial is turned. Retune either the radio receiver or transmitter to the "dead" spot and the transmitter is ready to operate. Final adjustments can be made with the transmitter located away from the radio receiver. The potentiometer serves as a volume control for the transmitted signal.

2. Making a Reed-Switch Variable Tone Generator.

Materials for constructing the reed-switch variable tone generator (Fig. 30-29):

1 Variable speed motor (see text)
1 Wood base
1 Cylindrical magnet, $3/16''$ or $1/4''$ diameter, $1''$ long
1 Piece wood dowel (see text)
1 Piece wood dowel, $1/2'' \times 5''$
1 Reed switch

or made by winding 130 feet of No. 32 enameled wire on the form shown in Fig. 30-27. Connect the parts as shown in the wiring diagram Fig. 30-28. If you wish to use a crystal microphone, connect a

Fig. 30-29. Reed-switch variable tone generator.

1 Small loudspeaker
2 Machine screws for terminals

This project demonstrates another application of the versatile *reed switch*. By means of a magnet, a variable speed motor, battery, loudspeaker, and a reed switch, musical tones that extend as high as 1,000 vibrations a second may be produced. The motor used may be battery operated or a universal AC-DC type with its speed variable with a rheostat.

Make a magnet holder from a piece of 1" wood dowel, as shown in Fig. 30-30. Drill a hole for the magnet so that its outer edge will be even with the face of the dowel. This may be done by first drilling the hole through a longer piece of stock, then cutting it to the desired length. Break the edges of the hole away to form a slot and secure the magnet in the slot with epoxy cement. Drill holes through the ends of two pieces of ½"

dowel for the reed switch. The holes should be located so that the switch will be parallel with the magnet mounted on the motor shaft. Secure switch mounting posts to the base so that the switch terminals will extend beyond the posts. Locate the motor on the wood base so that the magnet is not more than 1/16" from the switch and secure the motor to the base. Attach two terminal screws to the end of the base and connect them to the switch terminals with flexible wire. If the switch is to be used for other experiments, alligator clips may be used. Connect the sound circuit as shown in wiring diagram. One flashlight cell will operate the loudspeaker, but additional cells may be added for more volume. Test the generator by slowly turning the motor shaft by hand. If you hear a slight "click" when the magnet passes the switch, the unit is ready to operate.

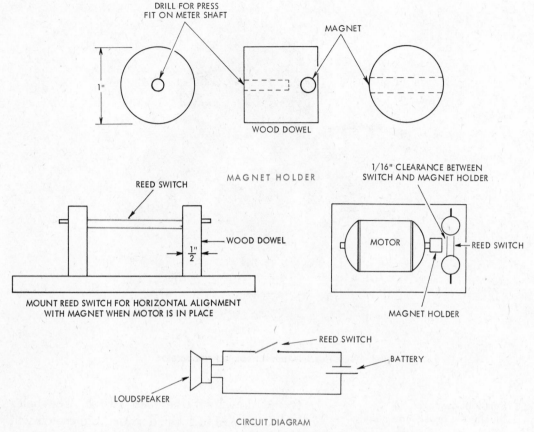

Fig. 30-30. Diagram of reed-switch variable tone generator.

REVIEW QUESTIONS

1. What is the purpose of a radio frequency signal?

2. What determines the frequency of a parallel *LC* circuit?

3. Explain the function of the tickler coil in a regenerative circuit.

4. In a Hartley oscillator, where does the feedback take place?

5. List the advantages of a crystal oscillator.

6. What determines the frequency of a crystal?

7. How does the tank circuit in a Class *C* radio frequency amplifier function?

8. Explain why it is not desirable for a radio frequency amplifier to produce self-oscillation.

9. Calculate the length of wire needed for a half-wave dipole antenna which will operate efficiently on 3,000 kilohertz.

10. Why should the transmission line impedance match the antenna impedance?

11. Name two kinds of transmission lines.

12. What is the function of a frequency multiplier in a transistor?

13. What is the purpose of a telegraphy key in a c.w. transmitter?

14. Name three methods of modulating a radio frequency amplifier in an AM transmitter.

UNIT 31
OTHER INTERESTING ELECTRONIC APPLICATIONS

The Television Camera Tube

Television (Fig. 31-1) has been one of the greatest inventions in the field of electronics. The ability to send pictures through the air waves and to make these pictures visible in a television receiver is a wonderful development.

A television station has two transmitters sending out high-frequency radio waves. See Fig. 31-2. One transmitter sends out the sound signals, and the other sends out picture signals. The picture signals are first picked up by a television camera. The camera uses a tube that is sensitive to light like the photoelectric cell. This tube changes light into a flow of electrons.

It is not possible to send a complete picture. It is necessary to break the picture up into a group of tiny parts of light. A beam of electrons called a *scanning beam* is made to move across the picture picking up the light received by the camera. The beam starts at the top of the

Fig. 31-1. Television cameras being used in a radio station studio. (Radio Station KFMB)

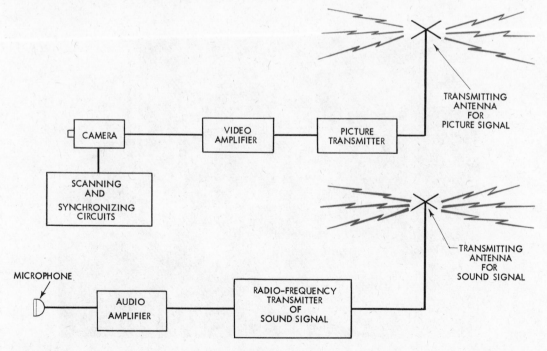

Fig. 31-2. A block diagram of a television transmitting station. One transmitter sends out the picture signal and the other transmitter sends out the sound signal.

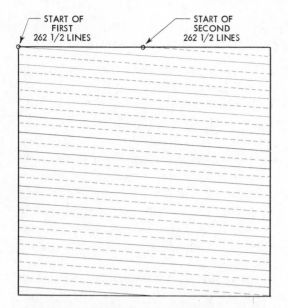

Fig. 31-3. A drawing of the scanning lines of a picture picked up by a television camera. Each picture takes 1/30 of a second to complete and it is made up of 525 lines. Two sets of lines are used to make the 525 lines of the picture. The beam scans half of the lines (262½) as shown by solid line. Then it starts back again between the first lines and scans the other 262½ lines as shown by the broken lines.

picture and goes from one side to the other to the bottom of the picture.

This scanning beam sweeps across the picture and breaks it up into 525 lines. Each complete picture is made up of particles of light found in the 525 lines. It takes ⅟₃₀ of a second for a picture to be completed; thus, 30 pictures are sent out every second. See Fig. 31-3.

The Television Transmitter

The electron flow from the camera is then made stronger by an amplifier called a *video amplifier*. These picture waves are combined with the high-frequency carrier of the transmitter (Fig. 31-4). A transmitting antenna (Fig. 31-5) then sends these waves out into the air.

Television signals travel in a straight line like a beam of light. For this reason transmitting antennas are placed in as high a location as possible so that the

Fig. 31-4. This high-power television station has an ultra-high-frequency transmitter with a radiated power of one million watts. (Radio Corporation of America.)

Fig. 31-5. Radio relay stations and towers, spaced about 30 miles apart, provide a line-of-sight route over which telephone calls and television programs can be relayed great distances. The radio waves that do the work are of super-high frequencies and travel in fairly straight lines, like a beam of light. (Bell Systems.)

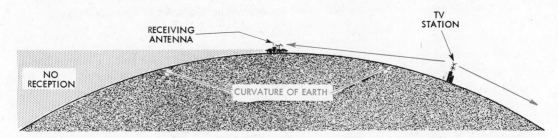

Fig. 31-6. Television signals travel in a straight line like a beam of light, so antennas are made as high as possible.

signals can cover a fairly large area. See Fig. 31-6.

Frequency Modulation

In a standard broadcast station the sound waves and the carrier wave are

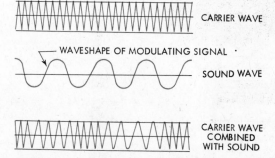

CARRIER WAVE

WAVESHAPE OF MODULATING SIGNAL ·

SOUND WAVE

CARRIER WAVE COMBINED WITH SOUND

Fig. 31-7. In frequency modulation the carrier is varied in *frequency* by the sound waves, while the amplitude remains unchanged.

sound waves vary the frequency of the carrier as shown in Fig. 31-7.

Frequency modulation is also used in ultra-high-frequency broadcast stations called *FM* stations. The main advantage of using frequency modulation is that noises made by such things as electrical circuits in the home, lightning, and automobile ignition are not heard in the receiver. Also, better sound quality is possible through the use of frequency modulation.

The Television Receiver

The television receiver (Fig. 31-8) has a tuner that is used to select the various stations. It tunes in both the sound signal and the picture signal. Since both the sound and the picture signals are on slightly different frequencies, they are

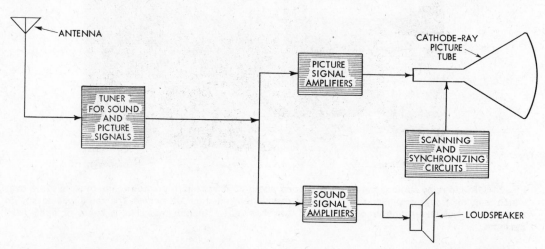

ANTENNA

CATHODE-RAY PICTURE TUBE

PICTURE SIGNAL AMPLIFIERS

TUNER FOR SOUND AND PICTURE SIGNALS

SCANNING AND SYNCHRONIZING CIRCUITS

SOUND SIGNAL AMPLIFIERS

LOUDSPEAKER

Fig. 31-8. This simplified block diagram shows fundamental arrangement of a television receiver.

combined so that the carrier wave is increased and decreased in strength by the sound waves. This is called *amplitude modulation*. Television uses another method of combining the sound waves and the carrier wave called *frequency modulation*. In frequency modulation the

separated in the receiver. The sound signal is amplified and is heard from the loudspeaker. The picture signal is amplified and is seen on the picture tube.

The Cathode-Ray Tube

The picture tube (Fig. 31-9) is called a

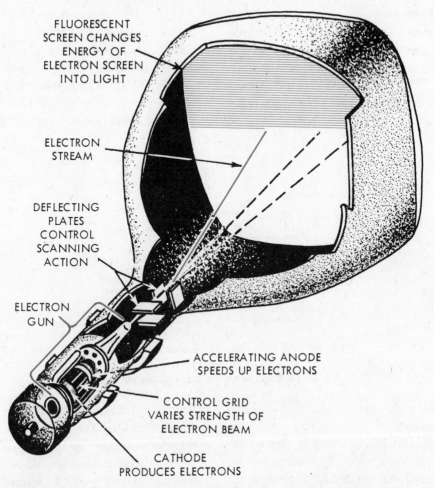

FLUORESCENT
SCREEN CHANGES
ENERGY OF
ELECTRON SCREEN
INTO LIGHT

ELECTRON
STREAM

DEFLECTING
PLATES
CONTROL
SCANNING
ACTION

ELECTRON
GUN

ACCELERATING ANODE
SPEEDS UP ELECTRONS

CONTROL GRID
VARIES STRENGTH OF
ELECTRON BEAM

CATHODE
PRODUCES ELECTRONS

Fig. 31-9. The video wave is picked up by your television receiver and fed into a picture tube, or kinescope. There it varies the strength of a stream of electrons. As the electron stream plays across the fluorescent screen at the wide end of the tube, it paints the same picture seen by the camera.

cathode-ray tube. It is the face of the cathode-ray tube that we see when we look at a television set. Inside the face of the tube there is a coating of a material that will glow when electrons strike it. The stronger the flow of electrons the more the tube will light up. This glow from the electrons hitting the face of the tube is what makes up the black and white of the picture.

The picture tube is adjusted so that the beam of electrons can keep in step with the beam in the television camera. Special circuits, called synchronizing circuits, keep the beam of the television camera and the beam of the cathode-ray tube together. As in the camera, the cathode-ray tube beam must move across the face of the tube making 525 lines 30 times per second. This means that the electron beam is traveling 15,750 times per second across the face of the screen. The beam moving across the screen paints the picture that the camera is picking up.

Color Television

If the correct proportions of the three colors—green, red, and blue—are added together, any desired color can be produced. This basic principle of combining these three colors is used to produce color television.

When the signal is received by the color television receiver, it is then necessary to synchronize the receiver with the signal produced by the transmitter and to separate the three pictures picked up by the three camera tubes. In a black and white cathode-ray picture tube, the

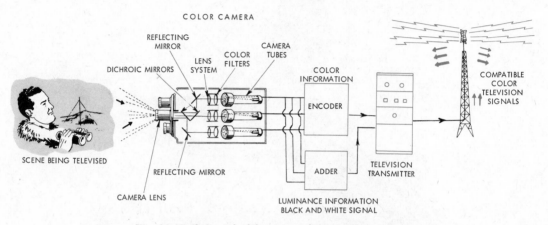

Fig. 31-10. Color television transmitting station.

At the color television transmitter, three camera tubes are used for the picture signal. A single scene is viewed by all three camera tubes, depending on the filter placed in front of each camera tube. A red filter passes only the red components, the green only the green components, and the blue only the blue portion of the picture, to the respective camera tube.

The TV color camera usually consists of one lens system focusing the picture to be televised onto and through special glass mirrors. See Fig. 31-10. These mirrors, called dichroic mirrors, will reflect the color for which it is made and pass all other colors through it. The three reflected color scenes are picked up by the three separate camera tubes (image orthicon or vidicon) which are synchronized together, and the signals are then amplified before going to the transmitter.

fluorescent material on its screen glows when struck by the electron beam from the electron gun. To make a color tube, it is necessary to have three different fluorescent materials. The inner face of the tube is coated with many thousands of dots of red, green, and blue phosphors which glow when electron beams hit them. The dots are distributed uniformly over the face of the tube as shown in Fig. 31-11.

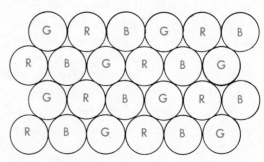

Fig. 31-11. Color dot arrangement in cathode ray tube.

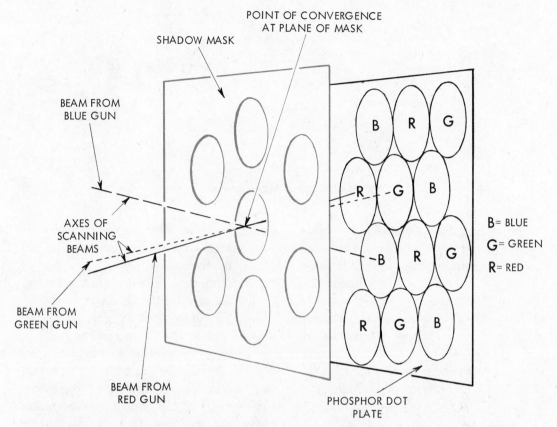

Fig. 31-12. Holes in the shadow mask keep electron beams lined up with the three color dots.

The color tube has three separate electron guns: a red one which bombards only red dots; a green one for the green dots; and a blue one for the blue dots. Each of the electron guns paints its own picture on the screen, and the three colors produce a picture like that viewed by the three color television camera tubes.

To assure that each electron beam will only illuminate its respective color dot, a shadow mask is placed between the electron gun of the cathode-ray tube and the fluorescent screen. The shadow mask consists of a metal plate with thousands of tiny holes which are lined up very exactly with the three color dots and the three electron guns. See Fig. 31-12. Through this arrangement, the beam of electrons

sent out by the electron gun that makes up the separate colors, strikes only the color that it is supposed to strike. Just as in black and white television circuits, it is necessary to have a deflection system to move the electron beam back and forth across the face of the cathode-ray tube. Since the color dots are so small and so close together, your eye brings them together into a true-to-life picture.

Color television broadcasting systems must send out a signal in either black and white or color that will work for black and white receivers (monochrome sets) as well as color receivers. See Fig. 31-13. Such a system is called compatible television. A black and white set tuned to a color broadcast uses the luminance, or

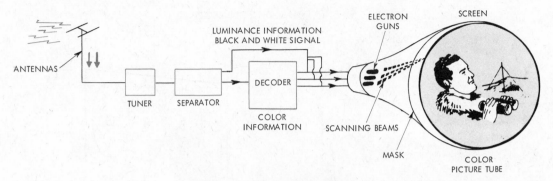

Fig. 31-13. Color television receiver.

brightness, signal to produce the black and white picture. The color signal plays no part in forming the picture. When a color set is tuned to a black and white program, the brightness signal is sent to all three electron guns. These electron guns omit beams whose intensities are such that when they strike the screen they give white light. In this manner, the black and white picture is produced.

Video Tape Recorders

Tape recorders that can be used for recording both sound and pictures are called video tape recorders. These recorders use magnetic tape similar to that used for sound recording. Tape widths may be ½", 1", or 2" depending on the type of recorder being used. As in sound tapes, these magnetic recording tapes consist of minute iron oxide particles evenly spread over a plastic backing.

The recording heads, for video recorders, have the same basic design as the audio heads in that they have a number of turns of wire wound on a core of permeable material. When the magnetic tape passes by the "gap" on the electromagnetic head while an alternating current is flowing in the coil, the iron particles will be attracted and repelled by the alter-

nating current. The magnetic pattern on the tape assumes the magnitude and polarity of the original signal.

In sound tape recorders, the audio frequencies range from 20 hertz to 20,000 hertz; in video signals, the frequency range is from 0 to 3.5 megahertz. Because of this tremendous frequency range required in picture recording, it is necessary to develop a method of increasing the spread of the signal over a greater length of the tape. If a sound recorder could be used for video recording, the high frequency response required would make it necessary to have the tape travel at a very high speed. In addition to the high speed tape travel, it would require a very large reel of tape to record a 30 minute program. The problem, of high frequency response and adequate playing time needed for video recording, has been solved by using a rotating playing head or by compressing the wide band width of the video signal. A carrier frequency is frequency modulated by the video signal before applying the signal to the recording head.

With video recording, the recording head, or heads, are mounted on a rotating drum which revolves as the tape is pulled in front of the rotating head. This method provides a high head-to-tape

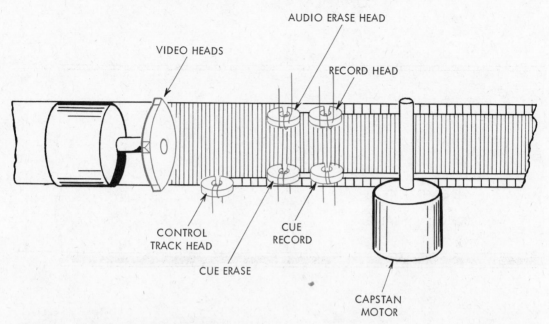

Fig. 31-14. A vertical scan recorded tape has three separate channels of information: the video tracks, the audio track, and the control track. (Ampex corp.)

speed which makes it possible to record the entire range of frequencies required for picture recording.

Two basic systems are used in video tape recording. The vertical scanning system, which was the first successful system, consists of four video heads located on a drum which rotates at high speed (14,400 rpm) perpendicular to the motion of the tape. A track is placed on the tape as shown in Fig. 31-14. Because of the near vertical track, it is necessary to use a 2″ tape. The other arrangement is called the helical scan system; it uses a drum around which the tape is wrapped. The drum may have either one or two heads. As the drum rotates, the tape moves and a track is laid down at an angle to the edge of the tape. See Figs. 31-15 and 31-16. An entire video field is recorded during each pass of the head across the tape. The helical scan system is used in most home type recorders.

In either the vertical or helical scan systems (Fig. 31-17), the audio track is placed on the outside edge of the tape. The audio recording head is entirely separate from the video head. Also, on each system, a control track is recorded on the outside edge, opposite from the audio track. The control track is used to maintain synchronization between the recorded tracks, the rotation video heads, and the movement of the tape. All recorders use an intricate servo system to keep the tape and the rotating heads at a constant speed as well as to synchronize each picture frame.

The speed of the head and the rate of movement of the tape are different for various types of recorders. For the vertical scan, used by most television broadcasting stations, a tape movement of 15 inches per second is used. For the helical scan systems, 7½, 8.57, 9.6, and 12 inches per second may be used.

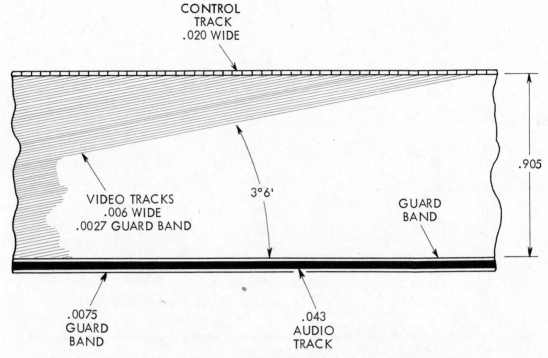

Fig. 31-15. The videotape recording format for a one-inch helical scan system. (Ampex Corp.)

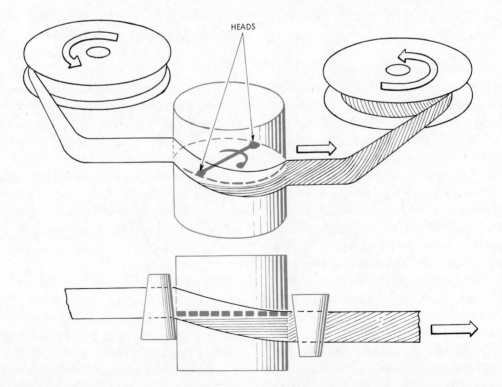

Fig. 31-16. A simplified drawing of the videotape in a helican scan system using a rotary drum with two recording heads. (Sony Corp.)

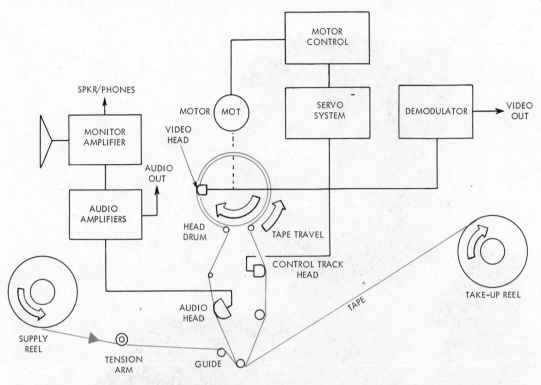

Fig. 31-17. The basic drawing of the function operation for a video recorder. (Ampex Corp.)

A simple video system consists of a TV camera, a microphone, the recorder, and a monitor screen. See Fig. 31-18. It is possible to connect some recorders to an ordinary television receiver so that the TV set becomes the monitor. Cassette type video recorders, similar to those used in cassette sound recorders, are available for easy loading and unloading of the tape cartridge.

As in the sound recorder, the tapes may be erased and reused. They may be easily edited by cutting out the unwanted sections of the tape and splicing the ends of the tape together. Another advantage of the video tape is that it does not require time for developing. It may be used immediately after taking the picture. In addition, slow motion or still pictures may be viewed.

Radar

Radar is an electronic development made during World War II that has been put to very valuable use during peacetime. In navigation, both at sea and in the air, radar plays a most important part. See Fig. 31-19.

You are familiar with an echo of your voice. The sound waves hit a cliff or building and bounce back. You heard your voice when you spoke, and you hear it again when it returns from the cliff or wall that it has hit. This is what happens in radar except that high-frequency radio waves are used instead of sound waves. The radar set sends out a radio wave that strikes an object and receives the same wave when it returns. The set then performs its most important duty by auto-

Fig. 31-18. A miniature videotape recorder, a hand-held camera and a cartridge using half-inch-wide video tape. Pictures may be played back for viewing on a standard television set. The system may be operated by batteries or household current, in color or black and white. (Ampex Corp.)

matically showing the distance that the object is from the radar set. See Fig. 31-20.

For example, an airplane can deter-

mine its height above the ground through the use of radar. A transmitter is used to send out a radio wave. The signal is beamed toward the ground. After it

Fig. 31-19. Airborne radar enables pilots to peer deep into thunderstorms, detecting areas where rough air may be encountered. Dotted lines or radar scope on cockpit show possible corridors pilot can follow for smooth flight through storm which appears solid to unaided eye. (United Air Lines.)

nal sent out by the transmitter shows on the screen of the tube by a little bump called a *pip*. The signal that bounced back from the ground also shows on the

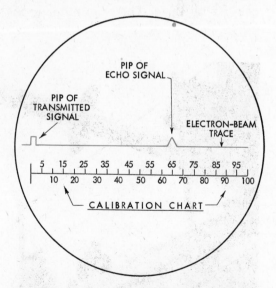

Fig. 31-20. The face of a cathode-ray tube used on a radar screen. The two pips on the screen show the distance between the original transmitted signal and the echo signal after it bounced back to the receiver. By using the calibrated scale below the beam, it is possible to determine the distance that the object is away from the radar station.

strikes the ground it bounces back up to the airplane. The wave that bounces back is picked up by a radio receiver that is connected to a cathode-ray tube. The sig-

screen by a pip. It only takes a fraction of a second for these radio waves to go to the ground and bounce back. The time between pips can be calibrated in distance since the speed of radio waves is known to be 186,000 miles per second. By looking at the scale on the front of the tube, it is possible to measure the distance between pips to determine the distance of the airplane from the ground.

Radar is used in many ways. Ships at sea can get a picture of the shore line near them with radar. Other objects in the air or at sea can be located by radar. More and more the principle of radar is being used for navigation purposes to make air and sea travel safe.

Radio-Controlled Rockets

Rockets and airplanes can be controlled through the use of radio waves. See Fig. 31-21. Rockets, or guided missiles, fired into the sky carry a radio receiver with them. The transmitter from the home station sends out radio signals that are picked up by the receiver in the rocket. All of the direction controls in the rocket are connected so that they can be moved by signals coming into the receiver. A radar station watches the rocket. It keeps the operators informed as to the speed and location of the missile. In this way the operators have complete control of the flight of the rocket.

High-altitude research rockets carry transmitters with them. These transmitters inform the ground stations as to how the rocket is performing. Information regarding air pressure, temperature, and other important facts is sent out by the rocket transmitter.

Satellites and Space Capsules

While rockets and missiles are valuable as a means of defense, their role in research has been replaced by the satellites and space capsules that are now being sent into space. See Fig. 31-22. These are

Fig. 31-21. Radio-controlled guided missiles shown aboard a Navy ship. The development of these devices depends upon electronics. (Convair)

Fig. 31-22. Telstar with its launching shell removed. Part of the 3,600 solar cells which provide
its operating power may be seen in the square
frames around its outer surface. The spiral antenna for telemetry signals is located on top of the
satellite. Two sets of microwave antennas for
receiving and transmitting TV signals encircle the
satellite at the center behind the small openings.
(Bell Laboratories)

capable of sustained orbits outside the
earth's atmosphere and provide information on weather, solar radiation and valuable new data on communication.

In the construction of these satellites
every component represents the latest ad-
vance in electronics. As a satellite must
be self sustaining in operation and provide the many forms of information necessary, it must be extremely compact and
reliable. This is accomplished by "pack-
aging" the electronic circuits in micro-
miniature component blocks and using
solar cells to provide for a portion of its
operating power.

Many satellites have been put into
orbit and have provided valuable information necessary for further exploration
in space. The Van Allen radiation belt
was discovered and plotted through the
use of these space devices.

Telemetering

Much data needed for space travel
preparation is being obtained from transmitters in satellites which respond to
signals from ground transmitting stations. The signals from the satellites are
in the form of pulses of such strength and
duration that they can be interpreted in
terms of the desired information. The
science of transmitting and receiving
measurements and other data from a distance is known as *telemetering*.

As many as one hundred fifteen forms
of data are available from the various satellites, among which are density of radiation, effect of radiation on the solar cells,
amount of sunlight hitting the satellite,
voltages on many of the components,
pressures within and outside the shell,
and condition of the power plant.

Communicating with Men on the Moon

With man's landing on the Moon now
an accomplished fact, we may wonder
what part electronics played in making
that historic event possible. Although
electronics had an important part in performing many of the tasks aboard the
Apollo spacecraft and the lunar-landing
module, (Fig. 31-23) its most significant
job was communications. Except for a
brief time, while Apollo was circling the
Moon and signals to and from it were
blanked out, the astronauts were in constant contact with each other and the
control station on Earth. Communications between the Moon and the Apollo
were with AM and FM very-high-fre-

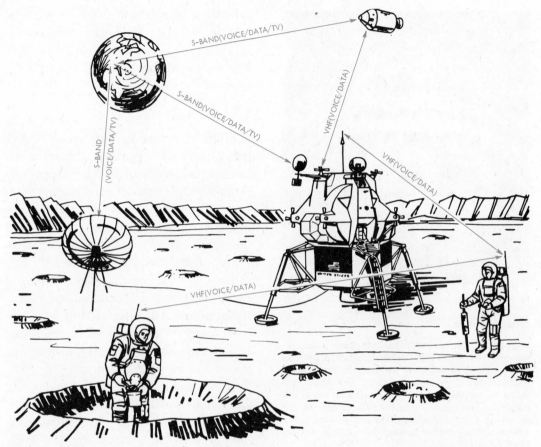

Fig. 31-23. Drawing showing means of communcations between Apollo II astronauts and control station on Earth.

quency signals in the range of 279 to 296.8 MHz (c.p.s.). Communications to Earth were by means of ultra-high-frequency signals of 2282.5 MHz, known as the "S" band.

The TV pictures transmitted to Earth consisted of 320 lines at 10 frames per second, since it permitted the camera to operate at a 500 kHz bandwidth. Our commercial television operates at a band width of only 4.5 MHz, so it was necessary to rescan the pictures received at the Earth control center to convert them so that they could be shown on conventional TV sets.

Much of the success of the transmissions to and from the Moon was due to a collapsible antenna that could be expanded to an umbrella-like dish 10 feet in diameter. This unique antenna focused its energy so that its transmissions covered the entire section of the Earth that faced the Moon at any given time.

The Laser

The laser beam, considered to be one of the miracle applications of electronics, was first conceived by physicist Charles H. Townes back in 1951. Since that time, its progress has been rapid, but for the many advances, credit must be given other scientists whose contributions have helped to bring the laser to its present state of development. Present day applications of the laser include eye surgery, precision measurements, surveying, astronomy, seismology, and welding. The science of *holography* also has made exceptional progress with the aid of the laser beam. Holography is a method of

Fig. 31-24. Laser beam being used for communication on a construction project. (Metrologic Instrument Inc.)

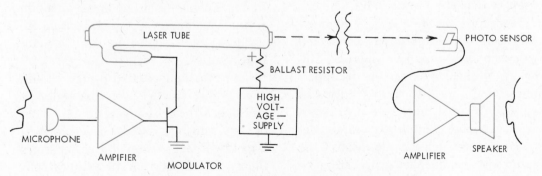

Fig. 31-25. Laser modulation and communication system.

creating a three-dimensional image on photographic film. Other uses of the laser predicted for the future are long-distance communications, three-dimensional TV, and data recording (Figs. 31-24, 31-25).

Basically, lasers based on physicist Townes' ideas operate on the principle of agitating the helium atoms of a helium-neon mixture enclosed in a glass tube, with a small electric current. The helium atoms collide with the neon atoms, transfer some energy to them, and raise them to an excited energy level. This starts a light wave to race back and forth, which triggers more atoms and causes a beam of brilliant-red coherent light to emit from the end of the glass tube. The term *coherent* means that the rays of light are concentrated in one direction instead of scattering in many directions as they do in an ordinary light bulb. An interesting demonstration simulating the two may be made with an ordinary garden hose and nozzle. Adjust the nozzle for a fine spray and note that individual streams spread out and extend only a few feet from the nozzle. They represent rays emanating from a light bulb. Without changing the water pressure, adjust the nozzle for a small solid stream and note its lack of spreading and the distance it extends from the hose, as compared to the fine spray. This will demonstrate the action of a coherent beam of light.

Heretofore, the high cost of commercial lasers and the dangers connected with their operation have deprived students in the field of electronics the opportunity of getting acquainted with this space-age marvel, but those restrictions no longer exist. Low power safely designed lasers which include most of the features of commercial types are now available for school use.

Infrared Intrusion Detector

Principles of a device that was conceived originally for military use have been adapted for equipment to protect industrial and commercial establishments from unwanted intrusion. Known as a *passive infrared intrusion detector,* the system will detect a man in total darkness at a distance of 1,000 feet, or a truck at 2,500 feet. The detector is termed "passive" because it requires no return beam for operation, such as is used for radar or light controlled equipment. The passive infrared detector is responsive only to heat that emanates from the intruder's body in the form of infrared rays. It is claimed that the detector will distinguish between the temperature of a person and a background such as a wall or building, with only his head and neck exposed. The device is unaffected by falling leaves, rocks, raindrops, or other natural occurrences that would trigger detectors which require a return signal to operate. Development of the infrared intrusion detector was made possible by the use of a type of resistor known as a *thermistor*. Thermistors have what is called *negative resistance*. Their resistance increases as their temperature goes down.

An infrared intrusion detector (Fig. 31-26) is made up of two units: an alarm section containing audio and visual indicators, and a detector. The detector unit consists of two thermistors connected in a compensated *bridge* circuit. A common refractive optical system provides each thermistor with its own field of view, which at 750 feet covers an area 2 feet by 6 feet. A similar area separates the two fields of view. See Fig. 31-27. When setting up the detector unit to pro-

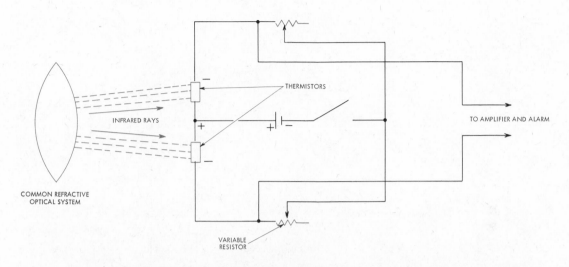

INFRARED RAYS

COMMON REFRACTIVE OPTICAL SYSTEM

THERMISTORS

TO AMPLIFIER AND ALARM

VARIABLE RESISTOR

CIRCUIT DIAGRAM

Fig. 31-26. Infrared intrusion detector. In the top photograph, detector system consists of infrared detector head on right, and alarm unit, that can be remotely located, on left. Telescope on detector unit provides alignment with protected area. (Barnes Engineering Co.) Bottom shows circuit diagram of detector.

tect an area, the thermistor bridge circuit is balanced against the background of the area by means of the adjustable resistors. When in a balanced state, there is no current flow to the amplifier input because one side of the bridge opposes the other. When an intruder enters the field of view from either side of the protected area, the circuit becomes unbalanced and permits a signal to actuate the amplifier to produce visual and audible signals.

Automatic Camera Shutter Control

The application of electronics to cam-

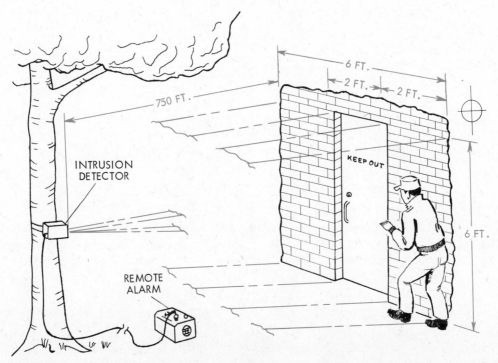

Fig. 31-27. Diagonal lines show size of protected areas from a distance of 750 feet. Alarm will indicate whether intruder enters from right or from left side of protected area.

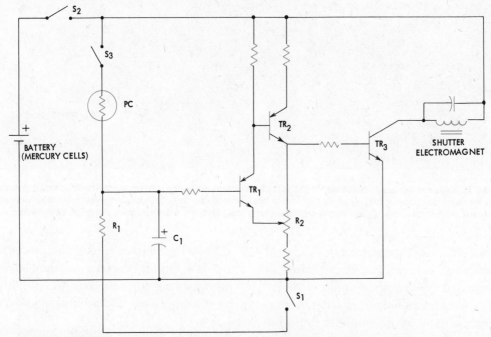

Fig. 31-28. Circuit diagram showing only automatic shutter control sections of complete camera circuit. Flash circuits which are hand-adjusted are omitted.

era shutter control has simplified picture taking to the stage where a photographer need do little more than point his camera at a subject and release the shutter. This has been made possible with the use of integrated and printed circuits. In one popular electronically operated 35 mm reflex camera the circuits contain 3 capacitors, 7 resistors, 3 potentiometers, 3 transistors, 7 switches, 2 mercury cells, an electromagnet, and a photocell. Yet the camera is no larger than many hand-adjusted cameras. When operating that particular type of camera, inserting the film cartridge automatically programs the electronic mechanism for the ASA or speed rating of the film. Winding the shutter closes switch S_1 which drains capacitor C_1, through resistor R_1, of any charge remaining from previous use,

Fig. 31-28. When the shutter button is pressed, the camera mirror flips out of the way and switches S_2 and S_3 close. This allows transistors TR_2 and TR_3 to pass current, which energizes the electromagnet and opens the shutter. Simultaneously, the photocell PC begins to pass current and charge capacitor C_1, the amount of current flow depending upon the intensity of the light striking the photocell. When the charge is enough to trigger transistor TR_1 it conducts current, which turns off the transistors TR_2 and TR_3. With no current flow in the collector circuit of TR_3, the electromagnet releases the shutter and its blades close together. The potentiometer R_2 determines the trigger point of transistor TR_1 and is adjusted only when the shutter speed requires correcting. The unmarked

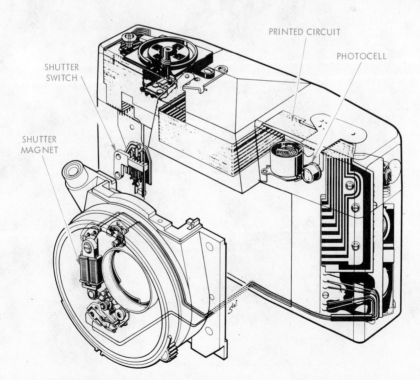

Fig. 31-29. Cutaway view of a modern reflex camera showing portions of printed circuit and electronic control mechanisms. (Eastman Kodak Co.)

resistors shown in the circuit diagram provide the proper voltages for the various transistor elements. The automatic sequence outlined may appear as requiring seconds of time, but all operations from the time the shutter switches close may be completed within 1/500th second. This is the top shutter speed of the camera. See Fig. 31-29.

Super-Power Transistors

Through the use of a new laminated construction technique, (Fig. 31-30) it is now possible to build transistors that ri-

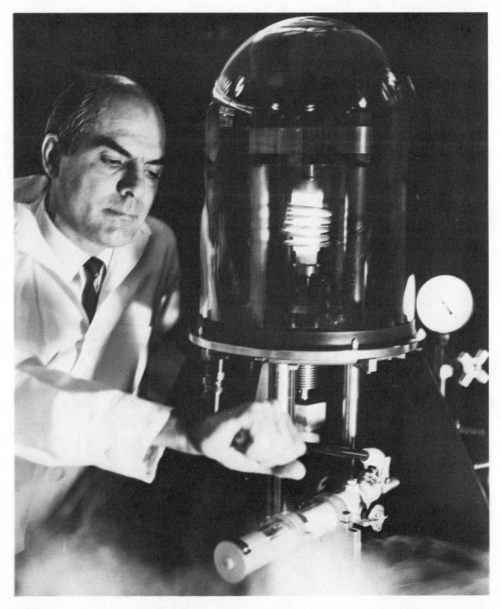

Fig. 31-30. Super-power transistors being fused together under intense pressure and heat, in a vacuum. (Electronic Components Div., RCA)

val large electron tubes in power output. Although the development of the super-power transistor is continuing, in initial tests they generated radio waves oscillating at 1 MHz (c.p.s.) with a power output of 800 watts. This is over three

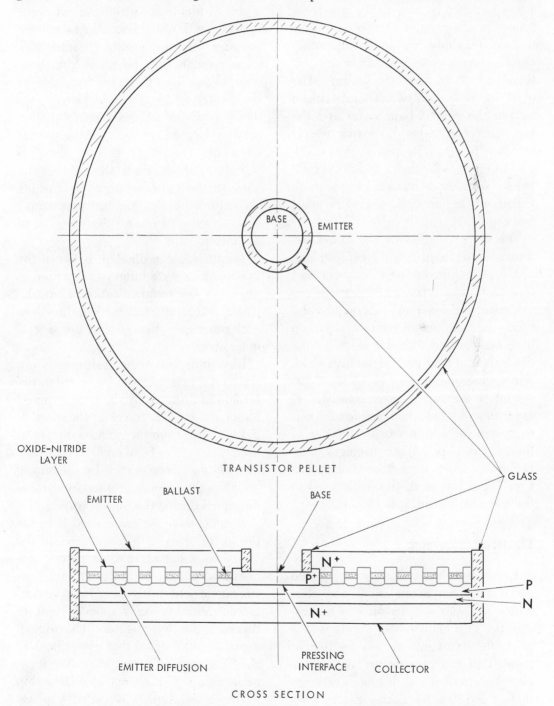

Fig. 31-31. Laminated transistor construction (800 watt type). (Electronic Components Div., RCA)

times the 250 watts generated by many standard radio broadcast stations. Considerably higher powers and frequencies are expected to be added. The new techniques which produced the super-power transistor includes fusing or laminating semiconductor materials, ultrasonic cutting, and glass hermetic sealing. The units are formed on two separate silicon wafers, the emitter-base wafer and the base-collector wafer. The two wafers are then fused or laminated into a single structure. After lamination, the individual sections or *pellets,* as they are called, are hermetically sealed in glass. See Fig. 31-31.

The active regions of the laminated transistor are located in the center plane of the pellet in contrast to conventional transistors where the active regions are at the surface. This construction provides solid and continuous contact areas on both emitter and collector sides for the dissipation of heat with metal heat sinks. Studies are under way to increase the output of the super-power transistor to as much as 5 kilowatts. Possible solutions suggested include increasing the size of the individual pellets, or placing a number of the pellets in parallel in one package. The diameter of the pellet used in the 800 watt transistor is 250 mils.

Electronic Surveying

Land surveying, civil engineering, and aerial surveying firms often use electronic systems for distance measurements. The measuring devices are portable electronic surveying instruments that can provide precision accurate measurements of distances between 30 feet and 30 miles. Such measuring devices are extremely valuable in rugged terrain or over water. See Figs. 31-32 and 31-33.

Electronic surveying equipment uses a pair of identical instruments set up at opposite ends of the line to be measured. Because the instruments are identical, measurements may be made from both ends of the line. One unit functions as the "interrogator" which provides a direct read-out of the distances on a counter located on the front of the instrument. The other unit is the "responder" which sends the information back to the "interrogator." By turning the control settings, the instrument may be changed either to a "responder" or to an "interrogator."

To provide coordination between the two instruments, a radio signal is used to provide voice communication. Thus, the two operators can talk back and forth to each other even though they are several miles apart.

Electronic surveying instruments operate on a principle similar to radar, determining distance by the time required for a radio wave to travel (at the speed of light) to and from the point being measured. They differ from radar in that they provide greater accuracy by measuring the shift that occurs in a modulated radio signal during the time of travel.

A microwave system is used between the instruments with frequencies in the 10 kilomegahertz range as carrier frequencies. The modulated microwave carrier signal sent out by the "interrogator" is transmitted to the "responder" and returned to the "interrogator." The original signal and the signal that comes back to the "interrogator" have changed in wave relationship. This change in relationship between the signals is called a phase shift. Such a phase shift is determined by

Fig. 31-32. In electronic surveying, two instruments are used for accurate measurement. (Cubic Corp.)

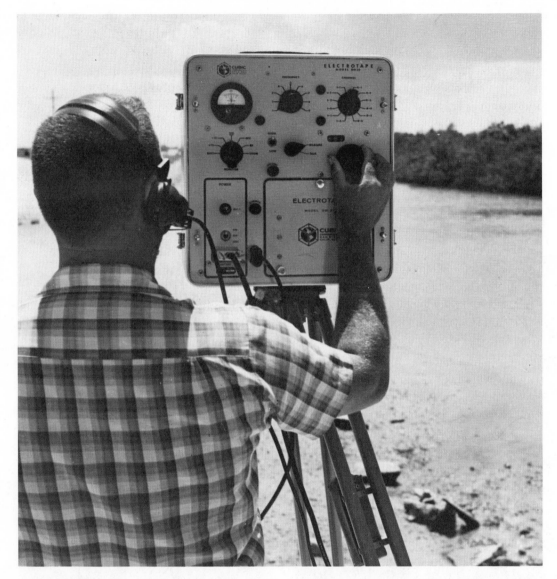

Fig. 31-33. This operator is using an electronic distance measurement instrument called an "Electrotape".
(Cubic Corp.)

(1) the distance of the wave travel, (2) the modulated frequency, and (3) the velocity of the wave (186,000 miles per second). This phase shift, or comparison of signals, is recorded as distance on the counter of the measuring device. For an immediate accuracy check, the other instrument is used in turn as a measurement unit. The second answer is then compared to the first.

Xerography

When a number of copies of an original document are needed, a duplicating system, employing a stencil or some other form of master, may be used. Another

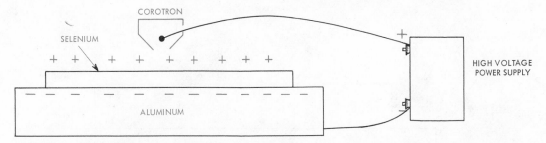

Fig. 31-34. With a high positive potential on the corotron and a negative potential on the aluminum, a positive charge is placed on the surface of the selenium.

system, called *xerography*, which is an electrostatic type of printing, eliminates the necessity of preparing a master; it reproduces the original material without ink or pressure.

Commercial xerography duplicators use an aluminum drum that has been coated with selenium. While the drum is in the dark, a positive electrostatic charge is placed on the surface of the selenium coating. This is done by having the positive terminal of a high voltage power supply (about 7,000 volts) connected to a fine wire, called the *corotron*, that is located above the selenium. The negative electrode of the power supply is connected to the aluminum drum. See Fig. 31-34. With such a high positive charge on the fine wire, the free electrons in the air are pulled toward it. These fast moving electrons in the air strike air molecules which lose electrons and become positive charges that move to the drum which is coated with selenium. See Fig. 31-35. The positive charges stay on the surface of the selenium since it acts like an insulator or "dielectric."

While the selenium has an electrostatic charge, a very strong light scans the surface of the document being copied. Light reflected from the original document is focused on the selenium plate. The image or printing on the document does

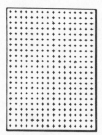

Fig. 31-35. The entire surface of the selenium plate now has a positive charge.

not reflect light, but the white portion of the paper reflects light. Since selenium is a photosensitive material, the area that receives light causes the positive holes in the selenium to move toward the aluminum which is located under the selenium. See Fig. 31-36. Thus, in the area where light strikes the surface of the selenium, the positive charges disappear. The dark area, which represents the original image or printing, does not reflect light and continues to hold a positive charge. The charged surface area of the selenium now represents the image of the document. See Fig. 31-37.

A black powder, called a toner, gains a negative electrostatic charge when spread over the selenium; it adheres to the positively charged zones. See Fig. 31-38. This powder now represents the printing or image of the original copy. Paper which has been positively charged

ARROWS REPRESENT LIGHT RAYS

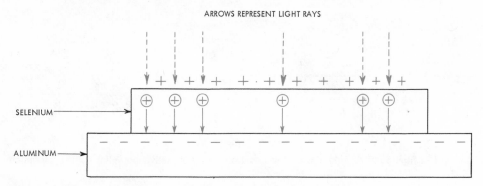

SELENIUM

ALUMINUM

Fig. 31-36. Wherever the light strikes the positively charged selenium surface, the charges move toward the aluminum base.

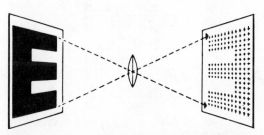

Fig. 31-37. When light is directed on a document, the printed area absorbs the light; the clear area reflects it. If the reflected light is focused on a charge plate, the charges remain wherever there is printed material.

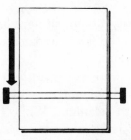

Fig. 31-39. A positively charged paper is moved near the plate that contains the black powder.

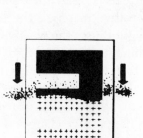

Fig. 31-38. Black powder is electrostatically attracted to the charged area of the plate. The powder gains negative charges when in contact with the charged area.

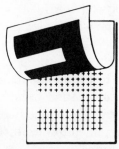

Fig. 31-40. The positively charged paper attracts the negatively charged powder so that the image is transferred to the paper.

is passed very closely to the drum (Fig. 31-39) and the powder particles are attracted to the paper. This powder, representing the original copy, is fused into the paper by heat. See Figs. 31-40 and 31-41.

Fig. 31-41. The paper is heated to fuse the image.

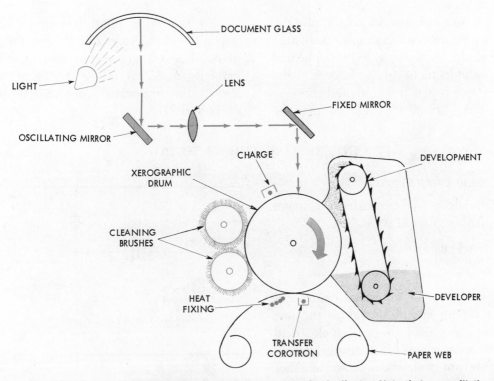

Fig. 31-42. This drawing shows the basic element of a xerography duplicator. Note that an oscillating mirror is used to scan the original document.

Fig. 31-43. Photograph of a xerography duplicator that can produce 60 copies a minute. The machine is also capable of collating 10 pages of duplicating.   (Xerox Corp.)

Operating commercial xerography duplicators is extremely simple, consisting only of placing the copy to be duplicated on the document glass, selecting the number of copies required, and pressing the start button. Photographs may be copied by placing a half-tone screen between the photograph and the document glass. Also, arrangements in some models make it possible to reduce or enlarge the size of the duplicated copy. See Figs. 31-42 and 31-43.

INTERESTING THINGS TO DO

1. Neon Lamp Flasher.

Materials needed to construct the neon lamp flasher (Fig. 31-44):

1 Neon lamp, Type Ne-2
1 Fixed resistor, ½-watt (see text)
1 Fixed capacitor, 150 volts (see text)

Many pieces of industrial equipment use a timing circuit similar to the one shown in Fig. 31-45 to turn an electrical circuit on or off. With its use extremely accurate timing may be obtained whether the time intervals are a fraction of a second or many minutes apart. The timing is governed by the values of the resistor measured in ohms and capacitor measured in farads. If we multiply the value

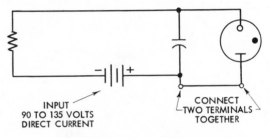

INPUT
90 TO 135 VOLTS
DIRECT CURRENT

CONNECT
TWO TERMINALS
TOGETHER

NEON FLASHER CIRCUIT

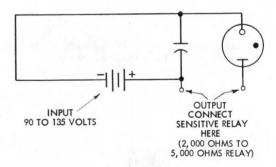

INPUT
90 TO 135 VOLTS

OUTPUT
CONNECT
SENSITIVE RELAY
HERE
(2,000 OHMS TO
5,000 OHMS RELAY)

NEON LAMP CONTROL CIRCUIT

Fig. 31-45. Diagrams of the neon lamp flasher and control circuit.

of the resistor by the capacitance of the capacitor in farads, the product will be the time interval in seconds at which the neon lamp will flash.

The flasher shown in Fig. 31-44 is arranged to flash at one second intervals by using a 1,000,000-ohm resistor and a 1 μf capacitor. The term *farad* represents such a large value that it is seldom used in electronic circuits, but since 1,000,000 microfarads equal one farad, we can see

Fig. 31-44. The neon lamp flasher.

that one microfarad can be expressed as .000001 farad. If we wish to increase the timing interval we have only to increase the value of the resistor or the capacitor, so that when both are multiplied together, the product will be the desired timing in seconds.

The input terminals should be connected to a source of direct current, 90 to 135 volts. If it is desired only to observe the flashing rate, a piece of wire should be connected across the output terminals. If it is desired to control another circuit, connect a sensitive relay across the output terminals.

2. Transistor Code Practice Oscillator.

Materials required to construct the transistor code practice oscillator (Fig. 31-46):

1 Piece wood, ½″ x 3″ x 3″
1 Transistor, GE 2N107 or Raytheon CK 722
2 Fixed capacitors, .01 μf (C₁, C₂)
1 Resistor, 47,000 ohms (R)

2 Pen light cells
4 Fahnestock clips

This transistor oscillator provides a very compact set with which you may learn the radiotelegraph code to qualify for an amateur radio license. Mount the parts in the approximate positions on the wood base as shown in Fig. 31-46. Wire the set according to Schematic Diagram, Fig. 31-47. Two of the Fahnestock clips should be marked "key" and two should be marked "phones." If all of the connections have been made correctly, a high-pitched buzz should be heard in the phones when the key is pressed. For the best results the phones should have an impedance of 2,000 or more ohms. To reduce current drain from the pen light cells, the headphones should be disconnected from the oscillator when it is not in use.

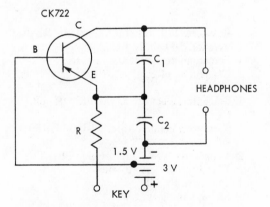

Fig. 31-47. Wiring diagram of the transistor code-practice oscillator.

3. High Gain Detectaphone Amplifier.

Materials needed to construct the high gain detectaphone amplifier (Fig. 31-48):

1 Transistor input transformer, primary 200 k, secondary 1k, T₁
1 Transistor driver transformer, primary 10k, secondary 2k, T₂

Fig. 31-46. Transistor code-practice oscillator.

Fig. 31-48. The detectaphone parts may be assembled into a compact unit that may be attached to a belt or slipped into a pocket.

2 Resistors, 470,000 ohms, ½ watt, R_1, R_4
1 Resistor, 100 ohms, R_2
1 Potentiometer, 10,000 ohms, R_3
2 Capacitors, electrolytic, 10 mfd, 10 volts, C_1, C_2
1 Capacitor, electrolytic, 50 mfd, 10 volts, C_4
1 Capacitor, ceramic disc, 0.01 mfd, 150 volts, C_3
2 Transistors, PNP, audio type, TR_1, TR_2
1 Transistor battery, 9 volts
1 Switch, S. P. S. T.
1 Microphone jack
2 Phone tip jacks
2 Terminal strips, 4 lug
1 Plastic case with cover, 1″ x 3″ x 4½″

This high gain amplifier is small enough to be carried in a shirt pocket, yet sensitive enough to pick up conversation within a house 50 to 70 feet from its source. If a sensitive microphone is attached to it and held against a wall, sounds occurring in a room beyond may be readily understood. If the microphone is suspended in front of a bowl or reflector, its range can be extended to several hundred feet.

Obtain a plastic case first, then cut a piece of insulating material such as bakelite or plastic, 1/16″ thick, for mounting the parts. Arrange each component so that the leads will be as short as possible. Connect a transistor to three of the lugs on each terminal strip and use the extra lugs for securing other parts. Secure the microphone jack and potentiometer to one end of the plastic case and the phone tip jacks to the opposite end. Although the potentiometer and switch are listed as separate items, they may be obtained in one unit. The high gain of this circuit is due to the fact that transformer coupling is used. While resistance-capacity coupling would provide better quality of sound, its gain would be far less than

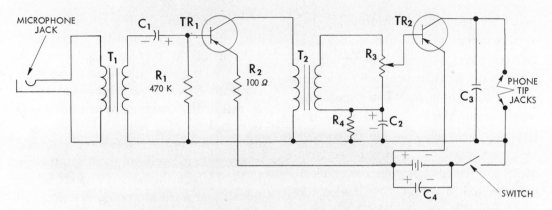

Fig. 31-49. Schematic diagram of high gain detectaphone amplifier.

Fig. 31-50. If a microphone is mounted on an adjustable rod in the center of a reflector, the detectaphone will amplify sounds such as bird calls from a distance of several hundred yards.

that obtained with transformers. Their audible range is more than sufficient to give excellent reproduction of all the voice frequencies, which fulfills the purpose of the amplifier. When transformer coupled amplifiers are used there is a tendency for them to break into a low frequency oscillation when the components are placed close together. This effect is called "motor boating" and it may be identified by sharp clicks in the headphones which occur two or three times a second. To eliminate that possible ef-

fect a capacitor, C_4, is connected across the battery as shown in the diagram.

Connect the parts as shown in Fig. 31-49, taking particular care to wire the capacitors so the polarities will be as shown in the diagram. When all wiring is complete, plug a crystal or dynamic microphone in the microphone jack and a pair of sensitive headphones in the pin jacks. Turn on the battery switch, adjust the volume with the potentiometer, and the amplifier is ready to operate.

Fig. 31-50 shows a microphone connected to a reflector on an adjustable rod.

REVIEW QUESTIONS

1. Why are two transmitters used in a television station?

2. How many complete pictures are sent out every second by a television station?

3. Each picture is divided into how many scanning lines?

4. Why is it necessary for a television antenna to be located as high as possible?

5. What is the picture tube in a television receiver called? Explain how it works.

6. Explain how a radar set tells the height that an airplane is from the ground.

7. How can radar be used to make airplane travel safer?

8. What is the advantage of having radio-controlled rockets?

9. How does an infrared intrusion detector operate?

10. In what way was it necessary to change the Apollo TV signals so that they could be shown on standard TV receivers?

11. What recent advances in electronic circuitry have made automatic camera shutter control possible?

12. What is *holography?*

13. How does the construction of a super-power transistor differ from that of a conventional smaller size transistor?

14. Name the three colors used to produce color television.

15. What is the purpose of the shadow mask in a color cathode ray tube?

16. What is the basic difference between the recording system used in sound tape recording and video tape recording?

17. Name two types of scanning systems used in video tape recording.

18. What type of printing is xerography?

19. Why is selenium used on the plate or drum of a xerography duplicator?

20. When using an electronic surveying instrument what is the name of the unit that records the distance? What is the name of the unit that returns the signal?

BASIC SAFETY FOR ELECTRICITY AND ELECTRONICS

In the electronic lab, safety includes safe and proper use of tools and equipment and in an attitude of RESPECT for ELECTRICITY.

1. Never overload an electrical circuit. Overloaded circuits may cause a fire. All circuits must be protected by fuses or circuit breakers.

2. When a circuit breaker opens or a fuse blows as the result of an overload, always report this to the teacher and correct the fault before turning the power back on.

3. Changes in the wiring of any circuit may be made only after the power has been shut off or the equipment has been unplugged.

4. Frames and housings of all portable electrical equipment must be properly grounded.

5. Wires shall not cross the aisle (a special setup) unless the arrangement is approved by the teacher.

6. When making temporary or permanent connections, carefully avoid leaving open splices or pieces of wire sticking out. Secure all wires properly. Tape or cover the connections.

7. Before replacing a fuse in any electrical equipment, disconnect the power source.

8. When cutting component leads, be careful not to let them hit anyone.

9. Be careful in handling component leads after trimming; the cut ends are sharp.

10. Extreme care must be used when using a knife to remove the insulation from wires. Enamels and similar insulations can be removed with sandpaper.

11. Always use a test lamp or suitable meter for testing purposes.

12. Consider all electric wires "live" until they have been proven "dead."

13. All live wires must be handled carefully. Low voltages can give a serious burn, and high voltages, a fatal shock.

14 Under NO circumstances give another person an electric shock. Remember! Electric shocks are dangerous and can be fatal.

15. The chassis of an AC-DC radio shall at all times be kept clear of ground wires and all other conductors, such as metal table tops.

16. In making adjustments when the power is on in an AC-DC radio, avoid coming in contact with metallic and grounded objects.

17. Filter capacitors may hold enough electrical energy to cause serious shock. Be sure that any capacitor has been discharged before touching its terminals or connections.

18. Before touching anything behind the panel of any electrical equipment, remove the attachment plug from the wall outlet to insure that all power circuits are off.

19. Never allow anyone to switch power on and off for you while you are working on radio and electrical equipment.

20. Remove headphones while working on transmitters or receivers.

21. Keep one hand behind your back or in your pocket when testing high-voltage circuits.

22. All chassis, cabinets, microphone cable shield, and any other shielding around transmitting equipment must be grounded.

23. Never draw a test arc from transmitters and TV power supplies. It is very dangerous.

24. High-voltage power supplies must be so constructed that accidental bodily contact with power circuits is unlikely.

25. All high-voltage power supplies should be equipped with a bleeder resistor to discharge filter capacitors.

26. Never touch a hot vacuum tube, resistor, or freshly-made solder joint. Allow cooling time before gripping them firmly.

27. Cathode-ray tubes (such as TV picture tubes) are dangerous because they can implode (collapse suddenly) and injure you with flying glass.

28. The chemicals used in picture tubes (TV) and fluorescent light bulbs are dangerous. Be very careful when handling broken glass from these items.

In all electrical work, good soldering joints are essential. Solder is intended to provide a good electrical contact, to prevent corrosion at the joint, and to add strength to the joint or splice. Most electrical soldering is done with an electric soldering iron or a soldering gun.

Procedures for Soldering

1. Clean the Soldering Tip

When using an electric soldering iron, it is advisable to remove the copper tip from the iron before filing. File the tip so that the four sides of the copper are smooth and come together to a point. If the tip is round, clean it with sandpaper or emery cloth. The tip should be taken out of the iron at least once a week so that the corrosion can be removed from the copper. If the tip remains in the iron for long periods of time, it will corrode in the iron barrel. Should this occur, it is very difficult to ever remove the tip.

2. Tin the Tip

Heat the tip and then apply a thin coat of rosin core solder. Sometimes the solder will not stick even though the tip looks clean. When this occurs, rub the heated point with steel wool and again apply the rosin core solder. The tip should now be tinned and will have a shiny appearance.

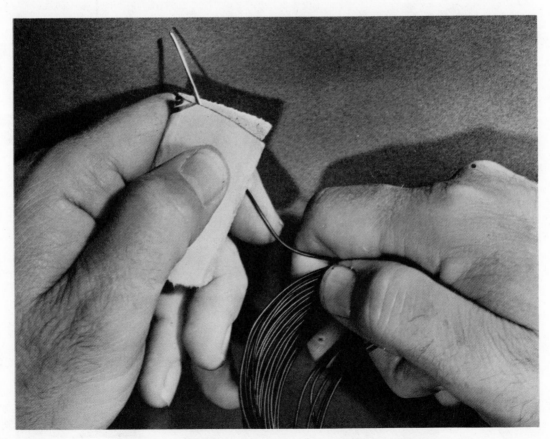

1. The insulation on small wires can be removed with sandpaper.

If excess solder remains on the tip, it can be removed by wiping the point with a rag.

3. Use Rosin Core Solder

Wire-shaped solder with a hollow core filled with rosin flux is recommended for all electrical connections. Acid core solder or paste fluxes are not desirable because they corrode connections.

4. All Parts to be Soldered Must be Clean

Solder will not stick to wire or terminals that have not been cleaned. Lugs, wires, and other parts to be soldered should be scraped with a knife until the metal appears bright. Thin wires covered with enamels can best be cleaned with sandpaper as shown in Illustration 1.

5. Make a Good Mechanical Connection

Before soldering, the wires should first be wrapped around terminals or securely clamped. After the wire is tight and secure, the solder can be applied.

6. Heat the Connection

The hot iron tip should be held against the parts to be joined until they are heated. Enough heat should be applied so that the solder melts when it touches the wires being joined together. The

2. To conduct heat away from transistors the leads should be held with pliers when soldering.

solder will then flow freely over and through the joint.

7. *Keep the Connection from Moving*

While the joint is being soldered and while the solder is cooling, the connection should be held perfectly still. Movement of the connection will result in a cold solder joint that may have a high resistance.

3. The small tip of a pencil-type soldering iron is preferred for printed circuits.

8. Use the Proper Amount of Solder

Use only enough solder to do the job. Excessive solder does not help the connection, and this extra solder may cause a short circuit. If excessive solder appears, re-heat the joint and remove the extra solder by wiping it with a rag.

9. Protect Certain Parts from Heat

Certain parts such as diodes and transistors can easily be damaged by excessive heat. To avoid ruining these parts when soldering, the leads should be gripped with pliers as shown in Illustration 2. The pliers will conduct the heat away from the part.

10. For Small Spaces Use a Small Tip

Crowded electronic circuits may have a number of components in a very small space. A large soldering tip can easily damage the parts or the other connections. In such instances, a small tip such as found on pencil-type soldering irons should be used. See Illustration 3.

STANDARD SYMBOLS FOR ELECTRONICS

ADJUSTABLE, CONTINUOUSLY arrow is drawn at about 45 degrees across the symbol	**CONNECTION, MECHANICAL**
ALTERNATING CURRENT SOURCE	**CORE** no symbol indicates air core iron core
ANTENNA general　　loop　　dipole	**CRYSTAL, PIEZOELECTRIC**
	FUSE or
BATTERY single cell　　multicell	**GROUND** used for either ground to earth or chassis
CAPACITOR fixed　　variable	**HEADPHONES** single　　double
COIL, INDUCTANCE or air core or magnetic core adjustable　　variable	**INSTRUMENT** *appropriate letter symbol is placed in circle A—ammeter　　OHM—ohmmeter G—galvanometer　　V—voltmeter MA—milliammeter　　W—wattmeter
	JACK

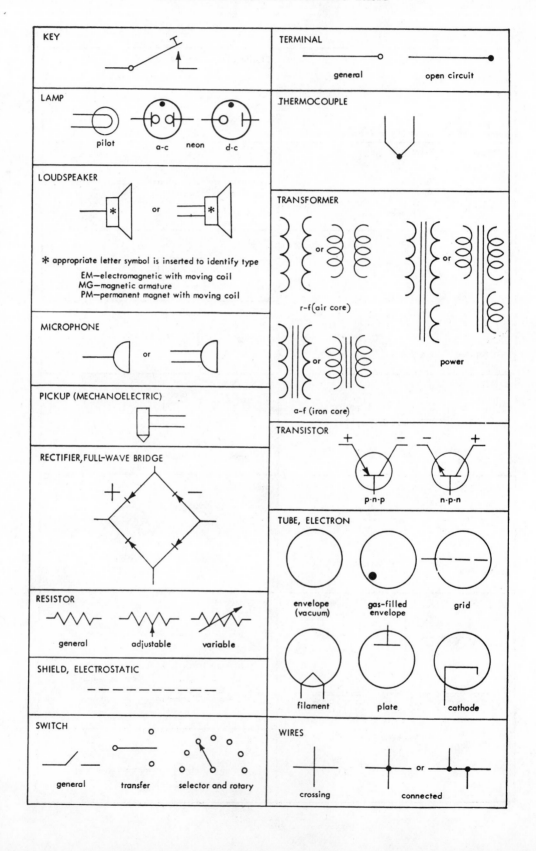

KEY

TERMINAL

general   open circuit

LAMP

pilot   a-c   neon   d-c

THERMOCOUPLE

LOUDSPEAKER

or

* appropriate letter symbol is inserted to identify type

EM—electromagnetic with moving coil
MG—magnetic armature
PM—permanent magnet with moving coil

TRANSFORMER

or   or

r-f(air core)

or   power

a-f (iron core)

MICROPHONE

or

PICKUP (MECHANOELECTRIC)

RECTIFIER, FULL-WAVE BRIDGE

+   −

TRANSISTOR

+   −   −   +

p-n-p   n-p-n

TUBE, ELECTRON

envelope   gas-filled   grid
(vacuum)   envelope

filament   plate   cathode

RESISTOR

general   adjustable   variable

SHIELD, ELECTROSTATIC

SWITCH

general   transfer   selector and rotary

WIRES

crossing   connected

or

Index